Dyadic Developmental Practice and Intellectual Disabilities

Integrating Attachment, PACE and Trauma-informed Care

Nic Jones, Cathy Harding and Mariëlle Wilcox

Pavilion
PUBLISHING

Dyadic Developmental Practice and Intellectual Disabilities:

Published by:
Pavilion Publishing and Media Ltd
Blue Sky Offices, 25 Cecil Pashley Way, Shoreham by Sea, West Sussex, BN43 5FF

Tel: +44 (0)1273 434943
Email: info@pavpub.com
Web: www.pavpub.com

Published 2025

A catalogue record for this book is available from the British Library.

ISBN: 978-1-803884-11-0

Pavilion Publishing and Media is a leading publisher of books, training materials and digital content in mental health, social care and allied fields. Pavilion and its imprints offer must-have knowledge and innovative learning solutions underpinned by sound research and professional values.

Authors: Nic Jones, Cathy Harding and Mariëlle Wilcox
Editor: Jo Hathaway
Cover design: Emma Dawe, Pavilion Publishing and Media Ltd
Page layout and typesetting: Anthony Pitt, Pavilion Publishing and Media Ltd
Printing: Independent Publishers Group (IPG)

About the Authors

Nic Jones is a consultant clinical psychologist and became an independent practitioner working in a specialist attachment trauma service, after 20 years in split posts, including an integrated autism service, adult learning disability services, and fostering and adoption services in the NHS and Local Authorities. Nic qualified as a DDP practitioner in both children's focused work and in her work with adults with intellectual disabilities. She continues to offer therapy, teach, support teams, supervise and work with services to develop their use of DDP.

Cathy Harding is a consultant clinical psychologist and has worked in community, inpatient and now supported living services for adults with an intellectual disability, primarily, in South Wales. She is interested in how our understanding of attachment and trauma influences our work with people with intellectual disabilities, individually and for staff teams. She has been sharing these ideas within the service with which she works and more broadly, including publications, conference presentations and through her work with BILD.

Mariëlle (Maz) Wilcox is a clinical psychologist and completed her DDP level 2 training in November 2017. She has a long-standing passion for supporting young people who have experienced adversity. Maz worked in an attachment service providing training and consultation for professionals in Health, Social Care and Education, before joining a therapeutic service for care-experienced children and, for the last five years, has been leading an attachment-informed intensive PBS service for children with intellectual disabilities in South Wales.

Acknowledgements

Most importantly, we are so very grateful to the people with intellectual disabilities we have met, worked alongside and from whom we have learned so much. Also, thank you to the families, supporters and staff teams with whom we have explored and developed these ideas. This book reflects so many of those discussions we have had about what helps and what does not. Those we have worked with have allowed us to be curious and have accepted our offers of connection, even when things have been difficult.

We are all thankful to those who have read versions of this book, especially Kim Golding who has not only provided a foreword for the book, but also read early drafts and generously commented from a DDP perspective. Her encouragement and thoughtful feedback have influenced the final chapters in this book.

Also, thanks to Vikki Langeford who has proofread initial drafts of many of the chapters. As well as to Alexis Quinn, Rachel Potter, Mark Smith, Julia Metcalf and Kirstie Davies for their expert opinions on sections of the book, and to Louisa and the Pavilion team for their faith and enthusiasm for its publication. Any mistakes or inaccuracies within this book are ours and we apologise for them.

In addition, Nic would like to thank her family and friends for their endless patience and encouragement to complete this project, and for the Clyro team at The Family Place who have been so encouraging.

Cathy would like to thank her parents for their ongoing support and provision of brownies; her husband, children and friends for tolerating the things she did not attend (to) due to writing a book and the amount she talked about the tribulations of it.

Maz would like to thank her husband, children, mother, sister, friends and colleagues for their listening ears when talking endlessly about the book and everything it entailed as well as for their unwavering encouragement.

Contents

The resources to accompany this book can be downloaded visiting the link or scanning the QR code

www.pavpub.com/dyadic-developmental-practice-and-intellectual-disabilities-resources

Foreword

Kim S. Golding

If I knew then what I know now.

Many years ago, as a young psychology graduate, I spent two years working in what were then called 'hospitals for the mentally handicapped'. Later, as a trainee and newly qualified clinical psychologist, I provided support to families who were parenting young children with Down Syndrome. As I read through '*Dyadic Developmental Practice and Intellectual Disabilities*' I am reminded of those times and everything I didn't do for the children, adults and families I worked with. We were so focused on reducing challenging behaviours and helping the children and adults learn and achieve that we were in danger of losing sight of the person we were striving to help.

Where did getting to know the child or adult fit in? What difference would a deeper understanding of their experience, hopes, and dreams, have made?

How did we facilitate the joys and comforts of relationships to happen?

When did we have the curious conversations with the carers and parents about the impact on them of caring for children and adults with a range of challenges?

What room was there for the grief and fears of parents caring for and loving their children? How did we support them to hold sadness for the child they didn't have and worries for the future of the cherished child they did?

I was compassionate. I was supportive. But looking back I can see how little space was available for relational care and support, and how much more we could have done.

Ah, if I knew then what I know now, I would have approached this work very differently.

I am so pleased that Nic, Maz, and Cathy have written this book. They have centred emotional connection and relationship at the centre of interventions and services for children and adults with intellectual disability. They have thoughtfully explored how we can be relationally informed when working with practitioners. They have expanded this to consider how systems can also be attentive to relational connections.

To do this these authors draw upon the DDP model and its theoretical foundations in attachment theory, intersubjectivity and neuroscience. They have combined their years of experience working with this vulnerable population with their knowledge of Dyadic Developmental Psychotherapy (DDP), DDP-parenting and Dyadic Developmental Practice (DDP-practice) to explore how we can adapt the DDP model to fully nurture the relationships that people with intellectual disability need and deserve.

With appropriate relational support, combined with a range of interventions, challenging behaviours will reduce and people with intellectual disabilities will learn and achieve. Most importantly, they will be seen as the unique individuals they are.

When I am providing DDP training I am frequently asked how we can use this model to help people with intellectual disabilities. I now have a comprehensive answer for them.

With this book, they will know what I didn't know back then.

Preface

We are a group of clinical psychologists who are interested in, and have a range of experience of, using Dyadic Developmental Psychotherapy (DDP) or Dyadic Developmental Practice (DDP-practice) in our relational-focused care for children and adults with an intellectual disability. Between us, we have worked in a variety of adult and child settings; in community, inpatient, supported living and family services. We have each noticed how a DDP-based approach to care has proved helpful in our work with people with an intellectual disability and their support networks, and we are keen to share, reflect and summarise what we've noticed so far, practically and theoretically.

We are at various points in our own training with the DDP approach. We all work with an attachment and trauma-informed framework in mind. We have all noticed the value and use of this model with indirect and direct therapeutic work, when creating formulations around a presentation that is being classed as risky or worrying, or where people are struggling to be in relationship with others, or when working with people whose behaviour is of concern to others.

In writing this book, we are embracing the idea that "we do not write a book because we know all there is to know about this area, rather we are writing the book to help us make sense of what we do know and to be in dialogue with others" (shared by Westoby, 2024). We are aware that in the process of writing this book, through drawing on others' work and in reflecting on our shared experiences, we have developed our thinking and also deepened our reflections about the work we do, and changed our practice accordingly.

We hope that this book will be of interest to parents and family carers from whom we've learnt so much, and who, like us, are asking how to hold relational care central for the children or adults with intellectual disabilities they care for, and how to support themselves and others do the same. We anticipate this book will also be of interest to DDP practitioners, familiar with the model but curious to offer and extend their support to children with an intellectual disability. We hope that professionals and practitioners working in intellectual disability services will also find this a valuable resource, a point of reflection and feel encouraged to explore DDP training. We have endeavoured in some way to capture the voices and experiences of parents and carers, team members and services we have been lucky enough to work with and who are dedicated to the care of children and adults with an intellectual disability. In this book we have used amalgamated or composite cases, which aid with ensuring anonymity, yet aim to be representative of DDP work.

The original concept for this book came about as a result of Cathy and Nic's ongoing conversations about responding to the attachment needs of people with an intellectual disability, most decisively in a pub garden at the foothills of Pen-y-Fan; we were two enthusiastic, but busy practitioners. At the time, Nic was qualified as a DDP practitioner and later became a DDP consultant. Cathy has completed Level 1 training (in 2017), but until more recently, given her work in adult intellectual disability services, there wasn't a route through to Level 2 training. Now, this can be on the horizon. Cathy and Nic kept the idea for the book alive, despite the demands in their working lives, a pandemic, caring for families, children and dogs!

Early in 2024, we approached publishers and included Mariëlle (Maz) Wilcox into our writing team. Maz has created a huge difference in pushing us to broaden our original focus (from adult-focused work) to include our experience and work with children. It is interesting and noticeable that this project moved and developed more because of a need to support each other in this endeavour, than had ever been generated by an incentive or goal!

So, now there is a book! We hope this can contribute to the shift in focus towards more relational care for people with intellectual disabilities and their parents, carers and support networks. It feels, in some ways, as though we are in the early days of considering relational-focused care as a priority in services for people with an intellectual disability and we hope that this book joins with the voices and writings of others to further these developments.

Chapter 1: Introduction

Thinking about Dyadic Developmental Practice (DDP-practice)

In this book, we aim to share our experience of how DDP-practice enables attuned, person-centred and co-regulated care for both children and adults with intellectual disabilities. DDP-practice emphasises the critical role of safety and relationships in emotional and psychological development, particularly for individuals who have experienced trauma or interrupted attachment, which is often referred to as attachment trauma, developmental trauma and, more recently, as relational trauma. We highlight the role of DDP-psychotherapy, parenting and practice in enhancing the relationships around people with an intellectual disability, whether this be with family, carers or the broader support systems.

Overall, Dyadic Developmental Psychotherapy (DDP) offers a powerful and effective approach to healing relational trauma and gaps in care during childhood. The approaches, models and theoretical bases for DDP are drawn on when offering distinct support to parents and carers (DDP-parenting) and also used to inform interventions across services and broader systems (DDP-practice). So much of the care experienced by children and adults is provided by those that know them well, either in families or in staff teams; who work hard to maintain connection, joy and curiosity in relation to the person they support. We acknowledge both the impact of care giving in general, and also the demands and joys that arise in caring for someone with significant cognitive impairments. Even resourceful services and loving parents and carers have noticed times when the connection between them and the person with an intellectual disability they care for falters. DDP-informed practice enables a way to make sense of phases of disconnection and offers a model for attuned reciprocal relationships. This focus feels crucial as we notice the loss of connection and dehumanisation that occurs in some settings where people with intellectual disabilities can be highly dependent on caregivers, yet may also be disempowered, othered and left vulnerable. In such settings, the risk of abuse increases. We are keen to support and champion the voice of people with an intellectual disability, whilst also understanding and supporting the work of their carers – paid or unpaid.

It is an exciting yet complex time to work in the field of intellectual disability, as many services are turning their focus to understanding attachment, trauma-informed care and the importance of relational connection, whilst services are cut or ill-resourced, financial state benefits are challenged, and caring work is poorly remunerated. Over the last 20 years there has been a growing emphasis on understanding the inner experiences of individuals with intellectual disabilities, moving beyond a purely behavioural focus. We welcome how the once-dominant lens of behavioural support is now challenged by deeper enquiries into attachment, trauma, relationships, and early experiences of connection.

We see this evolution as a positive and necessary step forward, and it is enabling people with intellectual disabilities to have more say in their care and more agency in their lives. In considering someone's attachment history, the push and pull of intersubjective connection and understanding more about neuroscience, we enrich our understanding of those we support.

An overview of the book

Throughout this book, we discuss DDP approaches and adaptations to consider when supporting people with an intellectual disability, illustrated through a range of case studies and practice examples. The initial chapters of this book provides a summary of the central components and approaches used within DDP interventions and reflections around why this model has become so relevant for our attachment and trauma-focused work with people with intellectual disabilities. The rest of the book is then divided into three areas, including theoretical models underpinning DDP, key concepts within the DDP approach and the application of DDP in psychotherapy and practice.

Section 1 includes chapters which detail the underpinning theoretical models for DDP, giving a historical overview of attachment theory and intersubjective connection. This is followed by insights from neuroscience to help us to consider how relationships directly shape our development and what might interrupt relational connection when caring for someone with an intellectual disability.

In Section 2, we outline the key concepts and frameworks used in all elements of the DDP approach when working with people with an intellectual disability. DDP promotes and prioritises learning from the individual, their parents and carers to better understand their experiences of connection, regulation and safety.

Within DDP, a key concept is the attitude that is summarised by the acronym PACE, which stands for being Playful, Accepting, Curious and Empathetic about the person's experience. We discuss the DDP framework for providing Two Hands of Care, which maintains safety and connection through our relationships, whilst also offering boundaries and clear structure.

We explore the concept of shame that might be linked with past experiences and/or triggered by our current interactions, both for the person and the carers supporting them, as well as how people may defend themselves from these feelings through the shield of shame. When in a state of shame, it is harder to connect, to feel safe, to present as calm or to articulate your worries.

We consider the additional complications and protective strategies (or shields) that people with an intellectual disability might need to rely on. This is followed by the relational process of Blocked Trust, which can occur when someone can no longer relax into and trust another and therefore blocks their capacity for delight, due to their fears of rejection. We note the challenges that arise when someone with an intellectual disability might experience Blocked Trust and how this increases the risk of Blocked Care for caregivers. This chapter also offers steps for support when carers and people with a disability experience these relational barriers.

Finally, Section 3 offers ways to apply and integrate DDP-focused work within an intellectual disability context. We have drawn on Kim Golding's Pyramid of Need (2013) to understand and identify care needs through thorough developmental assessments to create attuned intervention plans. The Pyramid of Need offers a framework that moves from the provision of safety at the bottom of the pyramid, through to relationships, comfort and co-regulation, empathy and reflection, resilience and resources and, finally, exploring trauma and mourning losses at the top. This model enables us to review the current care and support needs of someone with an intellectual disability as well as their carers.

This section then describes DDP as a dyadic therapy, as parenting support and how it can be used as a whole practice based approach (DDP-practice) when DDP interventions are incorporated within a service or through a system. We outline considerations to hold in mind, adaptation we use when offering DDP, and how to sequence the therapeutic process, before moving on to DDP-Practice with the system around the individual with intellectual disabilities. Chapters 13 and 14 promote the provision of trauma-informed care and the use of DDP-practice to support safety within systems and for those working within them. We specifically discuss DDP-informed service provision, including boundaries, staffing, restrictive practice, ongoing family contact and consent.

In recognition of the reality that the Positive Behavioural Support (PBS) framework is prevalent within services for people with an intellectual disability, in Chapter 15 Cathy and Maz describe the ways in which they draw on the DDP model to enhance PBS-focused work in a way that enriches meaningful connection, emotional safety and a deep and intersubjective understanding of individual's relational needs. Our experiences are that the use of a DDP-informed approach has highlighted that prioritising a more relational approach results in no longer needing traditional behavioural approaches. Nic has noticed how, through embracing DDP in her practice and support for those with the most complex needs for nearly a decade, she has switched her focus towards safety and improved relationships and no longer needs to draw on PBS. Cathy and Maz, however, present the weave of DDP and PBS for those who are working in services where the PBS framework remains central, offering suggestions for embedding an attachment and trauma-informed lens, through the use of DDP based approaches in PBS frameworks and support plans.

Finally, we have included some resources and ideas for future training and supervision, and final thoughts; as well as an appendix, making available copies of some key resources we have developed and shared throughout the book, here and online resources (see link in Contents Page).

Terminology – intellectual disability

As UK-based practitioners, we are aware of our bias here, and the services we have worked in and people we have met have used the term 'learning disability' to describe themselves (LD). However, we have opted to use the term 'intellectual disability' in this book as it is currently the more internationally recognised term and was recommended by the publishers. We hope people within the UK who are more familiar with LD can bear with us. In addition, for those working with children under five years of age, they may refer to the term Global Developmental Delay or a Developmental Disability. Again, this might be a UK-specific issue and our use of one term is not designed to exclude but to maintain the flow of the text.

In using a collective term, we are acutely aware that we do not bring nuance to the variety of lives, loves and diversity of experiences of those who have an intellectual disability and we entrust our readers to hold and apply these thoughts and ideas as needed amongst those they meet, support or champion.

Parents, carers and attachment figures

We are writing about a group of people who often need support from others, and we recognise that, in reality, people with an intellectual disability have a huge range and variety of different relationships. For ease of writing, we often use the term 'parent and carer' or 'caregivers' to encapsulate all these roles, rather than explicitly naming all the people who are responsible for creating safety and offering love and protection to the baby, child, young person or adult with an intellectual disability. Our family list might include a kinship, biological, adoptive, step family members or foster carers. We know that attachment figures can also include paid carers such as support staff, respite carers, teachers or someone from a multi-disciplinary team.

All-age perspective

DDP was originally developed for children who were adopted or living in foster care; they had typically experienced the trauma and the loss of an attachment figure. Over time, this model has been adapted for use with a variety of children including children living in birth families, for use in education settings and those in residential care. It is our intention to illustrate how DDP interventions are both applicable and useful for children and adults with an intellectual disability. We have included specific considerations for adult-focused work across the chapters as needed.

Intersectional relationships

We are keenly aware that we are three cisgendered, able-bodied, heterosexual white women, writing from a Western European perspective, and that our assertions are based on our experiences of our work in services in a Western culture, within a UK-based NHS and local authority set up, and often using theories drawn from white Western researchers. We do not have lived experiences of navigating many of the systems we write about, although we have each interacted with some of them professionally and personally. We work and write with an awareness of our potential for bias, but with a passion for bringing sensitivity and understanding to each person's experience and an attempt to acknowledge and recognise power imbalances. Our expectations about family life, or how we might even say hello to, or work alongside, someone with an intellectual disability, are informed by our own attachment, family, cultural experiences and prejudices. In focusing on adapting this model for use in intellectual disability services, we have not explicitly focused on diversity linked with family experiences, background, sexual or gender identities. These differences remain of great importance, regardless of ability or disability; we hope that the open and curious stance offered within the DDP model will facilitate responsive and sensitive support, especially when coupled with appropriate supervision. We remained conscious that there may be gaps in this book regarding inclusivity or implicit biases, for which we apologise. We have also not explicitly talked about neurodiversity, yet acknowledge it is a significant factor for many of those we support. Our intention in this writing is to bring a focus to the intersectional tensions within relationships for people, due specifically to there being distinct and significant differences in cognition and skills between those cared for and those caring.

The writers

We have co-authored this book; we have written together and separately, we have commented on, debated and supported each other. We have tried to share our knowledge and experiences around each area, and considered how each section relates to a variety of settings and ages. We have aimed to cover as much as we can, whilst avoiding repetition, but also recognise that the issues that affect humans are hard to put in tightly controlled boxes or chapters.

Final notes

We encourage all practitioners to access qualified trainers or supervisors. In our experience, DDP (and in particular one of the DDP approaches most commonly referred to, PACE) sounds intuitively easy to apply, but, in reality, it is often hard to slow down, to not quickly jump to a plan, to making people feel better or consider solutions. In slowing down, in maintaining connection and co-regulation, we are better able to help people to learn from and draw on the guidance on offer so that they can learn, consider new perspective, or narratives, understand relational challenges and develop new skills. All who access supervision notice how their practice improves, and we would encourage the readers of this book to access their own DDP supervision and support.

This book cannot and does not substitute training in DDP. It is our hope to offer an insight into why we are so excited by DDP in all its forms and why we recommend this as an essential approach to increase relational safety for people with an intellectual disability and their carers, and improve connections even in the most challenging circumstances. We recognise that this book reflects the start of a conversation and are keen and curious for others to join this exploration.

Chapter 2: What is Dyadic Developmental Psychotherapy? A brief overview

Summary

- Dyadic Developmental Psychotherapy (DDP) was initially developed by Dan Hughes as a therapeutic approach for children who had been fostered or adopted and finding it hard to adjust after their early trauma.
- DDP, as a therapeutic approach, typically involves working with the parents or carers and the children of concern. Over time adaptations have developed including the use of DDP for parenting support where a child is not directly involved in therapy meetings; known as DDP-parenting or DDP-informed parenting. Great success is being recognised when using the concepts from the DDP model within residential or broader services. DDP interventions, when used across systems, services, residential or educational settings is known as Dyadic Developmental Practice (DDP-practice).
- DDP interventions are focused on understanding and development of attachment; improving intersubjective connection by building or deepening connection; developing a coherent narrative to enable trauma-focused healing.
- This chapter will provide a description of the key concepts within DDP interventions with reflections about appropriate adaptations when supporting people with an intellectual disability.

Introduction

DDP was initially developed as a systemic psychotherapy for children and their adopted or foster parents to improve understanding of the child's experience, to increase safety within relationships and to support trauma-focused healing (Hughes, Golding & Hudson, 2019). The focus of this intervention is relational rather than about skills building or developing specific strategies. DDP has now evolved beyond Dyadic Developmental Psychotherapy for use with families, to include support for parents (DDP-parenting), and also for those working in residential or care networks, known as DDP-practice, (Golding, 2020). This chapter includes a summary of the key elements or approaches that are used within DDP, and considerations for DDP when working with people with an intellectual disability.

The aim of DDP

DDP was developed to create a way of supporting a more secure and trusting relationship between the child and the caregiver, which, in turn, can then provide the child with the support and guidance they need to develop emotionally and socially, and ideally, to recover or heal as best as possible from early trauma. DDP has been shown to be effective in working with children who have experienced trauma or other difficult life experiences, as well as those who struggle with behavioural or emotional difficulties (see Chapter 12, Hughes & Golding, 2024). The practice-based evidence is now extensive in children's services and rapidly building across child and adult services for people with an intellectual disability.

The extension of DDP, beyond therapy, to considering parent or carer-focused support (sometimes referred to as DDP-parenting or DDP informed parenting) and into education and residential settings (DDP-practice), aligns well and holds a clear relevance for people with an intellectual disability. The nature of cognitive impairment means that people often rely on carers and many live in residential or supported homes. Central to DDP-based work is the recognition that people who have experienced early childhood or relational trauma, neglect or other adverse experiences, such as gaps or mismatches in care, can struggle with attachment security and self-regulation due to these life experiences. Someone who has experienced early trauma is more likely to find difficulty trusting others, expressing emotions, or struggle to manage/regulate their own emotional states.

A DDP-focused approach aims to build confidence and autonomy, by first building connection and supporting the development of trust with safe adults. In other therapeutic approaches, where the focus is on the individual, there can be a push to develop skills, resolve upset, teach anger management or enable independence. These developments are, of course, important but will be hard to achieve or even consider for those who have a poorly developed sense of self and who have not yet experienced security in relationships, who do not yet know who to trust and who to listen to for guidance. However, with support this can change. The brain has huge plasticity and our work has revealed just how important it is to offer connection and build in safety into a vulnerable person's life. In order to develop empathy for ourselves or for others, we first need to experience it. With the appropriate foundational support in place, a person is likely to feel less confused by their reactions over time and, through repeated experiences of co-regulation, will hopefully be able to move towards their own self-regulation around challenging situations and difficult feelings. A DDP approach enables the conversation and supports the shift away from a more critical and even blaming stance about behaviours of concern, towards increasing understanding about how, when and what type of care to offer to a frightened or dysregulated person.

Figure 2.1. The theoretical base for DDP and use of DDP-focused interventions

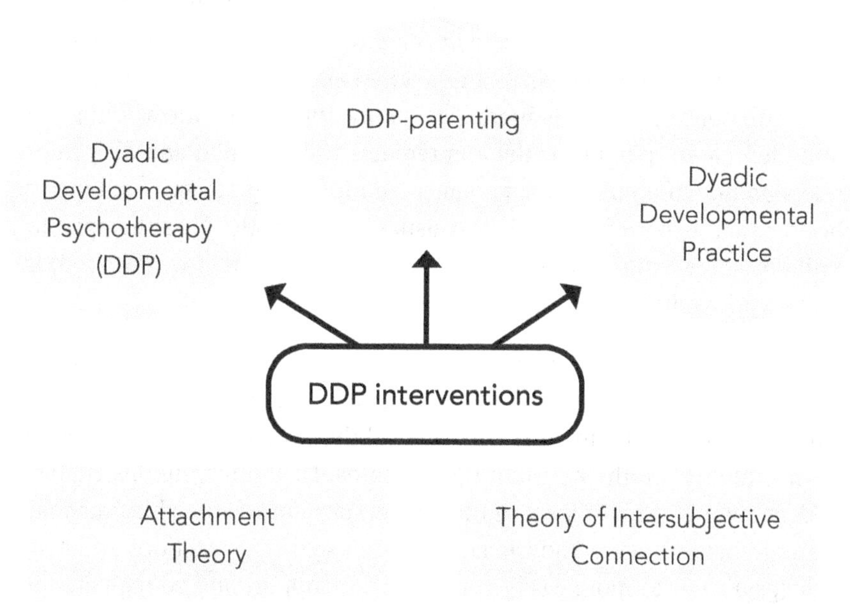

Dyadic Developmental Psychotherapy (DDP)

This psychotherapeutic approach was developed by Dr. Dan Hughes, in response to the families he was meeting, where there had been a form of early trauma and where traditional therapeutic approaches were not proving helpful. DDP was developed to help parents find a way to connect with the children they had fostered or adopted, to deepen their relationship, but also to form a coherent narrative of their experiences, (current and past) that are and have been impacted by trauma. This relational approach enables parents and carers to build an understanding of how early attachment patterns and possible early trauma are impacting their current relationships. By building deep relational safety and in creating coherence about experiences, DDP enables healing and recovery from early trauma or gaps in early care. DDP, as an approach, is directly informed by both the Theory of intersubjectivity and Attachment theory (see Chapters 4 and 5 for more detail) and, over time, our understanding of neuroscience has yet further refined and developed the use of DDP as an intervention beyond dyadic therapeutic work. DDP interventions draw greatly on our understanding of the types of input and support that work well in early child-parent/carer connections to inform ways to support families where connection is fragile, where trauma interrupts relational connection and where a child or adult experiences fragmentation or incoherence in their experiences, reactions or memories. We would recommend that anyone offering DDP has as a minimum attended Level 1 training and is accessing DDP supervision.

The Dyad in DDP: Who is involved and why

DDP was originally designed for dyadic work between the parent (or a key attachment figure) and child in order to develop the felt sense of safety and connection in their relationship between the child and their parent/key attachment figure. Our experience is that this model is equally appropriate for working with adults and their carers/parents as the aim remains to help build and deepen their understanding of a vulnerable person's emotional experiences, and increase coherence for their experiences. (It is less usual in this model for a therapist to meet with a child or adult without a key attachment figure but if this was needed, the focus in the work would be relational.)

This therapeutic work is sensitive to the presenting emotional age (generally younger than the chronological age) of the individual challenged by relational trauma and aims to help them better understand their own attachment experience and how this impacts on their current relationships. DDP interventions enable a better understanding of the impact of the past on current relationships; enables the parent/carer to better understand the child's/adult's current reactions and responses; and also helps a carer to more easily connect with, support and co-regulate the vulnerable person in moments of struggle. Deepening their understanding will improve a parent/carer's connection with their child/adult's emotional world and provide a different relationship experience. This, in turn, helps the traumatised person to develop a more integrated and coherent narrative about their experience and their past. A coherent narrative is important for healing from trauma and developing an authentic and healthy sense of identity. Where the adult with an intellectual disability is in agreement about working with key carers/parents, this dyadic focus would be the preferred route to follow.

Those who have experienced profoundly mis-attuned or dangerous care in the past will have learned to be cautious and might present as rejecting or excessively clingy in response to other attachment figures. This has been termed 'blocked trust'. When someone experiences blocked trust, a predictable pattern is experienced by those around the mis-trustful person: they will likely, over time, move into a blocked state described as 'blocked care', (Hughes & Baylin, 2012). When someone is unable to trust others, and responds by unconsciously creating distance or taking control by avoiding or becoming clingy, it can create a barrier to connection or even a sense of failure for the adult who is trying to offer safe care; this sense of failure occurs because the intersubjective connection has been profoundly interrupted. Repeated failure to connect can lead a parent or carer to experience blocked care. It becomes very hard to be around the traumatised person and the likelihood of family breakdown or placement disruption can increase. (See Chapter 10 for a fuller consideration of blocked care and blocked trust; intersubjective connection is explored in further detail in Chapter 4.)

The responses triggered by a traumatised person in their parents/carers often evokes reactions that are below consciousness; past experiences of relational failures or difficulties can be awoken which then further impact on the dyad. To better understand and support the adults or key attachment figures, it is also important to better understand their own experience of being parented and attachment patterns. We are each influenced in our parenting and caring by our previous relationships: whether that is to actively offer a very different style of support to the one we had when we were younger, or to adhere and incorporate the influence from our own experience of being cared for.

When there are breaks in relational connection, and when the relationship between an attachment figure and a vulnerable person (adult or child) comes under strain, we notice that the parenting or support style offered might not be quite attuned to the pattern that works for the child/adult needing support. DDP based approaches aim to help those in a tense relationship to better understand their patterns and what puts pressure on their relationship including ways to unpack misunderstanding, miscommunications and to deepen their knowledge about each other. Dyadic work with a vulnerable, traumatised person therefore always includes an initial focus on parenting (or carer) support.

DDP-parenting

DDP-parenting is a significant and essential component of traditional DDP when offering therapy meetings to parents/carers and a child/vulnerable adult. However, these parent or carer focused meetings can also be offered as a stand-alone intervention. This particularly applies where a child or adult does not consent or agree to engage in direct therapy, but where this approach could be of value and use to the dyad. It also is relevant when wanting to offer relational-focused support to families or services where an individual does not have sufficient language (due to age or cognitive impairment) for some of the conversational elements of DDP. We would again recommend, that anyone offering this type of support to parents or carers is has a minimum undertaken Level 1 training and is accessing DDP supervision.

There are some other situations where the parents or carers experience significant barriers to being ready to engage in dyadic work with a vulnerable adult or child. These barriers typically link with the parent/carer's own struggle to be regulated and in a position to explore relational connection. There can be a range of factors that interrupt dyadic work including:

- the trauma has impacted on parent/carer relationship so significantly that these issues need to be addressed first
- parents/carers are in blocked care
- parents/carers have their own trauma history that is being triggered in their care for another person with a trauma history.

Parent/Carer attachment focus and support

During therapeutic work, through play, talk and other forms of interaction, the therapist helps the child/adult and caregiver build a more secure and trusting relationship, in order to build an intersubjective connection (see Chapter 4). This a collaborative approach; with a therapist discovering and helping a carer to attune to the child/adult's emotional states, and to also help to consider the impact on the carer or parent of caring for a trauma experienced person. The work requires a commitment and readiness from the caregiver or primary attachment figure to be an active participant in the process. In order to better understand the tensions arising within a dyad it is helpful to explore the parents' or carer's experience. Often, this involves giving time to the parents and carers to consider their own attachment histories, or their triggers, when they are supporting someone who does not yet trust their care. In supporting the key adults around the child or adult with an intellectual disability, to better understand their own patterns and reactions, they are more likely to remain regulated and available for the child/adult they are keen to support. Over time, the aim is to change and develop the care and child/adult relationship, so that a closer connection forms that allows exploration and understanding of emotional states and what causes the barriers or tensions within their relationship.

Dyadic Developmental Practice (DDP-practice)

The DDP-based approach can also be used in residential care work with children, and when used in this way is referred to as DDP-practice (Grant, Thompson & Golding, 2024). DDP-practice integrates the principles of DDP across the whole system from the therapy room, to staff teams and families, to the classroom, extending out to the management team and professionals within community or inpatient services. Children with an intellectual disability will often have periods when they experience some form of residential or respite care; times when they are not in their family home, when the family might be needing some respite or when families are not able to provide the support required. Some children and many adults with an intellectual disability often require a team of supporters or carers, so experience multiple relationships and potentially repeated changes in key attachment figures. DDP based approaches can inform the support offered by networks and residential services, and help enrich an understanding about the increased complexity that working with people with an intellectual disability can bring. We would recommend that those offering to offer DDP-practice focused support is qualified in DDP (has completed the practicum) and accessing supervision.

This chapter aims to provide an outline of the key elements or approaches that are used within DDP, whether this is around dyadic therapy, parenting support or when working with a whole system. Throughout this chapter and every chapter that follows, we will consider the adaptations and adjustments needed when using DDP interventions to care for and work with people with an intellectual disability, their families and professional support network.

Features/approaches and considerations with ID-focused work

DDP has been used less often in adult-focused work, though our personal experience is that there is growing interest in this model (British Psychological Society, 2017) certainly in the UK and maybe further. Whilst DDP was initially designed for work with children who have experienced attachment trauma or Adverse Childhood Experiences, there is a recognised need for more attachment-trauma focused support for people with an intellectual disability who have experienced relational trauma during their development. Having an intellectual disability often includes experiencing significant complexity throughout life, especially around emotional regulation, communicating needs and sustaining relationships. All of us rely on others to some extent throughout our lives, however, people with an intellectual disability have an increased likelihood of needing to rely on others for support and help throughout their lives. This dependence on others, and the inevitability of having to be in relationship with others, is what has made the DDP model such a relevant framework with the services and teams within which the authors operate.

Whilst this section considers some of the approaches used within DDP, it is not a replacement for DDP training. The reason for considering them a little here is to highlight the considerations or adaptations to hold in mind with ID-focused work.

Follow lead follow

DDP interventions offer the opportunity to experience a very different way of relating. It is an attuned approach that draws on the use of self in a very deeply open manner. To offer a different type of relationship and connection the DDP practitioner needs to draw on what occurs within their own relationship to make sense of moments of upset, discomfort or joy. DDP interventions provide a route for tracking the issues that are of relevance and importance to the individual, but following their initial lead, rather than, for instance, the issues on a list shared by a referrer. In working at a client's pace, we can build trust but also relevance to the concerns facing the individual. However, this is a relational model, and so the DDP therapist or practitioner will encourage a reflection, or notice a link with the past, or build coherence around an experience. The therapist will lead this exploration of a theme for as long as the individual is interested or able to join that exploration, at which point we would revert to tracking or following what the client needs to focus on. In working in this way, we offer to join their world and their concerns, but offer a different reflection or co-regulation for their experience. In order to offer a new coherence and some healing to their experience of relationships, we must do so steadily in order to maintain or deepen trust, but we also need to be attuned to each person's tolerance of safety.

Adaptations for ID based work

In supporting a DDP-based conversation, we would start with the person with intellectual disability's concerns. Tracking their interests allows us to understand the pace at which they can explore topics and also helps someone to feel safe. When carers and parents lead with an agenda or topic it can reduce the sense of regulation and safety making it harder for the person with an intellectual disability to engage, learn or digest the conversation. A DDP-based interaction isn't just about listening, it is a highly active approach and the lead, whilst tracking the initial issues raised, allows for reflection, consideration, and connection with the affective experience around the issues the client shared. Again, this power dynamic feels respectful, but also important for a client group that can often be silenced. Sometimes, allowing a client to lead a conversation at the start of the meeting can be overwhelming; when this is the case the parent/carer might offer a few suggestions in order to help a conversation or some key themes evolve. Ideally, though, we follow the issues and interests of the individual with an intellectual disability.

PACE

PACE-based approaches will be explored in greater detail in a later, separate chapter (see Chapter 7). It is often the part of DDP that many remember, but it is a part of the overall picture, not the whole.

PACE is an acronym that stands for an approach or attitude that can be:

- **P**layful (or joyful, offering a lightness in approach
- **A**ccepting of someone else's experience
- **C**urious about what might be going on for the other person
- Based in a deep **E**mpathy for their unique experiences.

It is an attitude of mind or ways of being within relationships rather than a specific technique. It has proven to be vital within families and for those offering care in residential or staffed settings. We have also noticed how effective this way of being is in more challenging conversations or disagreements, even those associated with funding or resources, and has been helpful to maintain good working relationships with those considering broader complex commissioning processes.

Considerations for ID-based work

Offering a playful or 'lightness' approach needs to be tailored and attuned around each individual. The purpose of a playful approach is to support intersubjective connection through experiencing shared delight. The style of humour has to be adapted and attuned to what tends to delight or lighten moments for the person with an intellectual disability. It is vital for this style and these moments to be sensitive to the expressed style of the person with an intellectual disability which might require an avoidance of word play, puns or sarcasm/dry humour to achieve these connected moments. A playful approach or lightness of connection enables breaks between more intense or tender conversations but also captures the times when we relax into and enjoy the relationship. It describes the times when we experience being of interest to each other. Allowing for a lightness in our conversation not only reflects the natural rise and fall in conversations but also facilitates processing of more difficult though important themes that are being discussed.

For some, it can create a tension or confusion to both accept another person's experience and views whilst also feeling responsible for creating rules, providing safety or teaching new skills. Caring for or about someone with an intellectual disability can move some towards a more protective stance and can make it harder to first slow down and consider or accept their experience or perspective. People with an intellectual disability have shared how often they have been overlooked, their voice is sometimes lost or drowned out amongst the opinions held by the teams, professionals and family members. True acceptance can be a refreshing change of experience for someone with an intellectual disability.

Holding an attitude of curiosity and expressing empathy when supporting someone with an intellectual disability can require a way of being sensitive and holding in mind the multitude of potential experiences. It can be harder to communicate these thoughts and reflections but our struggle to find appropriate and accessible language must not diminish the depth of experience that we are exploring and offering connection or empathy about.

Creating stories

An important component within DDP, is the use of a storytelling approach. Storytelling is an ancient form of communication that has enabled humans to share their experiences, knowledge and support over the years. It can be a way of teaching at a very practical level or a method of communicating morals or values held dear by the family or community. More recent research has identified how song and storytelling are accessible mediums for our brains as they are less likely to activate our defence brain systems than someone who is teaching or offering advice within general conversation, (Baylin, 2024).

Considerations for ID-based work

When we consider a story-based approach within work with someone with an intellectual disability we need to consider how long each statement can be, what prosody or intonation of voice is most compelling. In general, the use of long and complicated sentences or introductions of metaphor is distracting and unhelpful. Telling the brief 'story' about feeling nervous or worried about coming to the first meeting would be a really clear starting point. It is vital to check if the story you are telling or maybe even drawing out/ or illustrating with a clay model, is clear and also whether you've told the right story for the individual. It can be really important to check with the parent/carer in the room if there might be additional facts to add and to see if a client is ready for the story to be a bit longer. A story is often used at intervals to explore an upsetting time or to draw together information towards the end of a meeting. The story doesn't need to be long but does need to be digestible!

Creating coherence

When we meet with someone with an insecure attachment pattern, especially those with a complex history of trauma or gaps in connected experiences as a child, we notice how hard it is for that person to talk about their day, a tricky experience or their past with a sense of coherence. A conversation with someone with such interrupted early experiences often jumps about, there are multiple tangents, or conclusions to a description that might not make sense. Anyone listening, who was also present at the same time, will likely struggle to track or maybe even recognise the description of any event or day. People who have experienced trauma or interrupted connection have difficulty processing events, and their own biases or state of anxiety/terror might make it hard for them to track all the information, or they might dissociate and miss a lot of information. The world can feel very muddled and this might exacerbate a pre-existing sense of disquiet, confusion and also mistrust in those around them. The focus will be around the experience of the child or adult with the complex early history. The aim is to bring coherence, whether this is around the child or adult's internal physiological experience, their reactions or another person's reactions to a recent event.

DDP can also be used to explore and create a 'Therapeutic LifeStory', where the coherence offered is deeper than a list of events or a story book, and instead enables an exploration of reactions and feelings triggered by key issues from the past. A component of trauma recovery is linked with having a coherence, or clearer understanding, of what has occurred. The process of building this coherence depends on an integration of all the approaches in the model.

Considerations for ID-based work

Often, we can stumble and struggle to find the right words that fully express or capture the experience of another; again, additional thought needs to be given to the verbal and nonverbal communication that suits the person we are connecting with. For some people we can rely on conversations and at other times we need to be more creative in the ways we help make sense of an experience or previous trauma. It is likely that emerging themes from trauma-focused discussion will need revisiting to support processing and to embed a new perspective or relationship to upsetting experiences and memories.

Talking for

Often, a surprising and remarked upon approach within DDP is the way in which those who are in the position of aiming to provide regulation or connection are often asked to suggest and explore or name out loud what the experience is like for another person. This requires skills and practice to move from "You are doing this to me or us" to "Are you feeling like this or that?". Talking for another does not imply that someone else knows better. Each statement or "Talked for" experience has to be checked out to ensure your guess about their experience is capturing the right mood. For those that find it harder to talk, or who have not yet developed language, we can communicate this with both our words and in our nonverbal expressions, as is offered to all young preverbal babies. In talking for, and in accurately understanding another's experience, we deepen the connection with them. In showing our empathy and understanding about their perspective and experience, by holding their issues as of central importance, we help increase the sense of their worth and value in our lives. This helps build or deepen the trust within the relationship.

Considerations for ID-based work

In the context of working with someone with an intellectual disability, this need to check in, and check if you are on track, requires huge sensitivity. People with an intellectual disability are often disempowered, silenced and have long experienced challenges with having their voice or experience heard. In a world organised around cognitively able people, many people with an intellectual disability have learned to be highly compliant or might be vulnerable to suggestion. The aim here is to work slowly and gently – to check in repeatedly to see if you are really building the right picture about their experience. Sometimes this 'talking for' can sometimes require us to use fewer words and to use all our ways of communicating - facial expression, prosody and rate of speech, to check we are in tune with their experience. When tracking if you have made sense of someone else's worries or delights, we need to rely not just on their verbal or facial expressions, but also their whole body and physiological reactions. This is highly individual as some people become still when their experience is being captured, whilst others might make a specific vocalisation. 'Talking for' and then pausing to see if you are correct, can in some relationships be a very active and intense process. When considering this approach with families, or with staff teams, it is important to be aware of the huge power differential present between those who experience significant cognitive impairment and those who do not.

Talking about

The idea behind 'talking about' is to offer someone support and connection with their experience but in a more indirect way. It is useful for those who find direct conversations about very personal or important emotions hard. Sometimes, talking directly about personal issues is too challenging, because this type of conversation feels unfamiliar, or direct conversations increase the risk of shame or dysregulation (see Chapter 9 for fuller information about these experiences). Talking about needs to be person-centred, and undertaken with an attitude of PACE and is always undertaken respectfully, often tentatively, and with the person within clear ear shot. It is a purposeful conversation, sometimes between a therapist and an attachment figure, sometimes between a therapist and a puppet or toy, or even a cushion. 'Talking about' is also a valuable approach outside of the therapy room between key attachment figures or carers. It is a time to offer an empathetic suggestion about the person with a complex history and experience, with the attachment figure wondering out loud to themselves (or even to a cushion in the room!) about how things are for the client. Sometimes, you can talk about a client's experience with another parent or carer, but this only works within the DDP model if you are both holding the same focus of making sense of the client's experience.

Considerations for ID-based work

When 'Talking for' or 'Talking about', it is important for the person without an intellectual disability to be open to being wrong, to checking and repeating the conversation, and to be aware of the risk of compliance and the need to please the more powerful person in the relationship. It can take time and repeated explorations to bring clarity and a shared coherence to events or feelings, but again, when this occurs it strengthens the relationship and builds trust.

Matched affect

In matching someone's affect we bring our energy up to match their current experience; we are not mirroring their mood. For instance, if someone is very low and sad we can tune into their sadness, and adapt our prosody by slowing our pace of speech, use a lower tone of voice than we would for a more excitable conversation. We can also slow down our body and facial movements by positioning ourselves quietly alongside if they are expressing sadness. Alternatively, if someone is presenting as if they are on high alert, they are not very likely to be able to notice a soothing and calming voice. Instead, we need to inject some energy into our exchange to enable both brain states to be more aligned. 'Matching affect' does not mean that we join or mimic a client's rage or sadness, but that we speed up or slow down in response to their energy. The aim of matched affect, is to join with the person's experience, to connect with their energy, in order to co-regulate their distress. Once in a co-regulated relationship with you there is a greater chance you will be able to help them feel more regulated.

Considerations for ID-based work

If a child or adult with an intellectual disability is upset, we often try to present with soothing and calming voices, and yet it is interesting how often this does not seem to help calm things down. At other times the emphasis is on 'de-escalation', often with approaches such as distraction. The impact of distraction, though, is that it means that the important feeling that is being aired has to once again be ignored, minimised, or just isn't heard. We might need to express things with our words but these must be attuned to each person's understanding. We can join in by expressing and vocalising their mood with other vocalising, or through our actions. Offering someone a place to stomp might interrupt the need to run; picking up bean bags to throw at the sofa might be safer than other objects that could be thrown in the room. Using the name and voice of a familiar TV/film character that might embody that feeling can be a quick way of aligning alongside the mood someone is feeling.

Co-regulation

As described in matched affect, the aim within DDP is to join, move and talk or be in step with each other. In offering this joined level of connection we can enable co-regulation, as offered with a baby or small child who is experiencing upset or distress. Co-regulation enables a regulated adult a way of both connecting and soothing, or calming down, the person who is upset. For children and adults who find it a struggle to regulate their experiences, they can be given a pathway out of their distress when being co-regulated. The person leading must be in a regulated state themselves, but in matching affect, in matching movements and energy we can first join and then gradually slow down our prosody and change our positioning so that our bodies move less, or we sit in a more relaxed position. This can be both a verbal and a nonverbal process and is not always linear; as someone might be reactivated if the co-regulation is too rapid.

Considerations for ID-based work

When working with people with an intellectual disability, the process needs little adaptation, though there can sometimes be more focus on the non-verbal and physical steps needed to offer care, comfort and co-regulation. It is a subtle dance, and it helps to know a person's method of communicating, their signs of distress and agitation; also of knowing what patterns a person might show that indicate signals of lowered arousal and increased regulation.

Affective-reflective

DDP supports a very deep discovery and inquiry about the emotional experiences, or affect, experienced by others, and offers a way to reflect on these experiences to develop a coherence around the feelings. This manner of inquiry about an experience in turn enables the parents or carer to deepen their knowledge about the affective experience of the child/adult in the room. Often, we need to slow down conversations, to enable this reflection. With the use of a PACEful attitude, this type of consideration of another's experience can deepen empathy for another; it is also a vital component within intersubjective connection between family members or client-carer relationships. When this conversation is contained, not rushed and undertaken with sufficient co-regulation, it can be surprising to understand the underlying beliefs, or internal working models that are revealed in this opportunity to reflect. When we rush this process and move too quickly towards solutions, strategies or skills development we effectively shut down this exploration and change to better understand and also then reflect together on this experience. Sometimes, this reflection can link more recent events though often an important affective experience links with a trauma or challenging experience.

Considerations for ID-based work

Holding a focus on affect is complicated and runs counter to behavioural focused approaches. There can be a narrow tolerance or heightened anxiety that moves family, professionals and carers towards solutions and management strategies. This need for solutions typically accelerates when there are significant challenges or when risks become heightened. However, when we offer solutions or strategies this pulls us into a cognitive stance and reduces the intersubjective connection in the relationship. In moving away from listening and connecting to a more teaching approach we've changed the dynamic.

Many people with an intellectual disability can struggle with their detailed autobiographical memory, especially where timelines are needed, and so the 'affective-reflective' exploration might need to focus on more recent events. In some situations, the therapist or carer can help by holding or co-creating details of the story for the person with an intellectual disability, to allow a deepening of an affective-reflective conversation. The coherence created is, therefore, not just around the affective experience/reaction but can also help make greater sense of, and compassion for, why certain reactions are triggered by key events/experiences.

Interactive repair

There are often mistakes and misunderstandings arising within our relationships which, when addressed, can ensure we maintain trust and connection. There are times when we do not focus or attend well enough to another, when our attunement is mismatched or when we are distracted. Parental focus is sometimes, especially as a baby develops, drawn to other things – putting the washing on, making food or talking to the baby's sibling. At a young age, this lack of focus can feel like the end of the world. If you are not held in the gaze of your primary attachment figure, who will protect you and make sense of the world? As the baby develops they are gradually introduced to brief pauses in connection with their parents. This often leads to momentary upset but, if offered care and understanding about their distress, the baby will settle again.

Being offered understanding about this feeling of loss is another way of attuning to a baby's experience and is their first experience of both rupture and repair. 'Interactive repair' is essential for the moments when there is a disconnect or rupture within the relationship. Younger children, whose attachment security is still developing, need help with repair and reconnection, sometimes multiple times a day or even an hour, on a particularly scratchy day! In the safety-exploration cycle (described in Chapter 5) this offer of repair and comfort works in the same way that being soothed and settled does after being startled or scared by something in the environment.

DDP assists people to not just offer repair within a relationship, but to better notice the times when there has been a rupture to the relationship. In attuning to someone else's experience, and holding attachment security in mind, and in moving away from a behavioural monitoring perspective towards a relational focus, it can be easier to notice even minor glitches and tensions. Within DDP we emphasise the importance of noticing these changes and checking for potential offence or upset that might then impact on your relationship. We notice that it is likely that when 'Talking for' or 'Talking about' we will misjudge, overstate or just make an error. Sometimes the repair is needed, not because a parent or carer has made an active error or misunderstood things, but because the client has experienced a hurt or slight (such as attention being offered to another person rather than to them first). Offering repair for such misunderstandings or upsets is very powerful.

Considerations for ID-based work

The value of this approach feels even more important to hold in mind for people with an intellectual disability, who are often surrounded by people who find the world easier to navigate, and so the person with an intellectual disability might be more likely to note or be reminded of another times when they made an error or did not fit in, or dropped something again. Being offered an apology is a powerful step towards rebuilding a relationship.

This need for making sense of mis-attunement, or not getting something right proves valuable, and sometimes vital, in busy settings such as school or residential care where there are competing demands for attention. For clients who experience marked rigidity, who experience multiple changes of carers, who might have to process let downs (transport hasn't arrived on time again, for example), the need for repair and to make sense of the disappointment can be marked. In opening up to a relationship we risk being let down. Many people with an intellectual disability are dependent on a huge chain or network of people. Whilst an increased network might often create buffers and overlaps to smooth over gaps, the larger and less interdependent networks are vulnerable to interruptions such as when a bus breaks down or key support workers are sick. The experience of rupture and the challenges to processing sudden changes makes the need for repair almost greater or more prescient when supporting someone with an intellectual disability.

Conclusion

DDP has evolved from a direct therapeutic model with a child and/or parent to a way of supporting interactions, deepening understanding and building relationships and managing risks within and across services or organisations. The flexibility and power of this intervention draws on its flexibility and sensitivity of support to both those who have experienced gaps in care and also for those who are offering this dedicated support. In caring for the intersubjective relationships and through improving connection and understanding - and also by helping people to experience new types of relationships - opportunities develop for healing relational trauma. By focusing on, not just the vulnerable children and adults, but also supporting their carers/parents, DDP offers a holistic model where coherence of support can be developed for both sides of the relationship.

Chapter 3:

Why explore Dyadic Developmental Practice with people with intellectual disabilities?

Summary

- People with intellectual disabilities are at an increased risk of experiencing relational disruptions, both in childhood and adulthood, including challenges to the development of a secure attachment, increased susceptibility to trauma, multiple moves and marginalisation. Within this chapter, factors contributing to these relational disruptions are examined, including individual characteristics, dynamics within the dyad, and broader societal influences.
- The role and impact of Dyadic Developmental Practice (DDP-practice) specifically with people with intellectual disabilities, is outlined. This chapter focuses on fostering a sense of safety and safe interactions, addressing shame and discussing blocked care. It also highlights the importance of these concepts across levels, of the system including with immediate caregivers, within teams and across services.
- We highlight how the key approaches within Dyadic Developmental Psychotherapy (DDP) are suited and attuned to the needs of people with an intellectual disability and those that care for them alike and how these can foster connected relationships and meaningful engagement within the individual's care network.

Introduction

'The brain learns best through constant repetition which means that the key therapeutic adults for severely traumatized children are their carers and teachers rather than traditional therapists.'

Furnivall & Grant (2014, p.12)

As outlined in Chapter 2, DDP is rooted in attachment theory and intersubjective relationships, aiming to support individuals who have experienced developmental or relational trauma. By fostering attuned and safe relationships, DDP and the resulting practice helps children and adults experience responses to their distress based in consistent, empathetic care. This chapter explores why DDP specifically should be considered with people with intellectual disabilities, by describing how this population group is more likely to experience attachment difficulties, and by outlining the risks and impacts of trauma. The chapter is consequentially split into two sections, the first considering the possible complexities in attachment when a person has an intellectual disability and the second considering the increased risk of traumatic experiences, including developmental trauma for this group. Throughout, we describe how these elements affect relational security and how DDP approaches offers a psychologically-informed relational model of therapy and care to offer therapeutic healing in response, providing a framework to address these challenges by engaging existing support networks and promoting relational-based care.

1. Attachment difficulties

The nature of our relationships is one of the most influential aspects on quality of life. Early attachment relationships can pave the way for our later relational experiences. Chapter 5 provides an overview of attachment theory, as well as a critique of that theory. In this chapter, we think about how these potential difficulties with attachment allow DDP to be a useful model for the person, their caregivers and the system.

For too long, people with intellectual disabilities were thought of as emotionally void and their emotional experiences were not considered or thought relevant. Thankfully, this is no longer accepted, and in 2017, the British Psychological Society published guidance on incorporating attachment theory into clinical practice for people with intellectual disabilities. Relationships and early attachment are important for us all, and of course, as it has been increasingly recognised that this is just as true for people with intellectual disabilities (BPS, 2017). There should not be an inherent assumption that secure attachment is harder for people with an intellectual disability, but there are some ways that developing a healthy attachment relationship might be more complex for people with intellectual disabilities (summarised in Figure 3.1, below; for fuller review, see Fletcher, 2016). Whilst we consider attachment complexities below, it is important to acknowledge that many parents can overcome these barriers.

Of note, assessing attachment security is incredibly difficult, and inaccurate (as discussed in Chapter 5). Some studies suggest that the proportion of attachment security in children with intellectual disability is broadly equivalent to people without intellectual disabilities (Larson *et al*, 2011), but a systemic review of studies from 1980–2019 concluded that children with intellectual disabilities are less likely to develop secure attachments and more likely to develop disorganised attachments (Alexander *et al*, 2024); although a further overview of this is given in Chapter 5, here we will discuss some of these factors in relation to how DDP can help.

Figure 3.1 Potential complicating factors to attachment security for people with intellectual disabilities

(You can also find this figure as a photocopiable resource in the Appendices 1).

Individual factors	Parental factors
■ Premature birth and additional physical needs alter the time they have with their parents and the availability of soothing touch. ■ Altered sensory experiences ■ Communication difficulties ■ Need increased physical proximity to feel safe and secure ■ Smaller social circles and attachment relationships ■ Challenges in experiencing co-regulation ■ Challenges in expressing their needs ■ Less responsive to parents' attachment cues ■ Need longer to process and respond to stimuli ■ Physical disabilities ■ Lifelong support needs	■ Dejection and overcompensating in context of diagnosis ■ Missing delayed or difficult to read attachment cues ■ Smaller social circle and isolation ■ Parental grief and feelings of loss ■ Overwhelm, guilt, frustration, helplessness, shame ■ Experiencing blame ■ Attachment history ■ Relationship to seeking help ■ Cognitive needs ■ Sensory preferences ■ Neurodiversity ■ Economic strain ■ Additional layers of practical care impact on emotional connection and reflection ■ Increased risk of mental health difficulties and marital strain

System factors

- Potential ack of available and/or quality professional and practical support in the context of needing lifelong support
- Changeable and professional support network, who lack adequate support and guidance in negotiating relationship boundaries
- Living amongst discriminatory and stigmatising cultural discourses
- Social exclusion
- Placement insecurity and multiple placements
- More likely to live in low socio-economic households and be exposed to poverty
- More likely than non-disabled peers to experience violence, abuse and neglect
- More likely than non-disabled peers to be exposed to a greater number of potential adverse life experiences
- Ongoing misunderstanding of needs and support offered

There are several reasons why developing stable attachments may be harder for some children (and later adults) with intellectual disabilities and their parents/key care givers. Although attachment patterns are unique, there are core elements which aid a healthy and secure attachment relationship to develop between a care giver and child. These include:

a) Factors within the child
b) Factors between the adult/child dyad (the two attachment partners)
c) Factors within the caregiver
d) Factors within the system – societal and systemic.

One of the reasons that DDP is such a useful intervention is that it allows each of these factors, and the interaction between them, to be thought about and worked with: DDP for the individual; DDP-parenting for the caregiver/child relationship; and DDP-practice for the wider system.

DDP is not the only model that aims to address attachment difficulties but, in part, this is a reason to consider it for people with intellectual disabilities; in addition it helps everyone in the support network who relates to and interacts with the person with intellectual disability, to incorporate the key elements of DDP into their care, including curiosity, building safety and connection and allowing everyone's vulnerabilities to be explored and supported.

a) Factors within the child

Separating attachment into factors that relate to the individual and the attachment partner (be that carer or parent) is slightly artificial, as attachment, by its very nature, is relational and requires active engagement from both people. It can be helpful to think of attachment as a dance, where neither attachment partner knows the exact steps at first, but both must learn to move together in a coherent and responsive way. Initially, this can seem a random phenomenon, with the adult responding to the random and unpredictable needs of the child, but over time, a pattern of a dance begins to develop. In this dance, roles of leader and follower naturally shift, and each person must adapt to each other's needs, creating a connection that is fluid and meaningful. Over time, this dance can grow to hold and soothe distress, fear, anger, and shame, fostering a sense of safety and understanding. As with any dance, the skills and abilities of both partners are important. For individuals with an intellectual disability, certain factors can influence this attachment dance, potentially creating unique rhythms and challenges that require careful attention and adaptation. The dance is always unique, yet overtime each dyad forms a dance, sometimes a secure dance and sometimes one within which there is a lot of anxiety.

Very early experiences

Babies born prematurely or with additional physical needs might need ongoing, complex, and invasive medical care, which may alter the time they have with their parents and the availability of soothing touch. They may be in incubators, receiving medical help with feeding or from an early age in specially adapted wheelchairs or positioning seats. All these factors can alter initial attachment seeking and responding behaviours.

Sensory and communication needs

There is also the possibility of altered sensory development experiences and/or sensory integration needs which, for some individuals, alters the way in which they experience touch and comfort from others. For some, this might mean that they need greater firmness in touch to feel connected and grounded; for others, there might be a need to avoid touch, as this is not soothing on a sensory integration level. Communication difficulties will impact how individuals can express their needs and therefore how parents or carers can accommodate this. These elements make the process of attachment in the early and later years more complex for people with intellectual disabilities and their parents. Of course, any parent can struggle to identify and meet the needs of their child, but this can be more prevalent for children within the intellectual disability population (Giltaij *et al*, 2015). Parents whose children have intellectual disability may also need extraordinary sensitivity to overcome the difficulty that their children have with expressing their attachment signals (Schuengel & Janssen, 2006). DDP's focus on intersubjectivity and attuned reactions can be helpful here, across the life span. In addition, there is some evidence that, due to reduced theory of mind, people with intellectual disabilities might need increased physical proximity in order to feel safe and secure (Fletcher

& Gallichan, 2016). The focus on routine and structure can also begin to offer this predictability and, again, transparently sharing this information with the person and parents can also be helpful to explore this in an intersubjective way.

Why consider DDP?

Many families can adapt and meet their child's needs, but the increased risks and challenges in doing so highlight the importance of a reflexive, intersubjective approach, which DDP-parenting and practice explores and aims to address. This approach offers to help build an understanding that allows the carers in the parent-child relationship (the dance) to be better able to be fully responsive to the child's unique needs. Instead of following the dance the parent/carer had envisioned or expected, parents learn to adapt to a different rhythm – one that may be slower, involve less physical touch, or require alternative communication styles.

DDP concepts of 'talking about' and 'talking for' can allow sensory differences to be verbalised for and with the person with intellectual disabilities; over time (as developmentally appropriate) this can allow carers to better understand sensory needs and increase the likelihood of this being matched for the person. Meaningful touch and closeness are helpful to hold in mind too.

A focus on intersubjectivity and attuned connections can support the process of identifying and meeting the needs of people with intellectual disabilities who might struggle to communicate their attachment cues and emotional needs. Routine and structure can offer predictability and support intersubjectivity.

Ongoing needs

In addition, ongoing additional health, social and educational needs can lead to multiple interventions, by multiple professionals; these may be experienced as supportive or invasive and families talk of having to tell their story many times to different professionals. In the context of an involvement from an ever-changing network of support, what is the individual's and families' experiences of permanence? And how are interventions attuned to the individual (as opposed to being done to them)?

We all need the support of other people we feel safe with to help us manage emotional distress and to learn an embodied sense of our own emotions; this is created in dialogue with our attachment figures, in co-regulation, so that in time, there is greater capacity to do this more independently. As we say above, people with intellectual disabilities may experience challenges in experiencing coregulation and developing self-regulation skills. The challenges in relationship can make it harder for individuals with intellectual disabilities to feel safe and secure enough in their relationships to express their needs openly, have those needs understood, and receive timely, attuned responses. The issue could be the limited availability of attachment figures in their lives or a lack of trust and safety in the relationships they do have.

Why consider DDP?

The relational focus of DDP, as the first step of establishing safety and improving regulation, allows us to place safety and relational connection at the base of other interventions; it is linked to the ideas of Maslow's hierarchy of needs (Maslow, 1954), Golding's Pyramid of Need (Chapter 11, Golding & Hughes, 2012; Golding, 2013) and recent the neuroscientific models (see Chapter 6). Safety and connection are imperative to enable relating and reasoning.

Within the DDP model, this development of emotional co-regulation, is based in curious narrative, in the reflexivity of acknowledging affect and cognition. If these verbal elements are pitched wrongly or are less accessible, this could impact on the persons abilities/opportunities to develop regulation skills, which in turn impact on developing healthy attachment relationships throughout life. The need for curiosity and reflexivity to do this is inherent within the DDP model. In this book, we also explore ways that this can be matched appropriately to the cognitive abilities and skills of people with intellectual disabilities.

b) Factors between the adult/child dyad (the two attachment partners)

Diagnosis

There is some evidence that receiving the diagnosis of a learning disability of itself may alter the interactions between a child and their parent (Fletcher, 2016; Alexander *et al*, 2024). Further to this, a child with an intellectual disability (and additional physical needs) might be less responsive to their parents, which in turn, can lead to parents overcompensating or becoming dejected within the relationship. For some, this may mean a mismatch develops within the attachment relationship.

Showing and processing attachment cues

Many people with cognitive impairments need longer to process and respond to stimuli, stimuli in the environment and stimuli provided by the caregiver. This slower processing can be missed by parents, who are keen to offer good attachment cues, and therefore unintentionally disrupt the rhythm of attachment. This can also lead a pattern of parents overcompensating and further missing their child's attachment cues, exacerbating an initially small mismatch to become more significant. Returning to the dance metaphor, the parent, in their haste to get the attachment dance right, may rush ahead, almost performing a solo, but in a way which does not allow the dance/attachment partner to be truly part of the dance.

Leaving and returning to the caregiver

Difficulties in child-carer mis-attunement may be further complicated by physical disabilities and carer concerns about the child's cognitive ability, factors which can alter the process of leaving and returning to the caregiver, either due to physical ability, and/or carer anxiety. This process of leaving and returning is important in attachment for several reasons:

- it allows the child to begin to explore and develop some increasing levels of independence
- it supports the natural development of object permanency: the skill of knowing that even though an object (or attachment figure) is out of sight, they still exist in the world
- it plays an important role in developing attachment security, as it allows emotional connection to the caregiver even when they are not physically present
- returning to a caregiver allows the child's feelings to be organised and for them to be delighted in (this is the beginning of co-regulation (see Chapters 4 and 5 for further information on this process).

As this process is multi-faceted in function, so is the potential impact on the person with an intellectual disability when this process is affected; see Figure 3.2, below:

Figure 3:2 Impact of leaving and returning in attachment

Impact on development of successfully leaving and returning to a caregiver	Potential impact on the person with an intellectual disability when leaving and return to a caregiver is interrupted/problematic
Allows the child to begin to explore and develop some increasing levels of independence.	Children may have less opportunity to develop their social, emotional and daily living skills as part of developing their independence in a more typical trajectory as they are not exploring and trying things without their caregiver.
Supports the natural development of object permanency: the skill of knowing that even though an object (or attachment figure) is out of sight, they still exist in the world.	Without object permanence, the absence of an attachment figure is more anxiety provoking, as the person cannot know that person will return (or even still exists), heightening separation anxiety.

Plays an important role in developing attachment security, as it allows emotional connection to the caregiver even when they are not physically present.	If children struggle to return to their caregiver, literally or figuratively speaking, children might experience distress more intensely and/or for longer.
Allows the child's feelings to be organised and for them to be delighted in. This is the beginning of co-regulation.	Co-regulation (and later self-regulation) patterns are likely to be more difficult to develop.

The attachment dance throughout chronological development

As children grow and develop, their attachment needs change and they utilise the leaving and returning process more (in a usually developmental trajectory from about 12 months plus). In later childhood, children begin to transfer their relational support to other adults, such as teachers or coaches. They also start becoming more independent from their parents, spending increasing amounts of time with peers – first through playdates, and later, sleepovers.

As they enter the teenage years, there can be a shift where teenagers seek greater (and sometimes excessive) independence, while parents may resist this. This push-and-pull dynamic, where typically children push and parents pull back, is crucial for developing appropriate levels of independence, though the need for co-regulation and connection remains. Attachment needs for children and young people with an intellectual disability might look quite different as they grow older, with the push for independence potentially less driven by the individual. To return to the dance, often, teenagers without an intellectual disability feel ready to pirouette across the dance floor before their parents are ready for them to do so. Often, teenagers push this separation, and parents accept (with whatever level of smoothness). However, a person with an intellectual disability and their attachment figure might wish to continue dancing together longer, sometimes whilst external others are suggesting the person is ready to dance solo (perhaps based on chronological age). In our experience, attuned parents are usually good at spotting when someone, even with a profound and multiple learning disability, will benefit from leaving the family home; but the dance is different.

The complexity of fostering healthy attachment relationships for people with intellectual disabilities is further compounded by the fact that they may have smaller social circles (whilst having larger professional networks) throughout both childhood and adulthood, which becomes increasingly significant as they grow older. Some research suggests that the principal caregiver, often the mother, tends to develop a particularly intense relationship with the person with intellectual disabilities. This bond includes a deeper and more intimate understanding of the meanings behind the person's behaviours and interactions (Pelchat *et al*, 2003). While this closeness can be beneficial in fostering a sense of security, it may also inadvertently contribute to limiting the individual's broader social network as others are less able to understand how to connect with the person based on their needs and wishes, exacerbated by the person struggling to express these.

There is a difference in the range of attachment figures for people with an intellectual disability, with there being more attachment figures in their lives whose relationship with them may be professional in nature, whereas people without intellectual disabilites have more personal attachment experiences with multiple friends, friends parents, extended family. The lack of variety of attachment experiences can also alter the developmental pathways typically associated with achieving greater independence and the process of separation. For people with intellectual disabilities, this narrowed scope of attachment, alongside practical barriers, can make navigating these pathways more challenging. Families may also struggle with this dynamic, as the strong reliance on a single/few primary attachment figures can reinforce dependence and make transitions toward autonomy more complex and emotional.

Why consider DDP?

DDP's very focus is on the dyad of the attachment, be that parent/s and child, or young person or adult and carers. This focus on the relationships that endure outside the therapy room means that the areas between the person with intellectual disabilities and their carers can have a coherent narrative established around them. Addressing these challenges requires a nuanced approach that supports both the individual and their family in expanding social networks and fostering diverse, meaningful relationships. The 'talking for' and coherent storytelling elements of DDP are particularly related to this area as they allow expression of relational elements that can be harder to acknowledge and discuss; DDP can give the framework for these to be talked about day to day. It also allows areas like shame and blocked care to be thought about for each person within the dyad (and the system) in a way which is safe enough.

One of the difficulties can be that what originated as a relatively minor mismatch in attachment needs, becomes a bigger difficulty, as parents lose confidence in their ability to offer attachment security and containment and withdraw from his process. Of course, parental resources, including access to support and previous experiences of parental roles and disability can reduce stress and might mean support is more easily sourced or resources are more easily accessed. A lack of familiarity could increase stressors as families need to navigate medical terms, genetics, teams of professionals and alterations in their family patterns of activities

c) Factors within the caregiver

Parental grief and loss

It has been proposed that parental grief and feelings of loss for the imagined 'healthy child' can impact parental attunement early in a child's life (Fletcher, 2016). While research suggests that most families adapt by representing their child's actual abilities rather than clinging to 'wished-for' or predicted abilities, the process of grief and possible emotional detachment can still hinder attunement. If parents struggle to develop an internal representation of their child's actual skill level and instead focus on idealised abilities, it can further disrupt this connection (Barnett *et al*, 2003). In the dynamic of a dance, if the parent's steps are guided by unrealistic expectations, it becomes difficult to meet the child where they are cognitively, emotionally, and relationally. It can also become difficult for the child to know what their parents' expectations are. They are less likely to be scaffolded and supported to work towards their skills, to experience success and develop a secure sense of self. This mismatch in the 'attachment dance' can affect parental sensitivity and hinder the development of secure attachment (Atkinson *et al*, 1999). In such situations, the 'in-the-moment' nature of DDP, with its focus on reflection and attunement, can help parents adjust their steps to align more closely with their child's needs.

When working with parents, it is important to recognise that families may not identify their experience as grief or view it as an explanation for their responses. Imposing such a notion (or any notion) without explanation or curiosity is unhelpful (BPS, 2017). While most families do adapt to their child's disability, complicating factors (such as physical disability, societal attitudes, lack of clarity regarding diagnosis and service availability) can influence this process; this is further explored later in this chapter. Talking for, curiosity and storytelling concepts of DDP can help explore these areas with parents/carers. If parents feel that there are difficulties in their child's development and yet experience blame or a lack of support in relation to these concerns, they may feel isolated and/or overwhelmed. This can lead to feelings of guilt, frustration, helplessness or shame, potentially impacting their emotional well-being and their ability to advocate effectively for their child. These emotions may also strain their relationship with professionals, making it harder to collaborate on interventions or support strategies. PACE-based conversation about parents' hopes and griefs, modelled alongside emotional distress can be helpful in exploring this in whatever form it takes.

Parental attachment history

The attachment history of the parent is also relevant, as some parents will be better equipped to adjust their attachment style to attune to the needs of their child with intellectual disabilities and others will find this more difficult. It may be that the difficulties in the parent-child interaction reignite feelings of rejection or inadequacy in the parent's own attachment experiences. Some parents will be better able to seek help and have more emotional and practical resources to do so. Other factors such as the parent's level of cognitive function, sensory preferences and neurodiversity are also of relevance in attachment, as well as the parents internal working model, and their relationship with help seeking can be helpful here.

Why consider DDP?

DDP-Parenting begins with a focus on parent-preparation sessions; these support parents/carers to develop a clear understanding about their own patterns of relating to themselves, others and emotions and how this might have developed in the context of their experiences of being parented (explored further in Chapter 12). Parent-preparation sessions also prepare parents to develop their own ways of offering a PACEful parenting style for their children; PACE allows for individually interpreted ways of embodying this stance, allowing parents a way to be PACEful and offers them tools to provide each element that that fits well for them and their family, culture etc. Unlike other psychological therapies, DDP actively involves parents as key partners in the therapeutic process. Through these preparation sessions, parents are better equipped to reflect on their own attachment history and have modelled the skills necessary for co-regulation – an essential role they will continue to play in the future. In an adult intellectual disability context, this approach extends to carers, offering a structured space to explore and refine their caring role in supporting individuals with intellectual disabilities. This emphasis on parental and caregiver involvement is central to the DDP model.

There are wider impacts of having a child with intellectual disabilities which can impact on the attachment relationship. Parents of a child with an intellectual disability may be more stressed, which can lead to less parental engagement. There are links between engagement and economic stability; having a child with intellectual disabilities may lead to financial implications for families, with estimates that it cost three times more to care for a child with intellectual disabilities than a child without intellectual disabilities (Joseph Rowntree Foundation, 1998) and that 55% of families of disabled children live in poverty (Sloper & Beresford, 2006).

The additional layers of practical care can also lead to caregivers finding it harder to create emotional space and practical time to make emotional connections, to think about attachment styles or to have space to reflect and allow connection.

Providing DDP-practice support for all carers allows a space for this to be directly addressed; the focus on non-verbal interactions, PACE and creating narrative can allow a different perspective on these areas, to deepen and (re-)establish fulfilling connections and attachment security.

In addition, the experience of having an intellectual disability and/or being a parent to someone who has an intellectual disability (and additional other challenges) can be highly isolating. It can be hard not to be consulted in one's own life and plans and to be talked about, talked for and excluded from society, which are the experiences of many people with intellectual disabilities. Support networks can be hard or impossible to establish, and more so when there are multiple moves, or placements away from an individual's family of origin or community. Furthermore, families may have ongoing disputes about the type and quality of service they want for their children/adult-children. This can occur at a range of times throughout the person's childhood and adulthood. It is increasingly recognised that navigating through health, social care and education systems can cause severe trauma to families of people with intellectual disabilities (Challenging Behaviour Foundation, 2021). This is perhaps more likely at times of key transitions, such as leaving school, leaving home, or parental ill-health. Parents of children with intellectual disabilities are identified as being more likely to have mental health problems, a general risk factor when it comes to developing healthy attachment relationships, and which has implications of the interaction and enjoyment they have with their children (Singer, 2006).

It could be that, due to the extra demands of caring for someone with an intellectual disability, and the lessening of societal support, parents are less available to offer attuned and attached care and, in turn, this can lead to unmanageable shame for parents. Shame occurs when someone is unable to manage the overwhelming feelings they have; over time a lack of support in managing and understanding these feelings can become a sense of "I am bad" or "I am unable to do this". Unmanageable experiences of shame can hold risks of blocked care/blocked trust occurring (see Chapter 9: Shame and shielding from shame, and Chapter 10: Blocked care, for further explanation). This can occur in parenting when a parent's attempts at establishing attachment are not reciprocated as they expected or hoped. Although many of these barriers do not belong to the parents or the person with intellectual disabilities, they can still be the ones who experience shame.

d) Factors within the system – societal and systemic

As well as child, parent and interactional factors affecting attachment security, there are also wider societal elements that can affect how both parts of the dyad (parent and child) function in their relationship with each other and with others, such as professionals, school and carers. Those who 'observe the dance' may comment on it or join in with it, invited, uninvited or through necessity of support.

The role of society in contributing to and perpetuating attachment difficulties and disempowered potions can be seen in the viral video "Assume I can drink a margarita", where our assumptions about the ability of someone with Down Syndrome to drink margarita, party, live independently and work, are challenged (Down Syndrome International, 2024).

> *'Everyone was being given tea in a cup and saucer apart from my daughter who was given a mug without any thought to what she might need or be capable of. Other people's low expectations create more of a problem than my daughter's needs... I can count on one hand how many times I have cried over Hannah's disabilities, but I have lost count of the number of times I have cried because of others' insistence to hand her that mug.'*
>
> Derbyshire (2013)

Cultural discourses

The cultural discourses/assumptions, such as those above, that we as carers may have about people with an intellectual disability can also hold the people we care for back from reaching their full potential or allow their experiences of disempowerment to become the norm. This also connects to re-traumatisation experiences, as new instances of disempowerment can evoke feelings similar to those experienced during past traumatic/abusive events. Whether DDP can alter cultural discourses is a big ask. However, the curious stance about the unique individual and family who practitioners are working with, and explicit conversation about these narratives, can allow discourses to be challenged at whatever level these conversations are able to occur; including within wider systems.

Needing lifelong support and the impact on attachment relationships

Attachment is a lifelong process and our attachment styles continue into our later relationship and interpersonal or romantic connections. As children grow up, attachment relationships move to peers and romantic relationships, whilst attachments are maintained with parents. Through attachment relationships, people develop internal working models of who they are, what is valued about them, how other people will treat them (their relational expectations), and their sense of safety in the world. The internal working model we develop when younger becomes our blueprint for relationship patterns going forward. People with intellectual disabilities are more likely to experience institutionalised care, where care is provided within a formal care/residential setting (Green & Goldwyn, 2002). They are also likely to have numerous agencies and individual professionals involved in their lives from an early age; this list can be extensive – schoolteachers, teaching assistants, Direct Payment carers, respite carers, social workers, psychologists, physiotherapists, speech and language therapists and occupational therapists (not an exhaustive list). The focus of these roles is often to help meet someone's developmental, physical and/or social needs, but perhaps attend less to their emotional and relational needs (and those of their wider family). There can be numerous paid people involved in the lives of people with intellectual disabilities, and this group of people can change in unpredictable ways, again impacting on the person's understanding of relationships and relational safety. Many people with intellectual disabilities need lifelong support and this pattern of unpredictable relationship changes can continue.

Many people with intellectual disabilities are reliant on carers throughout their childhood and adult life and risks are inherent (BPS, 2017). These risks include frequent changes in staff personnel, high workloads for staff, and a lack of continuity in staff presence, which limit opportunities for individualised support. This inconsistency can undermine the development and quality of relationships for people within the care settings. There is often an overemphasis on fostering independence that overlooks the universal human need for interdependence and intersubjectivity in relationships. This can neglect the relational aspects essential for emotional well-being and co-regulation. Additionally, it is recognised that paid carers frequently lack adequate support and guidance in negotiating relationship boundaries. This can result in mismatch in the caregiver-service user relationship, further complicating efforts to establish meaningful and supportive connections.

Why consider DDP?

Proactively addressing the challenges of negotiating boundaries with a DDP approach offers a way for carers of children and adults to be responsive to social, emotional, developmental, cognitive, relational and behavioural development and explicit about relationship boundaries (see Chapter 8 and chapter 14). Working with key attachment figures to ensure that the ideas of PACE, safety and co-regulation are being developed can help with these factors (see Section 2 on key concepts).

DDP-practice can foster a more stable and enriching care environment, enhancing the quality of relationships and promoting both independence and the need for connection and interdependence. DDP can help relate to children's or adults' experiences, meeting them where they are within their current abilities to manage emotional distress and be in relation with each other. This, in part, may reflect cognitive ability but also the quality of relationships and attachment experiences people have had.

Social exclusion

People with intellectual disabilities still often find themselves in the 'out of sight, out of mind' position in society, which undoubtedly impacts on their views of self (Oakes, 2012). Out-of-county placements can become the norm, especially for those who are considered to express their needs and distress in ways that are considered to pose significant challenges. Such provisions can have a potential to focus on the service provider rather than service user (King, 2005). These factors can be seen as indicators of society's interaction with disability and a social exclusion of this population, coupled with the fear and actuality of eradication for this group, written about so eloquently by Valerie Sinason (2021). This interpersonal and intrapersonal distress can add to a lack of interaction and opportunities thereof for secure relationships. DDP aims to help strengthen relational security and offer opportunities for co-regulation, which allows safety to be established.

Placement, relational and personal insecurity

People with intellectual disability can also experience multiple placement failures, especially for those who express their distress through behaviours that are challenging to others, or who keep themselves relationally safe through (verbal or physical) aggression aimed at keeping others away. Placement breakdowns mean the person repeatedly moving, and moving means re-establishing relationships with new and eventually multiple caregivers and managing multiple losses. Repeated placement changes will undoubtedly shape a person's views of themselves and others (internal working model, see Chapter 4) and therefore their way of relating to others. It might take a long time to establish trust in relationships; each move reduces the person's capacity to do this, as it risks eroding the trust from before (more on service risks in Chapter 14).

Why consider DDP?

The Golding pyramid of need can be helpful for us to better understand where the person's or systems needs are and allow focus on establishing what is most needed at that time, be that safety and/or predictability in relationships. In turn, identifying key attachment figures that are able to implement ideas of connection before correction and PACE can aid with reducing placement breakdowns.

Dan Hughes talks about how children cannot establish a sense of safety if the adults who look after them are not safe; this is true in all caring relationships. The DDP model allows a perspective to be brought to services about how service organisational structures and interactions can impact on safety and relational security for individuals. It is important to think about therapeutic endings, and endings to placements when necessary; also the importance of repair whenever possible, offered in a timely and regulated way (more on this throughout the book).

2. Adverse childhood experiences, developmental trauma and intellectual disabilities

Children with intellectual disabilities constitute approximately 9.2% of the UK's looked-after children population (UK Government, n.d.) This section gives a brief overview of the prevalence of trauma among people with intellectual disabilities.

> *'Traumatic events overwhelm the ordinary systems of care that give people a sense of control, connection, and meaning... Traumatic events are extraordinary, not because they occur rarely, but rather because they overwhelm the ordinary human adaptations to life.'*
>
> Herman (1992, p.33)

Psychological trauma has been defined as

> *'an event, a series of events or a set of circumstances that is experienced by the individual as physically or emotionally harmful or life threatening'*
>
> SAMHSA (2014, p.7)

Complex trauma is repeated, ongoing, and often involves extreme interpersonal trauma (Kezelman and Stravropolous, 2012). The interpersonal nature of this type of trauma means that, inherently, it impacts on trust and relationships, and is acknowledged to have significant impacts across a range of areas.

Over the past 20 years, there has been increasing recognition of the experiences of trauma and adverse childhood experiences (ACEs) and the impact on adult mental health, physical health and social outcomes (Kessler *et al*, 2010; Larkin *et al*, 2014; Mongan *et al*, 2017; Shevlin *et al*, 2015) in the general population. Equally, it is recognised that people with an intellectual disability are more vulnerable to adverse life events and abuse than their peers (Emerson *et al*, 2015; Wigham *et al*, 2011).

Emerson's review of the UK's Millenium study in relation to inequalities (Emerson *et al*, 2015), suggests that when compared with their non-disabled peers, children with intellectual disabilities are:

- more likely to live in rented housing, overcrowded housing, or housing in a poor state of repair
- more likely to live in low socio-economic households and be exposed to poverty

- more likely to be exposed to tobacco smoke
- at increased risk of exposure to violence, including bullying, physical, sexual, emotional abuse, or neglect
- more likely to be exposed to harsh parenting and chaotic family environments
- more likely to be exposed to a greater number of potential adverse life experiences; among other things.

The adverse life experience literature includes experiencing physical or emotional abuse; abandonment or neglect; losing a family member to suicide, or close bereavement; growing up in a household with substance misuse; have a mentally ill or incarcerated parent; divorce or separation of parents as adverse life events (ACEs). There is indication of higher rates of ACEs for children with intellectual disabilities, with a Dutch study concluding 82.6% of children with intellectual disabilities having experienced at least one ACE, and 49% having experienced more than two (Horner-Johnson & Drum, 2006). Parental separation and divorce were the most commonly reported ACEs, affecting 63% of people. Notably, parents of children with intellectual disabilities face a higher risk of marital strain and divorce (Glenn, 2007). Other ACEs included parental mental health problems (33%) and witnessing violence against parent (28%; Horner-Johnson & Drum, 2006).

Why consider DDP?

Historically, the emotional needs of people with intellectual disabilities were underestimated or dismissed. However, as service provision increasingly acknowledges, in the emotional and relational world of people with intellectual disabilities, DDP-practice helps us consider the early and ongoing trauma, the factors which make it hard for an individual and their carers to reciprocally relate and feel connected. DDP-practice provides a framework of how to align with these principles and those of trauma-informed care. Focusing on the importance of 'connection before correction' (Hughes, 2009) to empower individuals, families, and carers to overcome barriers in attachment and increased prevalence of trauma for people with intellectual disabilities.

Abuse and neglect

Prevalence rates of abuse and trauma among individuals with intellectual disabilities are difficult to establish, but consistently show higher levels compared to non-disabled peers. A population-based review of state records in 2000 found that 31% of children with disabilities experienced abuse or neglect, compared to 9% of non-disabled peers. Children with intellectual disabilities had a 25% prevalence, with a fourfold increased risk of physical, emotional, sexual abuse, and neglect (Sullivan & Knutson, 2000). Similar findings were reported in a UK-based study by Spencer *et al.* (2005).

A recent systematic review reported that 1 in 3 adults with intellectual disabilities experienced sexual abuse in adulthood, with higher rates in institutional settings and among those with greater levels of disability (though rates decreased for individuals with profound disabilities; Tomsa *et al*, 2021). Earlier studies provide varying estimates, including 25% of individuals with intellectual disabilities having experienced sexual violence (Sobsey, 1994), and 49% experiencing 10 or more sexually abusive incidents (Sobsey & Doe, 1991). However, contrasting findings exist, such as a 2006 review concluding no significant differences in maltreatment rates between people with and without intellectual disabilities.

There are also experiences of trauma in from someone's experience of having an intellectual disability including in relation to inappropriate management of challenging behaviours, and unnecessary restrictions in the environment and use of restrictive practices and the lack of consistency in staff (Kildahl *et al*, 2020).

Hate crime

Overall, people with intellectual disabilities experience more violence in general when compared to those without disabilities. In 2008, The National Crime Victim Survey found that people with disabilities experience higher rates of violence than people without disabilities (40 victimizations per 1,000 persons with disabilities, compared to about 20 per 1,000 without disabilities), and in the 'Living in Fear' report, over one third of people with intellectual disabilities experienced some form of disability-related hate crime (Beadle-Brown *et al*, 2014). Similarly, the Health and Social Care Committee (2016) launched a national survey focusing on determining the current level of autism and learning disability hate crime in the UK. It found 73% of respondents had experienced disability hate crime, with over half experiencing such acts within the last year.

In a scoping review paper, McNally *et al* (2021) concluded that the mental and social impact of trauma may be at least similar for people with an intellectual disability to that of others in the general population, including, but not exhaustively; aggressive or violent behaviours, self-harm, refusal to cooperate or disobeying commands, withdrawal and sleeping at inappropriate times, hypersensitivity, poor social skills, sensation seeking, task avoidance and relationship avoidance (Kessler and Stravropoulos, 2012); this trauma presentation is explored throughout the book (especially in Chapters 9, 10 and 15).

Hughes *et al* (2019) emphasised the importance of recognising abuse that specifically targets individuals due to their intellectual disability, terming 'childhood disability abuse' as a distinct category. Beyond the direct impact of disability, Schepens *et al* (2019) highlighted the need to consider factors such as a lack of self-determination, dependence on others for support, and feeling different; this was also stated in the '*Living in Fear*' report in which carers and families reported people acting differently from societal norms as a factor in adult abuse/ hate crime (Beadle-Brown *et al,* 2014). These experiences connect to the concept of micro-traumas – the cumulative impact of repeated small slights on one's sense of self and relational experiences.

Why consider DDP?

The DDP approach enables exploration of the impact of these experiences. It provides a way for carers and people with an intellectual disability to notice the shame or deterioration in trust that might occur when people have experienced hate crime and micro traumas. Elements of curiosity, a storytelling narrative and relational connection can allow vulnerabilities to be explored and experiences to be linked. DDP allows explorations of shame that people may experience in their own judgements about their own and others' presentations. The Golding Pyramid of Need (Golding, 2013)) also explicitly places safety has the foundational needs in someone's care – as explored in Chapter 11.

Reporting abuse

Intellectual disabilities can present inherent challenges that may affect or limit the identification or reporting of abuse (BPS, 2017). Potentially, there can be a lack of developmental clues that someone has experienced trauma, as developmental milestones may not have been met and therefore cannot regress. A lack of sexual and financial knowledge may hinder the person in understanding whether behaviour is appropriate or not (increasingly seen in the vulnerability of people with intellectual disability to exploitation and gang involvement). There are also potential difficulties with problem-solving and verbal skills which may delay or hinder the reporting of abuse and the ability to gain support, including difficulties with accessing support (Wigham & Emerson, 2015). Kildahl *et al* (2020) also referred to the need to directly ask people with intellectual disabilities about their traumas as they may not know the necessity of reporting it otherwise.

Trauma and the family/system impact

Why consider DDP?

As DDP is a systemic intervention, it is crucial to consider the wider impact of traumatic experiences on the support network of individuals with intellectual disabilities. Families, carers, and support systems often experience heightened stress when worrying about how the person they support will be received by others (Hastings *et al*, 2004). This stress can have a significant impact on the mental health of those within the system, potentially affecting attachment relationships and the cohesion of the network (Perry, 2006). When systems are overwhelmed, there may be a move away from positive risk-taking, or an increased likelihood of criminalising behaviours that stem from a lack of understanding of the relational and emotional underpinnings of such presentations. DDP and DDP-practice can help with this across multiple layers, offering a chance to curiously explore with the individual and/or their system why certain events may occur. The emphasis DDP places on relationships and co-regulation being central to all interactions may differs from other models of understanding and working through difficulties. Additionally, the focus on connection before (during and after) correction also allows relational elements to be at the forefront of care; with DDP aiming to make boundaries and safe limits feel safer for the person rather than aversive.

Carers and family members of people with intellectual disabilities are also at an increased risk of stigma and hate crimes, which further compounds their stress and impacts their relational capacity (Ali *et al*, 2012). Parents of children with intellectual disabilities may experience trauma related to birth complications or physiological challenges, which can disrupt early attachment behaviours and relational patterns (Fletcher *et al*, 2016). Insensitive or dismissive professional interactions can exacerbate these challenges, leading to vicarious trauma or re-traumatisation at critical points in the person's life (Davis & Gavidia-Payne, 2009). A PACEful approach offers carers an experience of feeling safe and heard; to feel regulated before exploring trauma. DDP also considers the impact of relational trauma on carers internal working model, emotions and patterns of interacting and caring for others.

For some people with intellectual disabilities, emotional regulation difficulties may be understood and labelled as behaviours that challenge, which can further strain their support networks. These behaviours can lead to vicarious trauma for parents, siblings, and carers, impacting their emotional resilience and the overall relational environment (Hastings, 2002). Addressing these systemic and relational challenges through a DDP framework emphasises the importance of building understanding, fostering secure attachments, and supporting all members of the network in navigating the complex dynamics of trauma and care.

This section finishes with a quote from someone with an intellectual disability who has urged us to do better in our approaches:

> *"...please listen to me and people like me. If people can't talk, find out about them and help them.... Everyone ...is a person with a story and a life to lead. Our voices should count."*
>
> Wilczek (2020, p.27)

How DDP can help with these experiences of trauma and attachment complications for people with intellectual disabilities

As illustrated in Figure 3.2, there are a number of barriers to attachment security when a child or adult has an intellectual disability. There are key features of DDP-practice which aim to help address this, either with direct therapeutic intervention, through parenting support or in wider DDP-practice. All areas of DDP can be helpful in relation to any difficulties in attachment, and ongoing relationships. However, as highlighted throughout this chapter, there are specific areas where there is more direct impact, which is summarised in the table below (Figure 3.3).

Figure 3.3: A Summary of barriers to people with intellectual disabilities and their support network experiencing attachment security and corresponding ways in which DDP can be helpful

Societal /system barriers	How DDP can be helpful
Stigma, hate crime and abuse	■ Curiosity ■ Building respect ■ Connection before correction ■ Allowing vulnerabilities to be explored
Multi-disciplinary staff with roles to meet developmental, physical or social needs, but less so to meet emotional and relational needs	■ Offers team and individual frameworks and tools for PACEful care that connects to emotional experiences and emphasises the importance of relationships ■ Connection before correction – that it is in a relationship where people feel connected and respected that there can be an offering of change and correction, and this is part of all aspect of care ■ DDP- practice allows this approach to be applied and utilised by all in the network and this increases connections and reduces the risks of staff changes impacting on relational security

Unpredictable changes to key attachments in support network /multiple placements impacts on the person with intellectual disability's understanding of relationships and relational safety: a discontinuity of staff presence and a lack of individual support. Inconsistency in presence and quality of relationships and overemphasis on independence as opposed to interdependence and intersubjectivity	■ Identifying and working with key attachment figures to implement the ideas of connection before correction and PACE ■ Fostering interdependence and intersubjectivity with all in the support network ■ Supporting therapeutic endings ■ Using Pyramid of Needs to create safety and predictability in relationships and day to day life ■ This Pyramid of Needs can be applicable to systems

Factors primarily affecting carers/parents and attachment	**How DDP can be helpful**
Shame and isolation (see Chapter 9: Shame and shielding from shame)	■ DDP gives the language and understanding to develop shame resilience: aiming to offer a non-judgemental and curious stance to allow; ■ Name shame ■ Recognise the patterns of shame ■ Share experience of shame with others
Experience of grief and loss	■ PACEful conversations about hopes and grief. Modelling being alongside emotional distress ■ 'Talking for', curiosity and the storytelling nature of DDP to help to voice some of the shame and emotional experiences which feel unacceptable
Experience of stigma and **vicarious trauma related to caring**	■ Explores vulnerabilities in a PACEful way to offer an experience of feeling safe and heard, regulating before exploring trauma ■ Considers the impact of relational trauma on internal working model, emotions and patterns of care

Blocked care: Parents/carers overcompensation or feeling dejected following struggles with attunement and intersubjectivity (see Chapter 10: Blocked care)	▪ Allowing these areas to be talked about and to model and comment on these in the room. ▪ Follow-lead-follow as a way to offer greater attunement ▪ Developing a coherent and non-blaming narrative about the mismatches in attachment and how these may have come into existence and the personal and wider factors that contribute to these.
Parent/carer attachment history and parents' skills and availability to attune	The coherent narrative of attachment and the focus on attuned interactions and intersubjectivity
Additional layers of care: financial stability, disputes about quality of service, emotional space, functional caring responsibility and reduced time to make emotional connections.	Offering a service-wide DDP approach can help with these areas being talked about across the service and connections being fostered which help to identify why and what people need

Barriers experienced by people with intellectual disabilities	How DDP can be helpful
Physical disabilities and cognitive barriers altering the process of leaving and returning to the caregiver. For example, people with intellectual disabilities may struggle to recognise or communicate their internal experiences and needs. People with intellectual disabilities may also take longer to process and respond to stimuli, including offers of attachment, connection, delight and co-regulation, which	▪ Attuned interactions, intersubjective approaches and rupture and repair aid with this ▪ Consistency of care and routines to aid with predictability (and object permanency). ▪ The storytelling nature can help voice this for some people with intellectual disabilities when there is verbal ability that allows this to resonate with the individual ▪ The ideas of intensive interaction, which emulate the relational security, predictability and reciprocity of DDP when there is less verbal ability can also be helpful

may cause a mismatch in the attachment relationship (and lead to parents overcompensating or becoming dejected)	■ The PACEful discussions with parents about shame and mismatch can help this be brought into awareness through coherent narrative (as discussed above); learning the different dance ■ Accepting and discussing that some people with intellectual disability do need greater proximity and we are not working to a model where independence is necessarily the end goal
Sensory needs: People with intellectual disabilities may need increased physical proximity, more, less or different touch, which may alter the way they experience comfort, emotional and physiological regulation	■ The ideas of meaningful touch and closeness can be helpful here, including sensory needs ■ Recognising these differences and talking about, storying how they can be best responded to
Smaller social circles and reliance on primary carer, who is very knowledgeable in the person's behaviours and overall needs	Talking for and a curious saying-it-aloud approach can be helpful in creating a coherent and non-blaming narratives and aiding others in the network to increase their understanding of the person with intellectual disabilities

Conclusion

In conclusion, DDP interventions are designed to support individuals who have experienced developmental trauma by fostering safety in relationships, enabling affective-reflective conversations, and building intersubjective connections with therapists, parents, and/or carers. For people with intellectual disabilities, who are more likely to experience attachment insecurity and trauma both developmentally and in adulthood, this relational approach is especially important and can address a number of the barriers to attachment security present in people with intellectual disabilities. In addition, people with intellectual disabilities' continued reliance on others for safety and meeting basic needs often amplifies feelings of powerlessness and lack of control, which can echo previous trauma or lack of relational security. The model also offers a route for not just helping the individual but also creating an approach for caring for carers. The long-term impact of this DDP-informed support across the network, family or system is that there is a reduced risk of placement breakdown with increased relational security.

As highlighted, many individuals with intellectual disabilities require lifelong care, and research demonstrates that viewing care staff as a secure base positively influences well-being and increases quality of life in adults with intellectual disabilities (BPS, 2017). Offering relational security is crucial for trauma recovery, and DDP provides a framework for creating this security through intersubjective relationships and co-regulation; through PACE and lead-follow-lead. This can be thought of as a 'dance' with the person they support, adapting to their unique rhythm, even if it differs from the expected steps, but tailored to individual need.

Moreover, DDP addresses complex relational dynamics, such as shame and blocked care, by fostering curiosity and compassion within attachment relationships. By depersonalising struggles and reframing them as opportunities for connection, DDP enables family members and carers to engage in more empathetic and attuned interactions. This approach allows individuals with intellectual disabilities (and wider carers) to reconnect with their emotions and experiences, both past and present, in a way that reduces feelings of shame and fear while promoting trust in others and themselves.

Later chapters in this book will explore in detail the elements of DDP theory and practice and how DDP can be held central with individuals and their parents/carers, as well as within broader caregiving systems, including paid carers in supported living or residential settings. Through this work, individuals with intellectual disabilities can build a foundation of relational safety, leading to more secure attachments and greater trust in others and in their own experiences, leading to less shame and distress and more relational security.

SECTION 1:

Theoretical models underpinning Dyadic Developmental Practice

Chapter 4: Intersubjective connection

Summary

- We provide an introduction to intersubjective connection; presenting an introduction to what this means, how connection develops for young babies and how it can be interrupted.
- During this chapter we highlight the impact of early primary intersubjective connection and how this connection influences and informs our readiness for secondary intersubjective connection with the outside world and meeting people beyond our immediate cared for experience when young. The style of interaction and experience of intersubjective connection is informed by all our cultural variations in expression of connection; which is vital to understand when considering any relational work.
- Our sense of ourselves and our own worth develops over time, but inevitably our early experiences have a huge and significant impact on how we perceive ourselves. This sense of self or internal working model influences how we approach others and the world around us.
- In this chapter we explore the potential interruptions to intersubjective connection for people with an intellectual disability and how these experiences also in turn shape the internal working model for people with an intellectual disability.
- Intersubjective connection describes and explains the reciprocal nature of all relational focused work. Dyadic Developmental Psychotherapy (DDP) isn't an approach that is "done" to another, but instead DDP interventions draw on the importance of truly connecting with another's experience. The use of self in this model is vital, and in offering a genuine relationship and in helping others to deeply connect we establish safety in our relationships which will enable and support healing.

This chapter leans heavily on the teachings, in person and written by DDP founder Dan Hughes, Kim Golding (DDP Consultant and Trainer) and Colwyn Trevarthen (Professor of Psychology who extensively explored and championed the theory of Intersubjective connection). It is lightly referenced, because using DDP rests on these ideas that at some point become ingested and therefore harder to reference.

Introduction

This chapter follows on from the previous chapter to explore, in detail, the importance of intersubjective connection, its roots in early childhood experiences, and how these early patterns remain important throughout our childhood into adulthood. This chapter, no doubt, reflects a bias in the author's experience of a more individualistic societal structure that is akin to the experience of key researchers and developers of this theory. We have endeavoured to introduce a broader, more sociocentric perspective, alongside the patterns that might occur in families, or teams of carers, when interacting with someone with an intellectual disability. We illustrate the importance, value and reliance of intersubjective connection in DDP.

> *'Attachment behaviour is not reciprocal. The child turns to the parent for safety. The parent does not reciprocate by turning to the child for safety. In contrast, intersubjective relating is reciprocal. The practitioner (or parent) has an influence on the child, and the child has a reciprocal influence on them.'*
>
> Hughes & Golding (2024, p.49)

Intersubjective connection describes the key interactive exchanges that occur, initially between a child and their key attachment figures, that then expands to relationships beyond this inner circle. This intersubjective connection is made through a range of verbal, non-verbal, and sometimes very physical, interactions. It is an important part of the bonding process and integral in shaping attachment security. Intersubjective connection is about the active connection between people and so fluctuates as it reflects the dynamic process within relationships: it can both develop and weaken over time (moment to moment and longer-term). An intersubjective connection describes the interaction occurring between people, often at a microlevel. Within traditional Western cultures, this reciprocal relationship has historically been held and nurtured between a baby and one, maybe two, key parent/attachment figures. Whereas in other more sociocentric cultures, this reciprocal interaction is established between a baby and a number of caregivers, all of whom are available and highly attuned to meeting the child's needs. The care and relationships available might be more diverse and across broader age ranges than in individualist cultures, but the relationships formed in any culture aim to be intersubjective and help to prepare the baby and, later, the child for the environment in which it is anticipated they will develop. In any culture, intersubjective connection describes the two-way experience or reciprocity within the relationship. Understanding the early experiences for the adult and children we meet in DDP-based work, will enrich our understanding of someone else's experience of connection, which will assist our own connections and reciprocity within our relationships.

Within a relationship, the child's experiences, mood, actions and behaviour have an impact on the adult and in turn the adult's response, actions and mood influence the child. This is true for relationships beyond a parent-child dyad and includes the pattern of relationships formed with key people, including extended family members, the community in which you are raised, teachers, care workers or therapists. Whilst the formative patterns for an intersubjective connection are developed in early childhood, the connections we experience with people and the interchange that exists, continues throughout our lives.

For those who require longer-term care and support, as commonly experienced by people with an intellectual disability, the importance of intersubjective connection is often pivotal. The majority of people with an intellectual disability experience barriers with communication. This can occur as a result of people not understanding the communication style of the person with an intellectual disability, or when they might not find it easy to interpret the gestures, facial expressions or pace of interaction needed for someone with an intellectual disability. In turn, the person who is more able can be equally indecipherable to the person with an intellectual disability; by talking too fast, communicating too many ideas all at once or using lengthy phrases, or unfamiliar words. Sometimes, carers' non-verbal patterns increase confusion for the person with a disability as they include the use of gestures or changing facial expressions in ways that are harder to interpret. Within a formal care setting, the rapid change of staff can also make it harder to have the time to get to know another person and to experience this reciprocal relationship. If it is initially hard to form a connection; this can trigger a loss of confidence and reluctance to keep initiating a connection, or at the extreme, it might encourage them to seek alternative employment.

Intersubjective connections can be described as primary and secondary. Below, we aim to describe these, how they apply in context of people with an intellectual disability and how these principles are considered within the DDP framework:

- Primary intersubjectivity: From birth, babies can coordinate their behaviour to relate to their caregiver(s). These interactions are the basis for development of social and emotional understanding.

- Internal working model: how we view ourselves, others and the world around us.
- Secondary intersubjectivity: extending beyond the key attachment figures to include the outside world; objects, toys and other people.

Primary intersubjectivity

Trevarthen's studies and research, in particular, have enriched our understanding of the importance and power of reciprocal intersubjective interactions. His work has shown that the care and love shown to a baby, this careful attentiveness, informs a baby's movement, their perception, and learning. This early connection creates the building blocks for mapping their bodies and developing regulation. This interaction helps a baby to learn how they are viewed and experienced in response to others (Trevarthen & Aiken, 1991).

Within an attuned relationship, where a parent/carer and baby are able to consider and discover each other, the process of intersubjective connection develops. A baby's most vital and close relationships with connection are described as the primary intersubjectivity (Trevarthen, 1979). As a young baby, this interactive pattern encompasses all our early experiences, from being fed when hungry to having the curtains pulled when the sun feels too strong. If a baby's interests are recognised, delighted in or explored, if the things a baby finds to be of value or distress are worthy of being understood and explored, this offers two things. Firstly, it creates a deep sense of being in the care and support of someone we can trust, but also conveys to the baby that they are worth the effort, care and love. This is all communicated with loving care and isn't about a formal verbal explanation.

What does an intersubjective connection look like?

When caring for a young baby, those caring for it are anticipating and making sense of the young child's every need. A high level of empathy is needed to try to navigate a baby's responses. It is often important and helpful to draw on, and remind ourselves of, the delicate interactions that occur between parents and their babies, to think about intersubjectivity generally and about establishing such connections with people with an intellectual disability. Before formal verbal language, there are many methods of trying to make sense of someone's experience. There are non-verbal facial changes, babbling and vocalisations that form a pattern, types of crying to indicate different types of distress and lots of whole-body gestures that provide our clues. A skilled carer is working hard to attune to the different cries, to piece together all the information from the vocalisations, mannerisms or way their child settles to sleep, to understand their level of contentment and their state of mind. This curiosity for the child's experience, requires a high level of attention and often huge patience, and considerable empathy for the baby are often needed on the days when things do not run smoothly. In order to continue doing this, the carer also requires empathy for their own experiences and the complexity of the job they are doing. The carers around the baby learn whether what they are doing is effective and soothing or exciting, whether their care and efforts feel worthwhile and can experience the delight of a baby who likes what they are doing.

Figure 4.1 Illustrating intersubjective connection

What the baby learns

A baby quickly learns whether what they are concerned about is manageable, and is of interest to, or on the radar of their carers/parents: they start to understand their impact and power in the world. They will learn it is ok to move in certain ways when they experience the approval or disapproval from their loved ones. They will experience a power or agency: they are having a direct impact on another. They also learn how effective their carers are in making sense of their experiences, such as whether expressing distress/joy is something that the key attachment figures can cope with, without making the baby feel bad for showing upset or having a grumble about things. A baby will learn from their parent's face whether the distress they feel is of concern and importance to the parent. This to-and-fro, reciprocal dance lets a baby know a variety of things such as:

- "I'm interested in you and what you say is of interest."
- "You are loveable and I love you."
- "Your distress and upsets are important and understandable, I know what to do to help you."
- "I understand why you cry in that way, and will be there for you to offer a cuddle."
- "You are delightful and I want to spend time with you."

When someone notices or attunes to us, we have a powerful experience that the things we do impact on another person; our actions are meaningful and have a powerful impact on the people around us, and sometimes, on our immediate environment; when exchanges are reciprocal, we are in an intersubjective relationship. When two people have reciprocal interest in each other and notice that they have an impact on each other, this increases their connection.

Internal working model – the story we hold about ourselves

Before being able to develop a sense of ourselves and our own worth, we learn to make sense of ourselves and the world through the eyes and reactions of those around us. If a parent shows a calm, gentle and loving attitude to their baby and young child, that child will be likely to grow with a sense of themselves as loveable, interesting and worth spending time with. Conversely, if a parent finds it hard to engage with a baby, to find ways to play together or if the baby seems unresponsive, the parents might lose connection and interest, and in turn the baby can learn that they are not so interesting, are not of central importance to their parent, or maybe feel they are not loveable. This is how we build our own story, and how our internal sense of ourselves and our impact on the world is created and sustained: this is our internal working model. This view or story of ourselves can be reinforced or challenged through and by future relationships.

Figure 4.2 Illustration of intersubjective connection and interrupted connection

Challenges to the primary intersubjectivity

In a disconnected relationship, or one where the parent is struggling to focus and attend to the baby or child, the message conveyed (even if not explicitly) is: "I'm not listening, I don't have time for you and don't care what you say," or " I'm listening and you're wrong and should shut up," or "I'm listening but you don't make sense to me. Your needs are too great for me". When this experience is repeated often enough, it will inform their view of themselves. This links to Tronick's ideas from the 'still face experiment', that in practical terms caregivers-infant relationships fluctuate and are sometimes attuned and responsive; that a third of the time they might get this wrong (be mis-attuned); and one-third of the time interactions will fall between the two (e.g. Tronick *et al*, 1978). What matters most is the process of repair, in which when there is a misreading of the child's needs the caregiver recognises and responds to this (repair is explored further in (Chapter 5).

Primary intersubjectivity and intellectual disability

Not everyone is able to use this early dance, and often, the parents and carers of a child with a disability will be the first to notice very subtle signs of challenges in communication. Skilled and attuned parents and carers are able to notice, track and attend to the communication style of a young child; sometimes, there are mistakes which can lead to a baby's tears and distress, but more often there is attunement and connection; however, the experience of connection for and with babies who have an intellectual disability might (at times) be complicated.

Depending on the context and environment into which they are born, and the level of understanding and insight their parents might have around their baby's challenges, it is feasible that there is a greater incidence of misunderstanding in these moments of connection. It might be that the world in which these babies grow is highly attuned and adapted around their needs, and it could also be that the world is too fast and the pace of information they are receiving, or the rate of transitions between activities, are too intensive to process. Furthermore, if there are additional needs, such as significant medical procedures, or times away from familiar carers or parents, these connections will be interrupted. This necessary input can intrude upon the connections being built between the baby and their parents. The early input of professionals, or hospitalisation, can further dilute this primary intersubjective experience; of being known and understood, uniquely and intimately by another/select attachment figures.

In these circumstances it is possible that the unintended message the baby experiences is "I've tried listening to you, but you aren't responding quickly enough," or "You should be able to do this at your age/stage of development – what's wrong?", "You are too much for me."

This connection is harder to build for stressed carers/parents who are feeling out of step with their child's needs, or for those parents with additional demands, such as marked mental health challenges or financial pressures. For parents who have experienced a paucity of attachment safety in their own lives, childbirth and parenting can be more complicated than they might have anticipated. Children with complex needs can, for some, challenge the ease of connection when milestones are not met, or when there is more muted, or no response, to interaction and care. Understandably, in some families, this can be a confusing time. Not for all families, but for many, it can be a time of uncertainty. Some parents might become disheartened and feel inadequate or ineffective, while others might work harder to 'get things right', all of which puts pressure on the connection and trying to find the 'spontaneous' joy of the experience. Under any of these circumstances, a baby might see a worried face rather than experiencing their parent's joy and delight about spending time together. Here, the connection is at risk of becoming strained and the message of understanding, love and unconditional regard can be overshadowed or only offered intermittently.

We need to consider the complications of trying to support someone with an intellectual disability who might find communication challenging: they might find that we are overlooking their experience, or that we have not noticed their discomfort. Often, the person in a caring role is responsible for creating safety for the child or adult with an intellectual disability. These power dynamics have a significant impact on relationship dynamics. How can we build or offer truly intersubjective connection at these times? We need permission to spend time with someone with an intellectual disability in this way, possibly easier in family life, but important to consider in whichever setting someone lives. We keep learning and listening to the dance. By offering to sit alongside, to notice the smaller things, to work at the right pace, to ignore the pressures of everyone watching what we are doing; in these moments we can enable connection. A lot of patience, curiosity and acceptance is needed to build genuine connection: not something that looks good from afar, but that is about the link between two people. Intersubjective connection also enables us to be more authentic and reduces the need to 'cheer' someone up or distract them from a worry. It instead enables us to be impacted by someone's worry or sadness, and in doing so, to more deeply know that person, to communicate that they are worth knowing, supporting and their experiences are not to be dismissed. When, historically, people with an intellectual disability were treated as if they needed to always be happy – and not allowed negative emotions of sadness or distress – they were less likely to experience genuine, reciprocal intersubjective connection.

The intersubjective trajectory

The pattern established in early childhood helps us to predict the pattern of future interactions; and determines whether we anticipate others will be interested in understanding our needs and then possibly also in, meeting our needs. If the story that we hold (or the internal working model that has developed about ourselves) is that we are not loveable or worth spending time with, then we will struggle to be open to current and likely future intersubjective connection. When connection has been unpleasant, it makes sense to reduce your availability and, therefore vulnerability, within relationships. The impact on the early child and parent's relationship is profound, but so too are the interactions we experience across the lifespan.

DDP and intersubjective connection

The use of intersubjectivity in therapeutic support is at the heart of DDP. This requires a huge amount of openness on the part of a parent/carer/therapist – to both note their own experience and reaction, and to also be interested in, and curious about, the reaction of the person they are caring for. This sensitivity is fully tested when the actions and responses of another person are not open, or even socially acceptable, or when someone is angry and cross about something a carer has done. When we match our affective response to attune to the experience of another, we offer connection and attunement to their experiences. We have not moved into fixing or teaching different skills, but slowed down to track and reflect upon how things are for the person next to us. When we attune to another experience in this way, it might be unfamiliar, and for those not used to this offer of connection, it can be overwhelming. At these times, the skilled and regulated person needs to notice the challenge the other is feeling about the closeness or connection that is being offered. Being attuned to the experience of another is so important: knowing their challenge with trust, or feeling worthy of interest, or coping with someone showing delight in their achievements is vital. At these times, we need to allow someone to retreat from our offer of connection, to lighten the mood, or allow the conversation to move to safer ground. Offering reciprocity means that we (as carers) have to follow the child or adult's pace; we need to track what they can cope with at all times.

DDP also enables time to consider complex and traumatic events. By offering **joint attention** to a difficult memory, the therapist or trained carer can support a conversation about the past. In 'matching affective' states, and offering regulated support, they can develop a joint focus on the difficult experiences. A story telling approach is often needed around these events, to help offer co-regulation, but this also helps someone sustain their focus when the events are upsetting and hard to revisit.

Within DDP we enable the development of **complimentary intentions** around difficult themes a child or adult has previously experienced in relationships. When offering to just get to know each other, without a plan to change or improve or to teach skills, the child or adult being offered this connection is more likely to open up and relax about being known and understood. This may be very different to their relationships and so it may take time for them to believe that there is not a desire to focus on change or correction. In this way, an openness to better understand each other is described as their complimentary intentions. In an intersubjective relationship, both individuals are actively engaging in the relationship, and this represents the joining of minds with complimentary intentions (Hughes, 2011).

Case Vignette: Nick

Nick is throwing things towards Sadie. Sadie has asked Nick to calm down and tried to sing Nick's favourite song thinking she just needs to distract him. She shows Nick the TV remote control to see if this would be of interest. This has not helped, in fact, the singing seems to make it worse and Sadie is wondering if she should get someone else to step in to help. Sadie has a cushion to shield her from any objects, and feels safe, but isn't feeling very effective in calming things down.

Sadie pauses for a moment. She notices that when she stopped singing, Nick threw slightly fewer things. She mutters to herself about how her singing wasn't helping – then she says this to Nick. "That wasn't helping, hey?" Her tone changes as she repeats this. "Hey, I wasn't helping there, was I, with my singing?" She notices that she is sounding a bit less bossy, or even less stressed. Sadie keeps talking, "I see you're so cross. I am sorry you are cross with me or about something I've done. You want to *get all* those feelings out. I want that too. It doesn't feel ok feeling angry, hey?"

During this, Nick is listening and the throw rate is slowing a little more. Then Sadie picks up some of the soft cushions and toys that had landed near her. Nick looks a bit surprised. Sadie starts to throw the cushions at the wall, far away from Nick, and as she throws she tries to name something that Nick might be annoyed about. She starts with "Sadie" and adds in a "hurruphh," then moves on to "College", then to "People saying NO," and "Sadie singing my song at the wrong time." She continues with a list of things she knows or guesses Nick dislikes and he joins her in throwing cushions and soft toys at the wall, but also in naming things. After a time, Sadie moves near to Nick as they throw some things at the wall. Some of the things they name are silly, or about things they've done together, such as making a cake that went wrong. Eventually they finish sitting side by side, no longer throwing but talking together about the things that were irritating and worrying Nick.

When Sadie stopped making suggestions or trying to distract away from the anger, and instead, connected with and voiced Nick's experience, things started to shift. Being impacted by this experience, he starts to open up about his frustrations. Being in a relationship that allows for upset, and that shows that these feelings are important and need recognising, Sadie and Nick move closer again in their connection.

Secondary intersubjectivity

Our attachment figures prepare and then introduce us to the rest of the world. Our initial experience of reciprocity prepares and orientates us for connection beyond our initial attachment figures, and in particular, helps in our exploration of the world beyond the experience of these initial close, more intense, relationships. The attitude of the attachment figures will inform a child's readiness to explore or communicate with others, as well as the child's core sense of being understood and supported to look into the world beyond their first relationships. Within secondary intersubjectivity, a child's developing internal working model informs how and where they will explore the immediate and more extended environment including how confident they might be to explore objects, and their broader more physical environment.

For example, imagine a child going to the front door with their parent, where the parent has shown an interest in who is at the door and sounds welcoming when they greet that individual on the threshold. A different child might hang back, stand by their parents, hold on to their parent's clothing for safety, or be carried. In each situation, they are witness to and learn from their attachment figure about how to have this exchange with the world beyond their familiar parent-child dyad. There is also a powerful pattern here, of a parent knowing how ready a child is to meet strangers; how a parent is ready to shield and protect their child from unwelcome visitors; or how a parent can teach their children about diversity and inclusivity through their own response to the world. Children are learning at every step about who is trustworthy, whether those in uniforms are to be given authority or dismissed, whether people with different family traditions, customs or those with a different skin colour to your family should be discriminated against.

Secondary intersubjectivity and intellectual disability

Sometimes, our early experience with the outside world leaves a difficult imprint which colours expectations for the future. It is important to build a picture of the past or hold in mind that someone with an intellectual disability might have experienced a range of intersubjective relationships. Processing and adapting to new events is often more challenging for someone with an intellectual disability. It is feasible that current carers will remind the people with an intellectual disability of a previous carer or family member. This can establish positive or negative expectations and reactions. Previous experience might influence future openness to people with specific hair colouring or certain perfumes, or who drive a type of car, through to feeling caution or worry about people with a certain tone of voice or way of walking. In an ideal world, we would try to maintain familiarity; keep carers consistent, reduce the number of sudden changes and, crucially, allow time for relationships to develop. Sometimes, the reasons behind another person's strong or cautious connections are hard to predict, but staying open to an array of variabilities will help us make better sense of their experience. From this position of understanding, we can start to support someone else's worries or excitement, even when they are struggling to articulate it for themselves.

DDP – intersubjectivity, internal working model and building coherence

> *'We are communicating meanings-emotional, social, historical-that express our inner lives and enable us, feeling safe, to be open and receptive to the inner life of the other. Within this dialogue voices are rhythmic and modulated, fully expressive of the subtle, unique meanings of self and other in ways that the words themselves cannot convey. Such dialogue holds the attention of both participants while each safety explores the inner world of the other.'*
>
> Hughes & Baylin (2012, p.140)

When we are curious and accepting in our approach or way of interacting, we will develop a better or clearer understanding of someone else's experience and their internal working model of themselves, others and the world. Our instinct is to counter sadness and upset with reassurance and love or connection, which are all important. However, in slowing down (and pausing this reassurance), we can connect with and understand the story and beliefs or view they have generated about themselves, others and the world in response to their environment, and the way in which they have been cared for. In understanding someone's story, we better understand the pressures they are experiencing, as well as their starting point for all future relationships. When working with people with impaired cognitive skills, we can risk brushing over this important stage of enquiring into their internal experience. We can miss out on reciprocal connection and rush to fix things or take over. It can be so powerful to connect with someone's experience, to show them our concern for their upsets, to honestly find shared moments of connection and delight. Within DDP we offer this authentic relationship and connection. In building this connection and trust we are better placed to identify and accurately articulate what might be going on for someone who isn't yet able to put their experience into words. This is often the case for someone with an intellectual disability, and the power of being able to show and share an understanding with both words, and non-verbal communication, can be profound. In co-creating the story of someone's internal world, we also have scope to possibly add to or amend their experience of themselves. If someone has developed an understanding of themselves as useless or bad, DDP offers a way to help explore this self-critical stance, and with empathy for someone's experience, introducing a different viewpoint to their story.

Case vignette: Charlie

Bailey noticed that Charlie is very quiet and withdrawn. Charlie hasn't touched their food and isn't really making eye contact with Bailey. Bailey is missing her connection with Charlie and after the meal they do the washing up together.

Bailey: "I don't think you're feeling ok right now, hey?

Charlie shrugs and says "Fine".

Bailey continues: "I wonder if you are feeling quiet because the food was wrong today?"

Charlie: "No."

Bailey: "Not the food, maybe something about me?"

Charlie: "No."

Bailey, aware there could be so many guesses (it's been a busy day), gets out a picture plan of the day. "Can you show me when it felt wrong?"

Charlie points to time spent in the candle-making project.

Bailey: "Ah, that didn't go well. Was it the noise again?" Bailey's tone is slow, softer and unhurried to match Charlie's mood.

Charlie: "I was shouted at and told off."

Bailey: "Oh I see. That's upset you a lot, hasn't it?"

Charlie: "Yes, like the teachers before, at school."

Bailey: "Telling you off?"

Charlie: "Yes, too fast and loud. And then the kids too, at the end of school."

Bailey: "That sounds big: at school some teachers went too fast, it was too noisy and the kids were mean."

Charlie: "Yes, saying names: stupid, dumb. I know I'm rubbish."

Bailey: "That is so horrible. When it got tough in candle-making today – did it feel the same? Did you start feeling rubbish again?"

Charlie: "YES." Charlie is no longer quiet but seems to be energised by talking together.

Bailey: "I guess that might have happened a lot. The people around you made you feel like you were rubbish. Maybe sometimes you got the blame for lots of things. People called you lots of names and you thought it must be true. Do you often feel like you are rubbish now?"

Charlie: "Yes, I mess up."

Bailey: "Messing up when things go wrong? Ok. Yes, there are times when things go wrong. And every time you worry? You worry and think it's your fault. I'm so annoyed that you landed up feeling rubbish. Maybe the teachers messed up a bit there as it sounds like they didn't know how to help you in that school?"

Charlie: "Yeah."

Bailey: "When you feel rubbish, I notice I feel rubbish for you."

Charlie: "Yeah?"

Bailey: "Yeah. I make mistakes and sometimes you do too. We are learning. I will notice though that it can make you worry. I will keep noticing that with you – is that ok?"

Charlie: "Yes."

Bailey: "Shall we have a hot chocolate and watch the end of that film before anything else today?"

Charlie: "YES!"

Conclusion

A meaningful and attuned connection with another person enables a reciprocal relationship; one person equally impacts the other. When we better understand someone's previous experience of intersubjective connection it can inform our understanding of their current approaches to relationships. A baby learns about their agency and builds a sense of self through people's responses to their needs, and learning, for instance, whether they are someone who is worth connecting with, saying sorry to, cuddling or having a giggle with. They learn whether they are someone others wish to spend time with or avoid. These early tender exchanges will help to establish a baby's sense of themselves and their importance in the world; this is their own story, their internal working model.

A baby's disability might interrupt the ease with which a carer and the baby can connect, make sense of each other's expressions and decipher each other's communication styles. The misunderstanding or mismatched connections that can arise for babies with intellectual disabilities can lead to relational trauma. For people with intellectual disabilities who have had struggles in the reciprocity of relationships or who have missed out on joyful or relaxed connection when young, within their primary intersubjective relationships, may have a dampened view of their ability to engage, delight or influence their carers. They might have an experience of being done to, cared for or cared about, but maybe not experienced intersubjective connection. A lack of joyful connection within a primary intersubjective relationship will inform future expectations when engaging in secondary intersubjective connections. Where there are persistent mismatches in communication within a dyad, where needs are not met, or when both sides cannot be their authentic selves, this will alter the closeness available; the felt sense of connection. These initial encounters will inform a readiness or resistance when meeting new people or exploring new environments. When someone's internal script or working model instils them with confidence and a sense of worth, their approach will be more confident than we would notice for people who have experienced mis-attuned or interrupted connection. These interactions establish patterns and expectations for future relationships. DDP recognises the importance of our intersubjective connections; building truly reciprocal relationships to develop enables us to share our delight and concern about someone else's experience; to repair when our relationship wobbles. An attitude of PACE enables us to explore and learn about another's world and be open to be influenced by another's reactions, concerns and experiences. From this authentic connection we can explore co-regulation, relationship repair, make better sense of the past, and support individuals to explore and reflect more deeply on their emotional responses.

Chapter 5: Attachment theory – an overview

Summary

- Attachment theory is the one of the central theories in use throughout DDP interventions. In this chapter we consider how attachment security developments with our primary attachment figures.
- There are distinct and important cultural variations in the expression of attachment security and also who might be an attachment figure. We share our understanding of the gaps in early research to highlight the importance of being attuned to each person's experience as this will help us to avoid misunderstandings and enable us to be aware of the bias our perspective may bring.
- In this chapter we describe attachment insecurity in the general population but also for people with an intellectual disability. We have considered the specific risks for people with an intellectual disability of developing insecurity attachments, even when their home lives have been loving and tender. Whilst people with an intellectual disability are no doubt at risk of adverse relationship, trauma and abuse, we want to consider the complications of caring for someone with profound needs and how this might impact on attachment security. The barriers in communication can, for some families, be so profound that people with an intellectual disability might experience multiple mis-attuned relationships. This type of mis-attunement might be better described as relational trauma.

Introduction

DDP is, in part, founded on the core ideas within attachment theory, around the importance of security of relationships and emotional connection to facilitate an infant's healthy exploration of their world. Attachment theory has evolved, and our understanding of attachment has, in turn, deepened as the gaps in the early, and later 20th-century writings have been recognised. We will be considering the key concepts that underpin attachment theory as these are of particular relevance in DDP, as well as outlining some of the common patterns and interactions that are associated with attachment security and attachment insecurity. The barriers to secure attachment are considered, with a key focus on pressures within early relationships for those born with an intellectual disability.

How this theory developed

Attachment theory, and what we have come to understand as 'safe' or 'good' care for children, was formative in the development of the DDP model. Donald Winnicott, a British paediatrician and psychoanalyst's initial work was a foundation for John Bowlby, another British psychoanalyst who was also a psychiatrist. It was Bowlby who first described a theory of attachment (Bowlby, 1969).

Winnicott's studies and observational work drew him to conclude that a baby is not a passive recipient of the careful care they receive, but that their engagement in the relationship with their carer is key. The attuned care offered by the attachment figures is vital in ensuring a baby's needs are met, but also the baby, in turn, experiences this love and care and reciprocates this connection (Phillips, 1988). Winnicott wrote extensively about the connection, or this reciprocity, between a mother and baby as being a strengthening part of the bond between a mother and child (Winnicott 1964/1992).

Bowlby was interested in mapping out a baby's early development and how they best thrived. He was particularly drawn to making sense of the impact of gaps in care and maternal-baby separation. His work concluded that babies benefited from a secure base, needed human connection and thrived where there was safety in the immediate relationships (1969). Bowlby extended Winnicott's description of the impact of the reciprocal nature of the mother-baby relationship indicating that this very relationship helps a baby develop their internal working model about themselves. Bowlby's view was that a mother's approach to their child helped the child learn whether they are interesting, important or loveable, for example (Bowlby, 1969).

Attachment security and exploration

Universal across attachment-focused research is the discovery of the important role of relational and attachment security in determining the extent and nature of a child's motivation to explore their immediate, and then more distant environment. When a child becomes worried or distressed, where there is attachment security, the child is able to seek out the comfort and protection of their key attachment figure/s. Powell *et al* expanded this framework more fully in their Circle of Security Theory (2014), where the back-and-forth checks by the baby to the adult, and the adult to the baby are beautifully illustrated. The parent or attachment figure attends to, and is drawn to, their baby's discomfort or upset, and offers support. When the support is attuned, or just right, this soothes and settles the baby. This interaction is not necessarily just functional or practical but often involves layers of communication on the part of the carer when making sense of the baby's upset through their words, facial expressions and gestures or actions. Security of attachment does not just offer basic but essential life-preserving physical safety to the child. The baby is also given an experience that they are worth being attended to, but also that they have the backup, help and support of a trusted adult who is there to protect, interpret and safeguard them in the world. Having this backup and support enables the baby to feel calmer, and once calm, they are ready to explore their environment: to experiment with moving their body or seeing what happens when they touch their carer's face, for example.

Figure 5.1. Safety-exploration cycle: how attachment security evolves through early experiences of care

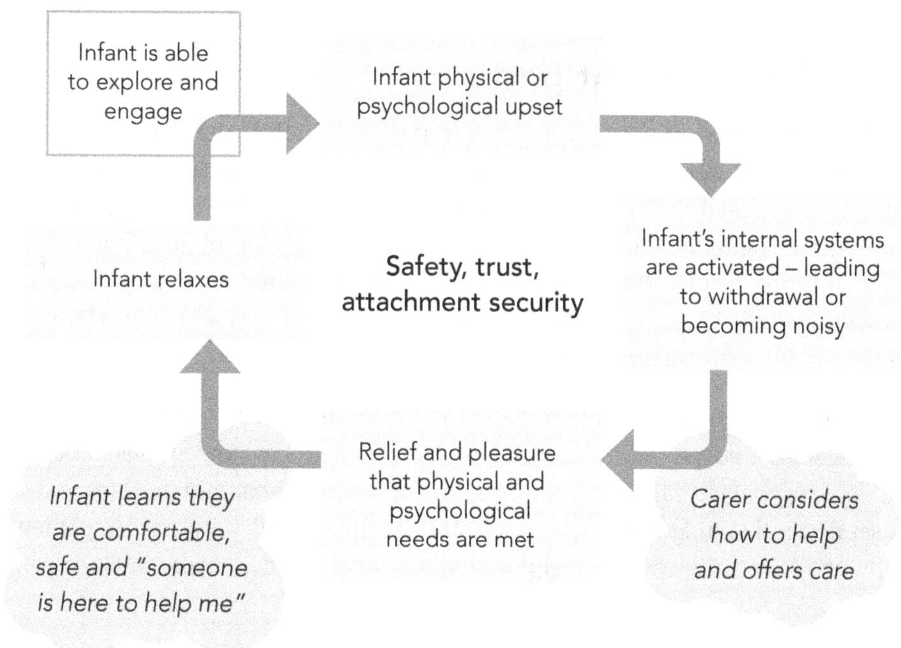

When this security, trust and exploration cycle works smoothly, a baby and their caregiver are connected and attachment security is high. The parent is able to be responsive and attuned to their baby's needs, and when they are able to successfully offer comfort, the child's attachment security increases. When a baby's needs cannot be made sense of; or when a parent doesn't notice their child's need for help; when what worked last time fails and the parent loses confidence and stops trying; when a parent does what someone says rather than what their gut and experience suggested is needed – this is when the circle of connection fractures.

Within all parent/carer and child relationships there will always be some fractures, often very small. However, where there are multiple fractures over smaller events, or fractures and gaps in connection at key points of concern for a baby, then interactions are more likely to become strained and the baby will feel less secure. Over time, repeated experiences of this pattern increase the risk that a baby will withdraw from reliance on the adults around them, and they might also limit their exploration for fear about what might happen next. Or they might be inclined to explore their environment, without the necessary guidance or boundaries about what is safe and appropriate for their age and ability. Other babies work harder to gain the attention and focus of their attachment figures by becoming noisier, or trying to present as the type of child that their attachment figures will spend time with – a more conditional type of interaction. Whilst this might increase their access to key figures, this pattern suppresses their own needs and means operating in a state of anxiety that will limit the energy available for exploration and playful engagement in their environment.

Types of attachment patterns

Mary Ainsworth, an influential researcher in the field of child development, worked largely in white western settings. She developed a scenario that set up a series of interactions, called the Strange Situation, to examine or make better sense of parent-child attachment. This research led to the classification of attachment into distinct patterns: secure attachment, insecure-ambivalent and insecure-avoidant (Ainsworth & Bell, 1970). A further insecure classification was added by Main & Solomon (1986) – disorganised attachment.

However, these distinctions around the classification of attachment patterns are increasingly understood to lean on earlier judgements or perceptions about 'good' and responsive care that have been informed by white, middle class and Western normative judgements (Keller, 2022). Distinguishing between attachment security and insecurity remains helpful within a family or care context. Once we understand the cultural patterns around how love and care are expressed or the way a baby might learn to raise an alarm or show upset, we can better understand the relationship dynamics. Attachment security and the need to provide safety around the young and vulnerable individual is universal, however, the expression of security, and who attachment figures might be varies across societies and communities (Van Ijzendoorn & Kroonenberg, 1988). Keller's work (2022) provides a useful worldwide perspective across various research, and studies considering attachment security being expressed differently depending on custom and continent. Note that children develop attachment security when there are multiple attachment figures, where those raising the baby are siblings, or that healthy attachment can be developed with key teachers or even peer groups. Chaudhary, Salali & Swanepoel (2024) observed relational safety and security can also be provided by a group of multiple caregivers if they provide dedicated, attuned and responsive care needed by the baby.

Attachment figures are vital and, across different cultural systems, are the person/people who understand, interpret or anticipate the needs of the baby and developing child, and who work hard to endeavour to meet those needs. The ways these are expressed vary across cultures, and indeed, across communities within cultures, including the relative significance of a primary attachment figure. Understanding the structures and norms of individualistic or collectivist cultures will enable a better understanding of the presenting attachment security in those we support. The cultural expression will directly influence and organise the expression of safety and relational connection both in the immediate family and broader community. Interventions that are influenced by attachment theory must be attuned to each family's, or a staff team's, unique experiences of attachment and the context in which they understand and experience attachment security. This pattern will be informed by each person's attachment history.

Safety-exploration strains and barriers to attachment security

Parental factors

Parenting is often exhausting, and huge resources are needed to maintain the necessary energy, attention and focus on meeting a baby/child's needs. If a parent has additional challenges, such as maternal depression, mental illness, an intellectual disability, substance misuse issues, financial or housing pressures, then the parent's own resources to attune to and focus on the young child can be depleted. In addition, if there are factors such as domestic violence or coercion, then the primary issue for the attachment figure is more likely to be focused on basic survival, making it likely that there will be gaps, or limited attention available for the nuanced needs of a baby or developing child. For families where there is an existing parental health challenge, this can again reduce the availability of the parents/key caregivers, such as where a parent, or grandparent, has complex health issues to manage, or where a sibling of the baby has complex health needs.

Factors or events around the child

Understanding individual attachment patterns, and the need for, or avoidance of, connection are central relational principles we hold in mind throughout DDP focused work. There can be many events that interrupt attachment security; sometimes through the experience of neglect and trauma that would be classed as abuse; but we also understand that attachment security can be made complicated at times when parents and children are separated by medical care, by ongoing parental stress, by misunderstood congenital factors, by early birth and through unforeseen events that overstretch a family. Attachment insecurity does not necessarily just arise when something actively aversive has occurred but can occur as a result of mis-attunement and a struggle with connection, despite the presence of love. This strain on relationships and connection, this **relational trauma**, is, we suggest, one of the patterns that might emerge when caring for, raising and generally interacting with someone with an intellectual disability.

Attachment security and intellectual disability

It is important to consider the potential impact for some families, of having a child with an intellectual disability. The degree of challenge experienced in families when their baby has an intellectual disability will possibly be mediated or informed by the family's prior experience, attitude, knowledge, support and, sometimes, cultural beliefs about disability. For some parents, it can be an enormously challenging and worrying experience to learn that their young baby has additional health, cognitive and social needs. The impact of processing significant news arises in the context of existing family, but also broader cultural beliefs about disability in general. Sometimes, the attitudes around or held within a family can be highly supportive; sometimes, they can be sadly stigmatising and isolating, especially where attitudes of blame or criticism are around in the family.

The introduction of a new baby into a home leads to a period of adjustment, regardless of ability or disability: a time to learn about their baby's likes and dislikes and the different pressures being solely responsible for another person brings. For families where a child has additional and complex needs, this period might take longer, as medical interventions need to be prioritised, or if baby/children's upset is particularly hard to soothe, feeding is complicated by differing muscle tone, or babies do not cry and alert parents to their needs. All children's reactions are unique, and some parents can feel overwhelmed or inadequate when faced with providing care for a child with a disability, while other parents might notice that they are finding it harder to read their child's reactions and responses or notice significant worry and pressure to get things right. Access to community and extended family support might become more or worse, less available, depending on the understanding and attitudes about disability held in the broader community.

In circumstances where a parent is already distressed and worried about how to care for their child's complex needs, this worry can interrupt or influence initial interactions, opening up the potential for relational trauma. When a baby is distressed and needing comfort, but is presented with the face of a worried, stressed or depressed parent (Astor *et al*, 2020), the baby is less drawn to looking at their parent and will learn to look away and avoid a distressed face. Such disconnect could be exacerbated by the miscommunication and misunderstanding that can occur when the baby has an intellectual disability, as these babies might be harder to map and decipher for some, because their ability to communicate is challenged and their development and readiness for their parents' chatter might be misunderstood. The pattern of safety and exploration is like a dance, and it starts with tiny moments of connection or disconnection, and these early experiences provide the foundation for our attachment patterns, whether that is secure or insecure. Each person's attachment style informs a variety of interactions, such as the extent to which we will look to others for support; the extent to which we will feel confident in leaving key people to explore the immediate world; whether it is beneficial to keep loved ones close or distant; how to ask for help when upset.

We all have our own attachment experiences from which our attachment patterns are formed. Increased awareness of our own styles, as professionals, parents, or carers of others, and also of the patterns we notice in those we care for, will only enrich our relationships. The variety of factors that impact on the development of attachment insecurities have historically been linked with early trauma, neglect and assault; however, gaps in care, relational ruptures and mis-attuned parenting (even with love) are better understood to be important variables (Shemmings, 2024).

Our experience is that there are increased risks for people with an intellectual disability to experience attachment insecurities, born out of the early challenges around communication and attunement, and not necessarily due to neglectful or harmful care. It is for this reason the terms **relational trauma** or **developmental trauma** can be more apt descriptions of the interruption that has occurred. Many families would benefit from support and guidance to slow down, take the time needed to get to know their child, and allow much more time for a child to respond to their gestures and care. In turn, parents need encouragement and sometimes emotional and practical help with the slower pace often required to help establish this early connection. Parenting and caring in this way minimises the risks of missing early attachment cues in the child.

Conclusion

Our understanding of the key and central tenets of safety, security, love, and connection between a baby and their carers, has evolved out of attachment theory. Although early attachment theory presents cultural bias, a refreshed and broader understanding of attachment continues to draw on the protective and connective importance of strong relational bonds, loving experiences and care in early life which remains central in early development. There are significant pressures for the attachment figures of children with an intellectual disability, especially where they experience or feel prejudice, a lack of support or if they are already coping with additional pressures. The challenges of taking time to attune to the potentially complex communication and physiological needs of a child with an intellectual disability can interrupt the smooth development of attachment security, despite the care and love from key attachment figures. The communication pressures around people with an intellectual disability could significantly increase the potential for relational trauma, despite a loving connection. Understanding these early starts will create a fuller understanding of the child (and later, as they grow into adulthood) and their interactions with others, particularly during times of stress and illness, as well as times of fun and mutual enjoyment. Understanding each person's response to offers of safety and help, alongside mapping out their willingness to explore the world, can illuminate and help us to better understand an individual's reactions, responses and openness to connection.

Chapter 6:
Neuroscience – brain development is tied to the care received

Summary

- This chapter considers the ways in which our understanding of brain development helps us to consider our sensory, emotional and cognitive development. We note how researchers and theorists are using recent findings to help us to better understand how our neurological processes can evolve in response to our early experiences of care or trauma.
- We draw on some key models and theories to illustrate ways to interpret and make sense of the impact of trauma, but also to help inform the type of support that might be needed in the moment. These models include the neurosequential model of development, polyvagal theory, the window of tolerance and 4Rs (regulate, relate, reason and repair).
- Our primary attachment figures are central in the development of our sensory, emotional and cognitive networks. In this chapter we consider how the use of a DDP based approach can support the development of these fundamental systems, particularly in the development of regulation and improving resilience.
- By understanding the impact of early attachment or relational trauma on the developing systems we can improve our formulations for people with an intellectual disability, and better understand if the reactions and responses we are observing are linked with underdeveloped sensory systems, or emotional and cognitive processes that are survival-focused.

Introduction

Why consider neurological development in a book about relational therapy?

DDP is a relational approach which aims to help deepen relationships, improve safety and increase coherence about experiences as a way of healing from the impact of past trauma. This chapter includes an overview of how models of the 'lower ' sensory and emotional level systems of the brain are influenced by early relationships and safety. Higher-order cognitive development, or our executive system, is organised in response to the levels of connection, and the strengths and weaknesses developed in the lower systems. In this chapter, we discuss emerging findings and theories about neural development that help us better understand and conceptualise how our brain and body systems work. For us, this seems especially important when we consider the neurological complexity faced by people with intellectual disabilities. When we start to ask or consider the range of sensory and emotional systems that might be underdeveloped in a child or adult with an intellectual disability, we will offer more accurate assessments, develop richer formulations and offer more attuned support for children and adults.

Overview of brain development

Over recent years, research has helped inform and improve our understanding of the impact of early neglect, gaps in care and the experience of trauma (such as the effect of being repeatedly scared or stressed) on the developing child. Bruce Perry (e.g. 2006) has written and talked extensively about this connection, developing the Neurosequential Model of Therapy (see https://www.neurosequential.com/). Other Psychologists and Neurologists have studied the impact of trauma on the developing foetus, baby and young child, including the development of the nervous system (for example, Hughes & Baylin, 2012; Porges, 2011, Dana 2018 & Shore 2000) . In this chapter, we draw extensively on their models. Their work, along with others in the field, has helped us to envisage how our early care experiences directly affect the way our whole body develops. Each network of neural connections influences how other systems are organised. Neuroscientific models describe how even early in-utero care impacts the development of these systems. They connect from the bottom-up and include, in order:

1. fundamental life-sustaining and sensory systems which precede
2. emotional development, followed by
3. higher-order cognitive systems.

Our core unconscious and more physiological processes connect and form the foundation for our more conscious development around our emotional, and later our cognitive, experiences. These brain systems are described by some as the 'upstairs ' and 'downstairs ' brain (Payne Bryson & Siegel, 2011). The 'downstairs brain' refers to sensory and emotional systems or networks, and the 'upstairs brain' describes our more conscious awareness (such as impulse control, planning, reasoning and holding a strategy in mind). People with an intellectual disability will, by definition of their disability, experience impairments in some, or maybe even all, key areas of their brain development. Their underlying brain structure might be organised as a result of their genes, chromosomal pattern, birthing complications (for instance that might lead to restricted oxygen to the brain) or other brain-impacting trauma (head injury during childhood or chronic illness). When the neural connections have this additional complexity, it is, we argue, even more vital that we consider how care can impact on and support brain development for people with an intellectual disability. When we reflect on the ideas around the tender processes and sequencing of brain development, this can help us build a clearer set of questions about behaviours that are challenging. When someone is reacting in a way that is hard to manage (or maybe make sense of at first), could they be unconsciously trying to regulate their nervous system? Are we seeing a purely 'behavioural' response or is someone trying to find ways to regulate their sensory system? Are they feeling overwhelmed with emotion? Are they having difficulty processing sounds around them? Do they have an underdeveloped vestibular system? Or a combination of all of the above? For instance, biting can, for some, be a way to show anger or be used as a method to get people to move away from you; for others, it might be a way of using whatever surfaces are available to regulate themselves (through regulating input in the oral motor system). When someone barges into you are they trying to hurt you or are they struggling with their proprioceptive awareness? All of our reactions and observable behaviour can be driven by a variety of internal (sensory, emotional and cognitive) systems; when we remain open to considering and exploring the variety of factors that could explain someone's responses, this will not only improve our care but also our connection with their experience.

Polyvagal theory – a framework for considering the impact of relational trauma on brain development

Porges' polyvagal theory, and the writing of others who have further explored this model (such as Hughes and Baylin, 2012 and Dana, 2018), helps us to consider the impact of early relationships and trauma on our unconscious neural networks in our sympathetic and parasympathetic nervous systems. The polyvagal theory provides a model to explain how our autonomic nervous system helps support us to explore, learn, or sense when to seek safety. This theory unpacks how babies develop in direct response to their early care, and how development can be interrupted or dominated by trauma experiences, including relational trauma (where there has been mis-attunement and misalignment in relationships).

The theory

The Autonomic Nervous System is made up of two networks:

1. the Sympathetic (SNS)
2. the Parasympathetic Nervous Systems (PNS).

The SNS links bodily functions that enable more activity, and the PNS enables our body to quieten and slow. Porges identified a key neural route: the vagal nerve (including the ventral vagal nerve and the dorsal vagal nerve). The vagal nerve is a bundle of fibres that uses both the SNS and PNS and provides connections across our body that increase our ability to survive, to explore our environment or feel in a state that enables learning. He outlines three pathways within the vagal system which are activated (without conscious awareness) according to how safe we feel.

- The smart vagal nerve or ventral vagal nerve in the parasympathetic nervous system, which connects key organs including our brain, heart, voice quality, lungs, diaphragm and stomach. The ventral vagal nerve responds to the experience or signals associated with safety and social connection.
- The sympathetic nervous system – with nerves located in the thoracic and lumbar regions in the spinal cord. The SNS triggers an adrenaline release that readies us for action – fight, flight and freeze responses.
- The dorsal vagal nerve in the parasympathetic nervous system, which connects the nerves in the back of our neck, throat, eyes and ears and enables a whole body response to quietening down and can lead, in extreme danger, to dissociation.

Dana (2018) outlines a ladder system to help describe our different stages of activation and openness, as described by the polyvagal theory. We are constantly responding to our sense of threat or relaxation posed by our immediate environment and, so, different aspects of the vagal pathway are activated at different times. Our early relationships will activate and strengthen the neural connections in the vagal systems, fine-tuning or helping our readiness or exploration, alarm or shutdown.

Figure 6.1: Illustration of Dana's ladder used to describe the polyvagal system

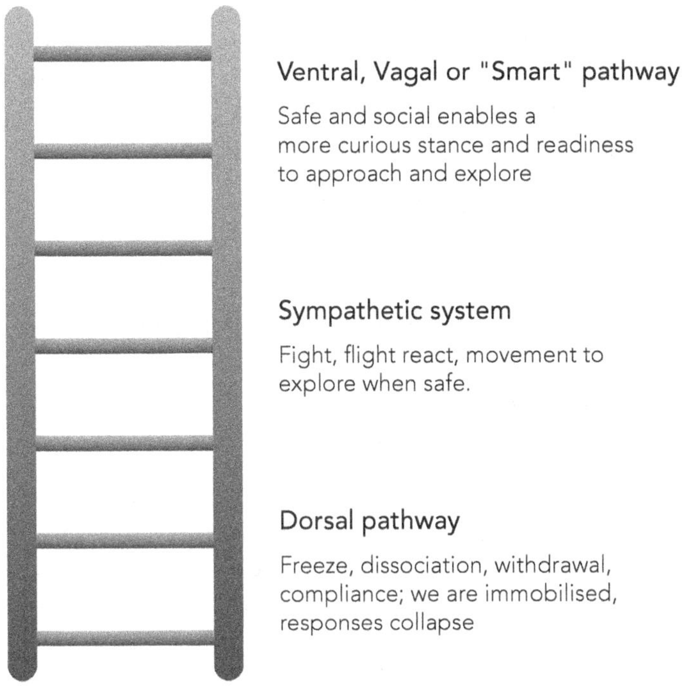

These pathways are activated and constantly changing in response to our past experiences, which informs our interpretation of the risks, threats or safety of the current situation. Our reactions are informed by our previous experience of similar settings/people or demands and are also mediated by the type of care and support provided by others. We need both the parasympathetic and sympathetic nervous systems to enable us to be alert to danger, but also to allow others to protect us when we are overwhelmed, to provide safety and teach us how to relax and enable time for play. A baby's development is dependent on, and informed by, how they can respond to both their environment and the people in it. Their development is therefore intrinsically related to the capacity and skills of their key carers in making sense of and scaffolding a baby's experience to maintain safety and support exploration.

Repeated experiences will influence the pattern of neural connections within a pathway. For instance, babies that are overwhelmed by sudden noise, lots of words, worried faces or maybe painful medical procedures, may be more practi sed at being alert and in a state of readiness or alternatively, might have learned to shut down and avoid demands.

Different systems are activated depending on the perception and experience of danger in the moment. If someone perceives or experiences a sense of threat, they will move out of a bodily state open to connection and will instead focus resources to enable the first move to action. If the danger is marked, or the activity enabled by the sympathetic nervous system hasn't helped them, the actions of the dorsal-ventral pathway dominate, leading to profound quietening of the internal systems including shutdown, falling asleep/not making a fuss, or dissociation.

Table 6.1: Summary of Porges' model

Neural system	Location	Responses
Parasympathetic nervous system (PNS) ; ventral vagal pathway	Connecting the brain stem with heart, lungs, diaphragm, stomach	Safety and connection
Sympathetic nervous system (SNS)	Located in the middle part of the spinal cord	Mobilisation for exploration and learning when blended with the ventral vagal system, when feeling safe or reaction to fight, flight
Parasympathetic nervous system (PNS) – dorsal vagal pathway	Connecting the brain stem with back of our neck, throat, eyes and ears	This system helps with monitoring and tracking an environment. When marked or extreme danger is noted it brings the body into 'shut down '; ranging from freeze, dissociation, hide, quiet, withdrawal

Questions to consider:

Might a lack of eye contact, or a fixed mid-distance gaze be indicative of an absence-type seizure or does it indicate dissociation and extreme overwhelm?

Is a person's state of flight or fight, due to an emotional reaction such as feeling scared, feeling aggressive (because they are scared), feeling intimidated, feeling panic etc?

Could any of these emotional reactions be triggered by a need to escape, or unconsciously shut down?

These sensations and emotional reactions can be triggered by a perceived threat rather than an obvious or active threat; this perception will be informed by past events and experiences.

Neuroception, interoception and attachment relationships

An attachment figure is central in making sense of a child's preconscious, internal bodily experiences known as neuroception. The neuroceptive system is located in the amygdala in the limbic brain. It is the system that enables us to process incoming sensory information from which we determine if a risk or threat is present, or whether this is a time to relax or explore our environments. Neuroception is below our conscious awareness, but over time, our sensory experiences help inform us about the world, and our attachment figures can shield and offer comfort around this sensory processing. This support and indirect teaching occurs within all the miniscule interactions between babies and their carers, where the carers chat through and name the patterns they notice, where they make sense of what the baby does, or speculate about what might be going on for the baby when they are upset (such as feeling, hungry, too hot, or in pain). Over time, this informal teaching brings awareness to the sensory and physical state; at this point our interoception or conscious awareness of our body has become clearer.

Our perception of danger and response to threat and safety happens before we are aware of it; at a pre-conscious, neuroceptive level. For example, people often can't explain why they like or trust certain people; but we have long referred to trusting our 'gut instincts ' to make sense of a situation or person. Those working in intellectual disability services are learning just how profoundly early disruptions in parent-child connections (whether due, for example, to communication barriers, gaps in care, or because of trauma) can skew or inform that gut instinct later in life. Our neuroceptive system is fast: sending information within 200 milliseconds (Baylin, 2024) and provides the information for our brain to prepare for what is coming next. One way our neuroception is triggered is by reading (or misreading) the facial expressions of the adults around us, such as raised eyebrows, a grimacing mouth or a furrowed brow. Over time, these signals help us determine whether we are in danger or safe, and activates our emotional responses (our limbic system) and our fight, flight, or freeze reactions in our brain's amygdala. The vagal nerve sends information between the body and the brain; enabling changes in our gut, alterations in our heart rate and even what we see to inform our responses. Even when we do not fully understand our reactions and gut response , the signals our whole body sends are strong and can guide our responses.

Embedded within this communication is the sense that carers understand, or can mentalise their child's world and their experiences and are not overwhelmed by the baby's needs. In terms of attachment, these repeated exchanges can deepen a baby's sense of safety and protection. When we consider the impact on the intersubjective connection between a baby and carer, at this point, the baby is able to relax and trust that their needs are being met. In turn, a carer might feel a range of reactions when they are able to decipher and meet a child's physiological needs – that could include feeling effective, like a brilliant parent, or maybe just sheer relief!

This understanding of another's physiological experiences needs to be tempered for those with an intellectual disability. The power of non-verbal communication is highly significant before verbal language is established, and for some, remains the central route for communication and connection. We also need to communicate and share our insights repeatedly with those with an intellectual disability, who will likely need more support or who might always struggle to learn about their internal states. By being attuned and attentive to someone else's feelings and needs, we can offer coherence for their bodily responses and help them to either make sense of their internal experiences with us or to feel better understood. Interoception describes our conscious awareness of our physiological state, and our knowledge is dependent on the formal and informal lessons shared by our carers. The personal and intimate moments of care, when another person is often more vulnerable, provide a pivotal opportunity for making sense of the body but also building or conversely undermining trust within a relationship. When we connect in these moments of care, we have the opportunity to help a baby, child, and adults, make better sense of their internal states and reactions.

To consider:

Over time, a child will associate a steady heart rate, an even body temperature, a settled stomach, and hearing singsong prosody of voices around them at a time when it is safe to explore. It might be that they come to link this feeling with a state of curiosity and safety. Conversely a child can learn that they are feeling anxious by the associated changes in their body state e.g. increased heart rate, feeling flushed, wanting to move quickly, feeling snappy with others.

Understanding someone's formative experiences can enable us to better understand what their experience of 'normal' might be.

Over time, with repeated experiences, we can link certain feelings to certain events or people in our lives, even before we fully understand those feelings. For example, we might feel uneasy about a situation before we are able to differentiate between nervousness, anxiety or mistrust. Rothschild's work on the Autonomic Nervous System (2017) is a valuable resource for understanding how our bodies react in different emotional states (how our internal primitive neural systems are activated in various states of arousal). It explains the basic ways our nervous system works, which can help parents and carers better understand the sometimes subtle or confusing reactions of the person they care for. This is especially important for people who struggle to cognitively process, let alone communicate, their emotions to others, or who may be restricted in movement or immobilised due to physical disability; where the potential to misread or not understand signals and changes can increase. Carers often become adept at noticing idiosyncratic changes ; interpreting these signs and patterns can be vital in better understanding what someone with an intellectual disability is experiencing and again, review what might have become their normative experience.

Nervous systems are co-regulated

The polyvagal theory explains that we need to be in a calm physiological state to be open to connection and engagement. As humans, we are born oriented to and dependent on receiving care: social connection is a biological necessity for our survival. When key attachment figures make sense of the baby's experience, and offer calm or soothing support, this process is called **co-regulation**; and it relies on both verbal and nonverbal communication. It is the first step in helping the baby to master their own regulation over time (more on co-regulation below).

Porges emphasises that this early dependency mediates how a child's nervous system develops and responds as they grow. Part of attachment security comes from knowing that parents or caregivers will protect the child from threat, danger, or overwhelming situations, such as with food, stimulation, noise or other dramas. At first, a baby's world benefits from being small, or, in a protected bubble, to help a baby and a parent/carer to get to know one another. Ideally, this is when the baby's calming ventral vagal pathway is activated and a responsive carer soothes and settles a baby when they feel scared, in pain or discomfort, when hungry, hearing frightening sounds or needing a nappy change. But, if for instance, a parent is the source of danger or has invited unsafe people into the baby's world, or does not understand the baby's needs, the child's nervous system will respond. The sympathetic nervous system will enable a child to escape from the situation and the parasympathetic nervous system facilitates withdrawal to reduce the focus on themselves, for safety.

Co-regulation of sensations and intellectual disability

The type of connection between a parent and child, would, it follows, link with the degree to which the parent can feel open and connected to their child. A parent's confidence, or sense that they are feeling effective in caring for their child, comes in part from being able to offer comfort which in turn allows the child to relax into a state of openness and engagement. Where a child has any type of developmental delay, there is an increased possibility of some interruption in their response to their carer/parent; such as the person with an intellectual disability might struggle to make sense of the care being offered or the words being used. When a child doesn't respond in the predicted way or it's hard to read their physiological cues, there is a risk, for some families, that it can challenge and interrupt the bonding experience. For other families, they find it easier to adjust and will be the first to notice that predicted milestones are not likely to be reached, and that their child might need additional time or support at various stages of their development.

Children with an intellectual disability often become known to a wider network beyond their immediate household and those in the network; extended family or professionals can be well or poorly attuned to their presenting needs. The opinion and views of others can greatly assist parents/immediate carers when the needs of the child are understood, but when there is misunderstanding, or when parents are misdirected, or worse, their concerns are dismissed, it can reduce the attachment figures' confidence in their actions to care for their child and undermine their knowledge about their child. Such feedback from the wider network can be incredibly stressful for parents, which in turn, will impact their confidence when caring for their child.

In utero impact

Some children experience toxicity during pregnancy, whether this is linked to prescribed or illegal drugs or alcohol, or from the stress hormones/chemicals linked with domestic violence, coercive control, difficulties related to maternal mental health, or housing pressure/homelessness. The impact of toxins in the womb on a developing foetus is multiple and depends on the age of the foetus, the frequency of toxin exposure and the type of toxins ingested. These toxins have a wider range of effects, from interfering with protein production in early development, to contributing to childhood disorders (Thompson *et al*, 2009). Proteins are essential for early neural development and are needed for the development of healthy neurotransmitters, which help brain cells communicate with each other. Specific toxins are noted by Michael, Kinsella & Monk (2009) to have certain impacts:

- cocaine impacts dopamine pathways (needed for pleasure and rewarding experiences)
- alcohol is linked with lower birth weight, hyperactivity cognitive deficits, lower birth weights, reduced brain volume
- nicotine use is associated with lower birth weight, hyperactivity and cognitive deficits
- maternal stress whilst pregnant (not just post birth) is associated with increased risks of children developing neurodevelopmental disorders, anxiety or depression.

In utero toxicity will directly impact the foetus's tender developing neural and sensory systems, and again, this sensitivity to possible impact, helps us to better understand what each individual child's 'normal ' internal experiences are and predicts their preparedness for new challenges.

Impact of premature birth

The protective ventral vagal system is not yet fully developed or myelinated for children born before 30 weeks (Dana, 2018). The absence of a fully developed ventral vagal system means the baby has to draw on the dorsal vagal systems at a time when they are relying on the support of neonatal care with machines, wires and tubes to provide essential support. They also often have limited access to their parents at this time, as a mother might need medical attention herself, and whilst necessary, these interventions can also create a barrier to skin-to-skin contact or even general access and soothing touch with their child. Children who are born very prematurely, such as at 28 weeks or less, are 66% more likely to be diagnosed with an intellectual disability (Behrman & Butler, 2007).

Until more recently, the impact of the hospital environment on a premature baby was not always considered or understood. Beyond meeting essential medical needs, other adjustments might have been overlooked with regard to the brightness of lighting, the amount and pitch of sounds in the essential monitors, the humidity in the room and the degree to which they heard their parents' voices or experienced their contact (Séassau *et al,* 2023). An additional pressure at the start of life comes with the often-complex, physical health needs that people with an intellectual disability experience, which sometimes require intrusive, yet vital, medical intervention. At the start of family life together, it is typical for parents and their babies to become immersed in each other, to the extent the outside world often fades into the background. However, there is a higher likelihood for someone with an intellectual disability to experience a disruption in this cocoon-like phase, whether through the support needed due to an early delivery or medical care linked with seizures or heart/lung conditions. Each of these stages can cause a necessary intrusion into the immersive connection with parents and teaches the baby about what to expect from care, how to respond to pain and who to trust. These processes can be terrifying and overwhelming and, again, might help us to better understand the level of development or interrupted development in essential sensory systems.

Trauma and underdeveloped sensory systems

The work of highly specialist occupational therapists such as Eadaoin Bhreathnach (2009) and Sarah Lloyd (2016), amongst others, is providing vital insight into the ways our tactile, olfactory, visual, auditory, vestibular and proprioceptive systems develop. When responsive care has been available, the neural pathways develop, enabling a baby and developing child to process and respond to the world around them. Where this development is interrupted through early trauma, such as gaps in care or even through mis-attuned connection, those sensory systems are less likely to thrive and might remain underdeveloped. This means that a child might be having to cope with a range of sensory challenges, making it harder for their bodies to be adequately prepared for other stages of development.

To consider

If a child is feeling wobbly and have to concentrate very hard to sit on a chair without falling off, because of your underdeveloped vestibular system, it will be very hard to listen to lessons in school or learn about the importance of turn-taking during a game of snap. Their body will need to put resources into coping with sitting rather than attending to anything else in the moment.

When a child repeatedly experiences sensory overload, those underlying sensory systems might develop to become super sensitive to certain input; struggling to cope with or process the information received. When sensory input has not been offered, these systems are likely to struggle to develop. Some systems are over-sensitised, meaning lower input is bearable, whereas other systems need greater input for the signal to be received and recognised. Sometimes the challenge is in modulation; working out how much of a type of input works well. When we get the sensory input we offer another person wrong, it can, in the extremes, feel painful. Considering sensory development and connections in more detail can help carers and parents to better understand and respond to an individual's support needs.

As our sensory systems develop in response to the environment and context in which we experience the world, attachment figures are central in scaffolding the support or stimulus a child needs in order for their sensory needs to develop at the right pace. Carers ideally understand, or are guided around, the type of exploration that their child is seeking at different points in their early development. This can often be more complicated for children with an intellectual disability. The exciting news about our sensory systems is that, given the right support and opportunities, our sensory systems have the potential to change and develop.

Those born with an intellectual disability might have highly complex neural systems due to their chromosomal patterns, or co-occurring medical conditions; so experiences need to be tailored around, and attuned to, any additional conditions or needs. As a population, there is a higher likelihood that a child with a disability might experience necessary but intrusive and painful medical input (Séassau *et al*, 2023). Therefore, there might be physical or practical restrictions on the range of sensory exploration that someone with an intellectual disability is able to access and engage in. There is growing awareness around the impact of gaps in sensory input and exploration, or the need to offer repeated sensory input where development has not yet taken place. Drawing on Perry's Neurosequential Model (2006), helps us to better understand how vital these early steps are, as our emotional and cognitive neural connections and regulation rely on the foundations of sensory systems. People with an intellectual disability have an increased risk and likelihood of experiencing underdeveloped sensory systems and these are worth assessing to ensure we are understanding and correctly attending to presenting needs.

- If the ability to modulate the information received via the auditory system is impaired we might notice some people seeking ways to control the sounds they hear and might do this by generating constant vibration in the inner ear. For an onlooker or carer, they might observe a child needing to create or have noise around them to feel regulated. This might look like constant chatter or a stereotypy attributed to a specific disorder, but could alternatively be linked with a specific auditory processing pattern.
- People who need to move and wiggle, who position themselves upside down or need to crash into others or walls might also be trying to meet a sensory need due to underdeveloped vestibular and proprioceptive systems.
- When proprioceptive (body orientation) systems are not yet fully developed we can note patterns for those seeking input to maybe better regulate those sensory systems. For example, those who need to hit out when upset do have behaviours of concern, but it might be important to consider their sensory systems first before considering an affective or relational explanation. Do we know if they need to regulate themselves through finding proprioceptive input at their extremities rather than targeting an individual or showing anger?
- A broader walking gait might indicate underdevelopment within the vestibular system and indicate underdeveloped gravitational stability or core strength.

Relationships and neural development

Sensory and neural systems

The process by which attachment figures chat to babies and essentially soothe, calm and co-regulate the babies' experiences, echoes the way DDP-based conversations are also structured. DDP is founded on the basis of what safe care and close connection looks like in line with theories of attachment and intersubjective connection (see Chapters 5 and 4 respectively for further detail). Attachment security develops where an attachment figure is attuned to the baby's needs and able to offer responsive care that aligns with the infant's emotional state, which enables the baby to explore and navigate their world. Whilst the early established pattern shapes our relationship security across our lifespan, children and adults continue to be influenced and respond to changes in relationships. Intersubjective connection describes the pattern and type of connection and influence that the baby and attachment figure are having on each other; it is a reciprocal experience. Intersubjective connection is a very active process, and moments of distress such as a change in a child's physiological state, will lead, in turn, to concern and upset for a carer. If distress is heightened, it can disrupt an intersubjective connection.

Dan Hughes, the founder of DDP, originally developed DDP as a therapeutic approach that could help restore care and connection for children who have experienced trauma and who were no longer living with their birth families. The approaches in DDP draw on the patterns of successful parent-child connection which includes an attitude described by the term 'PACE '. (A PACEful approach is described further in Chapter 7.) The acronym stands for a way of allowing for **P**layfulness, offering **A**cceptance for the baby's experience, feeling **C**urious to discover more, and leading with **E**mpathy for the child. The parent or carer's curiosity and empathy enables the child's experience to be better understood and often named : *"Ah, you need to keep singing so that you know what sounds are coming"* or *"No wonder you have been grizzly, you must be feeling hungry!"*. In offering a deep concern about someone else's interoceptive sensory experience, and helping to make sense of it with them, we offer coherence for their experience but also deepen connection and trust.

The fear and terror of sensations in the body around feeling hungry can lead a child to cry, at times, ferociously. There can be a similar reaction in terms of decibels, to feeling wet or experiencing trapped wind. With an attitude of curiosity to work out what the upset is about, a parent is able to learn the different types of crying signals and can even start to explain this to their baby with kindness and empathy for their experience. To the baby, these sensations are overwhelming at first and can seem life-threatening if we track the reaction of the baby, but the regulated or calm and responsive care of the adults around the baby helps to make sense of this with soothing tones, a calm face and a clear explanation about what is going on with a reassuring prosody of voice. When a parent accepts the baby's upset, rather than shaming them or telling them to be quiet, a baby learns that their distress can be contained or co-regulated, and over time, a child will be able to learn to not feel so scared and they start to better understand their physiological reactions; " *This sensation means I am thirsty and this one means I need to eat* ", " *This means I am going to be sick*", and so on.

We learn about our internal states or understand our interoceptive states in part through other's reactions, who teach us how our bodies are functioning, but who also share their thoughts, judgements and opinions about those bodily reactions. People with intellectual disabilities are likely to have gaps and challenges with processing information or understanding language, which can make it harder to make sense of internal experiences. Day to day, this can look like confusion or frustration and will be the types of reactions that are challenging for the individual or to others. For instance, someone might lash out as a response to feeling scared or worried when they have a stomach upset. This lashing out towards another might, however, be misunderstood as being cross or wanting to be alone at lunchtime. When we better understand the underlying issues, we understandably improve our care for another, and teaching someone about their upset stomach is of equal importance here whilst maybe also increasing support and increasing space between people to ensure others remain safe during lunch. In finding the right solution, we might assist with interoception and avoid introducing a plan that could be bewildering and isolating.

For those living in uncaring and unsupportive settings, sometimes, personal care is also associated with times of shame or worse, abuse. Experiences of poor care increase the confusion about bodily functions, and sensory experiences, and do not offer the scaffolding for development that could be seen. Sensory systems are constantly receiving feedback from the environment and importantly, are open to repair, but require attuned and connected adults available to support such change.

Case vignette: Toby

Toby is 45 and requires considerable personal care as he is doubly incontinent. His father used to find personal care very embarrassing and difficult and always pulled a face of disgust whenever changing Toby. When Toby was introduced to a new male member of staff in his service they initially got on so well. However, when this staff member offered to support Toby with his personal care, Toby reacted with sadness and anxiety. Toby was experiencing marked shame and anxiety linked to his previous experiences related to a male supporting his personal care needs.

Case vignette: Sam

Sam is 10 and permanently relies on a wheelchair to move about. His dad finds it easy to talk to him about his body and is often the one offering care massages when Sam's legs are in spasm. Sam was keen and eager for his dad to show his respite carers how to look after his legs on the afternoon his dad was going to be at work.

Emotional development

In a similar fashion to how we are taught about our different physiological and sensory states by a trusted adult, so too can we learn about our emotional responses. Without guidance, the different physiological reactions triggered by a range of emotional or affective states would, and could, be overwhelming. Within our brain, the limbic system (our emotional hub) is tied to, and linked with sensory feedback systems , enabling us to experience physiological changes with emotional changes. Again, without safe adults to make sense of and teach about these fluctuations, the difference between excited or nervous, happy or sad, might remain a muddle. Growing up in an environment where caregivers essentially offer a PACEful approach enables a more rounded development of different emotional states. Our emotional development is bound to our attachment experience and connections.

The limbic system in the brain enables us to identify and make sense of our emotions and some of our behaviour. This is key to our motivation and is tied to our longer-term memory systems. A parent-child relationship includes a mix of direct and indirect education, though often implicit or modelled through direct experience. The limbic system, as with sensory systems, develops in response to the experiences, opportunities and feedback gained in the early stages of life. Learning that certain actions or activities are fun helps us to seek out opportunities to achieve this emotional state again. When a baby's experience is one where their carers can be responsive, and effectively soothe and settle upsets, this has a direct impact on the limbic structures in the brain: the amygdala (flight fight, freeze, or dissociation response centre) is less likely to be triggered into response. Babies who grow in safety, or who are supported by protective parents who are able to meet their child's needs, are less easily triggered into a fight-flight response than babies who are frequently scared, or who have a sense of isolation because their needs are hard to meet (Balbernie, 2001). When needs are consistently not met, children experience heightened stress and distress. Their neurocircuitry is adapting; the networks and connections form in the area of the brain where there is the greatest demand or activity.

Window of tolerance

The optimum arousal state is when we are calm and regulated. At these times we are able to be open and engaged in relationships, to play, and to cope with the surrounding demands whilst remaining calm or regulated. Siegel's Window of Tolerance framework (2020) has provided a valuable way of understanding the variations in the state of arousal that occurs within each of us as we react and respond to the world, the people and sensations around (and within) us. This model works well when considering our responses to all input, whether this is sensory, emotional, cognitive or social.

There are times when our emotional experiences are strong and overwhelming , at which point we are operating outside of or beyond our window of tolerance. For children who have not been protected or for those, perhaps, who were born with an intellectual disability, whose needs are more complicated to predict and harder to resolve, there are increased risks that they live in a state of readiness, anxiety or even depression and withdrawal in response to their environment. Day to day, this means that people with an intellectual disability might be more likely to have a smaller window of tolerance or narrower tolerance of changes in their emotional experience. It also might mean they are more reactive or overwhelmed when their emotional experience is challenged. Their narrower tolerance increases the risk that they will be more rapidly pushed beyond their window of tolerance.

Our resilience and openness to experiences is described as operating within the ideal banding, or within our window of tolerance. The experiences and sensations that have become familiar, that our attachment relationships have helped decipher, in turn help predict our window of comfort or tolerance. We know that our sympathetic nervous systems are activated when our reactions are longer, bigger, louder, and generally more active. This is a state of hyperarousal and indicates times when we are no longer feeling calm and safe, but are dysregulated. In a state of dysregulation, behaviour tends to be out of step, disconnected, or an overreaction to the situation.

Conversely, when we notice someone shutting down, becoming markedly withdrawn, quiet, or hardly present, this would indicate that their parasympathetic, dorsal vagal pathway is dominant. Potentially, if that situation is too aversive or is not resolved it is likely that they will experience a dissociative state, which often looks like, or is mistaken for, an epileptic absence. Within the window of tolerance model, this is referred to as hypo-aroused.

Consider the pattern of someone who has a passion for and seeks out time to bounce on a trampoline; they actively seek out this experience and are thrilled by the spin, whizz and fun of this activity on their body and how it makes them feel in their mood. However, for some this sensation is too intense to process but they still want to bounce, to leap and crash on the trampoline. Ending it would feel so awful but this whizz is making them boisterous, feel invincible, reject any offers of help and this feeling blocks out the need to connect with other people or engage in other less satisfying activities. For those who are not able to easily regulate this experience you will notice their pupils dilate, their respiration rate increases and they become extremely hot (more rapidly than might be noticed when someone else is on the trampoline).

Example of hyperarousal

Someone has walked into Ali's room and moved things around. This is so upsetting to Ali especially since their request and hopes for a lock on their door haven't been accepted. Ali becomes angry, shouts abuse at the staff for not looking after their stuff, that no one cares, and then Ali slides all the furniture against the door and effectively barricades themselves in. Ali is also picking things up and throwing them at the wall and door. At this point Ali's heart rate is rapid, their blood pressure is elevated, the breathing rate has increased but is shallow, they feel sweaty but feel cold and they might feel a bit sick.

Examples of hypo-arousal

Ken is worried about going to school. He slouches in a chair, and seems to be very heavy, almost floppy and slow in his movements, his breathing is slow, and his pupils seem smaller. He seems to have trouble speaking as his mouth is dry. He is quiet and doesn't respond much to his family and their help.

Nina has just seen someone in the local supermarket. This person looks like the person who taunted her when she was little. She became silent, and didn't want to talk or to move anywhere. She looks to the staff team like she is having a panic attack – her heart rate has increased, her pupils are very small, she looks pale and she is in a cold sweat. Nina has also wet herself and been sick.

Figure 6.2: Window of tolerance and how this can change with relationship-focused support.

Adapted with kind permission from Jones (2021), originally published in Beail, Frankish & Skelly (eds) *Trauma and Intellectual Disability: Acknowledgment, identification and intervention* (Pavilion Publishing, 2021).

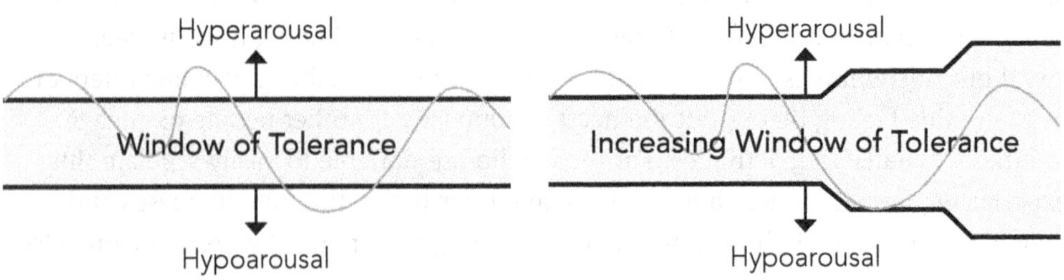

The impact of co-regulation on coherence

Children develop an understanding of their arousal levels from our primary attachment figures who guide and teach the developing child about their different states and also offer comfort and care to make sense of the environment in which the child is living. When someone offers to connect with, and support their child, regardless of the child's affective state , they are offering to support the child in making sense of whatever muddle is presenting. These carers are offering co-regulation. When in a state of hyper or hypo-arousal it is very challenging to return to feeling steady and calm. Young babies, older children and also adults often benefit from help to feel regulated. In offering this help it is likely that a greater sense of coherence will develop; another person makes sense of the upset and shares their understanding.

Within a DDP approach we start with a stance of curiosity and empathy to make sense of any upsets, in order to offer helpful co-regulation. Carers and therapists can connect with the person in front of them by modulating their tone of voice, expressing concerns with their words and also through facial expressions and in their more active responses (opening their arms to offer a cuddle). These are just a few of the steps carers might take in response to someone else's upset or confusion. In offering our connection and being open to understanding and finding out about another's experience, we must be authentic and face the current context. Within a reciprocal relationship, where what distresses one person impacts the other, we can accept another's experience and work to co-create meaning around these feelings. This means not moving too quickly to solutions, and not reminding people of the agreement or contract in place. Prioritising our attention on increased sensory or emotional regulation when someone is upset or scared can be challenging as we might be motivated to take action and fix things. However, in slowing down we can focus on safety through re-building trust and deepening the relationship. As the caregiver, when we accept another's experience, when we sit alongside and show that we take their feelings seriously and are impacted by their concerns, we can support someone to become more regulated and reinforce the safety that is available through our relationship. The world can become more manageable and predictable when we are known, understood and have alliances in the world. This brain-based connection enables someone who was dysregulated to become ready to reflect or learn new strategies.

The 4Rs: Regulate, relate, reason, repair

Figure 6.3: Illustrating the sequence of Perry's 3Rs model around regulation-focused support with the additional step suggested by Bombèr to create the 4Rs

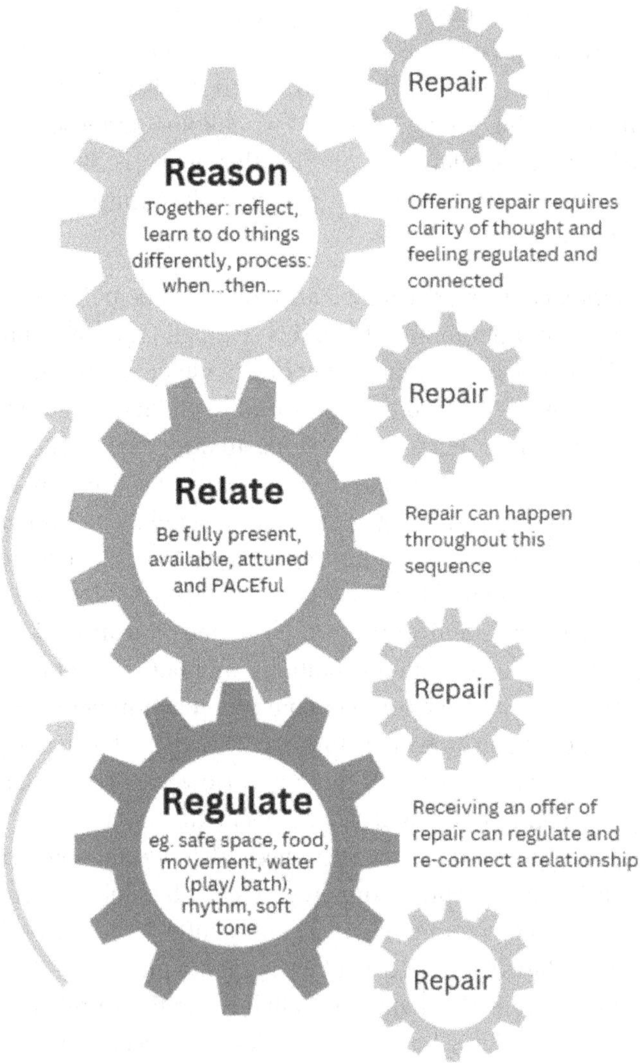

Perry (Beacon House, 2022) developed the 3Rs model to understand the different ways of connecting in the moment with a particular focus on reducing dysregulation and increasing reflection. Bombèr (2020) has added repair – a 4th R to this model, which we've entwined into our diagram above. The 4Rs illustrates our ability to move into reasoning once we are regulated, within safe relationships and when relational ruptures have been repaired.

Regulate

When someone is dysregulated, we initially need to offer or find ways to establish **regulation.** This involves helping the individual regain a sense of calm and control over their physiological and emotional state. In order to provide this input as successfully as possible, the supporting person must also be in a regulated state. Trauma impacts the lower regions of the brain responsible for survival responses, such as fight, flight, or freeze or dissociation. Activities that promote regulation, such as rhythmic movements, breathing exercises, time in a quieter room, using a soft tone of voice and giving time for processing information, can be the essential steps to reduce distress and allow engagement and relating to occur. Without regulation, higher-order cognitive processes like reasoning and problem-solving are less accessible.

Relate

Supporting someone into a regulated state will mean they are more likely to be able to **relate** or to experience intersubjective connection. When offering to relate to someone, we are connected with their experience, not necessarily agreeing with it, but offering acceptance about their experience. In doing so we will be impacted by their experience. When we draw on an attitude of PACE, we can first accept another person's distress and then offer curiosity and empathy to make sense of their perspective. Creating meaning about events might be assisted by our best guesses often explored when 'talking for' and 'talking about' an experience (see Chapter 2) matching their energy and working together to make sense of their perspective or experience. When we accurately identify and co-create the story about an experience we can deepen our connection with another person. There is a huge and significant power in being seen, known and understood. The focus on safety and connection in relationships allows the social and emotional parts of the brain to become activated (drawing on the ventral vagal system). The safety of this relational connection enables us to move into exploration or more playful approaches. Relating and deeply connecting in this way requires a carer to offer empathetic and attuned interactions, validating the individual's emotions and creating an environment where they feel understood and supported.

Reason

Reason involves engaging the individual in more reflective and draws on higher-order executive processes, such as problem-solving, simple sequencing tasks, orientation to time and place, learning, or reflecting on their affective response. Once we are able to reason things through we are ready to learn new skills, consider the consequences of our actions, review the support plans in place for specific triggers, consider different explanations for events and consider different perspectives about ourselves. We later consider the Two Hands of Care model (see Chapter 8), where we are reminded, that within DDP, we need to constantly maintain connection whilst offering correction. We can better engage with correction (such as safe boundaries, house rules) when we have the resources and support in place to enable reasoning.

When someone is regulated and experiencing safety in their relationships they will be better resourced or able to reflect on their trauma experiences. Perry emphasises that reasoning is only possible once someone is regulated and relational connection is established, because trying to consider, teach or explain things, when someone is in distress or does not trust those around them will make it too hard to focus on or process the information being shared. The impact of dysregulation is captured in Siegel's model called 'Flipping your lid' (2024). This model provides an explanation of the way in which our upstairs brain (the executive, reason, planning and impulse control part of our brains) becomes inaccessible, shut down or 'off-line ' when we are dysregulated. In order to enable the resources needed to reason we first need to help that individual become more regulated. We have to actively respond in ways that increase safety for the dysregulated person and work out the pattern that best enables them to re-establish connection. Supporting regulation, relationship and reasoning will help develop resilience to our different arousal states, and, over time, this can expand our window of tolerance.

Repair

As stated, Bombèr (2020) extended this model to include: **Repair**. It is a helpful addition to Perry's model, as the impact of dysregulation and likely relationship rupture can commonly include the need for repair to relationships (and maybe property or damage caused). We can only repair the impact of our actions or words when we are regulated, and wanting to be in a relationship (relating) with others. We will need our full reasoning and higher-order skills when trying to repair a relationship. Conversely, if we, as carers, have triggered shame (see Chapter 9) for someone else, then the priority would move to support regulation and re-connecting within this relationship. If we move too quickly to asking someone to say sorry or think through their actions, they are very likely to become dysregulated again and move out of their window of tolerance.

Cognitive development

The higher order, or executive systems in the brain are the last areas of the brain to fully develop, and even in typical development the systems in the pre-frontal context are not fully formed until the age of 25. The pre-frontal cortex or cerebellum is the part of the brain that is activated when we are talking to someone – tracking the words, making sense of their meanings, searching about in our knowledge centres for answers to questions and ordering the words needed to respond. Whilst we are retrieving the right information, we are needing to remember the question so that we try to stay on track and focused.

The prefrontal cortex is central, not just in attending to or focusing on information, but helps us filter so that we do not blurt out the insult that might be coming to mind! The processes are open to conscious awareness and need to reason, weigh up and balance information, find solutions to a problem or develop a new strategy when the last one failed. The demands and range of computation are to be marvelled at. Higher-order brain development can flourish when preceded by solid sensory foundations, and where there has been support for emotional development. However, when this sequential development is interrupted and the foundations remain poorly connected, it is harder to develop and draw on the skills needed in emotional control and regulation and, as outlined in Perry's model, fewer resources will be available for the development of the upstairs brain, and higher-order cognitive skills. Without firm foundations, is it harder to learn techniques for managing anxiety or distress and to stay regulated when facing uncertainty.

If there is an associated genetic or congenital disorder, life-impacting in utero care or complication that has arisen during birth, this sequential development is put under further strain. The experience for many people with an intellectual disability is that they are not just struggling with cognitive impairment but that the foundational processes are often not yet developed, which hinders access to support around their learning and skill development and their sensory and emotional development. We need to hold this neurosequential framework in mind when we formulate, review and tailor support and care to the individuals with, and the families and staff teams around someone with an intellectual disability. The question in mind is always: have we identified and addressed all the developmental gaps that we can, so that we can understand someone's needs, and in turn, offer the best opportunities for this individual's development?

Conclusion

The complexity of care needed to raise a healthy child, let alone a child with an intellectual disability, is marked. The early experiences around safety and co-regulation will significantly impact a child's neurobiological sensory and emotional development and overall readiness for support. Developmental models highlight how the strength of the foundations of the fundamental life-sustaining processes will impact on the emotional development (limbic system), and finally the higher-order cognitive elements (cortex). Early environments that are attuned and soothing enable the development of healthy sensory processing systems, emotional regulation, and higher-order cognitive processes. The care available to support these processes shapes how a child, and later a vulnerable adult, navigates and interprets their world, and whether they experience a sense of safety and develop resilience. When considering each individual's progress in their development and their window of tolerance for either sensory or emotional support, we will be better placed to connect with their experiences, and further the development of healthy neural systems. Understanding early influences on our nervous system also increases our understanding of a person's readiness to be regulated, their openness to relationships and when they are ready to reason things through with us or even move into repairing misunderstandings. Central to these processes is the understanding that the relationships around the developing child, and also for those that need ongoing support, can make a huge difference. When we hold a curious position about the internal experiences of people with an intellectual disability, and if we reflect on the variety of ways their development can be interrupted, we are more likely to provide attuned support. It is exciting that neural systems are open to repair or development and that this development can be influenced most greatly within safe, key relationships.

DDP focuses on connection with another's experience, drawing on the models that work so well to create safety for babies when they are needing to make sense of their internal worlds and surrounding environments. DDP provides a structure for holding a variety of hypotheses in mind, an approach for exploring experiences, and a way of building and sustaining connection even at points of distress. Neuroscience helps us to shape and better understand the complexities that people with intellectual disabilities can be experiencing, all of which is essential when drawing on or tailoring DDP approaches when we offer care and connection.

Resources

Window of tolerance (Beacon House, 2022): https://youtu.be/0ehq5-P5OSs

Flipping your lid (Seigel, 2024): https://www.youtube.com/watch?v=qFTljLo1bK8

SECTION 2:

Key concepts of Dyadic Developmental Practice with people with intellectual disabilities

Chapter 7:
PACE: What is a PACE-based approach?

Summary

- We introduce what a PACE-based approach is in this chapter. PACE is a way of thinking, feeling, communicating and behaving to help those around you feel safe. It is an approach that runs throughout any DDP focused work and was developed from keen observation of the patterns that help build and sustain connection.
- PACE is not a technique but a way of being alongside another - whether that other is someone you care for or work alongside.
- We consider in this chapter ways that a PACE based attitude might be adjusted or attuned when supporting someone with an intellectual disability.

Introduction

PACE stands for a way of being Playful, Accepting, Curious and Empathetic: each of these elements are interconnected and are hugely important ways to offer genuine, authentic connection with another person, and provide the foundations for a respectful and sometimes very deep relationship. This chapter focuses on the key components of a PACE-based way of being. In this chapter there are illustrations and examples of adaptations for teams, services or families to hold in mind when drawing on a PACEful approach, and for all to note when engaging with someone with an intellectual disability.

Figure 7.1: Summary of PACE

Playfulness	Acceptance	Curiosity	Empathy
A light approach, shared joy, pauses in intensity	Genuine acceptance for another person's emotions and experiences	Exploration of someone else's experience: learning rather than evaluation	Showing verbally and non-verbally that you see and understand another person's experience 'no wonder'

What is PACE?

PACE is an acronym used in DDP to describe an attitude or way of being within a relationship and is the style held across the DDP framework. An attitude of PACE enables a deep and direct, but also highly respectful and authentic relationship.

'PACE is at the heart of emotional connection' (Hughes & Golding, 2024, p 86) and is central to how attachment security develops and is the way in which we share and deepen intersubjective connection. Importantly, it is not a technique or a way of interacting at a certain point in a care plan: it is a way of being alongside and with someone. A PACE-based approach sounds beguilingly simple, but it is more challenging to maintain a PACEful approach than at first appears. An attitude of PACE also needs additional consideration when working with someone with cognitive impairment, or when working with staff teams and trying to help them consider how to develop a more PACE-filled relationship with someone with an intellectual disability (see Chapter 15 for consideration of use within services). It is not a stance or approach to switch on and off, but an attitude that should run through the culture of a whole service, department or home.

DDP's focus on the relationship helps us consider the ways in which we can deepen, enhance and strengthen our connection with another person. In tuning into and accepting or exploring another person's experience without prejudice or bias we can move into an open and interested stance. When another person relates to, or understands, our experience, we feel more able to trust that person because they see or want to understand all of our experiences; the difficult and positive. A PACEful approach is the way of offering, responding and being in a relationship to establish and maintain this connection.

PACE stands for Playfulness, Acceptance, Curiosity and Empathy: each of which we will describe in more detail. PACE is not a linear process; every conversation or exchange doesn't need to include each element of PACE. These are, however, central elements that help us to communicate unconditional regard, love and/or respect.

Playfulness

The playfulness denoted in PACE highlights or captures the points within relationships when we can share our delight and interest in another adult or child. When we are playful or light in tone, we are offering an openness; our guard is down. In being more relaxed, we can be open to new experiences, new approaches, and new ways of relating.

Playful approaches sometimes feel easier or less complicated to imagine when working with children, as there is an expectation that children like fun and games. However, we need to be ever thoughtful with our approach, as the role of playfulness within PACE is not to cheer another person up or to play games, but to share our joy about being with them. The playfulness in PACE is not, therefore, about making someone laugh as a form of distraction technique or playing a game (as an activity). The use of playfulness is to allow a lightness, to have some rise and fall or tonal aspect to your conversation and to your relationship. The rise and fall that comes in our voice also supports the storytelling approach often drawn on in DDP interventions (see Chapter 2). Our minds are noticeably more open when we are relaxed. Experiencing worries and sitting with, and alongside, someone else's serious feelings are vital approaches in DDP, but you will notice that in many conversations we need breaks or pauses within a conversation. There are natural rise and fall points in flowing conversation, and when the topics are around tender feelings or feeling vulnerable, playful or lighter moments can sometimes help to maintain regulation. There is something important about noticing the silly moments in life alongside the trickier and sensitive experiences. Playfulness helps us to connect and build an intersubjective connection.

Ways to offer a playful attitude or approach

- Blowing a cotton ball along a table to each other is often ridiculous but also great fun.
- Dancing or singing together.
- Tapping your fingers to the same beat.
- Echoing the noises another person might use.
- Intensive interaction.
- Playing a note on an instrument and trying to sound like it!
- Enjoying a joke or moment when you noticed something silly together.
- Sharing a silly YouTube clip.

If your style of playfulness or lightness does not work for the other person, you can always offer **Repair** (see Chapter 6, or later in this chapter, for more about this) to the relationship. It is important to note and name these moments as by apologising and letting the other person know you did not intend your words or actions to seem silly, that you did not mean to be mean when you teased, enables us to capture and repair or heal this relational interruption. By noticing that you might have created a possible rift is very important, given the aim of PACEfulness is to support connection! Noticing that you might have gone too fast with your words, or too far with some 'banter' is about being attuned to and sensitive to the other person's experience. It also reflects the intersubjective and reciprocal nature of the relationship, that you are not more 'right'; that you are both working out what feels good together.

An attitude of playfulness when with adults

Being 'playful' might trigger an understandable concern, especially when working with adults, that you will be required to offer games to grown-ups that are meant for children. Nirje's work (1969) updated with Wolfensberger's principles of Social Role Valorisation (1983), advocated the importance of sensitive and respectful attitudes towards people with cognitive impairment. This direction emphasised the distancing impact of the power imbalance between those with and without an intellectual disability. They also argued for the importance of treating people with respect to their chronological age. However, if we hold that a position of playfulness in PACE is about how we share and communicate our joy in being with someone, then the fears about being patronising or treating someone in a childish manner should diminish. A playful approach needs to hold a chronological age in mind alongside an individual emotional age in the moment. All adults have moments of lightness or a specific sense of humour, and an attitude of PACE supports a way of connecting with that pattern to share in what brings another person joy.

To consider:

What are the things that thrill the person you are holding in mind? Is it about access to new soft-textured cushions? Is it the sight of your favourite dog/kittens on YouTube? Is it dancing to specific music? Getting your hands busy with craft? Watching birds feed from a bird feeder? Can you recall the look of delight on someone's face when you share the right present or you turn up unexpectedly.

At all times, the aim is to experience connection and be aware of someone else's humour, but also what brings them happiness. Knowing that your dry style or delight in puns might be misread by others is helpful; it can help you check whether you need to explain or unpack a statement to avoid misunderstanding or unintended hurts/slights. Some adults are a little more structured with their playful escapes: the late-night gamers, engrossed online; playing team-based sports; watching sports with friends; knitting and chatting social circles. All of these offer moments for lightness but also for genuine delight about levels achieved in a game, the number of goals scored or the thrill of the creative endeavour. Often, such groups and activities are the vehicle that facilitate deeper connection in how we value and share our support in what is important to someone else. It can be important to explore ways to introduce lighter, joyful moments to our days, but also to consider how such approaches are a vital part of our therapeutic or PACEful conversations.

Acceptance

Acceptance is about exploring and not disputing the experience another person is having. Acceptance is not about agreeing with someone's actions, behaviour or attitude but about accepting that each person has their own reactions, reflections, interpretations and priorities. In accepting someone's experience we are focusing on their internal experiences, in particular, their inner emotional world. Offering acceptance therefore requires an openness where we must drop our agenda and truly consider what might be going on for the person with us. At its very simplest, this can be listening without trying to offer a solution, encouragement, reassurance or any problem solving. Acceptance of another's position, views or worries can be a truly challenging experience: listening to someone explain how great their football team is again and again can be wearing (especially if you support another team!). For most of us, it is likely easier to be accepting of someone's positive experiences; we will be able to engage in and most often share in the joy of their experience. Conversely, it can be so difficult to hold an accepting position when someone's internal world and experiences are negative such as being linked with depression, anger, fury or heightened distress, or when someone expresses love for a person that has also caused harm. At these times, it is harder to hear someone out, to listen to them explain their love/pain and hear the same pattern of worries be explained again, to notice someone getting into the same muddles and not drawing on all your (maybe great) advice from before. Hearing someone else's distress triggers many different responses in us, and they are worth noticing, and ideally understanding, as they will impact on your relationship (explored further in Chapter 10: Blocked care).

Bearing witness to someone we care about being in distress is challenging, and there can be a number of factors that make it hard to hold an accepting attitude. We have to note our own readiness to hear this distress: is it a day when other things are piling up for you? Are you already tired or worried about other pressing issues, such as a change in your own health, financial worries or just keeping an eye on the flow of the day so that you can pick someone up from school on time for once or ensure that activities of daily living are completed. It is interesting how quickly we move to reassure another person, to offer a solution to try to find a way through their muddle. Often, it can seem very obvious what someone else should, or could, do to make things better.

If we can hold all those competing ideas back, and 'just' focus on someone else's distress, it is interesting to note what happens. Offering comfort is vital and a huge part of the way we care for another, but in slowing down, in pausing before we offer solutions and comfort, we can allow space for someone to explore more fully, their experience. In going at this speed, we can learn more about, and deepen, the exploration, and enable someone to fully share their worries, their concerns and/or their upset. If we skip this step, such as when we offer advice or step in to reassure, we risk shutting down the other person's voice, however well-intentioned all our comfort is. This is part of our connection with another person; it is hard hearing about the times when things don't work out, or when they have been hurt, or when they are struggling. Meanwhile, in being heard and in letting someone explain their experience, they will feel respected, and hopefully, better understood.

So, acceptance; it sounds simple? It really isn't!

One of the particular challenges with acceptance is that when we ask 'Why?' or 'What is upsetting you?' we often experience a shrug in reply. Sometimes, our role is to be open and accepting of all possible explanations, and to be the one helping to explore what might be going on (See Curiosity, below).

Sometimes, this can mean that we have to be open to criticism of us as the upsetting issue, as the trigger for the upset might sit with us and could be something we have done. On these occasions, it means that we have to listen, and make sense of someone else's perspective, rather than stepping in and explaining, or even defending why we acted, responded or did the thing we did. This can feel highly unfair, especially during the times when our actions were around increasing their safety from immediate or marked danger (as in the example below). Sometimes, we have to hear that we haven't previously been as helpful as we hoped we were, when we offered solutions/ideas the last time this was discussed. Some people with an intellectual disability find it very hard to process information, and to process and really digest their feelings, so the rate and pace of change around an issue can take time. In offering acceptance, we need to also accept that this is the processing time that is required. There are other ways in which we need to draw on our patience; it is understandably hard to create time and space to hear the same worries being described again and again; this takes energy on our part and can be a common pattern in supporting people with an intellectual disability.

An example of moving a conversation to a PACE-based approach

In the following example, the carer/parent starts with a more factual conversation and quickly moves to a more PACE-based approach:

Client: Why did you just try to break my arm?

Carer: What? I didn't. I was trying to stop you running in front of that car.

Client: You are always trying to hurt me.

Carer: That's not true. I am always looking out for you.

Client: You hurt me.

Carer: Oh, I get it. I held your arm and it hurt a lot. I am so sorry about your arm. Can I check it over?

Client: Why are you always hurting me?

Carer: That was a horrible shock wasn't it. I held you really hard, didn't I? I think it felt very strong – maybe too strong? Maybe it scared you as it was really quick. You worried I was going to break your arm. Oh, that's horrible. I am so sorry to give you such a shock.

Client: People always push me about – you're like all the others.

Carer: You have been really hurt before. Maybe you felt like I was going to do the same. That would have been so frightening.

Client: It was.

Carer: I am so sorry for scaring you. I don't want to hurt you, I want to keep you safe. I do want to check on your arm now and maybe talk about this some more. Is that ok?

Curiosity

We use our curiosity to help make sense of things, for and with, the person we are talking to, with the aim of creating coherence for them, and hopefully for us, too. This is about increasing understanding, particularly in relation to emotions. Without this support to make sense of events, some people can be left trying to fill in the gaps themselves. Sometimes, the explanation or account we hear is a confabulated explanation that connects A to C, but the route there just does not make logical sense, or might not match what you witnessed occurring. Filling in the gaps and building the story together is an important aspect of DDP, and the process can build and deepen trust.

Another vital aspect of being curious is that it requires us to be non-judgmental or to remove preconceptions. I have repeatedly observed deeply entrenched judgemental patterns in the exchanges in both general children's services and especially in services for people with an intellectual disability. Fortunately, these judgments are often very positive, and take the form of "Well done", "You have done such amazing work there", or "That sounds great". Each of these statements seems so innocuous and it might seem strange to highlight this pattern. However, these statements often reflect the speaker's views, opinions and values and so aren't necessarily offering true acceptance.

Case vignette: Aspen

Aspen has been at school and returned home with a medal for his sporting achievements. His father is full of praise and keeps telling all their relatives about Aspen's fantastic ability on the football pitch. Aspen responds to this story with either a fixed smile whenever this is mentioned or a quick exit from the room. He doesn't seem to be shining with pride in the way his parents anticipated.

Aspen's mother takes a moment to make better sense of her son's reaction and explores this during a car journey when it's just the two of them.

Mum: We've been showing so many people your medal!

Aspen: Yeah.

Mum: We are so pleased for you about winning it. We are just so proud of you. Do you know that?

Aspen: I know.

Mum: But… you don't seem quite as happy about it. I am wondering if we might have got something a bit wrong?

Aspen: *doesn't say anything but is facing his mum and seems to be listening.*

Mum: I think we've done lots of talking about your medal but haven't checked in with you. I wonder how you are feeling about the medal?

Aspen: S'okay…

Mum: Ahh, I see. So, it's ok, but maybe not as brilliant as Dad and I have been saying. So can I check with you then, what do you think about this medal?

Aspen: It's okay. Not great.

Mum: Can you tell me more about that? Why isn't it great?

Aspen: It's not a cup.

Mum: Are cups better than medals?

Aspen: Yeah – much better.

Mum: And you wanted a cup and maybe think a medal isn't as good?

Aspen: Yeah that's it. Cups are bigger and better.

Mum: So if you get a medal it feels nice, but if you ever get a cup – it would be a wow?

Aspen: Yes! I wanted a cup.

Mum: Well, that makes so much more sense now. Shall we tell Dad when we get home?

Aspen: Can you explain it? I want to practise football outside.

Mum: Of course. You go and practise and I'll let Dad know you like the medal but would LOVE a cup more.

Curiosity, again, is harder to embody than it sounds: finding out more about someone else's experience, not just the facts but their emotional experience. Even if you have shared and been part of the same experience, working out what it was like for someone else is very revealing and can be incredibly powerful as it creates a sense that someone's experience is of value and important. Listening or offering to work out what happened gives the vulnerable person a voice about a difficult time, a time when they might have felt overpowered or confused.

We can all be good at the 'Who?', 'What?', 'Where?', 'When?', 'Why?' questions when we try to find out the details around an event. It can be harder to bring into focus the DDP aspect of *"What was this like for you?, Does this link with the past?"*

An additional advantage of curiosity is that holding an open and curious approach often enables a more accurate explanation to emerge. Without this support to make sense of events, people might need to stick to their version of events, in a more defensive stance, or due to confusion about how things occurred. They might also worry that they are at fault for their emotions and actions, or even that they are out of control, and whilst there may be some factual truth to this viewpoint, a genuine offer of curiosity can help make recent events become more understandable.

This is the starting point for supporting reflection; but it needs to be done together, and this modelling is vital when supporting people with an intellectual disability. A worry about being at fault, for some, can be a deeply worrying experience and might mean they stick rigidly to their first explanation if challenged too hard. People who struggle to understand the connections between events, and leap to an unhelpful, or even self-critical or blaming explanation, are often accused of, or considered to be, lying or making things up. It is hard to be lied to; it can break, or at least shake, the trust that had developed within the relationship. It is possible that the wrong explanation is offered, because they are scared, through their past experience of getting into trouble for doing something wrong, or because they genuinely don't remember, or because they actually do, and don't want to let you down. Being curious is not about being right, it is about offering the idea that there is an explanation (for these feelings and reactions) and that we might not even know what that is yet, but we are curious to see and to find out alongside the person, because we care about them and their experiences. Being curious is also about giving the message that these feelings or behaviours are understandable – there is a way of understanding them and you: *"I am curious to work it out with you. We might not get there straightaway, but you can be understood and I will work hard with you to try and do that."*

We are also working with children and adults who often get lost within a conversation, who might not have all the words to hand for their experience, or who only have non-verbal communication to share their reactions and experiences.

Working with someone who has experienced trauma, especially early trauma, helps us appreciate just how disorienting trauma can be. You might be working with someone who finds it hard to understand or make sense of their interoceptive or sensory experiences and cues, or who might be so scared by their emotional response that they cannot process anything else because they have dissociated. Often, we notice how our brains react to trauma with dissociation or a milder shutting down to protect us when we are overwhelmed; linking us back to our Porges's Polyvagal Theory (see Chapter 6: Neuroscience) about our somatic response to the times when we are overwhelmed.

When we help someone to create, or co-create, their experience, without blame and with a curious stance and full acceptance of the challenge of working through events, we offer order and coherence. In doing this, we can increase a sense of safety. Making events and reactions more predictable or accessible can help all of us to understand the world around us better. For someone who might be reactive, explosive or dissociative, this is an important step in helping an individual to understand that maybe they are not to blame for the terrible things that happened, or it might be a good way to help make better sense of their reaction to specific triggers or settings. We are offering the ideas that they, and their emotions, are understandable: their feelings have meaning and we can (in time and together) make sense of these. By offering to co-create the story around what happened we become an ally, but also a decipherer of their world and experiences, in much the same way as we offer newborns at the start of their lives – with both our words and the tone and prosody of our voice and the totality of our non-verbal reactions.

When building the story together, we can enable a focus on the bigger events and feelings, or we can notice how events in our current lives are linked with experiences from the past. We can also use our curiosity to help make sense of reactions to both wanted, and unwanted events, from food, or seasonal anniversary triggers, to smells, or even the weather.

Curiosity in DDP often takes a gentle and enquiry stance and can often include wondering out loud, offering a best guess, making a suggestion and then checking if what you've said sounds right. Sometimes this curious approach is part of a direct conversation with someone or might be more of a spoken wondering stance spoken between two carers in ear shot of the person with an intellectual disability.

Types of questions that help us to stay focused on the emotional experience

- Did this feel the same as when this happened before? How was this time different?
- Is this how it always feels when someone is mean to you?
- Is this the worst it has ever been?
- Does this link with other times when these sorts of events have happened?
- I wonder if Bill didn't like the way we rushed off the shops today and didn't say where we were going?

When we ask these questions, if we cannot expect an answer, we need to hold these questions and this position in mind. Our non-verbal expression will convey so much – that we want to gently understand what an experience has been like for them and how it has affected the rest of the day, or how their body feels.

An example of what curiosity in PACE might sound like

Client:	You were all shouting at me. Stop it.
Parent/carer:	Just now, we were all shouting at you?
Client:	Yes.
Parent/carer:	Oh, so it was loud, too loud?
Client:	Yes, too loud.
Parent/carer:	The singing was too loud or the words were too loud?
Client:	The singing.
Parent/carer:	The song was too loud. Did it hurt your ears?
Client:	A bit.
Parent/carer:	Maybe you don't like the song or there's something about hearing it before.
Client:	Dunno.
Parent/carer:	You might have heard it on a birthday before – it's often sung. People sing that and bring in cake too?
Client:	Yes – with cake.

Parent/carer:	So you remember the song from before. Are those memories ok for you?
Client:	NO!
Parent/carer:	I see so this song brings back a memory?
Client:	YES!
Parent/carer:	Maybe not a good memory?
Client:	No. When Grannie died.
Parent/ carer:	Ah you remember when Grannie died on my birthday – we'd all been singing that song and later that day we heard that Grannie died.
Client:	Yes.
Parent/carer:	That's a huge memory. This song makes you think of Grannie dying. It's very sad isn't it.
Client:	I miss her.

Empathy

All therapeutic approaches are founded on the need for empathy for another's experience, so ideas about empathy feel very familiar when learning about PACE or DDP. However, there are different levels for the empathetic response; at a cognitive or emotional level, and also in understanding someone's core sensory and physiological needs. All therapies are based on a strong need to have empathy, or at least understanding, for another person's experience, but DDP differs from many traditional approaches in how that empathy is shown or shared.

Within DDP, we are not focusing on skills teaching, considering strategies or offering solutions, but on offering or deepening connection; when we show our empathy for another, we communicate our understanding for someone else's experience. Empathy is more than validation; we are offering an intersubjective connection (see Chapter 4).

Offering a connection with someone shows that you are interested in them and willing to build a relationship, and in doing so, we enter a two-way process. DDP is truly collaborative; the issues that impact the child or adult in front of us are going to have an impact on us. This enables us to join, and truly celebrate another person's joy, to share this and show this in an active way. Conversely, it will mean that we will connect with, and be impacted by, another person's sorrow. If we are in a therapeutic relationship, it is important that we are not dysregulated by our empathy for another, but there is no doubt that, at times, we will be deeply impacted by this, and we need to be able to show that we are moved by their experience. In focusing on a relationship, we are agreeing to allow another person's experience to impact us: this is our intersubjective connection. To know and sit alongside another person's experience and to let them see we are moved and affected by their reactions is important; as our reactions can help make sense, in part, of what they have been through or are recalling. Imagine your reaction when a friend describes a terrible event happening to them: we are active and demonstrate our concern for them. A truly empathetic response means we should respond (whilst remaining regulated) with honesty when we sit alongside someone who might be recalling times when they have felt marked distress, been hurt, assaulted, rejected or denied a basic need. When we open up a relational approach, when we allow ourselves to truly empathise with another, we open ourselves up to being impacted and being moved or saddened by another's experience.

Many children and adults have learned over time to mask or minimise their reactions. There could be many reasons for this, including the reactions of others when really challenging experiences have been previously discussed. Alternatively, it might link to times when they have been blamed for the incident, or not been believed about a terrible event. If someone has experienced their reactions to events being repeatedly dismissed, minimised or overlooked, a great confusion can build up about understanding their affective experience; identifying and showing their experience might be highly challenging. This can be the case even following the most marked assault or saddening event. With the offer of deep connection and empathy of their experience, your reactions to events might mean that your non-verbal expressions are out of sync with the person who has experienced significant emotional upset. This mismatch will be important to note and gently explore. Often, holding empathy for another helps the individual start to learn, or at least see how they can be empathetic towards themselves.

An example of holding empathy

Client: I miss Dev.

Parent/carer: I bet you do. It's horrible when he's away from home, isn't it?

Client: Yes.

Parent/carer: Are you missing Dev the same as before or is it different?

Client: More.

Parent/carer: More? Oh, that is so hard. Let me check – you normally miss him this much (pulls arms a certain distance apart). But today you are missing him maybe this much (pulls arms even further apart)?

Client: Yes, that much.

Parent/carer: It's so hard missing him, isn't it?

Client: Really bad.

Parent/carer:	That bad feeling is hard to cope with, hey? Does it make you want to hide under the duvet or maybe under the bed?
Client:	My duvet, AND the bed.
Parent/carer:	It's so bad you want to be wrapped up in a duvet under your bed maybe. It's so sad to be thinking about Dev and not seeing him.
Client:	Yes, I want to cry but don't want to.
Parent/carer:	Missing Dev makes you want to cry – sometimes you might cry I guess?
Client:	Yes – I did today.
Parent/carer:	Today is a really tough day, isn't it?
Client:	Yes. When can I call him next?

Context and parent/carer attachment history

A readiness for a PACEful approach is often determined by the context or environment. It can be challenging to keep offering a connection and reflecting approach if this is being done in isolation and others draw on more traditional approaches. Similarly, on some days, on some occasions when we ourselves are not feeling regulated, we might struggle to feel light or playful, we might feel more judgemental, we could be far less interested in someone's experience, or might move quickly to solutions just to get things resolved. Our ability to demonstrate a PACE-based attitude is also influenced by our own background, including our attachment history and, for professionals, by our previous training. For instance, for myself, as someone trained within a fairly traditional Cognitive Behavioural Therapy framework in the 1990s, I was taught to demonstrate empathy for another through kind words and supportive summaries about the enormity of their experience. However, empathy can be expressed more deeply than with just words. When we experience connection, their sadness brings us deep sadness and their joy, likewise, lifts us. Appearing to sit calmly, in a neutral stance, whilst we talk about events where someone has been hurt, abused or assaulted is something we are taught (for good reason) to do as contained therapists, but what message does it also send: to sit and not react at all when we consider such painful memories together? Sharing some of our reaction or empathy for someone's experience is vital. In doing so we share our level of engagement and how much we care, it deepens our connection to that person and also normalises or maybe even models what their expression of their experience might be.

Figure 7.2: The connected attitudes in PACE based approaches and key influences in our expression

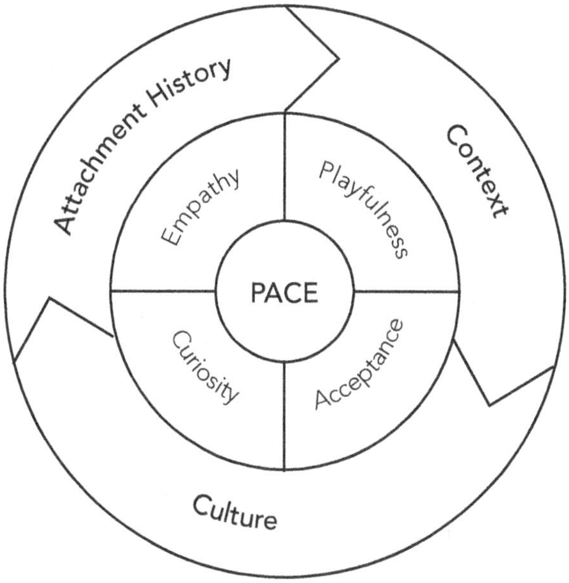

Cultural differences

There are important differences in each community/family or culture in how we show and share a playful approach, and it is important to be sensitive to how our approach is received by another. In some families, a dry or teasing approach is considered playful, or showing that you care, but this can easily be misinterpreted or misunderstood by others who are not expecting or do not know how to interpret your dry humour. If your humour is to tease when showing affection, please be cautious, especially when talking to those with a history of being ridiculed, or those with an inner working model that quickly leads to feeling of shame. It is hard to get teasing right, especially if the person you are teasing has had previous relationships or experiences where they have been subjected to, or felt, humiliation, been belittled or just felt confusion because it has been hard to keep up with the rate of the conversational exchange. Teasing in some cultures is offered as a sign of affection, whereas it can sometimes offer the opposite and reduce the closeness in your relationship.

There are important differences in each community/family or culture in how we show and share or develop a PACE way of being. In some families, a dry or teasing approach is considered important and as a way of showing that you care. In some cultures, directly expressing and naming affection felt for another would feel inappropriate and, instead, empathy for another is demonstrated with acts or gestures of kindness. In some families love is more conditional, or care in a service is offered within a model of positive regard, both of which run counter to a more PACEful approach. When love is conditional, or expectations are pre-determined or high around a person, it is harder to develop a more curious or flexible stance. In services where an emphasis rests on positivity, it is very challenging to hold a more accepting attitude that helps us to explore another's experience.

Our approach and use of PACEful approaches will be informed, not just by our experience of these attitudes in our own development, but also in the cultural expression of these attitudes. Understanding the experience of the people around you, and being open to not knowing and to finding out more about their experiences, helps us to understand our differences but also develop more honest ways of understanding and connection with each other. In deepening this connection and understanding we enhance the experience of safety.

Conclusion

Often, a PACEful or PACE-based approach comes to the forefront of our thinking when we see someone in distress. However, it is also important to hold this stance in mind for exploring neutral, and even positive and happy circumstances, experiences and memories. Feeling calm or excited are just as important to make sense of, as feeling nervous or angry. Holding a PACEful way of being in all experiences will make it easier and more familiar to everyone, including the person with an intellectual disability and their family member or carer, and will hopefully make this style of relating easier to sustain or hold across the day. Bringing or offering coherence and understanding to enjoyable experiences should not be overlooked, especially if they are novel to that individual. Sometimes, we might just offer praise or congratulations when something has gone in a way we think or judge to be ideal or great. However, in holding a curious and accepting approach we can check out how another person views a situation before offering our comment. Within an attitude of PACE, ideally our comment should track and support their reaction; whether that is joy, confusion or feeling overwhelmed.

In addition, when working with people with an intellectual disability, we need to be aware of the huge power imbalance present for those without and with cognitive impairment. In holding a PACEful approach, we can help be supportive of redressing some of this imbalance. The vital stance of acceptance and curiosity of another's experience provides, or strengthens, a voice for many who lack, or have their agency and power undermined. This means that our judgement about whether something was 'good' or 'bad' is not the leading issue; we first need to explore the experience and the affective state and opinions of the person with an intellectual disability. In holding back from imposing our judgements, we will be better connected to, and better attuned to, the experience of the person with an intellectual disability.

People with an intellectual disability are highly vulnerable to coercion, and the need to please the adults around them can be a huge pressure. In moving away from a reward and praise focus through DDP, to helping them identify and better understand their own experience, we can be supportive of, or strengthen, their own identity and challenge any pre-existing self-critical internal working models.

Chapter 8:
Two Hands of Care – connection before, during and after correction

How to communicate: "You matter, no matter what"

Summary

- People with an intellectual disability can experience potential barriers to the development of attachment security and their primary caregivers can struggle to fully understand their individual and additional needs. These factors can lead to an increase in dysregulation, and what can be referred to as 'behaviours that are challenging to manage'.
- Traditional behaviour management strategies, such as reward systems, time outs or other correction-based consequences, even in the presence of (and especially in the absence of) empathy and warmth, can lead to underlying needs being misunderstood, not prioritised or even rejected. Long-term, this can lead to an experience of love and attention being conditional, an experience of shame and boundaries being associated with a sense of "I am bad".
- This chapter describes the approach of "two hands of care" and how the one hand can offer warmth, connection and is attuned to needs of the person, whilst the other offers structure, boundaries and opportunities for learning through correction. We need both hands to work in unison to offer safety, connection and the chance for repair.

- This balance of connection and correction allows the message "Everyone needs to be kept safe, including you (the person with an intellectual disability) and me (the carer)" to be given.
- It is possible, and in fact important, to help people with intellectual disabilities we care for to live within safe boundaries and develop the skills to interact in less hurtful and more meaningful (to them) ways, within the foundation of our unconditional relational connection. This can be possible through parenting and caring within the two hands approach: engaging with people with curiosity and emotional connection and, using this connection to determine the appropriate boundary or correction (for ourselves and those we care for).

Introduction

This chapter provides an exploration of the *Two Hands of Care*, an approach that emphasises the importance of balancing connection and correction in parenting and caregiving. It examines what the Two Hands Approach entails, why it is essential, and its specific significance for individuals with intellectual disabilities. The chapter also gives examples of traditional behavioural management techniques, contrasting these with the Two Hands of Care approach, which integrates both emotional attunement (connection), and structure and boundaries (correction) to create a more balanced and responsive approach. A key focus of the chapter is the practical application of the *Two Hands of Care* approach in real-life parenting and caregiving situations. It provides strategies for maintaining balance between correction and connection, even in tricker situations. Connection fosters a sense of safety, which in turn allows for repair.

Additionally, this chapter introduces the *Parenting in the Moment* cycle, a model designed to help caregivers navigate tricky interactions, by responding thoughtfully and intentionally. Examples and reflective questions are included to facilitate engagement in this cycle, encouraging readers to apply these principles to their own experiences.

What is the Two Hands approach?

Two hands of parenting (caring/teaching), was originally developed by Dan Hughes (2009) as a way of describing how to create a balance of meeting the needs for 'connection' on hand one, alongside meeting the needs for 'correction' on hand two. Correction within the Two Hands approach is thought of as emotional and behaviour support, in order to move away from the idea of correction as punishment (more on that later in this chapter).

Although originally written as a parenting approach, we have noticed how well this concept works as 'two hands of care', when considering all immediate and extended attachment figures in the lives of people with an intellectual disability, such as teachers, direct payment workers and care staff. With appropriate adaptations, this approach works well for attuned support to people with an intellectual disability of all ages and levels of ability.

Figure 8.1: What might Two Hands of Care look like when supporting someone with an intellectual disability

(You can also find this figure as a photocopiable resource in the Appendices.)

Hand one	Hand two
Provides warmth, nurture, connection and is attuned to needs of the person with an intellectual disability, communicating *"You matter, no matter what."*	Provides structure, boundaries, opportunities for learning and making corrections that are carer-led, communicating *unconditional love, with conditions on behaviour (Golding, 2015)*
Be open and engaged, calm and regulated. Watch, be with, listen, really listen (with intention). Be playful, allowing for light exploration without pressure or expectation. **Spend time** with and delight in the person you care for. **Attunement and mind-mindedness:** View the person you care for as an individual, with their own thoughts, feelings, needs and motivations. Wonder, be curious and aim to understand and meet both hidden and expressed needs and any shield against shame	**Safety first:** Boundaries for harmful behaviour to maintain a sense of safety. **Time in** (as opposed to time out). Stay near the person you care for and ensure they feel safe. Although this will not always be appropriate. It might look like an explicit offer of space and 'time' instead for the person to be regulated before considering other correction-based strategies below to ensure correction is not reactive. **Set limits and routines:** Consider what structure, routines, boundaries and limits are needed for the person you care for to feel safe and thrive in the context of (dys) regulation and developmental needs.

<table>
<tr>
<td>Acceptance and empathy: Show acceptance for the thoughts and feelings underlying their actions (remember, this doesn't mean you accept the behaviour, but you accept the underlying feeling).

Co-regulate: Help the person you care for to manage emotions and feelings of shame with empathy and acceptance.

Intersubjective interaction: Interaction that maintains the key links between you both as a dyad whether this is around sensory, emotional, social and communication needs.</td>
<td>Problem-solve: Consider what corrections/adjustments you need to make to your own approach, the environment and activities to better meet the needs of the person with intellectual disabilities. Start with addressing and meeting the presenting dysregulation. For example, where a person is struggling to manage an activity, you can offer to assist to maybe just be near them to help them manage their anxiety or sense of feeling overwhelmed.

Teach (not punish) in a calm, clear and empathic manner.</td>
</tr>
<tr>
<td>Repair: Help the person you care for to know and feel they are cared for and liked. Your relationship is stronger than whatever has just happened within it.</td>
<td>Logical teaching: Ensure any correction/consequence is logical and linked to fixing/making right/repairing the behaviour, not abstract consequences. For example, where a person is struggling to manage an activity on their own, you will offer to support them and be closer to them in that activity in future.

Cause and effect: Help the person you care for understand cause and effect with 'if-then' statements. For example, "If you break the tablet, then it won't be there when you want to watch your programme. That will be so sad you won't be able to watch your programme".

Provide guidance and suggestions and opportunities to practise new adaptive behaviours.</td>
</tr>
</table>

X Delay conversation about behaviour **X** Avoid leaving the person **X** Delay problem solving	**X** Avoid punishments (e.g. withdrawing a planned and much anticipated activity because of distress earlier in the day) **X** Avoid relationship-based consequences (withdrawing love, attention, interaction) **X** Avoid responding with anger or shame-ensure you have taken a deep breath and any other necessary steps, so you are in your upstairs brain, feeling regulated and calm **X** Avoid giving complex or unrelated consequences (e.g. if you break the tablet then we won't be able to go out later) **X** Avoid lecturing or talking at the person you care for

Connection

Within the Two Hands of Care approach, Hand one can be thought of as representing care, warmth, nurture, autonomy and connection, building and maintaining a relationship with the person we care for through our repeated offer of loving interactions, understanding nurture and play. Within this connection, the aim is for the person we care for to feel safe and secure, to feel you are wanting to understand their inner experiences, including their thoughts and feelings. Connection requires an effort on the part of the carer, to remain open, curious and engaged with the person's internal world, needs and motivation. It is powerful to show another that you will sustain warmth, empathy and positive regard, despite their recent upset or dysregulation, being accepting of this and offering warmth and empathy (as discussed specifically in Chapters 4, 5 and 7). Connection must always occur before, during and after correction. By offering connection before correction, we not only maintain our relationship, the experience of safety for the other, but also improve the likelihood that they will remain regulated enough to hear the next steps, the new idea, the reminder etc that comes next in the correction stage.

Correction

Within the Two Hands of Care approach, Hand two can be thought of as representing supervision, structure, routines, activities, boundaries and supervision, so that the person we care for can feel safe and secure. Correction does not include a punishment of any sort; this is not advocated. The correction, when we get it right, offers the best way for the dyad to continue to feel connected whilst moving on from the tricky issue. Correction involves an effort on the carer's part, based on a thorough understanding of the person's needs, more so than an effort on behalf of the person we care for. The correction is informed by mind-mindedness, attunement and curiosity to meet needs of attention, communication, social interaction, sensory integration and overall development. Correction within two hands of caring offers the message "Everyone needs to be kept safe and cared for, including you (the person with an intellectual disability) and me".

When considering the Two Hands of Care approach, it can be especially helpful to consider the DDP principles of PACE, talking to, talking for and talking about and draw on affective-reflection dialogue or understanding around the underlying pressures. Depending on the social and emotional developmental needs of the person with an intellectual disability you care for, you can consider whether, for example, it is more helpful to make most guesses as an internal dialogue, or whether to wonder out loud without expecting an answer (*"Let me guess what's going on...."*) or whether to wonder with other key carers in front of the person you care for (talking about). Of note, the DDP concept of 'talking about' needs to be considered sensitively to ensure it is helpful and respectful, strengthening your relational connection (for more reading around this, see Chapters 2 and 7).

Why consider Two Hands of Care for people with an intellectual disability?

People with an intellectual disability are more likely to experience early and ongoing trauma and are potentially more vulnerable to experiencing attachment insecurity, throughout childhood and into adulthood (see Chapter 5: Attachment theory, for further reading). Alongside this, often, people with an intellectual disability experience ongoing reliance on others to ensure their safety and needs are met and this in turn may increase their feelings of powerlessness and lack of control. People with an intellectual disability can struggle to understand, identify, label and express emotions, experience potential barriers to the development of attachment security and their primary caregivers can struggle to fully understand their individual and additional needs. These factors can lead to an increase in dysregulation, expressed through, what can be referred to as, behaviours that are challenging to manage.

Traditional techniques of parenting, teaching and caring can be the wrong match for those who have not yet established trust and relational security in their relationship. Yet these techniques have tended to, until more recently, dominate the support offered to people with an intellectual disability. Prioritising more traditional approaches, such as reward systems, time outs or other correction-based consequences to manage undesired behaviours, means that the underlying needs contributing to those responses are often misunderstood, not prioritised or even rejected. Techniques that focus directly on eliminating or reducing undesired behaviours, without the consideration of the person's underlying needs and experiences, are likely to exacerbate and perpetuate distress, relationship difficulties and the experience of feeling rejected and misunderstood. In systems where behaviours are the only focus or consideration, people are at risk of becoming objectified or the sum of observable and measurable behaviours, missing the fundamental thoughts, emotions, sensory and relational needs and interests of an individual.

Correction-based techniques, without prioritising connection, can reinforce an experience of connection as conditional (I am loved if...), as opposed to connection that is unconditional (no matter what I do...) (Golding, 2008). Furthermore, those on the receiving end of such approaches are likely to associate discipline with seeing themselves as bad, experience high levels of shame (further explained in Chapter 9: Shame and shielding from shame), a nervous system that develops based on a lack of felt safety (Porges, 2011) (further explained in Chapter 6: Neuroscience) and perpetuate relationship difficulties. There is a danger that a focus on correction, communicates that in order to achieve a connected, loving, calm and understanding approach from their carer, they need to keep their emotions, and the associated responses 'in check' or hidden; that their emotional, dysregulated and 'messy' self is less worthy, or even unworthy of, connection.

Longer-term, this can contribute to confusion and mis-cueing, whereby the person on the receiving end of care expresses their needs based on their *expectation* of their caregiver rather than on how they *actually* feel. So, they may experience and express, "I am fearful of your response when I cannot do something or when I need you, so I will not show you I have a need for help/comfort/soothing. I will do this by myself."

In contrast, embodying the Two Hands of Care approach allows connection to come first. To first be curious about what is happening for the person in front of us, about the underlying reason for any dysregulation and distress; and only then do we consider a correction (in the environment or our approach, for example) that aims to set a person up for success. In prioritising connection, we give a message that the person you care for is enjoyable to be with, whereas an approach focused on the behaviour only, can move the person providing correction into an authoritative position. This power imbalance is particularly complicated and inappropriate for adults with an intellectual disability, who, by nature of their additional support needs, are already very likely to experience relational interactions where others do for and to them, as opposed to alongside and with them. Prioritising connection ensures that you are doing *with,* rather than *to* someone and have a drive to understand and better meet the underlying emotions and needs of any undesired behaviour with changing the context and circumstances. Additionally, connection before correction offers clarity. For example, "We are still friends, but when you throw things at me it hurts, you seem angry. Let's create a new, less lethal plan!"

Figure 8.2: Traditional behaviour management example and how this might be perceived without connection first

Traditional behaviour management: "Sit down to eat your food nicely please!"

The person you care for with intellectual disabilities struggles to sit at the table to eat with others. They often get up, distract others from eating, bring things to the table to play with or mess about with their food.

Traditional behaviour management	Potential perception and impact
"If you don't sit down to eat properly, you'll have to leave the table, because it's disrupting others."	"I'm disappointing you. You are fed up with me. You don't understand."
"Look at everyone else sitting nicely. Can you do the same?"	"I need to be like them. I'm not good enough. I should hide my feelings."
"Sit down nicely and eat your dinner or I can't take you to the café tomorrow, because you won't manage there either."	"I'm so dumb. How will I ever learn? I can't go out now. I feel so angry."
"Eat your dinner nicely and we'll put a sticker on your eating nicely chart. Look your chart is nearly full and then you can choose something nice from the shop."	"You don't seem to understand how hard this is for me. I should learn to keep my needs and feelings to myself, so people will like me, and I get nice things."

It may be that a correction-only approach changes behaviours, as the person modifies their behaviour to avoid the unpleasant feelings in the image above. However, neither the carer nor the person is any wiser as to why the behaviours occurred and therefore there is no possibility of learning from these internal motivators. It is also worth noting that from the care provider's perspective, traditional behavioural approaches without warmth and empathy might feel unpleasant to them as well, as the usual genuine and honest connection feels interrupted or momentarily ruptured. Yet, it is understandable that seeing a change in behaviour with this approach would lead to a pattern of parenting/caring in this way, as the impact on your relationship and the well-being of the person you care for by eliciting behaviour change like this, is not immediately obvious. On reflection, correction-based approaches may be more likely to become the default when caring for a person with an intellectual disability, as a two hands approach of care has the extra layer of complexity of needing to understand and connect with their inner world, which can be challenging in the context of the person's additional needs. Additionally, behaviours that challenge can elicit concerns for the carer, the person with intellectual disability and their functioning in the world and caregivers are likely to be under pressure to help the person they care for fit in with what society expects.

For any correction or limits to be helpful, it is essential to co-regulate the person's emotional and associated physiological experience and calm their nervous system. Connection and coregulation helps the person you care for to feel less threatened or scared, maintains your relational connection and engages the necessary brain pathways for learning (see Chapter 6: Neuroscience for more information around the importance of feeling safe and learning). Connection places priority on regulation, relationship, underlying experiences and the well-being of both parties (see Chapter 4: Intersubjective connection and Chapter 5: Attachment theory for more information), with the added benefit of allowing more successful management of behaviour, as illustrated in Figure 8.3.

Figure 8.3: Example of Two Hands of Care and how this might be perceived

Traditional behaviour management: "Sit down to eat your food nicely please!"

The person you care for with intellectual disabilities struggles to sit at the table to eat with others. They often get up, distract others from eating, bring things to the table to play with or mess about with their food.

Two hands of care

Potential perception and impact

Hand one: Connection

Sitting and eating is feeling hard right now isn't it? There is lots going on! It's noisy, everyone is chatting, and the food is smelly! Eat what you can. When we both feel calm, we will plan how to make dinner times easier."

Hand two: Correction

"You need to sit down to eat, so the food can go from your mouth to your tummy safely. We sit down when we go to the café too don't we? Let's make a plan to help you. Do you have any ideas?"

Based on your understanding, you might make some suggestions: *"You could choose to sit with me? You can have a stretchy band on your chair? Maybe, you would like the sauce and pasta separate?"*

You see me and my struggles. You love and care for me. There are rules and things I need to learn. I'm not alone in learning. You want to help me. You mean the best for me.

Hand two: Correction (another suggestion)

"If you don't eat now, *then* I am worried you will be hungry later. We know it is not nice when you feel hungry. Let's try and eat our food now, so that then we are not hungry later."

Maintaining the balance of the Two Hands

To allow those we care for to thrive, it is important to maintain a balance between the two hands of caring, in our overall approach. If one hand takes over, it is likely to have an impact on our relationship with those we care for in the immediate and long-term. It can also have a less than desirable impact on well-being, learning and development, immediately and in the longer term. For example, if we only provide connection attuned to the needs of the person with intellectual disabilities, without routine and boundaries, it is not just hard to understand the limits or parameters that help make the world more predictable, but the individual also doesn't get the opportunity to practise making choices or learning to cope with frustration, turn-taking, waiting or other day-to-day frustrations.

Case vignette: Connection without correction

A carer is wonderfully attuned to the needs of their child with an intellectual disability; they enjoy high levels of interaction, sensory regulation and drinking fizzy drinks. The carer doesn't accept offers to have breaks from their child, instead choosing to always be with them, lets the child throw balls inside the house and ensures a bottle of fizzy pop is always available. This approach without predictable limits and boundaries could lead to carer burnout, can create difficulty with accessing other environments where throwing balls inside is not safe, and consuming endless amounts of fizzy pop is unlikely to benefit physiological well-being. Additionally, the child with intellectual disabilities isn't learning that having boundaries and limits are both safe and a very tolerable experience. Lastly, the child is also not learning to communicate their needs or exerting autonomy, as their every need is anticipated.

The balance is needed to ensure the person we care for (and us as caregivers) knows what to expect, what's expected of them, that they are consistently cared for and to teach the person we care for how they can navigate life, to make good choices and to set boundaries themselves. If the person we care for feels that their caregiver(s) is unable to set boundaries, they are less likely to feel safe. The boundaries are essential, if not desirable for all of us, so that we are not overwhelmed with responsibility. In the absence of carers setting limits, the person with intellectual disabilities is likely to attempt to take control over situations themselves and may make demands that are not in their best interest. Having too much autonomy without structure and boundaries can be anxiety-provoking and frightening, which can invite further controlling responses to re-establish predictability and a felt sense of safety – exhausting for both the child and parent/carer.

Likewise, boundaries and structure alongside low levels of nurture, playfulness and connection, is likely to result in the person we care for feeling that love is conditional on their actions and to feel misunderstood and/or not deserving of care. Repeated experiences of correction without attunement and repair can cause the person we care for to learn their behaviour reflects them as a person (e.g. I did something bad, so I am bad). This, in turn can have a powerful influence on the person's future care of/responses to themselves and interactions with others. If a person believes they are bad in some way, without caregivers' consistent connection, they are likely to experience huge shame and shame responses (see Chapter 9).

Revisiting the case vignette: how to introduce connection-based correction

Carer correction: Within the Two Hands approach, correction includes consideration of carer approach. DDP therapy or consultation could be a helpful space to offer a PACEful affective reflective dialogue around the underlying experiences surrounding the carer's approach to caring. How has this come about? What are the carers worries? What are the carers hopes? How come the carer struggles to accept offers to have breaks from their child?

Delight in the person and your intersubjective connections: Consider what interactions would bring shared joy and maintains connection between the carer and the child. Incorporate these throughout the day. This could include together singing in the car, watching a favourite TV show or having a drink together on the sofa before the rush of the day. Alongside this, introduce shared ball games outside for shared joy and to teach that ball games happen outside.

Attune to and be curious about the child's underlying needs and respond accordingly: Show acceptance and empathy for the thoughts and feelings underlying the actions that might be cause for concern. What are the child's underlying needs for social and emotional connection, for communication and sensory regulation? Consider alternative throwing activities that could be appropriate inside, such as beanbags in a bucket. Consider sensory needs are met throughout the child's day, not just at home. Is the underlying need drinking through a straw or a certain cup, as opposed to the taste or sensory experience of the drink? Consider healthier alternative drinks that could be made available with free access instead of fizzy drinks.

PACEful teaching: Consider the use of videos and social stories to communicate planned changes (and the reasons for this where helpful/appropriate) with accompanying visuals made available to provide the child opportunities to ask questions and share their response. Depending on child's communication skills, consider visual communication aids to support the child to express their needs, wants and wishes. This will help carers to really attune to, connect with and support the child's inner world. Additional communication strategies will also support the child to exert agency by asking for playing ball/time with carer/a drink.

Maintain a PACEful approach: Be open and engaged, calm and regulated. Watch, be with, listen, really listen (with intention).

PACEful boundaries and limits: If child brings ball inside, show visuals (no ball inside, ball outside) and take ball outside offering to play there together or offer alternative inside activity. Decide together (where appropriate) on a daily limit of fizzy drinks and consider healthier alternatives. Consider how/if/when the child might experience shame and plan for this with a response of connection before, during and after correction, so the child understands they matter, and your relationship is okay.

How and why to use the Two Hands of Care approach when faced with a tricky situation

> *Use 'connection before correction and no correction without understanding.'*
>
> Golding (2015)

In response to challenges we might face in our parenting, caring or teaching roles for people with intellectual disabilities (when, for example, they have done something that crossed a boundary or hurt someone), the mantra *'connection before correction and no correction without understanding'* (Golding, 2015), is worth remembering.

As discussed earlier in this chapter, correction without connection to manage behaviour can lead to behaviour change, but is likely to have an adverse impact on your relationship, lead the person you care for to experience feelings of (and responses to) shame and affect their internal working model, well-being and future ways of relating. If behavioural change is fear or extrinsically dependent (i.e. *"If I don't sit down to eat my food nicely, I don't get a sticker or I don't get to go to the café tomorrow, so I best do what I've been asked"*), it is less likely that the learning is truly embedded or understood. Instead, it is a conditioned response that might only be applied to that setting or with that person.

So, when considering correction, only do this in a way that will guarantee that the person you care for will continue to feel regulated and connected with you (as opposed to experiencing a rupture in your relationship together). If regulation and connection is not guaranteed, the boundary/correction is unlikely to be supportive of your relationship and well-being or effective in teaching skills in the long term (see Chapter 6). Conversely, connecting first empowers the correction, guidance and learning that follows (Golding & Hughes, 2012) – see Figure 8.4.

Connection increases your empathy

A PACE-based attitude ensures that you are establishing a better understanding of the thoughts, feelings and motives that underlie the responses that require correction. It supports your acceptance that the person you care for is innately a good person and doing the best they can – true empathy for their experience. It helps you understand that the undesired behaviour is a response to meeting underlying needs; a way of meeting these needs in the absence of skills or desired responses for different ways of communicating these needs. Pausing and connecting with the person with intellectual disabilities and their needs before responding to the behaviour that was unsafe/undesirable, can help diffuse your own potential feelings of personal offence, hurt, frustration or defensiveness. Understanding the behaviour as a response to dysregulation and unmet needs, shifts accountability and attribution and make things more shared. It ensures a caregiver-led correction that might include making changes to your approach, the environment, relationships and skills that ensures the needs of the person with intellectual disabilities are better met, as opposed to an approach that is reactive to eliminating 'bad behaviour'. Any occasions of a person you care for being dysregulated or showing behaviours that challenge are opportunities for learning for you both and as a support network.

Connection communicates unconditional love

Connecting first allows the person you care for to experience the correction within the parameters of a trusting relationship, confident in the security of the relationship you have and safe in the knowledge that you will be there and have their best interest at heart. This unconditional connection is likely to have a longer-term, potentially subconscious experience of unconditional love: *"I'm okay, we're okay, and I know we can figure this out together."* Correction in the context of a safe relationship will reduce the risk of the person you care for experiencing shame (and an associated sense of self as bad) and the empathy-fortified correction that follows, will be more easily accepted in the knowledge they are loved unconditionally. For example, *"I know you really wanted to go swimming. It's so disappointing that we can't go. No wonder you're annoyed. It's not okay to hurt me when you feel angry and disappointed. I'm here. Let's make bubble mountains and book a taxi to go swimming tomorrow."* The person with intellectual disability is more likely to experience acceptance of who they are underneath their outward behaviour alongside experiencing the safety that a combination of empathic boundaries and discipline can provide.

Connection engages the body and brain

As described in earlier chapters, connection sends the message that we are emotionally and physically safe, which helps soothe a nervous system that is in survival mode, regulate our bodies and engage the necessary neural pathways for learning within a lasting relationship; for yourself and the person you care for (Hughes & Baylin, 2012). Maintaining a connection, regardless of the incident, also enable the person with an intellectual disability to remain less defensive and so more ready to talk about and learn different ways of responding in future.

Connection identified patterns

Truly speaking to underlying needs helps reduce the risk of triggers that push the person with intellectual disabilities out of their window of tolerance into dysregulation, linked with shame-based or needs-based responses (for example, connection, stimulation, escape or something tangible). Ongoing connection before correction is also likely to highlight patterns within which difficulties arise. It can help to identify patterns of when the person with intellectual disabilities you care for has struggled in similar situations, interactions, transitions, environments or activities. This raised awareness allows you to establish long-term corrections in addition to the in-the-moment corrections. It helps to consider, based on the pattern of responses over recent times, what can be corrected to set the person with intellectual disabilities up for success.

Parenting in the moment

The following Parenting (Caring) in the Moment cycle (see Figure 8.2) demonstrates steps that can be helpful to consider when employing the Two Hands of Care approach. Each step might read simply but can be complex in the context of providing a relationship, especially when interactions and responses are challenging. It might take minutes, hours or even days to move between the stages described. We might not always be able to go around the whole cycle or be PACEful in all our interactions. It can be helpful to consider how this might look for you as an individual carer or for whole staff teams. Becoming aware of and learning one stage at a time might be a more realistic way of drawing on DDP approaches when faced with tricky situations. It might be helpful to stick it on the fridge or to have to hand in reflective practice or supervision.

Figure 8.4: Correction only vs Caring with Two Hands of Care

Experience: Weekly swimming cancelled, because the car is in the garage for repairs.

Behaviour: Person with intellectual disabilities puts paper in sink plug and plays with water.

Correction only

Correction: *"What's this?! What a mess! I'll get binbags and a mop. You've made this mess, so you can help clean this up!"*

Connection before correction

Connection: *"Wow! (Takes a deep breath!) You've made your own swimming pool in here! You wanted to have fun with water because we couldn't go swimming today! We'll need to dry the floor. You and I can do that together. Which cloth will you use? Can you take the paper out of the sink, before we find a different game? I think your idea for a game with water is great. How about making some water balloons or making a bubble mountain?"*

Correction: *"If you block the sink, then the floor will get too slippery. That is not safe. I'll dry the floor. You can take paper out of the sink. Then we can play water balloons or trampoline."*

Long-term connection-based correction: offer time in and choice of alternative activities based on individual needs and interaction when plans change.

Figure 8.5: Parenting in the Moment cycle. Adapted with permission from Golding, K. S. (2017)

1. Notice

What is happening?
Do I need to step in? Do I need to take any immediate steps to ensure everyone is safe?
Try not to shout, criticise or lecture.
If you do, repair later.

2. Connect with yourself

Calm yourself: Take a breath and check your own response

Am I regulated? Can I stay open and engaged? Am I becoming irritated, angry or defensive? Do I feel useless? Do I need a break? Can I be compassionate to myself?

3. Calm the other person

Are they in upstairs or downstairs brain?

Give a simple acceptance and empathy response – NO curiosity yet! Then consider: Do they need me to help them **regulate** their emotions or senses?

4. Show curiosity

Real interest through tentative exploring

Even if you know they did something 'wrong', stay curious about *their* experience:
"I wonder what was going on when ...?"
"How come...?"
"No wonder you did...if you felt..."

5. Connect

via acceptance, empathy and meaning-making

Explore thoughts, desires, urges and motives underneath the behaviour. How can I help the person I care for to know and feel that I'm trying to get it? This is a deepened acceptance and empathy based on your increased understanding

6. Correct

Respond to the behaviour

Do I need to do anything further based on what I understand now? What should I approach this situation differently next time? Are there skills I can support the person I care for to develop?

7. Relationship repair

Do I need to repair the relationship so that the person I care for knows what has happened has not affected our relationship?

1. Notice what's happening

Take a breath and clock what's happening. Do you need to step in immediately to ensure everyone is safe? Take a breath! No shouting, no criticising, no lecturing (if you do, you can repair later!). Noticing and stepping in early is key.

2. Connect with yourself first

Take another breath and learn a mantra that works for you to give yourself a moment. This will help you to check what impact this situation is having on you.

- Are you able to continue engaging as a '**care**'giver?
- Are you able to respond in a considered way or are you feeling irritated, defensive or feeling useless?

Calming yourself first is so important. The way you feel will impact on whether you will be able to manage this situation well. You may need to swap with someone, take a break, go for a walk, splash cold water in your face, or open the window for some fresh air to take care of yourself. It is also important to ensure others know that this is about you looking after yourself, not punishing with the relationship (*"I just need to take a break to calm"*). You may need to use visuals and a timer to communicate you need some fresh air and will be back once calm.

3. Calm the other person

Are they in upstairs or downstairs brain? Have they 'flipped their lid'? Look and listen in a PACEful way and connect with that feeling. Even if you don't like the behaviour that's been shown, acknowledge or even embrace the feelings in front of you. Show acceptance and empathy for now, no curiosity about why, no lectures about behaviour, no questions! Of consideration here might be how to create safety when the person you care for is not safe. Time in and a connection-based approach doesn't necessarily mean physically stepping in or having the expectation that the person needs to be close, as, for some, this can increase dysregulation and distress. Connection might look like an explicit offer of space, whilst communicating that you will stay available. Consider a go-to sentence: *"I see you feel...I'm here."* Give yourself time to consider:

- How can you help them feel safe?
- How can you calm their senses and the intensity of their feelings?
- How can you let them know they are safe?
- Do they need a hug? Or space with you staying nearby?

4. Show Curiosity

Once you and the person you care for are ready, feel connected and calm, curiosity can commence to ensure you can attune to and connect with their experience (step 5) and learn what corrections might be helpful to consider (step 6). It may take time to get to this stage. Consider using visuals as tools to explore thoughts, feelings and/or triggers and changes moving forward.

- What are the underlying emotions or needs that might help explain what's happened?
- What was going on when...?
- How come...?
- No wonder you did...if you felt...

Depending on the social and emotional developmental needs of the person you care for, it might be more helpful to make most guesses as an internal dialogue (and then try one out loud); you may just wonder out loud without expecting an answer as such, or you might wonder with other key carers in front of the person you care for (talking about):

> *"I wonder if Bobby is feeling sad and lonely today, because his friends haven't phoned today like usual. Then he threw his cup at me, because I was talking about going out for dinner with my friends after work today. No wonder Bobby feels annoyed with me talking about that."*

5. Connect

Name it, to tame it. State your best guess of what might be going on to build a story from the perspective of the person you care for about what happened:

> *"I'm guessing that you feel sad today, because you couldn't see your friends. That was such a shame. Then you shouted at me when I asked you to help clear the plates away."*

This is a deepened acceptance and empathy based on your understanding of the emotions and needs underlying the tricky response.

6. Correct

Once you have a better idea of the emotions and needs underlying the tricky response, you are better informed to decide whether you need to do anything else. If you do need to consider a correction, you are now better informed to ensure this is effective and truly connects with the underlying emotions and needs:

- How can I better meet an underlying need of the person I care for? Increased structure or supervision, incorporate sensory regulating activities? Tailor communication boards?
- What do I need to learn?
- Should I do, say or approach this situation differently next time?
- What do I need to change to ensure the person I care for feels more heard and safer?
- What would the person with intellectual disabilities like to be different?
- Can we reframe a 'no' into a 'yes' with conditions?
- Is there something the person with intellectual disabilities would like to know or learn? Can I help with that?
- Do I need to help the person I care for repair a relationship with others?

7. Repair

If you messed up along the way in this *Parenting in the Moment* cycle, acknowledge it, apologise and repair in a timely way when both you and the person you care for are regulated. You might have a key phrase you use just between the two of you, or a certain connecting activity that lets the person you care for know that your relationship has withstood this tricky time.

- Do I need to repair the relationship so that the person I care for knows what has happened has not affected our relationship?
- Does the person know that they matter to me no matter what, that they're okay and your relationship is okay?

Conclusion

People with an intellectual disability are more likely to experience relationship insecurity and associated difficulties such as mistrust and shame. Caregivers may also experience difficulties, anticipating they may be unable to read the needs of the person they care for or experience behaviours that are difficult to manage.

Traditional parenting and caring techniques of setting boundaries, limits and consequences, in the absence of empathy for the needs underlying the behaviour, are likely to only alter behaviour in that context, risk exacerbating relationship difficulties and maintain shame responses and unhelpful ways of expressing needs. Two hands of caring helps to contain and manage distress, dysregulation or behaviour in a way that preserves and builds on connection security.

In the Two Hands of caring approach, hand one presents care, warmth, nurture, autonomy and connection, building and maintaining a relationship; hand two symbolises supervision, structure, routines, activities, boundaries and supervision, that the person we care for needs, to feel safe and secure. The combination of connection before correction, and not correcting without understanding, offers a focus on relationships and ensuring truly person-centred boundaries are provided.

Connection before (during and after) correction provides a sense of your care being unconditional; it communicates to the person you care for that they are safe and that your relationship is safe. Connection is the vehicle to a sense of safety within which you and the person you care for can learn helpful and appropriate ways of responding.

Chapter 9: Shame and shielding from shame

Summary

- The experience of shame is a normal part of child development and important for the socialisation process. Shame can become toxic when someone has not had repeated experiences of repair following a rupture in their relationship with their caregiver. When shame is not regulated, a child begins to internalise the experience of shame as a sense that they are unbearable to others and innately bad.
- Toxic, unregulated shame is so painful that we develop behaviours that shield us from shame.
- Throughout our lives, shame continues to be experienced within the context of our relationships to a greater and lesser extent, depending on our experiences of being shamed and our experiences of relationship-repair and care whilst feeling distressed. The experience of shame is shaped by our experiences of shame and by the responses of others once we are in a state of shame. The biggest trigger for shame is having a sense that we have done something wrong. Without experiences of repair, shame can be triggered by fear of rejection, loss or not feeling good enough.
- People with intellectual disabilities, their carers and support networks are at an increased risk of experiencing shame, due to a multitude of personal, interpersonal and socio-cultural factors.

- The antidote to shame is connection and co-regulation whilst in a state of distress, to learn that ruptures and interruptions in joy-filled relationships will be followed by repair and are not a reflection of being unbearable or bad. In other words, when relationships rupture but are then repaired, the experience of shame is regulated and becomes smaller.
- This chapter will also discuss the idea of developing shame resilience: learning to recognise what brings about shame and reaching out to others to talk about it, instead of defending against shame by shutting down or running away.

Introduction

This chapter explores the concept of shame and the role of intersubjectivity and repair in its development. It examines how shame can emerge in relationships, particularly in the context of abuse. It also considers the development of toxic shame, where co-regulation has not helped repair the rupture.

The chapter then outlines the ways in which individuals develop strategies to shield themselves from shame, often by disconnecting from relationships, and introduces the concept of the 'shield of shame'.

Following this, the chapter discusses the factors that may heighten experiences of shame for individuals with intellectual disabilities. These include stigma, discrimination, socio-cultural influences, powerlessness, repeated relational ruptures, developmental needs, and the complexities of long-term care. The impact of toxic shame on relational connections is then explored, alongside practical approaches to reducing shame. This begins with strategies for reducing shame within oneself, by recognising our own shame patterns, and fostering curiosity and engagement in relationships to counter these.

The chapter concludes with various ways to build shame resilience, proposing that through consistent connection and attuned support, individuals can regain power over shame.

What is shame?

Feeling shame is different from feeling guilt. Guilt involves an awareness of "I have done something bad/wrong, but I'm an okay person worthy of love and belonging". However, shame can be understood as a deeper and intensely unbearable feeling of "I am bad". It can be held central to the individual's sense of self, it is pervasive and self-directed, rather than occurring in relation to another person. Shame can be so painful that we end up pushing people away, at a time when we need connection most, as being with others intensifies our feelings of shame. When we are unable to connect with those around us when we experience shame, this feeling cannot be easily regulated or understood.

> *"Shame is the intensely painful feeling or experience of believing that we are flawed and therefore unworthy of love and belonging."*
>
> Brené Brown (2012, p.39)

In terms of the ideal factors for developing attachment security, the first year of life is about key attachment figure(s) providing safety and security. However, as babies and young children first begin moving around and exploring, they will inevitably do things that are less than desirable – pulling the cat's tail, knocking over a vase, digging in the house-plant soil, playing with the dogs' water bowl, rubbing hand-cream over the sofa... the list goes on! When 'good enough' attachment has been present up to this point, children are likely to have experienced their parent delighting in their every move and attempts to connect. Suddenly, the child's behaviour leads to a different response from their parent, who now might have a tense or even angry facial expression and may have a loud tone of voice. There is an important dyadic shift here, as the parents are having to negotiate the boundaries, and the child is no longer just experiencing their parent's delight and warmth. Unsurprisingly, this has a significant impact on the child, with their whole world seemingly falling apart, often resulting in whaling cries and tears. This rupture in the relationship is the experience of shame. The child's internal working model suddenly is challenged, which, up until now, is likely to have been developing into a sense of "I am wonderful and loveable, others are always predictable and happy, and the world feels fun". Now, with their parents letting their child know that some of their actions are not okay, the child starts to experience this relationship slightly differently. They start to experience shame. Shame leads to distress; at a neural level, shame moves us out of a regulated state and moves us into a more defensive or affective experience, predominantly to our amygdala's fight, flight, freeze reactions. Once in this affective state, we are less able to draw on the range of skills or memories about feeling safe with this person, which would enable us to relax into their guidance (Hughes & Baylin, 2012). Co-regulation, whilst in a state of shame, repairs the rupture between the parent and child. The child can then learn from the experience and, with the parent's support, develop behaviours acceptable to the parent.

A note about intersubjectivity and repair

Intersubjectivity needs to be considered as part of this picture too. The child begins to learn the influence their behaviours can have on others' responses. This will be happening in lots of positive ways as well. Through consistent experiences of primary caregivers scooping their child up and giving words to what has just happened, the child's emotional experience and nervous system are regulated. This reconnection reminds the child that they are innately loved and wonderful, despite any poor decisions they might make; they are loved and an innately good person, they just did something that wasn't 'good' (that was undesirable). They learn their parents' reaction was about keeping them safe. This helps to regulate their feelings of shame and helps inform their developing sense of themselves, their attachment security and, over time, will support the development of their theory of mind. Sadly, for all parents and caregivers, the need for correction and reminders is not a one-off event, as it can be great fun to explore what it is like to push your hands through soil, or to push soil into the cracks of the sofa and then clean your hands *on* the sofa! Parents can have different reactions, in the case of soil on the sofa, one of anger or upset (or finding it funny but still not ok!).

Through repeated experiences of regulating the child's sad, disappointed and shameful reactions to being 'told off' (the rupture and repair cycle), children learn that relationships can withstand interruption. The parents express their reaction as a way to increasing safety (of the child), and not as criticism of the child. Within a relationship in which the child feels overwhelmingly loved, good enough and cared for, the child can begin to understand that there is a difference between "I am bad" and "I *did* something bad". Repeated and consistent rupture and repair cycles within this context also mean that, emotionally, children begin to experience a feeling of guilt, as opposed to feeling shame when they have done something that is unsafe or less than ideal. Guilt is focused on how our behaviours affect others (it helps us to develop rules and morals and helps hold us to account against our values), whereas shame is a purely internal self-directed emotion.

What is toxic shame?

Shame, without regulation, means a child is unable to develop guilt and their experience of shame becomes toxic; it brings fear of disconnection, and complete rejection, an underlying factor of some of the most challenging of interactions and difficult behaviours. Children who have not had repeated experiences of comfort, when in a state of pain, fear or other distress, begin to internalise a sense that they are unbearable to others and innately bad. The feelings associated with unregulated shame are so unbearable that children will strive to try to avoid them. Children may become vigilant to signs and situations that might increase the risk of not feeling good enough. The more shame they experience, the more quickly this emotion will be triggered and the more vigilant they will become. This struggle makes engaging in relationships increasingly risky, as it is in relation with another that shame has been experienced. So, the child/young person may become controlling within relationships to establish a sense of predictability. In contrast, they may become very avoidant of relationships; the reaction to shame can vary, but children will attempt to avoid feeling that way again, even if that means not seeking out care and relationships. The apprehension of interacting with others becomes more complicated and aversive when interactions lead to repeated ruptures to the relationship. These relational ruptures and the discomfort of shame make it hard to put any trust into either specific relationships or maybe all relationships. The experience of deeply embedded shame can also lead to fundamental changes and blocks in trust and care (see Chapter 10: Blocked care). When someone is unable to trust, it hampers the responses and reactions the other person in the dyad experiences; the resulting connection between people fractures, leaving a cycle of blocked trust and corresponding blocked care on behalf of the adult carer.

What about abuse and shame?

Shame originates within the experience of a relationship, so in relationships where abuse occurs, the experiences of shame are more likely to occur and to be more potent, and unmanageable. There is no way that a person engaging in abusive behaviour can regulate the shame their victim (whether that be a child or adult) feels as they are the source of that shame. The abuse (whether physical, sexual, emotional or neglect) raises shame in the person as they are not being cared for and their needs are not even being considered, let alone met. Abuse is never about the needs or behaviour of the person who is abused, although they may be told that it is. Abuse is only ever about the needs and desires of the perpetrator; and so the victim is left with shame at what has occurred, which they cannot have regulated and cannot explain to others. The shame is part of why people do not talk about abuse, as they are too ashamed. They may also feel responsible (or blamed) for what has happened and the internalising of these experiences adds to this. We explore below how shame can be re-ignited in people; for those for whom the shame relates to abusive experiences the feelings associated with this, such as powerlessness, lack of control and feeling 'done to' can lead to overwhelming feelings of shame and shielding (more on that next).

Strategies to shield against the pain of shame

In childhood and throughout our lives, shame continues to be experienced in the context of relationships to a greater and lesser extent depending on our experiences of being shamed and our experiences of relationship repair and care whilst feeling distressed. Shame can be triggered by fear of rejection, loss or not feeling good enough (this also relates to the idea of an internal working model, as described in Chapter 4: Intersubjective connection), where our sense of self develops in response to the experiences and reactions that others have in response to us. Everyday situations that might trigger shame can include the potential of not knowing an answer to a question, not being able to put on your own socks, not winning a game of tag, not being able to do a task, being told "no" or feeling told off, especially if the person has experienced relationships where these things have led to disappointment or disapproval. There are two ways in which we, people we care for and those we work with might avoid shame (also known as **shame shields**) or defend ourselves/cope when shame arises (**shields against shame**).

Shields against shame

Golding & Hughes (2012) describe how we defend ourselves from, and cope with, the unbearably painful feeling of shame, especially if these feelings have become toxic, with a number of different strategies (see Figure 9.1). To shield against shame, someone might deny or minimise their behaviour, act tough as if they do not care, lie about what has happened, blame others or – if all else fails – rage against themselves and those around them. These behaviours defend the person from the responses of others.

Figure 9.1 Shield against shame (adapted from Golding & Hughes, 2012)

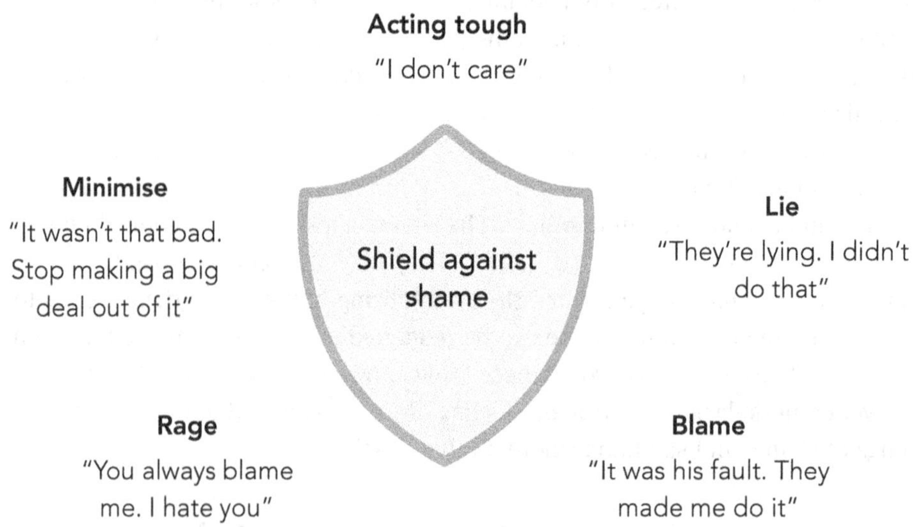

Everyone reacts differently to feeling shame, likely dependent on the situation and the persons with whom we're interacting. Shame-shielding strategies inevitably have a significant impact on relational and emotional responses from others, trust, attributions and future relationship patterns. For example, in a parent-child relationship, shame-based behaviours can draw the parent into reactive responses. They may also feel judged by others, themselves experiencing shame that their child's behaviour reflects their parenting. If the parent responds to their child's behaviours with frustration and without understanding the feeling of shame underneath, their response will strengthen their child's shield against shame, and their relationships are likely to become more disconnected, with perpetuating patterns of shame responses (Golding & Hughes, 2012). A similar pattern can occur with adults in supported living placements, for example, where support staff may seek help and advice around a person's risky behaviours, but are told that, as the person has capacity, they are okay to continue this behaviour, such as leaving the service late at night or over-eating. Staff may feel that others are minimising the potential severity of the risks, or that the adult with intellectual disabilities is acting tough in this situation, unaware of potential dangers. Staff may therefore feel shame that they cannot help the person to be safer. Alternatively, someone with an intellectual disability may be asked to reflect on incidents of 'behaviours that challenge', but feel shame about what happened, so may well minimise, act tough and as if they do not care about people who have been hurt or deny what has happened. This is upsetting for staff to hear and, although it comes from a place of shame by the individual, it can prevent repair in relationships and create distance (e.g. blocking trust).

Shame shields – future proofing

Based on previous painful experiences of shame, we may all use subconscious strategies of disconnection to reduce the risk of experiencing shame again in future. Disconnecting in the relationship aims to help us disconnect from the feelings of shame. Linda Hartling and colleagues (2000) identified shame-avoidant actions within three disconnection-based domains, which Brené Brown (2012) describes as 'shame shields' or 'strategies of disconnection' (see Figure 9.2). These are strategies of disconnection that are used to reduce the risk of experiencing shame. It is entirely possible that a person might show a mixture of these responses at one time and different shame shields in different situations.

Figure 9.2: Shame shields: strategies of disconnection (Hartling *et al*, 2000; Brown, 2012)

Strategy of disconnection to avoid shame	What this strategy could look like
Moving away Avoiding contact and interaction, playing small, avoiding at all cost	■ Numbing, keeping secrets and isolating or dissociating ■ Avoiding all uncomfortable situations, people and interactions at any cost ■ Addictive/risk taking patterns to shut out the possibility of shame and distract people from the original 'shaming behaviours', including running away or promiscuous sexual behaviour
Moving towards People pleasing, working hard to make everything perfect	■ People pleasing – making sure everyone is happy (especially with you and because of you) and getting others' approval ■ Saying yes when you want to say no ■ Perfectionism: working hard to show how valuable you are ■ Fitting in at the cost of one's own well-being and authentic sense of self
Moving against Creating pain or shame in anyone we feel might cause shame	■ Power over others ■ Judging those who might cause us to feel shame ■ Being defensive in your responses ■ Anger and/or blame towards those we feel might cause shame ■ Rageful behaviour and aggression towards anyone who we feel might be the cause of our shame

Shame in context of people with intellectual disabilities

"When our existence is reflected back to us tinged with contempt, disappointment, distance or not at all it has a profound effect on identity."

Greenhill (2011, paragraph 17)

Shame-increasing factors

There are numerous ways in which shame can be more prevalent and less contained for people with intellectual disabilities; as with many areas discussed in this book, this is not necessarily for all, but for many. Shame can also be experienced by their immediate carers and the wider support network and society. It is worth noting, too, that there can be an interaction of shameful experiences between the carers and the person with an intellectual disability, which can therefore be hard to separate.

Stigma, discrimination and socio-cultural context

People with intellectual disabilities are amongst the most stigmatised population groups, being criticised rejected, excluded and humiliated by others, affecting how people are accepted and can participate within their community (Ditchman *et al,* 2013; Scior & Werner, 2016). Jansen-van-Vuuren & Aldersley (2020) describe various forms of stigma of relevance when considering the experience of shame for people with intellectual disabilities and their support network:

1. Public stigma from the broader society
2. Self-stigma – when a person with intellectual disabilities internalises socially devalued status, having internalised societal prejudices against them. This can lead to vigilance for signs of rejection and lead to misinterpretation of ambiguous social interactions
3. Courtesy stigma – when friends, family and carers of the person with intellectual disability experience prejudice or discrimination

Shame can be considered the emotional core of stigma. Constant messages of "You are different", "You don't belong here", "You don't meet the criteria to participate in this" and "You are to blame" are likely to increase a felt sense of worthlessness and inner working belief of being unlovable.

Pregnancy screening

From the moment of pregnancy screening, there is a risk of sending a discriminatory message to people with intellectual disabilities and their parents. In Western cultures, as part of standard antenatal care, pregnant women are offered screening for Down's Syndrome, Edwards' syndrome and Patau's syndrome. If this diagnostic test shows the unborn baby has a condition, this can lead to a decision about whether to continue or end the pregnancy. This means that, for some expectant parents, the pregnancy and birth of a child with an intellectual disability can occur against the backdrop of stigma and fear. A positive result in screening influences a decision around termination of the pregnancy (especially with the technical advances of non-invasive prenatal screening), which has been argued to be based on a burden assumption (Rubeis & Steger, 2019). Western culture values independence and, consequently, people with high levels of dependency are more likely to be stigmatized. There is an assumption that people with an intellectual disability are a burden to parents, family members and society. It is a sensitive issue to raise, as it deals with the conflict between the principles of promoting the rights of people living with disabilities and preserving women's reproductive autonomy (Perrot & Horn, 2022). There are also cultural differences in the experiences of giving birth to a child with disability, including intellectual and physical disabilities. In some cultures, having a child with a disability has negative implications about the parents as well – that they have done something wrong during the pregnancy or it is someone's fault; this can be shaming for parents.

Developmental and diagnostic stigma

For some parents (and older children), the experience of not meeting milestones, or being sent to specialist professionals or needing adaptions to their home or educational settings, might result in feelings of shame. There can be a lack of support for parents of babies who cannot engage in informal play group and coffee dates; as these differences in ability become apparent, the parent may be left with feelings of shame that their child cannot participate in the same way – and this can hinder connection. There might also be assumptions made within a cultural context about life as a parent of a child with an intellectual disability being one that is potentially less fulfilling than having a child without an intellectual disability.

The process of diagnosis, although hopeful for some, can result in ongoing battles, stigmatisation and shame. Needing to repeatedly name what your child cannot do is a potentially shaming experience. Similarly, for adults with an intellectual disability negotiating the welfare system and the need to repeatedly outline deficits can also lead to shame. We meet family carers who were given diagnosis in a way which evoked shame and hopelessness in them; and the impact of stigmatisation is reported (e.g. Wiseman & Watson, 2022). This can lead to families not seeking help or minimising the difficulties that someone is having as they hope that they will not be pervasive or long-lasting. We have talked about how this can set up mismatches in attachment connections and this can also be shaming for the parent, which can be passed on to the child or adult in that caring dyad. The experience of being cared for by someone who is themselves experiencing high levels of shame resonates with the ideas of blocked care explored in Chapter 10.

Shame related to developmental and diagnostic stigma is also impacted by the parents' own experiences of being parented, of being supported through difficult times, or not achieving things they may have wanted to achieve, or their family may have wanted for them. It also reflects the family and societal views on independence and worth. For example, if worth is about financial security alone, then this is harder to achieve when you have an intellectual disability. Yet, people have worth in a multitude of ways.

Education and ongoing care can lead to segregation and isolation

Whilst accessing education, it is also more likely that children with an intellectual disability may not attend the same primary or secondary school as their siblings or neighbours. There are different points through the education system where difference becomes more apparent. There will be academic achievements which people with intellectual disabilities do not gain and, depending on the emphasis on the importance of those achievements, within a family the person could be exposed to unregulated levels of shame. Some schools, cultures or families are more ableist and focus on and measure success around achievements.

As children grow older and/or their needs become greater, it might not be possible for these needs to be met close to home. Some children and adults may attend education, or even live, many miles away from home and have limited contact with their families. Oftentimes, people might move without giving consent, or the move being discussed with them, as they are deemed by their funding authority to need a different sort of care (see Oakes, 2012).

The media

Although there are shifts in culture and in the presence of people with intellectual disabilities in mainstream media, there are estimates that only 4% of media content depicts disability, and acknowledges that this is most likely to prioritise people with physical disabilities (WECIL, undated). This means that many people with intellectual disabilities grow up never seeing themselves represented within mainstream or social media, and this lack of representation can perpetuate the feeling of being different or excluded, the idea that they are in some way shameful and not to be seen.

Bullying, hate crime and abuse

As discussed in Chapter 5, people with an intellectual disability are more likely to experience bullying and hate crime. The British Crime Survey (2011 as cited in Beadle-Brown *et al*, 2014) notes that rates of disability hate incidents 2010–2011 were higher than the number of homophobic hate incidents and religious-based incidents. Mencap reports that 88% of people with an intellectual disability have reported to experience bullying or harassment; 66% of those were frequent victims; and nearly a third were bullied on a daily or weekly basis (Mencap, 2000 as cited in Beadle-Brown *et al*, 2014).

These experiences are exacerbated by the recognition that there are also systemic failures in preventing disability-related harassment and tackling it effectively (EHCP, 2011 as cited in Beadle-Brown *et al*, 2014). Even when hate crime is reported, resulting prosecution is rare (Beadle-Brown *et al*, 2014).

> *"He has impacted on me and promoted my very low self-esteem... but I felt that I deserved it, it was a deep down instinct, I didn't belong in the world"*
>
> Interview 4003, Beadle-Brown *et al* (2014, p.93)

Not only does bullying and hate crime affect people with intellectual disabilities, it has also been reported by their carers too. Beadle-Brown *et al* (2014) describe how carers of people with intellectual disabilities experienced incidents of hate crime, including being filmed, having things thrown at them or members of the public damaging their property. Such traumatic experiences evoke repeated survival responses and a felt sense of rejection and worthlessness.

In relationships where abuse occurs, there is no way an adult engaging in abusive behaviour can regulate the shame the person with an intellectual disability feels, as the perpetrator is the source of that shame. The abuse (whether physical, sexual, emotional or neglect) raises shame in the person as they are not being cared for and their needs are not even being considered, let alone met. The perpetrator may actively place the responsibility for the abuse on the person with an intellectual disability. Shame is part of why people do not talk about abuse, as they are too ashamed. This is likely exacerbated for people with an intellectual disability, who may have a compromised ability to recognise and label their emotions and/or communicate their needs. These communication barriers can get in the way of being responded to with acceptance and empathy to feel truly heard and safe.

Powerlessness

People with an intellectual disability experience ongoing reliance on others to ensure their safety and needs are met and this, in turn, may increase their feelings of powerlessness and lack of control. Independence can be tricky for people with intellectual disabilities, as they may not have the naturally occurring opportunities and skills to explore this and develop independence in the same way as their peers of similar chronological age. Similarly, for adults with an intellectual disability negotiating the welfare system and the need to repeatedly outline deficits can also lead to feelings of powerlessness and shame.

When the feeling of shame relates to abusive experiences, the feelings associated with this, such as powerlessness, lack of control and feeling 'done to', can lead to feelings of shame and shielding (as described below); for example, if, as an adult, you need to seek help from services and need to (possibly repeatedly) state what you cannot achieve without support. Alternatively, not having the autonomy to choose who cares for you, where you live or needing to access services miles away from home and having limited contact with family – these are all further examples of powerlessness that people with intellectual disabilities are more likely to experience.

We also know that restrictive practice (such as physical and environmental restraint, confinement, blanket rules, restricted access, observations that invade privacy and medical restraint) can lead to people feeling disempowered, objectified and does not aid with relational care and connection (e.g. Quinn, 2024). As described in Chapters 13 and 14, restrictive practices place further shame on the individual with an intellectual disability, as they might be deemed too risky to leave or have sanctions/restrictions put on them. This is described by Silver (1986) – ideas of sanctuary trauma, where a person moves with the hope of receiving care and support, but instead finds further trauma. Furthermore, people may find themselves sharing accommodation with people they do not initially know and may not like. And if, as mentioned above, people need to move placement regularly, they experience repeated losses and relationship ruptures.

Repeated losses and relationship ruptures

People with intellectual disabilities rely on those around them for support likely to be provided by a large professional network. By their very nature, professional networks change, but people with intellectual disabilities often don't have clear messages about these relationship changes and repeated, unexpected endings. Here are just a few examples:

- Staff might go on holidays, be unwell, be allocated to work with others or leave their jobs (and this can happen across different settings at the same time – school, respite or supported living
- Parents may feel unable to care for the person with intellectual disabilities at home (sometimes a move is planned, sometimes a move happens in critical circumstances). Often, support networks struggle to explain to a person with an intellectual disability why they are moving and whether they continue to see their parents, peers and key workers
- Fellow residents or class pupils might move without explanation
- Some children might be supported by direct payment workers, respite foster carers or overnight respite providers without an explanation around when and why this happens

Without involving a person with intellectual disabilities in changes to their network, especially why, how and when there are changes to their care and peer relationships, it is highly likely that they will believe that any changes are related to them, increasing a risk of rejection and shame.

Developmental needs

Aside from stigma, there are other factors specific to cognition experienced by people with an intellectual disability that can have an impact on their intersubjective relationships and experience of shame. Developmentally, the understanding that other people have thoughts, feelings and needs that are different to our own, tends to develop around the ages of 3 to 5 (Wellman *et al*, 2001) and is thought to develop through language and social interactions (for example, during family conversations or interactions in school) (Carpendale & Lewis, 2004; Ricard *et al*, 1999 as cited in Jacobs & Nader-Grosbois, 2020). As we know, children with intellectual disabilities can experience difficulties in these prerequisite skills and theory of mind. Therefore, it is possible that when a person with an intellectual disability makes sense, subconsciously, of the responses of those around them, the only person that they can comprehend being in control and responsible for this reaction, is them. In other words, the person with an intellectual disability, through a lack of theory of mind, feels solely responsible for all the actions and reactions of those around them, whether nurturing, available and responsive or, dysregulating, neglectful or abusive.

The experience of and responses to shame can continue to occur as the young person progresses into trying to assert their independence as they grow and develop. In a usual developmental trajectory, teenagers become focused on separating from parents, which is accompanied by appropriate risk-taking, boundary pushing and seeking new roles and relationships with peers. This striving for independence can be altered in people with intellectual disabilities, due to limitations in independence skills and peer groups.

Challenges of caring for/working with additional needs

People with intellectual disabilities require additional support and guidance with their social interactions, skills and day-to-day behaviour. They may have developed coping strategies (to get their needs met in the best way they know how) that are considered challenging to those around them. These factors mean people with intellectual disabilities are more likely to be corrected by those around them. An increase in correction-based interactions means consideration of connection-based interactions can quickly tip the wrong way, with co-regulation and meaningful connections less frequent. It can be that, as conversations and interactions become focused on distressed behaviours, this becomes the dominant need responded to, reducing the focus on the whole person and their relational needs. Repeated patterns of correction-based and functional interactions without connection and repair, risks the person with intellectual disabilities experiencing themselves as a burden and not good enough.

As discussed in earlier chapters (particularly in Chapters 3 and 5), people with intellectual disabilities can struggle to express their emotional needs, and carers may struggle to pick up attachment cues and support regulation – attachment patterns that are essential to developing an experience of shame to one of guilt.

Parents and carers are especially vulnerable to experiencing shame when they may rely on a support network to help meet the needs of their child or when their parenting or support is being challenged. A sense of failure or not managing to get through to the child can lead to a sense of not being good enough. This might be more likely for those who struggle with their confidence or levels of energy in the first place, because of, perhaps, a lack of support, discrimination, bullying or personal experiences of being parented.

> *"The last time I had a big shame experience was when we were playing chocolate bingo in the hall of my child's school. I had nothing in the tank to keep chasing my child around the hall. It was a game of cat and mouse, instead of being calm, connected and talking my child through it. I thought: 'We're not going to engage in this. I'm not coping here in this moment. I'm not coping here with my child. And you're all watching me. We're leaving."*

In addition, there is the possibility that those in the wider support network might experience shame too. For example, teachers might feel shame that they cannot help their pupil to learn – or to attend; that the teachers might wish to blame the person with intellectual disabilities (and the system) rather than themselves – we all wish to shield against shame; and this might lead to the person with intellectual disabilities feeling more shame.

Shielding against shame in context of people with intellectual disabilities and their support network

As described, people with an intellectual disability and their support network are more likely to have had repeated shame-inducing experiences and are at an increased risk of not having their needs fully understood and met (including whilst experiencing a state of shame, pain, fear or other distress). Due to lack of connection in regulating shame they may develop survival strategies to protect themselves against shame, but these ways of surviving can be challenging to others.

For people with intellectual disabilities, shielding against shame can be understood within models of behaviours that are challenging. These responses can be the person's ways of shielding against shame (lying, blaming, minimising, showing rage) and helping the individual avoid shame in the immediacy. These responses can oftentimes be met with strategies that focus on behaviour, as opposed to the underlying needs. Such interventions can draw attention to behaviour being undesirable, which, by that very nature can perpetuate and increase experiences of shame in the medium to longer term (Chapters 8 and 15 explore traditional and DDP-informed approaches to behaviours that challenge in more detail).

> *"As a child development advisor, parents often show anger sometimes towards me. I wonder whether my involvement made the gravity of their child's needs apparent. Some parents disengaged, others would desperately show photos or videos of everything their child was able to do."*

When someone's responses, especially those with an intellectual disability, become more challenging, curiosity becomes more limited, and a variety of behaviour-solving or behaviour-reducing focused strategies can be introduced – including behavioural contracts or token economies – with the explicit aim of improving and altering the behaviours. When these approaches are delivered in the absence of a regulated and connected relationships, it will be harder for the person to feel calm and to use the structure provided (as discussed in Chapter 8: Two hands of care). Sadly, the implementation of such strategies or techniques, in the absence of safety and connection, can amplify the person with intellectual disabilities' distress and shame; their reactions reflect this.

As described in Chapters 10 and 11, patterns of shame amongst carers and support networks can play out in different ways, often with patterns of disconnect, defensiveness and a state of stuckness, reflective of the shame shields and shields against shame described earlier in this chapter.

Reducing the experience of toxic shame

"When our boy was young, we saw a specialist as he was having so much tummy pain, particularly at night. When I gave the developmental history, I mentioned that our son had changed after his MMR. I received a very angry rant from the paediatrician about how he had personally overseen the bowel results from the Andrew Wakefield trial and about how children had died from not being vaccinated. All I had done was mentioned the change I had seen. All my children were vaccinated. I did feel cowed, and then again, angry to have been dismissed. That scenario has played out more than once and I've stopped mentioning it, erased it from the narrative and decided it's easier not to think about that."

DDP aims to improve a person's felt sense of safety in key attachment relationships, with an experience of acceptance and empathy for the full range of emotions and experiences, whereby it's possible to hold the very opposite beliefs to shame: a belief that "despite my flaws and mistakes, I am enough". When considering interventions to reduce shame, attention needs to be drawn to the myriad of sociocultural factors, alongside the more intimate relational factors, that increase the risk of shame for people with intellectual disabilities and their carers. As described throughout (and particularly in Chapter 2), DDP is a system-based practice approach as well as a psychotherapeutic model. It can help to make sense of distress and open a path to more fulfilling relationships at all levels. This chapter highlights the pressing need for DDP-informed ecological systems, extending the key elements from the therapy room to the policy, guidance and community cohesion initiatives which aim to recognise and reduce the perpetuating pattern of relational trauma, shame and shame shielding behaviours (see Chapters 13 and 14 for further information).

Alongside tackling shame-increasing factors at a sociocultural level we – as professionals and carers for people with intellectual disabilities – can also develop the skills to become DDP-informed in our parenting and practice. Supporting others to reduce their experience of shame requires your ability to show genuine acceptance, curiosity and empathy. So, learning about our own shame responses can be a helpful place to start, as our own shame shields will get in the way of our ability to engage these skills!

Reducing shame: starting with yourself

Shame is an affective experience. You can experience shame in any interaction with any person! You might experience shame when supporting a person with intellectual disabilities, when working with a parent or when working with other professionals. Responses that have originated from an experience of shame are usually defensive and based on fear.

> *"I feel unproductivity shame for being off work and sick. I try to cram in loads of work on my return, to look and feel productive and try to make up for feeling useless."*
>
> NHS staff member

For any of us when experiencing shame, you are less able to draw on your usual repertoire of connection-based skills such as playfulness, acceptance, curiosity and empathy. The worksheet on shame (see Figure 9.4) is designed to help you and colleagues/carers/parents reflect on their shame and their shame-shielding strategies and think about when they might move away, move towards and move against people in relation to shame.

Figure 9.4: Reflecting on your experience of shame: a worksheet for parents, carers or professionals

> *'I thought it was just me (but it isn't): Making the journey from "What will people think?" to "I am enough".'*
>
> Brown (2007)

Through connection and consistently available relationships, we can gain power over shame instead of letting shame have power over us. Brené Brown developed a theory described as Shame Resilience Theory, which she defined as the ability to 'recognize shame, move through it constructively and grow from our experiences' (Brown, 2007). Developing shame resilience requires a deliberate effort to lean into the experience, as opposed to running away from it, learning to recognise and name the shame, and reaching out just at the time we would be shutting down or running away (see Figure 9.5).

Figure 9.5: The four steps of developing shame resilience (Brown, 2007)

1. Name it	2. Learn about it	3. Reaching out	4. Own it
Recognize and understand your shame triggers	Develop awareness of what experiences lead to shame	Talk about it with others to receive and offer empathy	Share your story

Steps 1 and 2: naming shame and learning about it

To develop an awareness of what triggers your shame experiences in different circumstances, it can be helpful to consider questions such as those outlined in the worksheet: When do I feel shame? How does shame look and feel like for me? Why do I feel shame? (elaborated in the worksheet, Figure 9.4).

Steps 3 and 4: reaching out to others and owning shame

Once you have identified triggers and an awareness of what shame can look like for you, it is time to reach out. Shame struggles to survive in connection with others, so reaching out and talking about it and receiving empathy is the best way to disperse feelings of shame. Brown (2007) writes about how talking with others about our common experience of shame ensures we are not feeding shame with secrecy and silence, instead creating change by helping yourself and others build an understanding of shame and strategies to developing resilience.

Reducing others' shame: (re) building safety and connections

We all need connection when we experience shame. Shame diminishes when we feel connected. The time when people most want to turn away, to hide their shame - possibly by lying, blaming others and minimising what has happened - is when they need connection the most. Paradoxically, these behaviours are aimed at pushing people away and so they are counterproductive. When thinking about how to reduce the experience of shame for people with intellectual disabilities we care for, it is important to acknowledge this entire book is dedicated to supporting people with intellectual disabilities to experience healthy attachment relationships where they know they are cared for and respected no matter what, and that people will 'stick with them' - all of which reduces shame. What follows here are nods to some areas, such as 'connection before correction' and PACE, described in further detail throughout this book.

Connection before correction

For the person with intellectual disabilities

Shame is most certainly not a tool for change. Setting boundaries are vital, but they are hard to use when you or the person you are caring for is in a state of shame.

Disconnect from the behaviour and connect to the emotion. Saying "*Don't speak to me like that*" speaks to the behaviour. Saying "*You are angry right now, I get that*" speaks to the emotion.

For example, when a person with an intellectual disability you are caring for experiences shame, they will be less able to draw on memories about feeling safe with you, which would enable them to relax into your guidance (Hughes & Baylin, 2012). So, aim to give a narrative to survival responses (name it) (as described in Shame Resilience Theory, Brown, 2007) and build a genuine connection, by holding in mind all the ways that increase a sense of safety at a sensory and emotional level for the person you care for. To calm their nervous system, we need to be curious about, accept and offer empathy for the emotional experience underlying shame; disconnect from the behaviour and connect to the emotion. In Chapter 8: Two hands of care, we describe how, as well as a day-to-day approach, we can respond in a way that meets the underlying emotional needs of shame-based behaviours that are difficult to manage, without compromising your relationship and connection.

Connection before correction allows you to offer a message that's the antidote to shame *"I see how you feel. What you did was not okay. You are loved no matter what. Let's figure this out together"*.

Remember, you can tailor how you offer PACEful connection to the emotional experience of someone with an intellectual disability, by, for example, joining their play, offering something of comfort, such as a favourite drink, or engaging in intensive interaction; whatever will increase the chances that the person you care for will feel regulated and connected with you. Correction can mean making a change to a routine or making changes to your approach or the environment, to ensure the needs of the person with intellectual disabilities are better met.

For the support network

Reducing shame requires an explicit and deliberate engagement of curiosity and building connections, not only with the person with an intellectual disability, but also with carers and, as professionals with one another in the support system. Where you may see scope for a different way of parenting, caring or working or when faced with shame-shielding behaviours, it can be helpful to offer our support with two hands of care. Only when there is a genuine experience of trust and connection, are people in systems able to feel safe enough together to explore challenges in a curious way and together embark on making day-to-day changes in practice. PACEful connection can look like really hearing about experiences, concerns, emotions, and ideas in a completely open and genuine way. PACEful correction might look like, together thinking about potential training needs, increases in supervision or role-playing a PACEful approach with carers for specific situations they find difficult. This approach aims to build a sense of safety in your working relationship, reducing the risk of a sense of blame and triggering shame.

Within a support network, regular PACE-based reflection can also be useful to allow staff to talk about shame in a safe way (see Chapter 11 for further reading around this idea). Consider the four steps of developing shame resilience:

1. Name it;
2. Learn about your shame roots;
3. Reach out to others;
4. Share your story.

This can include PACE-informed discussions in team formulation, supervision (using John Adair's model, for example, as cited in Grant *et al*, 2024) and team meetings.

> *'I regularly meet with a headteacher from a specialist school for autistic children with an intellectual disability. Whilst discussing a behaviour shown by a pupil we are jointly working with, the headteacher noted: "If the child shows us that they are in distress with, what might be considered, behaviours of concern, then we're not getting something right and we need to change our approach. That doesn't mean that we as a setting are not good enough, it just means we need to do something different".'*

This reflection showed how, as a system, the school embraces a curious stance that comes from a position of feeling safe.

Conclusion

Toxic shame can develop in the context of not having repeated experiences of comfort, when in a state of pain, fear or other distress. Consequently, a sense of being unbearable to others and innately bad develops. Shame is an emotion which comes from disconnection and a sense of ourselves as bad and unworthy. It is self-directed, rather than held in relation to another. When people are exposed to repeated experiences of shame and do not have access to repair in connected relationships, to help make sense of this experience, they can become defensive and stuck in their fight, flight and freeze responses. In these situations, day-to-day experiences that might elicit a risk of failure or not being good enough, can trigger these overwhelming feelings of shame.

When experiences of shame have become toxic and overwhelming in this way, people will try to defend against the feeling of shame by pushing others away at the time when they most need connection, curiosity about and empathy with their experiences. To reduce the risk of feeling shame, they may move away (avoiding connection and interaction); move towards (pleasing people and working hard to make things perfect); or move against (creating feelings of powerlessness, pain or shame in those we think are causing shame in us). In the thick of experiencing shame, to shield against these painful feelings, someone might deny or minimise their behaviour, act tough as if they do not care, lie about what has happened, blame others or – if all else fails – rage against themselves and those around them.

There are several reasons why shame might be more acutely experienced for someone with an intellectual disability, including the socio-cultural context of stigma and discrimination; the high prevalence of bullying, hate crime and abuse; experiences of powerless; repeated losses and relationship ruptures; developmental needs and the challenges of caring and working with additional needs.

As is also acknowledged throughout this chapter, experiences of shame can occur for the person with an intellectual disability and throughout their support network – for parents, carers and professionals. In thinking about supporting people to reduce their sense of shame, we need to seek ways to offer connection at times when shame is experienced. This can include helping ourselves and others identify times when shame is most prevalent and exploring what helps to build safety and connection when we/others experience shame. This would likely include a stance of connecting with the emotions and not the behaviours, offering curiosity and PACEful connection at these times of shame, especially when shielding against shame.

Chapter 10: Blocked care

Summary

- Blocked care is a term given to a reaction that occurs when we notice we are unable to connect with another's experience. It occurs in response to the repeated rejection or barriers we feel when someone else cannot trust us. It can be a disquietening and confusing experience, especially for those whose key aim and role, and maybe paid work, is to offer care for others.
- We consider in this chapter what blocked care might feel like and some of the warning signs that are more indicative of blocked care. There are terrible examples in institutional settings, where members of teams have become abusive, where we anticipate the staff are likely in blocked care. The risks of blocked care to family or placement stability are understandably high.
- There are potentially higher risks for blocked care arising when supporting someone with an intellectual disability as communication and misunderstandings can increase, the barriers to connection can be more pronounced placing strains to our intersubjective connection.
- We consider how to repair the loss of our connection and ways to address blocked care when it arises.

Introduction

So far, this book has focused on ways of building or deepening connection. The emphasis throughout has been on supporting the adults to better understand and relate to the person with an intellectual disability that they are caring for. Sometimes, we create extraordinary changes in relationships when we facilitate a better understanding about trauma; when we reveal how we can misread the person in front of us; when our expectations become clear, because we have learned about neurosequential development and revealed gaps in development. Sometimes, deepening understanding or holding in mind a more PACEful approach can lead to significant changes in closeness and connection. However, this is sadly not always the case.

This chapter will focus on trying to decipher and make sense of what is happening when we do not feel close to, or connect with, a person with intellectual disability we are caring for, what the risks are when this happens, and how these risks may, potentially, increase if not addressed. This struggle and its consequences can be described as 'blocked care'. Blocked care has, to date, been linked with times when a child is unable to trust others due to their earlier trauma experience. We also observe this pattern with adults.

Signs of blocked care

Is this blocked care? A quick check

There might be times, for some, when they notice a profound change in their connection with others. When this is experienced across multiple settings – with family, friends and at work – it is feasible that this denotes a change in mental health in the carer, rather than a specific instance of blocked care. It is feasible that this pattern indicates possible signs of stress, anxiety or even depression, especially if this is a distinct and new pattern. Changes in mental health will impact on a relationship and the ability and energy to be able to connect and consider another's needs. In this instance, the priority is more likely to be around increasing self-care, reviewing sleep hygiene, considering access to exercise, reviewing the range of life stressors and possibly accessing an initial mental health check with a GP.

In this chapter, we will be describing what happens when you notice that you do not want to spend time with someone or are noticing that you are actively finding ways to avoid a relationship with someone. When this avoidance, or switch-off, occurs it can be very strange and is often hard to articulate. Experiencing a block in care is a pattern that is at risk of occurring when caring for someone with a trauma background. It is a pattern that can emerge even after a very strong and loving connection has been formed and occurs at an unconscious level. The experience of blocked care is difficult to describe but emerges as a way of creating self-protection, making it hard to notice or make sense of at first. We've offered the converse experience to help highlight the experience of blocked care.

Recall for yourself what it is like to feel relaxed about returning home, or to a meal, with people you feel connected with. You will notice your own internal physiological and affective experience, or your positive reflections on the moments. With those with whom you feel connected, you will not just be more likely to feel relaxed during and after an exchange, but also will be able to look forward to spending time together. Within these relationships we are more relaxed about being physically closer or sharing contact, we might be able to be alongside each other in an easy silence, the gaze between people will feel easier, the volume or prosody of our voice will feel unforced and probably not even part of conscious awareness.

When thinking about blocked care, we are recognising a relationship where you are experiencing the opposite feelings to the description above; when you want to move in reverse and increase distance between you. You might also be aware of a strange tension in your body, how your voice feels polite or strained, how much louder or more quietly you are speaking. You might try to mask your true experience by putting on a fixed smile; only when you come away will you notice the tension in your body. The impact can feel so heavy, in our bodies but also our hearts, and leave an empty feeling inside. Here, there is no anticipated joy about your time together and instead you might be watching the clock whilst you're with them, and the sense of relief when you can leave can be marked.

Description of blocked care from a foster carer

A friend of mine is a highly skilled therapeutic foster carer who kindly described the experience she noticed around blocked care, and the resulting loss of connection with a foster child. She was fostering two children at the time and recalls not wanting to spend time with one child, and seeking out ways to be busy with active care tasks (the cooking, washing, tidying, planning activities) rather than spending meaningful time together when in the company of this particular child. There was also a disconnect for the foster carer with the comments that others made about how lovely this child was and how beautiful the child looked. The foster carer felt guilty for not feeling the same but also self-critical about not feeling connected to, or really even liking this child. The foster carer had started to doubt themselves and worry about doing a good job. This wasn't something that she could talk about easily because her job was to be 'good at caring for and liking children' – it was a very lonely and unpleasant experience. This foster carer was accessing relationship-focused support with a practitioner who was trained in both DDP and Theraplay. During their therapy meetings, the therapist named how hard she was finding it to connect with the child. Identifying this disconnected experience helped the foster carer start to talk about how hard they were also finding it to connect with the child. In naming and making sense of the experience the foster carer not only felt understood, but she also started to better understand the dynamics of her relationship with this child.

The ideas behind blocked care have been elegantly drawn together by Hughes and Baylin (2012), and for those who wish to consider this topic in more detail should direct themselves to their book, *Brain Based Parenting*. We are using the model of a parenting brain and applying this outline to include all those who are in the role of close, protective care around someone with an intellectual disability: those who potentially hold the role of attachment figures and who will be the key adult available when things are not feeling very safe.

Figure 10.1: An example of blocked trust

Hughes and Baylin have helped to map out the impact on the adult brain of caring for a child who does not trust others and with whom connection is truly challenging. The mistrust is founded on their early experience of care where the young child's needs have not been understood or met, or worse, where they have been hurt by those who should have protected them or excluded from receiving care. Our neuroceptive system (our unconscious bodily and sensory reaction to events or people) is central in determining our stance and openness to trusting another. The rapidity of processing within neuroception means that this is outside of the reach of reason and explanation, but past experience enables our other brain systems to move in a state of readiness. (See Chapter 6 for further details.)

Our suggestion is that it could very well be harder for someone with an intellectual disability to fully trust others; that they are very likely to have experienced repeated small and maybe larger mis-attuned moments, or that there have been significant miscommunications. In addition, the communication barriers between a carer and a child with an intellectual disability might make it harder to offer repair to any mis-attuned moments in a way that is accessible for the developing child. Often, those with no cognitive impairment talk too fast, forget to decipher the complex world for the person they are supporting, or struggle to connect with the internal experiences of the person they are caring for. Someone with an intellectual disability might become familiar with experiencing confusion around misunderstandings, being talked over, or just not being understood very well. Over time, it might be harder for those with an intellectual disability to stay open to others and instead, they might develop a need to feel cautious during interactions. People with an intellectual disability can be so vulnerable to the sensitivity and skill of those they know, and sometimes upon whom they depend. This increased vulnerability heightens the importance of being able to trust others.

Figure 10.2. Blocked care cycle for a carer and trauma experienced person with an intellectual disability

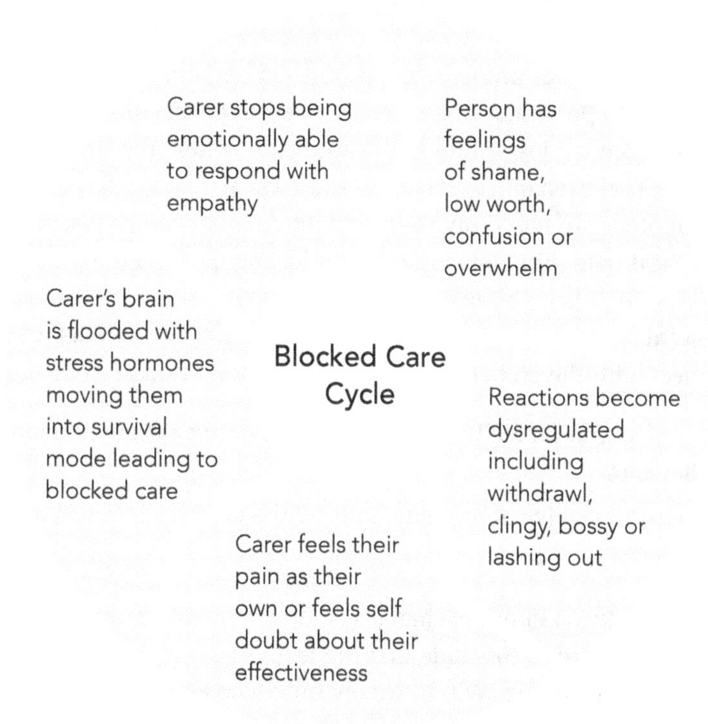

Breaking the cycle

Within this book we are highlighting the conversations, but also more importantly the stance and types of interactions that DDP-focused interventions can bring to a relationship to help avoid blocked care, and to re-build trust when needed. In working within this framework, DDP interventions can help make sense of and resolve both blocked trust and blocked care. DDP can be highly preventive because it focuses on real, attuned and meaningful connection for both parties. When we help carers to learn more about relationships, including their own expectations or to learn about their own triggers and pressures we can help make sense of the current shut down or uncomfortable interaction within a dyad. As a therapist or practitioner we can support and explore blocked care and how to make sense of the mistrustful person's defences. In offering a framework we are offering support but also effectively de-personalising the process of feeling mistrusted. DDP offers a way to bring awareness to the carer/parents about patterns in the dyadic relationship that can both prevent and also resolve the experience of blocked care.

Risks associated with blocked care

When we disconnect and no longer have empathy for another person, we are more at risk of providing functional care where we miss the stories about or the inner experiences of the individual. At worst, blocked care will lead to punitive care. When blocked care becomes pronounced, protracted and endemic across a service, there are huge risks to providing safe care. The warning signs of blocked care are linked to no longer feeling joy within the relationship; where the experience of Playfulness in PACEful exchanges feels lost; when we are aware that our exchanges and time with another are based on a sense of duty, obligation or just routine. When we notice not wanting to join a meeting, or not feeling motivated to pop in for a chat with key people, it is possible that the connection we once had is becoming blocked. When this pattern continues, and when the carers or parents haven't found ways to reconnect with the child or adult we are holding in mind, they might:

- Become more focused on feeling the need to win or always be 'in control' of the bad behaviour.
- Notice the need to resolve arguments, to have the last word, to teach important lessons.

When our dominant focus in our exchanges is functional and around 'managing or reducing behaviour', we can conclude that the feelings of care are blocked. This is because, when we focus on behaviour, we are only focusing on one aspect of an individual and it's likely we have lost sight of our relationship with, or enjoyment of, the person and no longer see what is special about them. When we narrow our focus, we no longer hold in mind a person's needs, hopes and wishes or the personal, internal experience that underlies their presentation. We are at risk of reducing someone to a chain of cause and effect, rather than being able to hold in mind the richness of someone else's life, the range of reasons for their reactions and the depths of their possible internal experiences. When we ascribe or attribute blame wholly and repeatedly to the vulnerable person, it is likely that we have lost our ability to empathise with or feel curious about them, to feel delight or even relaxed when with them, and will find it harder to accept rather than evaluate their actions, words or attitude.

Institutional risks

These are the clear warning signs around blocked care; when held across an institution, these are likely to be the precursor to some of the horrific and saddening instances of institutional abuse that have been reported (e.g. in 2011 at Winterbourne View Hospital caring for vulnerable adults, the children's residential homes in Cornwall in 2006, and more recently at Whitefield School between 2014–2017). In common amongst the inquiries are the lack of supervision, training, and appropriate oversight for staff teams with a pattern of dehumanisation of or depersonalisation in response to the vulnerable adults and children deserving care and protection, rather than assault or humiliation. In all of these reports it appears that the professional teams around the children or adults with an intellectual disability no longer empathise with and are blocked in their care for those they are responsible for – which seems both remarkable and horrific as the staff in these services have chosen roles where they are caring for more vulnerable people. The experience of blocked care moves us away from understanding, and can move people towards control, which is likely a helpful way of making sense of (but not agreeing with) the deterioration in these services. In understanding these complex patterns we are more likely to be able to identify, interrupt and improve relationships and avoid instances of such institutional failure in the future.

Blocked care and our five systems of caregiving

Hughes and Baylin (2012) outlined five systems that influence our readiness or availability to be open to a relationship; we have adapted these for those in a caring relationship with someone with an intellectual disability.

Figure 10.3: Five systems of care giving

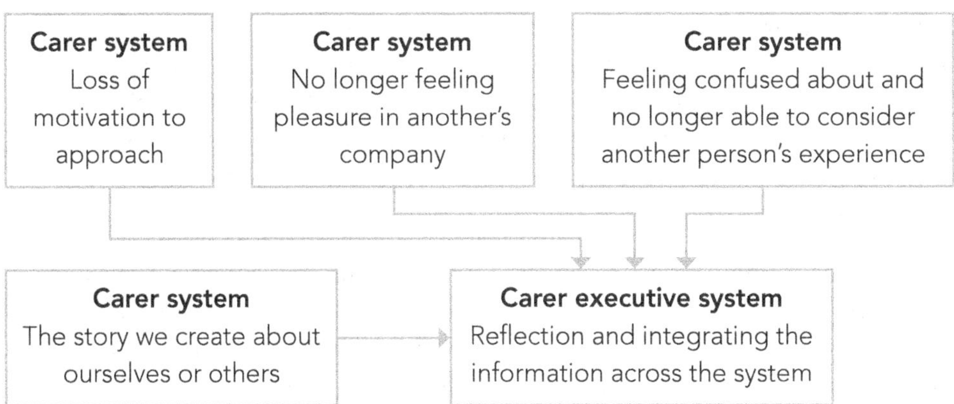

Hughes & Baylin's model was founded and developed with child-parent relationships in mind, and we have extended this framework to consider the interactions that occur in important relationships for anyone with an intellectual disability.

Figure 10.4: Model of Blocked Care and Blocked Trust - adapted from Hughes and Baylin (2012)

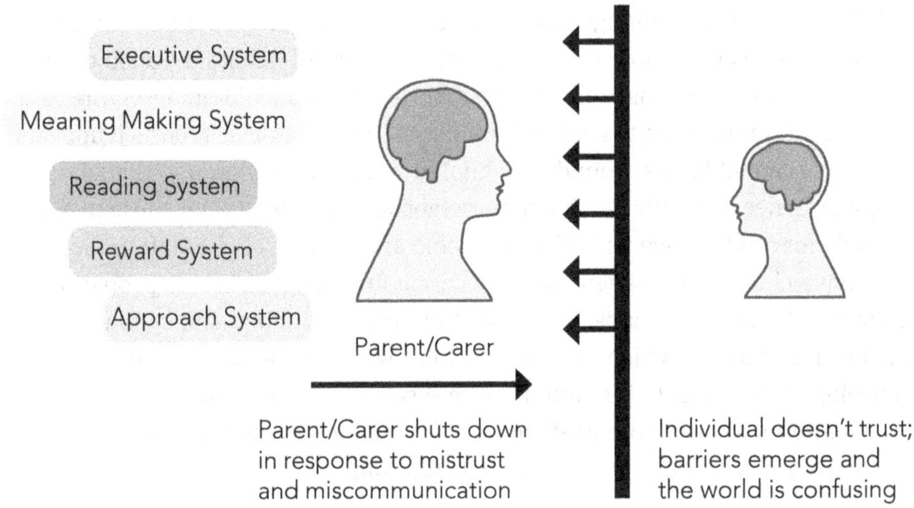

1. Carer approach system

When we anticipate connection going well or being well received, especially when our previous experience has been positive, we notice how easy it feels to approach another person. The person who is making the approach is likely to be in a regulated and calm state of mind, and does not need to be thinking defensively or having to consider self-protection. They would be best described as being in a physiological state where the nervous system is actively responding to move us into safety. Our willingness to approach is often based on our previous experience of connection and informed by the release of key hormones and peptides, including dopamine and oxytocin. These chemicals, oxytocin in particular, effectively block our defence systems in our brain and enable us to be ready for social engagement. When in such a state of readiness, it makes sense to want to approach and spend time with the other person.

Our openness to approaching or moving into a more defensive stance is also in part determined by our own genetics and our own early experiences as babies. We can either inherit a readiness to explore and approach, or we can learn that approaching people leads to feeling afraid or stressed or even hurt. When there are repeated experiences of feeling stressed or hurt, the brain connects 'approach' with key consequences.

This is vital if the approach is made, for instance, around touching an electrical socket and getting a warning voice from a kind parent, but the same tone can, similarly, also teach a child to be cautious about seeking out comfort or a cuddle in case they are shouted out or dismissed again. All the adults around the people with an intellectual disability have their own experiential learning to hold in mind, when we need to consider their readiness to approach another. When a child or adult is rejecting, or their responses feel challenging or undermining to their carer, this will chime in alongside whatever learned approach system the parent or carer brings to the relationship. When we meet someone whose own approach-avoidance system is activated, when they are experiencing mistrust, it is harder to stay in a caring relationship – to physically move towards that person and to keep offering connection. This very reversal of being able to offer what we think we should be offering can trigger confusion and shame in the carer.

Risks linked with intellectual disability

Bernard-Bonnin's (2004) literature review highlighted research which indicated the significant and negative impact of maternal depression on children's cognitive and interactive style. Whilst it's important to emphasise that we are not proposing all mothers and parents of children with an intellectual disability are depressed, it is feasible to consider the impact of a mismatch in expectations that can occur if the parents are not yet clear on how much time their child might need to process information, in order to engage, or for parents who might not, at first, understand their babies' way of communicating. If the intellectual disability is not yet known, there might be a period of confusion and of feeling ineffective or self-doubting as a parent. The Still Face experiment (when a parent purposefully becomes unresponsive to a child for a short period) is challenging to watch (Tronick, 2007) and resonates here: there is increased potential for disconnection and confusion for the parent around a child with information-processing challenges. It is feasible that the parent's own approach system switches off or dials down, because their own brain stops producing the 'approach' chemicals.

Similarly, this pattern can continue to exist as a child with an intellectual disability grows into adulthood. It can be helpful to understand the adult carer's previous experience of offering care, their own genetic disposition to approaching others, and also their expectations and understanding of the communication style/pattern of the person with intellectual disabilities. When posing a recent search term on the internet 'meeting someone with an intellectual disability for the first time', I was saddened to see that the first result was a site that started with 'Don't be afraid'. Our brains can become scared or worried about how to approach anyone, or any situation that is not familiar to us. Sadly, for many, that includes not feeling confident about approaching someone with an intellectual disability.

2. Carer reward system (no longer feeling pleasure in another's company)

When interacting with a child or adult we are caring for (or just caring about), and when this interaction goes well, our brains experience a neurochemical reward. The approach system enables the release of oxytocin which, in turn, impacts on the release of dopamine, a central chemical for the reward centres in our brains. This is the reward system that is triggered during craving and addiction and is clearly a powerful mechanism. The 'approach' and 'reward' systems are highly interconnected and finely tuned. The rewards centres of the brain can be triggered by just looking at pictures of your own child or hearing their voice, and these experiences are activated in anticipation of similar interaction in the future (Hughes & Baylin, 2012).

When the carer's approach system is impaired, the reward system will receive less or no feedback and might raise questions such as, "Am I a terrible person, that I just don't like hanging around with X?". If the higher order (executive brain or prefrontal cortex) reward is not activated, it becomes harder to keep both the approach and reward centres engaged. There are fewer and fewer stored memories of pleasurable encounters to draw on, during tense or tough moments in offering care. Dopamine is needed to provide motivation, and the lack of, or lowered dopamine in a carer's system, combined with the limited number of pleasurable memories to draw on, means that there is a higher risk of blocks in a relationship.

Risks linked with intellectual disability

For some families, certainly not all, making sense of a learning difference, especially when not yet diagnosed, can be lengthy and confusing. There is a heightened risk of parental depression with lowered dopamine. A child born with an intellectual disability has an increased likelihood of also experiencing additional physiological conditions and health challenges. Learning about these additional care needs can be complicated and stressful and, again, significant stress can dampen both oxytocin and dopamine systems. When the cognitive impairment is not yet clear, there can be a phase of feeling inadequate or losing confidence as a parent. Once a child's cognitive impairment is clearer, there can remain a sense of feeling overwhelmed and inadequate as a parent to meet their child's additional needs. It can be hard to adapt expectations and to feel effective as a parent during the early, often tiring, months of caring for a baby. It can be highly challenging to stay open and engaged with a child who does not provide immediately rewarding feedback (Hughes & Baylin, 2012).

In later life, this pattern for many people with an intellectual disability can, in our experience, present this same challenge in relationships. If carers' understanding of someone's needs or their way of showing happiness or distress is unclear, then it is feasible that the sense of reward during contact diminishes.

3. Carers reading another system (feeling confused about and no longer able to consider another person's inner world or experience)

Our ability to empathise with someone means we need to be aware of our own internal reactions and notice how, and in what way, we are moved by another person's experience. We need to notice any change of state in our own bodies and in our mood, noticing that we have been impacted and affected by their experience. The experience of empathy draws on both a visceral experience of connection and higher order brain processes where we hold in mind and make sense of another person's experience. Hughes and Baylin's (2012) insights from the neuroscientific literature help us understand a mechanism behind a parent-reading system. This parent-reading system draws on the parts of the brain that interprets non-verbal communication to help us make sense of the emotional and physiological needs of a baby. The systems involved in empathy are also intriguingly open to expansion and contraction (Cozolino, 2006) and therefore adjusts and varies in response to each situation.

Mirror neurons play an important role here, a mechanism by which we are thought to deepen our experience of caring for and understanding someone else. Mirror neurons are activated when we observe another person, and these mirror cells are thought to enable the process of empathy and attunement. Mirror neurons are a two-way process: the child can mirror the parent's reactions and vice versa.

When a parent or carer is inadvertently triggered into a stress state and a child mirrors this back, a challenging feedback loop can be triggered (Cozolino, 2006). The reading system is heavily focused on facial and eye moments, and when either a parent or child's facial expression is hard to decipher, or is unresponsive to our interactions, then empathy and the ability to care starts to falter. The reading system is mediated by our interpretation: if a parent or carer's interpretation is that the child/adult in front of them does not like them, their own reward and approach systems will be impacted, making them more likely to emotionally and maybe physically withdraw. Again, oxytocin is emerging as a key hormone informing our ability to accurately read and interpret facial expressions (Ross & Young, 2008). The absence of oxytocin in the context of challenges with our approach or reward systems, can further impact on our empathy and people's reading systems.

Our reading systems are also informed by our own experience and expectations that develop through our previous relationships, and in particular a parent or carer's own attachment history will often be illuminating. We build an understanding about how others behave or should respond to our care based on our own experience of being cared for as well as drawing on our more recent experience of being within a relationship. Blocks in a carer's ability to make sense of or empathise with the child or adult in front of them might require a deeper exploration of the carer's own history.

Risks linked with intellectual disability

The risk around misinterpretation of meaning can be elevated around people with an intellectual disability if we are not yet synchronised into their communication style. This is particularly poignant in early childhood and for those who, as they grow up, either do not develop formal language or who struggle to articulate their feelings accurately or as easily as those around them. In cultures that are highly reliant on words to smooth over misunderstandings, or that rely on words to connect and communicate, there are heightened risks for people with an intellectual disability that others will misread, and misattribute their reactions and feelings.

Parents and carers who find it hard to read or decipher facial expressions and reactions due to their own stresses, pressures or work demands, will notice that it requires more effort to approach. Over time, there is a risk that avoiding contact and misunderstanding within this relationship might become more pronounced, increasing the risks of blocked care. If a parent or carer has themselves been raised in a stressful environment, they grow up being more sensitised to detecting signs of anger or fear. This interpretation bias is more likely to trigger defensiveness in the carer if a child or again, in later life, an adult with an intellectual disability, presents in a way that feels rejecting or in some way critical. Cozolino's (2006) research indicated that these feedback loops are rapid and reciprocal – once the mistrust and gaps in empathy begins, the effects can become cumulative, especially if there is an absence of help to challenge or interpret this misreading of each other. Improving relationships improves oxytocin functioning (Gouin *et al*, 2010). This is a powerful research finding for those who also experience lower levels of oxytocin, including those on the autism spectrum (Andrai *et al*, 2010) and highlights the need for developing therapeutic relationships as a way of increasing oxytocin systems for people experiencing blocked care.

4. Carer meaning-making system (the stories we create about ourselves or others)

It takes time for the systems within our brain to reach full maturity; for these different systems to be fully developed and fully connected. Safe and attuned care is needed for the developing brain. Injury or significant stressors will markedly interrupt the ease with which the brain systems can link, and it is this linkage that enables the integration of all the information that allows a parent or carer to make sense of the experiences they are noticing in front of them. A mature brain can integrate information from their own sensory feedback, their emotional reactions to make sense of someone else's patterns. Someone who is in a calm and non-defensive state will be more nuanced in their ability to consider and make sense of another's experience, and to also understand their own pressures are influencing their readiness for connection.

However, if there is parental or carer stress and their other approach, reward and reading systems are not engaged, the brain will have moved into a more defensive state producing vasopressin, not oxytocin (Hughes & Baylin, 2012). In a defensive state we have evolved so that less of the brain is activated, we are primed for caution and more likely to think polemically or in black and white terms. At these times, a parent or carer is more likely to be critical or self-blaming and rather than think of a baby as tired and colicky, might feel that the baby doesn't love them, or that they are being a rubbish parent. Here, the parent or carer is not holding a perspective of drawing on the meaning-making skills that today the baby is really hard to soothe and settle. Instead of being able to solve the upset their role might be to offer comfort and company whilst the baby is feeling so upset. A defensive system often means we move into blame or upset and are less likely to be able to generate alternative and empathetic explanations. If carers are dysregulated, then the interpretation of events and the story around an interaction with another is more likely to be biassed, skewed or narrow.

Risks linked with intellectual disability

When we offer attuned care to someone with an intellectual disability, we need to change and adapt the content of our conversation and discussion so that we are not overwhelming that person with too many words or concepts all at once. This tailoring is an important part of respecting potential communication challenges associated with cognitive impairment.

The risk of simplifying

It is important to notice whether when we simplify or adapt our communication to suit someone with an intellectual disability that we are not also simplifying or toning down our consideration about another's experience. When we simplify the words around a person, there is a risk that we also move towards simpler affective explanations or frameworks around someone with an intellectual disability, not acknowledging their full experience.

Parenting and caring for and about someone with complex needs, such as a child or adult with an intellectual disability, is likely to cause moments of dysregulation and doubt. It is feasible that the worry and communication challenge, and/or level of responsibility, increases the likelihood of carer dysregulation.

The need for breaks and helpful networks around the carers of people with complex needs is salient here to help challenge and bring in different perspectives or accounts, and make better sense of the relationship patterns at play. The narrative we all hold about ourselves (as effective, loving, calm or caring etc), that is formed through our early childhood experiences, are often tested to the limit in parenting and care work. This can particularly be the case when caring for people with an intellectual disability, whose rate of development and process is likely to be impaired or delayed. These delays can, for some, make it more worrying and challenging to know if what you are offering is having an impact or whether you are doing the right thing. Sometimes the story or narrative becomes distorted or lost and we might even move more to action and practical care, and lose confidence, or even openness to connection and relating.

5. Carer's executive system (reflection and integrating the information across these systems)

The executive system integrates information across the different parenting or caring systems. It will integrate information from our older 'reptilian' brain (physiological/ sensory systems), to our limbic brain (emotional processing systems) up to our higher order neocortex or executive systems. A carer's executive system therefore enables self-understanding, people-reading, reflection, emotional regulation, reasoning, and the capacity to adapt to new situations. This overview enables us to consider and reflect on our interactions and the usefulness of our approach.

These different processes have been described by Payne Bryson & Siegel (2012) as our upstairs brains and downstairs brains.

Figure 10.5: Key areas of the brain that are impacted during blocked care

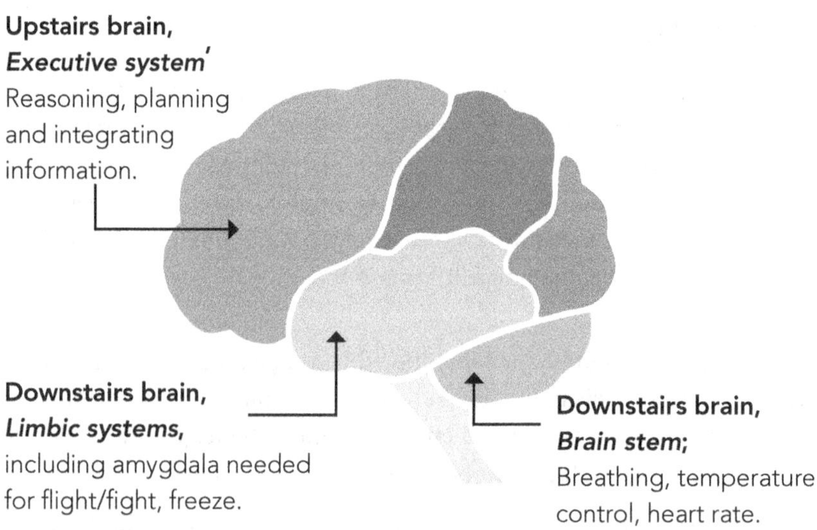

The executive system enables us to reflect and adapt in order to respond to changes in a relationship. When we become rigid in our thinking or understanding about someone else, our perspective can significantly narrow. The executive system enables us to pause and notice the negative effect experiences and allows us a way of reflecting. When the other systems shut down and it's hard to want to approach, have empathy for or experience any joy in caring for someone, it is the executive system that aSllows us to continue to move through the steps of providing care. This system allows us to reflect and can enable a pause or consideration about asking for help, and also helps to monitor how effectively you are resolving any possible conflict.

The ability to monitor and review the impact we are having on another person, or to track the ups and downs of a relationship is mediated by stress. A stressed, tired, highly worried or distracted parent or carer will find it hard to change their approach, and this change of approach is needed in response to developmental change in the child or adult, or when we better understand a key thing about another person's experience.

Risks linked with intellectual disability

When a parent or carer is given more information about their child or the person they care for, possibly new information as a result of a diagnosis, or an assessment that reveals an important issue about the person with an intellectual disability, there is often a need to pivot or change approach. Sometimes, this includes developing a richer understanding about the degree of challenge someone experiences in their receptive or expressive language, or making better sense of the impact of underdeveloped sensory systems. Integrating new information requires huge flexibility and adaptation and, often, those caring for people with an intellectual disability are tired and have insufficient support, formal and/or informal. Sometimes, information is shared in a way that makes the parent or carer feel criticised, or is just hard to process because it is different from their previous understanding. Already-stressed parents or carers, those who might be young and offering care before their own brain has reached maturity, or those whose own childhood experiences might not have prepared them for huge relational challenges, are more at risk of experiencing blocked care.

Finding ways to repair blocked care

These ideas are adapted from Hughes & Baylin (2012) and include reflections from our own experience in intellectual disability services.

1. Focus on relationship and connection

When supporting a carer or parent we might need to help them consider the activities or support that might release oxytocin, a hormone that arises when we care about another. Alternatively, as well as offering curiosity and empathy for a carer's experience, a therapist can also help a carer to attend to and track moments, however short, of connection. When we help others to notice nuance or fluctuations or that a whole day wasn't necessarily "rubbish" we can remind a carer of their successes; reframe their experiences, opening them to noticing connection.

2. Know about blocked care

Understanding how we connect and stop connecting with another person is vital. It seems particularly salient when offering care to someone with highly complex needs and when relationship demands are high, and might include offering a lot of personal care, advocacy and coping with challenging reactions. Knowing about blocked care helps us to track the experience for ourselves and may help prevent us feeling defensive when someone notices the pattern for us. This knowledge and perspective truly draws on the executive carer or parenting system, when we integrate our learning and experiential information together.

3. Check your own warning system

It is important to spend time reflecting on whether you are reading the situation accurately or maybe are interpreting things with a particular slant, and checking whether you are being given false warning information – have you moved into defence and reverse when it's maybe not needed? This helps us to check in on both our approach and reward systems.

4. Understand your own attachment history or patterns

Understand when you are tired or exhausted, or when 'your buttons have been pressed'; understanding how a pattern or issue from the past might be being triggered as you get to know the person in front of you can ensure you are conscious of the potential for blocked care.

5. Engage your reflective brain

As a parent or carer of someone with intellectual disability it is important that you notice your instinctive or visceral reaction and reflect on the picture that is emerging. Linking your affective and cognitive skills is vital here; if you are working in a system where there has been professional involvement, can you go back to a formulation, or an assessment document, to refresh your brain about the challenges the person with an intellectual disability is experiencing? When we hold their story in mind, we are better able to reduce rigidity by engaging the parent/carer reading systems and also the parent/carer meaning-making parts of our brain.

6. Reflective buddy

It can be very helpful to have someone you can talk to honestly about the unwelcome and unpleasant reaction to a child or adult who is vulnerable and who is triggering strong reactions in you. This needs to be a person who responds kindly and without judgement. Caring for others is also tiring and it is easy to lose track of the caring person that you used to feel you are; taking breaks and connecting with regulated people, and doing things where you feel effective and valued are an important part of the mix.

7. Being honest

Be kind to yourself and remember your skills and strengths. Offering support to another person, whether as a parent or carer is hard – it can be tedious, it's not always rewarding and it might be hard to sustain the effort and energy needed at all times. Being kind to yourself will enable you to reflect on both your experience, and the experience of those around you as well.

8. Make a plan

List some things you like to do together. Draw down on the knowledge of a clever occupational therapist to find an activity that interests both you and the person with an intellectual disability.

Use 'Intensive Interaction' (Nind & Hewett; 1994) or Theraplay (Booth & Jensen, 2010), to find ways into small moments of joy and connection.

9. Repair

When things go wrong – and they no doubt will – offer yourself some forgiveness, and also make sense of the wobble or misunderstanding with the person you are caring for. Making sense of things rather than avoiding talking about it, re-builds and strengthens a relationship. (See more on repair in Chapter 2 and Chapter 6.)

10. Working with attachment-trained professionals

It can, for some, be very rewarding to understand that you are offering sensitive care to a child or adult that has serious and complex needs. It is important that this is recognised and acknowledged, as there are significant and important skills needed by staff and family to connect with someone who has a different basis for communication; with someone who might have a fixed range of words or noises to engage; or who might not be highly expressive about their joy, but highly reactive around distress. There should be respect afforded to those who offer this additional care, who attune to people who are maybe very different to themselves. Sadly, too many people lack the confidence to, or maybe the experience of exploring what it is like to care about someone who is different to themselves. Not everyone finds this easy. Professionals in the system can be pivotal here in maintaining respect and support for the care and support that immediate carers and loved ones bring to the life of someone with an intellectual disability. These professionals can also champion and help you to sustain a focus on the strength of your relationship. They will ideally be the ones that help teach and remind you about the risks of and experience of blocked care, but also how to change this dynamic.

Example of building connection when in blocked care

When my foster carer friend learned about the patterns associated with blocked care, things started to change; just having a name for it and a framework was an important first step and helped reduce the sense of shame or self-criticism she'd experienced until then. Understanding what happens to our brains when children are deeply mistrustful was an important starting point. At this point, the foster carer noticed that this blocked experience occurred only when she was in the company of the child. At night or when the child was at school, the pause and gap enabled her to feel more positive about the child, but as soon as they were in the same room she noticed the heavy feelings again. In addition, once this pattern was identified, she noted with interest her small reactions: when the child walked in the room, she recalled how her face physically and instinctively turned away from the child, or her active avoidance of eye contact with the child – all patterns that are markedly different from her typical interactions with children to this point.

Having someone truly accept and acknowledge this pattern, enabled the foster carer to share these profoundly unpleasant feelings she had been carrying on her own. Being able to explore this in a non-judgemental manner was vital, as well as learning about blocked care and how to counter this experience. The therapist explained the steps needed to bring the warmth and empathy into the foster carer's experience of this child. A considerable amount of trust is needed to follow these steps, as it requires the adults to actively initiate change and move towards a child that their brain is instructing them to move away from. However, the trust established between the adults enabled the foster carer to actively seek out and actively offer care, and spend time with this child. Over a few weeks the relationship changed dramatically:

"Our relationship went from a 1 to a 10."

When the child was due to be adopted, the foster carer was truly upset about having to say goodbye. Their connection was extremely close by then.

Conclusion

There can be great shame as a parent or carer in not feeling close to your child or the person you are employed to care for. This shame and confusion can increase further for those who generally find it easy to connect, and who generally want to engage with others. When we make sense of how trust can be eroded and when we better understand how our brains and bodies are organised to respond to blocked trust, it can interrupt this shame. In naming this process of blocked trust and blocked care we do not just create an understanding, but also start to identify ways to better support the relationship. The risks of blocks in trust and care are potentially more likely within relationships where there are communication challenges or where it might be easier to misinterpret ideas and intent behind behaviour. The risk around blocked care, especially in institutional settings can be incredibly high and have, at times, been catastrophic. The clarity and support offered within DDP interventions at those points of disconnection are therefore vital, not just for relational repair, but also for family coherence, to avoid family or placement breakdown, and to also reduce the terrible risks associated with dangerous, disconnected care. A DDP model enables staff, parents and carers alike to find and explore non-shaming ways of making sense of interrupted care and a route to recovering connection.

SECTION 3:

The application of Dyadic Developmental Practice for those working with people with intellectual disabilities

Chapter 11: Assessing presentations and tailoring DDP interventions according to the Pyramid of Need

Summary

- The Pyramid of Need is a six-level framework developed by Kim Golding and Dan Hughes to tailor and guide the provision of DDP intervention plans for children who have experienced developmental or relational trauma.
- This chapter offers a framework for assessing and understanding presenting needs at each level. Understanding presenting needs at each level can contribute to a wider formulation, tailor a plan of intervention for the person with intellectual disabilities and their caregivers, and help navigate working roles throughout the wider support system.

Introduction

In this chapter, we will consider how presenting needs of people with an intellectual disability and their support networks can be considered at each layer of the Pyramid of Need framework. We will also consider the steps that might be taken either in therapy or with the network around the person with an intellectual disability. Throughout this chapter, each level of the Pyramid is laid out in the following way:

- A brief introduction of the Pyramid level.
- An 'Assessing for signs' text box describing several presentations corresponding to the Pyramid's level, intended as a guide to identify different needs and experiences of the person with an intellectual disability, their carers and wider support network (see Appendix 6 for a Pyramid of Need assessment summary).
- A summary of 'Supportive steps' that correspond to the needs identified at each level to guide the provision of DDP-informed therapy, intervention plans and systemic working.

What is the Pyramid of Need?

The Pyramid of Need (Golding & Hughes, 2012; Golding, 2013) and corresponding assessment grids (Golding, 2019) were designed to tailor and guide the provision of DDP informed intervention plans for children who have experienced relational trauma. The Pyramid is a useful framework or paradigm in which to create individually tailored support that meets the needs of the child and their family/ support system. The pyramid consists of six levels, with each level building on the foundations being created by needs being met at the earlier stages for the next. It is not a linear or sequential process as individuals' needs and support varies depending on their environment, what is happening and who is present at the current time. It is also important to note that it is possible to be at different levels at the same time and to move up and down depending on what is happening, who is around and what the environment is like at any moment. Therefore, be mindful to review and adjust the intervention accordingly, as levels further up the pyramid will be compromised without intervention to establish each preceding level.

Figure 11.1: Ensuring needs are understood and met within these domains of safety – adapted from Golding & Hughes (2012)

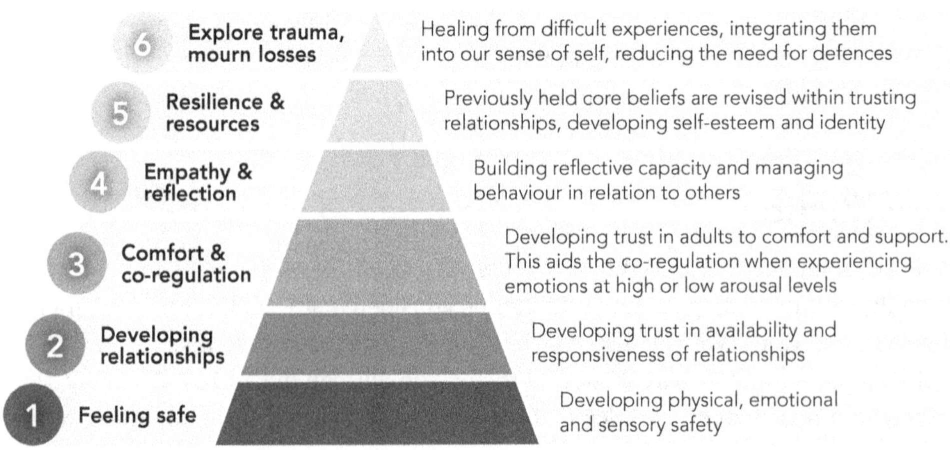

Level 1: Feeling safe

Level 1 addresses the basic need to be and feel safe, both physically and emotionally. Physically, we all need shelter, warmth and food. Emotionally, we need to feel understood and supported. When we feel safe, we have a regular heart rate and muscle tone, we are relaxed and engaged, curious and creative.

To consider this level of 'feeling safe' more deeply, you can delve into Chapter 6, which outlines that it is the way our basic physiological needs are met, that helps determine how our sensory systems connect and regulate. The approach and attitude of the parent/carer has a profound impact on the experience of safety and forming a close bond. When we receive responsive and attuned care, where our fears are understood and managed, we are more likely to feel safe. The experience of safety directly informs how we respond to threats (such as calling out when feeling alone) and helps inform someone's resilience to and tolerance for emotional challenges. Responsive and attuned care builds resilience and improves the 'window of tolerance' to big feelings such as distress, upset, or excitement. If someone perceives or experiences a sense of threat, they will move out of a bodily state that enables them to be open to connection and engagement and, first, move to action or defence (to reduce the threat). Feeling safe therefore involves an internal experience, a state of physiological, sensory, emotional, cognitive and social regulation.

Assessing for signs that a person with intellectual disabilities isn't feeling safe

- Almost constantly distressed or dysregulated.
- Finding it difficult to feel safe when away from parent(s) or primary attachment figure. Struggling to separate from carers.
- High levels of fear and anxiety, displayed through anxious (often distracted and fearful of change, new situations or places) or angry behaviours towards self and others.
- Often closed off and/or defensive.
- In blocked trust of relationships, often taking charge, demanding or conversely falling into submission, isolated, withdrawn and superficial in interactions, seeking out places to hide and lack of eye contact.
- Moving quickly; always 'on the go' and chaotic or conversely static and a bit sedentary.
- Hungry and never satiated or indifferent to food offered.
- Poor temperature control.

Supportive steps to develop safety for people with intellectual disabilities

When we feel unsafe and dysregulated, our brains and bodies are busy dedicating resources to survival, and our ability to develop trusting relationships, seek help or comfort or engage in activities will be significantly compromised; this is the case for us all. Simply stopping 'bad' things from happening to someone is not enough to repair the damage of them (Hughes, 2017). So, developing safety is not just about stopping the traumatic things from happening. Experiences of trauma and significant adversity, although in the past are joined to the safety of now 'by the fragmented sense of self with significant challenges to emotional, reflective and relational functioning' (Hughes, 2017, p 597). And so, even though people may find themselves in relationships which intend to keep them safe, unwavering safety needs to be demonstrated repeatedly; even in the light of anger, difficulty, or difference of opinion, communicate that safety will be preserved.

Individuals with intellectual disabilities may experience challenges in learning, differences in sensory processing, and/or a reduced understanding of object permanence. Additionally, there are instances where people with intellectual disabilities are subjected to interventions or decisions being made *for them* rather than *with them*. This can occur either because they lack the capacity to make decisions or because services themselves lack the resources to tailor interventions or provide accessible information. Such practices can further undermine a person's sense of agency, leaving them feeling powerless and further compromising safety. It may also result in significant life changes, such as relocations or decisions, of which they are unaware. Furthermore, since many individuals with intellectual disabilities are unable to self-advocate effectively, they may be disproportionately subjected to restrictive practices, limiting their autonomy and reducing their feelings of safety.

To increase safety for a person with intellectual disabilities, focus needs to be on stability and predictability (rather than on progress) in relationships, environments and activities. Offer supportive sensory regulation proactively and in response to challenges that might arise. Some ways in which safety can be tailored to people with intellectual disabilities needs include the following:

Your approach

First and foremost, embody the DDP approach and attitude in all you do, as it will increase emotional connection and safety in the relationship and enhance the provision of all the other suggestions written hereafter. Provide consistent and PACE-informed care (see Chapter 7: PACE for further information and examples). Remember, PACE is a stance with the aim of connection, not a strategy. For example, a PACEful approach can look like using intensive interaction, talking in a light tone, accepting that what lies beneath difficult-to-manage reactions and responses are feelings based on years of difficult experiences; put yourself in the person's shoes (if you'd had their day, week, life, how would you be feeling and responding?); and show up/ stay available with compassion during the person's hardest times.

Lowering your expectations of what you might achieve or do together and reminding yourself that ensuring the person with intellectual disabilities feels safe is your priority right now. Keep things simple – your presence and availability make a difference to instilling a sense of safety. Spending one-on-one time together in a safe and calm environment is essential, rather than being preoccupied, out or overly busy (distracting will not allow this connection and felt sense of safety). Remain fully available and responsive to the person's needs. Maintain a predictable, available and responsive approach even when the person with intellectual disabilities is defensive or unresponsive.

Boundaries and limits should always be provided in the context of a safe, connected relationship to communicate accepting and unconditional care whilst upholding boundaries and consistency (see Chapter 8: Two Hands of Care for more information). When things have become tricky and interactions have become dysregulated, the parenting in the moment cycle can be helpful to have to hand. If the person is away from their key attachments, ensure the previously mentioned strategies are implemented, with particular focus on providing increased nurture and presence.

Maintain/re-establish routines, structure and consistency across all environments

Whilst the world (external, and internally to a person with intellectual disabilities) might feel unsafe, predictability and consistent routines can reduce a sense of perceived threat from the unknown and bring a predictable flow to the day (waking routines, mealtime routines, hellos, goodbyes, evening routines, etc). Prioritise spending time together, but in a low-key way. Reduce the number of changes and avoid big excursions, which are inherently unpredictable.

Processing verbal information when we are dysregulated is a challenge, so increase predictability with visual supports, tools, reminders and resources too. This can include daily schedules, now, next (then) schedules, video walkthroughs and Social StoriesTM (as developed by Carol Gray, see https://carolgraysocialstories.com/). Well established visuals are especially important for creating safety, by enhancing predictability, the opportunity for clarification and amendments to activities. Ideally, visuals are used proactively and when change is afoot, such as:

- Staff going on holidays or maternity leave.
- New peers joining a support home.
- A change of vehicle or taxi drive.
- Moving house or building work.

Visual supports reduce the amount of processing that needs to occur and therefore frees up capacity for other processing (e.g. of safety cues and relational interactions). Visuals need to be used consistently, so they are a constant aid for the person in their processing of information. Visuals can communicate these changes and reduce the need to depend on less reliable and more effortful verbal communication.

Core staff teams

Shackleton (2016) emphasises the importance of people with intellectual disabilities having a core staff team of 6 or 7 staff to allow for predictable and attuned care, with 2 or 3 link workers or key workers leading this core team and being identified as key attachment figures.

Develop a coherent support plan

Consistent support from different carers across environments is essential in increasing predictability and providing a sense of safety too, so consider the development of a simple-to-follow support plan co-created by all those in the support network (see Appendix 5 for templates).

Provide limited choice

Limited choice will maintain a sense of agency while minimising the risk of overwhelm. People with intellectual disabilities are likely to have much less control and choice than their peers who do not have intellectual disabilities. Making choices gives a sense of autonomy and is incredibly important to our well-being, especially when people have had previous trauma in their lives. Giving opportunities for choice (between 2 or 3 things is likely to be best) of clothes, food, drinks and activities, *whenever possible*. Depending on receptive and expressive communication needs, adapt how choice is presented alongside verbal communication, using pictures or objects. For example, choice can be incorporated into a visual schedule with a choice symbol, which corresponds to a choice board with activities that are likely to lead to enjoyment and sensory regulation (such as a walk, music, crunchy and favourite foods, singing together).

Even if the person you care for has good verbal communication, it is important to think about tailoring choice so that people understand their options and can make meaningful choices which are in keeping with what they genuinely want (and not made to please others). Complicatedly, we need to hold alongside this that people who have had very little choice in their lives might not know what they want, want that like or how to make choices. The limiting and provision of choice needs to account for people's mental capacity and discussion about this directly with the person or their parents may sometimes be needed.

Provide safe objects, places and regulation

Ensure environments provide a sense of safety and available, individually-tailored activities to meet sensory and developmental needs, at home and across all environments the person accesses. Regulating and rhythmic movement is likely to be important, soothing the senses and therefore providing physiological feelings of safety: indoor or outdoor swinging, walking, trampolining, singing or drives with the window open! Also consider the use of objects, clothes, favourite foods, places and music that increase safety, such as, for example, clothes without seams, tight/loose fitting clothes, a teddy with a recorded message, a scarf with a familiar perfume, snacks and a safe space or hiding place can help to establish a sense of safety, comfort and regulation with familiar sounds, textures, tastes and smells. This might be especially important during times of transition and change in activities and locations (such as to and from school or family contact).

Ensuring safety throughout the system

Safety for the person with an intellectual disability will be compromised when their carers, teams and support systems for not feel safe themselves. Consider system-wide DDP practice and consultation, to ensure that all those responsible for creating and maintaining safety can do so and build the foundations necessary for developing relationships and co-regulation.

Assessing for signs that immediate caregivers, teams and support networks are not feeling safe

- Home/placement at risk or broken down.
- Difficult interactions with others in the support system.
- Information concealing and/or incoherent with the rest of the system or person with intellectual disabilities.
- Often, reactive and emotional in responses and emotional in interactions with others in the support network and in meetings, showing signs of hopelessness and negativity.
- Saying they do not feel heard and supported.
- Feeling unsafe in their care of the person with intellectual disabilities, for example:
  - struggling to use boundaries, by fear of the reaction of the person with intellectual disabilities
  - having to manage high levels of violence and risk with the person with intellectual disabilities

- Not engaged in discussion, starting to work as individuals as opposed to part of a team.
- Socially isolated and unsupported.
- Showing signs of blocked care or struggling to be attuned to and engaged with the person with intellectual disabilities, quickly defensive, irritated or hopelessness.
- Hypervigilance to signs of anger or rejection.
- Finding it hard to be available for, enjoy being with and caring for the person with intellectual disabilities.
- Difficulty attuning to and understand the inner world of the person with intellectual disabilities.
- Struggling to provide safety and containment in parenting style, by being too strict or too lenient.

Additional signs that the support network, specifically, isn't feeling safe

- Often unavailable to others in the system and missing correspondence from others.
- Showing signs of blocked care or struggling to be attuned to and engaged with the person with intellectual disabilities, quickly defensive, irritated or hopelessness.
- Not enough capacity in the service, so often seeing unmet needs, feeling responsible to fill gaps in service provision, not taking breaks, working longer hours than contracted or double shifts.
- Work environment not meeting needs of the carers or person with intellectual disabilities- lack of office space, training space, meeting space, kitchen, space for breaks.
- Jobs not secure, shift patterns given at late notice.
- Management struggling to use boundaries by fear of staff leaving.
- No clear risk management and safeguarding processes or training to manage highly risky situations.
- No clear understanding of job role.
- Too much responsibility in context of resources available, skill and training.
- Lack of appropriate supervision structures, reflection or debrief structures or that these are in place but not attend.

Case vignette: A parent's experience of a support network feeling unsafe

Our son showed behaviours of concern that were misunderstood. The situation was badly managed, and we were openly shamed when trying to explain what our son was trying to communicate with his behaviour. What it showed was a lack of understanding of behaviour as communication and those accusing were defensive and angry. It made us question whether we were at fault or bad parents for not being as 'horrified' as they were. We tried to resolve it directly. Unfortunately, this worsened relationships as the parties wouldn't engage in open discussion.

Supportive steps to develop safety for caregivers

Carers are likely to feel unsafe when the person with intellectual disabilities they care for feels unsafe. It can be useful to consider the following steps to increase a sense of safety for the carer, but also equip them to access personal resources and provide safety to the person they care for:

Model acceptance and empathy

When supporting a carer who is feeling unsafe, going straight to meaning-making for the person they care for is unlikely to be helpful. When in a position of support to the carer, ensure to check and reflect on your personal responses to the carer first. Then, embody a PACE approach: be curious about the carer's feelings and responses and show acceptance and empathy for this experience:

> *"I wonder what this experience has brought up for you? When you're in this state, it must be difficult to be curious, as all your resources are taken up with trying to keep yourself safe/ from losing it all."*

(See Chapter 10 for more suggestions for engaging the five parenting brain systems.)

Link attachment history to current caring experience

As part of really connecting with the carers' experiences of caring for a person with intellectual disabilities, it can be important to consider the impact of their own experiences of being cared for. This can gently help carers become more aware of any potential triggers to them losing empathy for the person with intellectual disabilities. It can also be relevant to explore experiences of becoming a parent to a child with additional needs and intellectual disability. Were they supported when their child fell behind on milestones? What was their experiences of help seeking and diagnosis? For paid carers, it can be helpful to be guided through similar questions, as well as unpicking reasons for their roles. The sociocultural attitudes that are held about disability which we all have and bring (carers, extended family, professionals and communities) will also have an impact on our way of relating

(sociocultural considerations are highlighted throughout this book, but particularly in Chapter 3 and Chapter 9).

Reflection: what might influence the way you connect with others' emotions?

- What was your experience of being cared for? As a child, were your attempts at connection (such as eye contact, playing alongside, crying, asking for help) seen and reciprocated with offers of connection?
- How were you kept safe when you were young, physically and emotionally?
- What are your fears, doubts and hopes when caring, in joyful interactions, but also when things are hard? Does this remind you of any other patterns or responses you've experienced before?
- Do you feel safe when caring for XX?
- Do you think XX feels safe?
- What are your strengths in and barriers to accepting and empathising with the underlying experiences of the person(s) you care for?
- Do you (or influential people around you) feel your role is to support people with intellectual disabilities to increase skill levels over attending to emotional needs?
- What is the role of stigma and the media's representation of intellectual disabilities on your approach to developing emotional safety with those you care for?

Explore and model key principles of DDP-informed care

It can be helpful to teach carers about key principles of DDP-informed care, as well as exploring how attachments and patterns of relating develop, how these shape our sense of self and our caring styles and responses. Learning about intersubjectivity, attunement, PACE, shame, blocked care and caring with two hands can also help carers feel and be equipped with understanding of themselves, the person with intellectual disabilities they care for and the interactions between them. It can help to develop an understanding of their own underlying needs and those of the person with intellectual disabilities they care for and equip them with the skills to offer DDP-informed care.

Case vignette: PACE-informed introduction to attachment for parents in distress

I regularly meet with a couple in relation to their 12-year-old autistic son with an intellectual disability. When we first started to meet, my main hope was that the parents could trust that they would feel heard. They often spoke about their son's difficult to manage presentation and not knowing how to respond. This was an opportunity to model a PACEful response, gently exploring their emotional experience: *"When that happened, what did it bring up for you?"*

Parents would answer along the lines of feeling sad about their son's distress and Mum felt angry with herself about her emotionally charged reaction. I offered acceptance and empathy: *"No wonder you felt a big emotional response to being scrammed and hit! When you're in that state, it's difficult to respond in a way you might have done if you felt safe and calm."*

I often needed to resist the urge to problem solve the behaviour or explore alternative ways they might have wanted to respond. Instead, depending on how open and engaged parents would present, I approached their honesty with curiosity about their emotional experience, their experiences of attachment and deepen their experience of being accepted and empathised with, asking a question along the lines of:

"You describe feeling angry with yourself for your reactions in that moment. Would it be okay if we try to unpick that a little bit together? Without expecting an answer as such, we could just think together about whether being hurt by your son and your response remind you of any other patterns you've experienced in other relationships? Are there particular things you are fearful of when caring for him?"

Gentle explorations of difficult emotional experiences within relationships past and present often opened up discussion around attunement, inner working models, blocks to connection and shame. This led the parents to not only consider their parenting style, but also the relationships they held with their parents and with one another in their marriage. They shared that that understanding of these concepts gave them a language, saved their marriage and helped them understand the possibility of acceptance (connection) and boundaries (correction) being compatible. We sometimes finished a session with parents saying they wanted to do things differently. During those times I might have said: *"I guess you'll go home and try to… don't worry if it doesn't quite work out"*.

Supportive steps to develop safety for staff teams and wider network

Everyone in the system needs to feel physically and emotionally safe, which means working with each other and in an environment that fosters safety. It is likely that some of the following guidance might apply more to those in positions of leadership.

Clear structure

We all work best when our working patterns and job roles are clear, and we know what is expected from us. It can be helpful to have a working practice agreement between all carers and professions in the network around people with intellectual disabilities, specifically detailing whose job it is to do what and who to go to for what. For example, who is the key person to review and update support plans, alternative communication strategies and resources and equipment. Who will arrange and chair multi-professional meetings, who collates information around glimmers, hopes and difficult times. Structure can also be provided with regular network meetings, team meetings, supervisions and set meeting structures.

Training

DDP-informed training can include concepts around neuroscience, attachment, intersubjective connection and DDP-- practice with teams and families. In sharing information about the ways early relationships can influence later development and interactions, we can make better sense of the patterns in front of us and ensure we are offering attuned and responsive care, in a way that also sustains or enhances relationships.

DDP consultation

Consultation can be a one-off event but often needs to be embedded into the systems around an individual with complex needs, so that this support is more readily available. The power of DDP consultation is that it offers reflective time, using the DDP model, to a broad variety of people, all of whom might have very different experiences and connections with the person with an intellectual disability. Consultation facilitates the connection and joining up of all the experiences between people and ideally across agencies. A DDP-informed consultation offers a reflective space, where individual views and emotions can be explored. The DDP practitioner's role is to support the exploration of these experiences whilst containing or co-regulating the emotions. This reflective process helps all to better understand the impact of trauma on all their relationships and on the systems in which they operate. A DDP practitioner will explore or co-create the common threads between the group members which builds a more accurate picture but also can lead to a coherent story, which in turn supports the development of a shared plan for the future.

Network training

DDP principles that inform training and consultation enhance Network Training days, offering extended time to consider the presentation, history, diagnosis and pressures that an individual with an intellectual disability brings to family life or a service. Based on a structure developed by Jenkins & Parry (2006), a network training meeting (originally designed to last for a day) aims to include as many key attachment figures, family members, carer workers and professionals as is feasible. Each person will have a different relationship with the person with an intellectual disability; as family member, as a teacher, as a respite worker, as an employer or as their psychiatrist for example. In drawing on such a rich pool of knowledge, we can create a fuller picture or story about an individual. The impact of trauma is that different experiences of a person can lead to people taking sides or splitting of views about what is right or true about a person. This can be particularly pertinent for those individuals who cannot directly express or share their experiences with us in words. The power of such a holistic approach is that we can create a clearer formulation including mapping out the impact of earlier experiences and now these inform their current responses to our care. Network training days typically include a teaching element, where some of the key DDP concepts can start to be introduced. This process often reveals what increases safety for the person with an intellectual disability.

Clear and concise support pathways and plans

Help to ensure consistency and an agreed way of supporting and approaching different situations, such as how to communicate placement moves or staff changes. Service processes and an individual support plan is great for a team to come back to when questions arise or practice needs to be reviewed.

Leadership informed by DDP-practice

This involves a PACEful, non-blaming approach that fosters a sense of safety among carers, leading with two hands to offer a PACEful, non-blaming approach whilst also maintaining clear and consistent boundaries and expectations. This fosters a space for carers to be open and feel safe to reflect on more difficult experiences. DDP-informed leadership also comes with the role of addressing environmental safety concerns – breaks, rotas, staffing ratios and so on – and ensuring policies and guidance around safeguarding and risks processes are clear and up to date.

Support and supervision

DDP-informed leadership or management draws on a PACE-based approach, amongst other DDP approaches, to enable reflection about challenges and frustrations. This type of supervision is mindful of shame responses, blocked care and blocked trust. DDP-informed supervision needs to ensure an overview of the task, the team, the individual and their intersection (Adair, 1983 as cited in Grant *et al*, 2024).

Reflections on the impact of the wider context on increasing safety

We can look to politics and broader systems in creating safety too (see Chapter 9 and Chapter 13 for further reflections). To create safety throughout the systems supporting people with intellectual disabilities, we can each take action (relative to our emotional and practical capacity, remit and resources!) (Public Health England, 2023). Persistent action to tackle stigma, address gaps in research, improve care coordination on a personal, multi-agency and national level and to make better use of funding streams and resources in ensuring access to the right help at the right time. DDP has a place within this context too with a PACEful approach required to create safety in reflective discussions and challenging practices, narratives and structures in a way that doesn't trigger shame and promotes a fairer way forward.

Level 2: Developing relationships

Level 2 of the pyramid of need emphasises that relationships are the primary means for achieving Level 1: Feeling safe. Building trust within these relationships is essential to fostering this sense of safety.

Assessing for signs of a need for support to develop relationships

Person with intellectual disability

When a person with intellectual disabilities is struggling to develop (trust in) relationships, it might look like they are:

- Struggling to manage own emotions and struggling to accept others' efforts of being present or offer comfort during times of dysregulation.
- Drawn to inappropriate interactions or social groups.
- Struggling to trust the availability of parents/carers, which can result in behaviours that appear to be a communication to want to push away efforts of connection or are testing boundaries.
- Struggling to initiate interactions.
- Struggling to allow others to be present or join in play or activities the person with intellectual disabilities is engaged in.

Immediate caregivers

When carers are struggling to support the person with intellectual disabilities to develop trust in their relationship and when carers struggle to relate to the support network around them. Signs of struggle may include difficulties with the following:

- Not being or making themselves available for interactions.
- Having difficulty to make connections, with responses often being irritable and defensive instead of light and playful.
- Finding it difficult to stay calm and open when the person with intellectual disabilities is dysregulated (potentially defensive, shut down, pushing away), and needs them most.
- Struggling to understand the needs and communications of the person with intellectual disabilities; having difficulty with reading their cues and make meaning.
- Experiencing barriers to feeling and offering empathy to the person with intellectual disabilities or colleagues and their internal experiences, to acknowledge their struggles, instead quick to offer solutions, shutting down or minimising expressions of need. For example, *"There's no need to be upset. Come on, let's watch some TV"*.
- Relationship with person with intellectual disabilities feeling more functional and practical, whilst struggling to find joy, delight or fun in the interactions together.
- Navigating social interactions and people in their support network (partner, colleagues, professionals).
- Feeling unsupported and defensive.
- Experiencing difficulties managing day to day, whilst also struggling to trust or other personal barriers to accessing support from others.

Whole teams and services

Teams and systems struggling to relate to one another might look like:

- Services struggling, but practising in isolation as opposed to sharing the load or and working collaboratively.
- Lack of genuineness; systems blaming (*"they would never understand"*) and passing responsibilities (*"that's not our remit"*), as opposed to thinking creatively about meeting needs.
- Struggling to navigate social interactions.
- Defensiveness in interactions, shutting down creativity and flexibility.

Supportive steps to developing relationships

Find opportunities for successful interactions

Given the additional needs of people with intellectual disabilities, carers are likely to do lots *for* and *to* them as part of their care.

- Practise being *with* the person with intellectual disabilities and delight in who they are and what they do (drawing on the P of PACE); fill their cup to overflowing and have joyful interactions!
- Lower expectations of what you want to achieve in a day, where possible, be more flexible in your own routines and expectations of what you want to do and by when, with more time together and less time rushing to fulfil a schedule.
- Consider how to slow down some day-to-day routines and demands to create opportunities of low-key interactions that are likely to bring small wins and glimmers of positive connection.
- Protect time at specific times every day of uninterrupted interaction led by the person with intellectual disabilities (such as play or intensive interaction), and schedule this. This will help the person with intellectual disabilities process the day, connect, experience shared joy and build relationships (as opposed to simile complete tasks).

PACE

Alongside the fundamental provision of physical and emotional safety, in order that carers can provide this for the person with intellectual disabilities, it is also important that it is accepted that to trust in the presence of safety the person with intellectual disabilities may first have to test the system, which can be difficult for the system. Understanding and responding to miscuing or attempts for extreme independence or extreme clinginess and an overreliance on others to do for them; are ways that people may test the safety and relationships being offered. Offering a PACEful approach across the system are some of the broad ways this can be provided.

Carers also need to feel safe in the relationship with the person with intellectual disabilities before they are able to offer connection in a way that helps the person they care for to trust connection. If carers find themselves needing support at this level, they may be struggling to connect with the person with intellectual disabilities (and their support network) for various reasons. It is the carers who spend most of their time with the person with intellectual disabilities, so truly connecting with their experiences, concerns, emotions, and ideas is central to effective change. If supporting a carer, allow them to experience you witnessing, accepting and empathising with their emotions and turmoil - and resist the urge to solve, reassure or distract. Developing trust in this approach and your interactions helps carers to experience safety in relationships and emotional expression. It also models the PACE approach, which you can label and describe, with the aim of helping caregivers to develop their own PACEful caring approach to responding to the needs of the person with intellectual disabilities.

Once carers show more openness, it is possible to show curiosity for and build on discussions around the impact of experiences on relationships and emotions (in, for example, carer discussions, supervision, team meetings, etc).

- "I wonder if when the person did X you felt frustrated, like nothing was working, even though you are working so hard?"
- "What's it like when the person you are caring for/ the carers you are supporting pushes you away?"
- "I wonder whether the way this person interacts with you reminds you of any other patterns or responses you've experienced before?"

This can gently help carers, teams and systems become more aware of any potential triggers to them losing empathy for/ wanting to pull away from the person with intellectual disabilities (see Chapters 9 and 10 for further reading).

Understanding attachment

Learning about intersubjectivity, attunement, PACE, shame, blocked care and caring with two hands can help carers feel and be equipped with understanding of themselves, the person with intellectual disabilities they care for and the interactions between them. It can help to develop an understanding of their own underlying needs and those of the person with intellectual disabilities they care for and equip them with the skills to offer DDP-informed care.

Reflect on what you consider successful interaction to be. DDP proposes successful interactions to include moments of the person with intellectual disabilities showing vulnerability by sharing distress or emotion, and carers responding with PACE, rather than problem-solving, frustration or distraction. These interactions with moments of delight, joy or playfulness are crucial for developing relationships.

In terms of support for staff teams and the wider system, finding opportunities for successful interactions can also help develop relationships. Join the system where they're at. For example, if a school doesn't accept invitations to a network meeting, consider the possibility of joining an existing educational review – purely with the agenda to develop relationships, as opposed to the agenda you might have in mind.

Ensure to practise acceptance and empathy in interactions. Consider the importance of celebrating glimmers and successes in every interaction, such as supervision, team meetings and modelling sessions. Remember, only when the relationship starts to feel safer with some openness/reduced defensiveness, can we bring in gentle curiosity and playfulness.

Ensure predictability and structure

Structure and predictability are paramount for all and have been shown to be part of successful DDP (Casswell *et al*, 2014). Structure and routine allows a sense of safety within the predictability of events and interactions, and allows opportunities for mutual joyful experiences. When considering structure and predictability for people with intellectual disabilities, the two hands of care (see Chapter 8: Two hands of care, for more detail) offers a DDP-informed way of offering structure and predictability alongside connection.

In terms of support for staff teams and the wider system, plan regular discussions in a predictable way and ensure safety within the discussion by offering some structure within these, whilst modelling a PACEful approach. This helps ensure that the system clearly understands your motives and feels safe in the knowledge that they know what will happen and how they might prepare for this, reducing the risk of them practising in isolation and increasing opportunities for genuine connection – feeling heard, accepted and understood.

Again, a working practice agreement can be helpful, as well as sharing/inviting meeting agendas, different formats of meetings (remote as opposed to face to face). Consider an external facilitator who is able to navigate discussion with a 'caring with two hands' approach. This might also help create systems to show and safely experience vulnerability (in not having all the answers) and open up creativity around *how we can work together to better meet needs.*

Level 3: Comfort and co-regulation

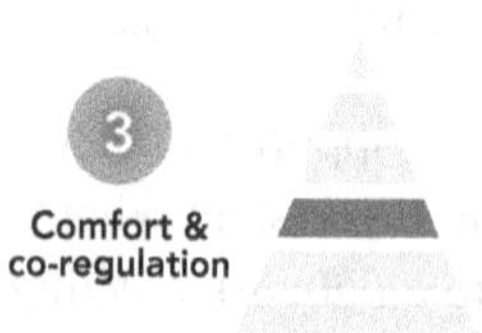

Level 3 focuses on developing trust in key adults to provide comfort and co-regulation when experiencing emotions at high or low arousal levels.

To provide comfort and support to the person with intellectual disabilities (or to one another in the support network), carers and professionals need to be regulated themselves first.

Assessing for signs of needing support to accept comfort and co-regulation

Person with an intellectual disability

- Person with intellectual disabilities is increasingly regulated and finding moments of joy and some sadness, and is becoming more secure with their main carers; however, they still struggle when experiencing strong emotions, with this often leading to them coming out of their window of tolerance, dysregulated or dissociating.

Immediate caregivers

Carers are struggling to provide comfort and co-regulation when the person with intellectual disabilities is experiencing dysregulation and needs them. This might look like:

- Withdrawing or shutting down.
- Trying to talk the person with intellectual disabilities out of their sadness or anger, distracting them or minimising the emotion (as opposed to showing acceptance and empathy).
- Becoming dysregulated themselves and showing, for example, frustration or anger.
- An imbalance in the two hands of care: providing discipline or corrections when the person with intellectual disabilities needs connection first, or being too lenient and not upholding limits.
- Struggling to repair after there has been a rupture in the way they might usually respond.

Teams and systems

Teams struggling to remain PACEful when the person with intellectual disabilities or others in the support network show distress or dysregulation. This might look like:

- Teams or support networks no longer open and engaged with one another.
- Splitting and becoming fragmented.
- Staff withdrawing and isolating themselves.
- Staff or systems being defensive and showing shame responses, minimising, blaming, judging, anger, with-holding information.
- An imbalance in the two hands of care: providing discipline or corrections when the person with intellectual disabilities needs connection first or being too lenient and not upholding limits.
- Teams struggle to meet one another, name challenges and repair.

Supportive steps to developing comfort and co-regulation

Take a breath

When things have become tricky and interactions have become dysregulated, the Parenting in the Moment cycle can be very helpful (see Chapter 8). Develop awareness of your triggers and patterns of unhelpful ways of responding when you are dysregulated:

- Do you usually end up shouting? Do you usually withdraw? Do you usually tell them to calm down?

Consider what strategies you can use (that are achievable in moments of crisis) to regulate, so you are able to offer a more PACEful response instead:

- Can you stick your head outside, splash water on your face, squeeze and stretch your hands or toes?
- Can you swap with someone to take a break?
- Can you talk to a safe person before deciding on your next steps?
- Do you need to hold on to a one-line reminder, such as "They're not being difficult, they're having a difficult time"?

The same supportive steps can be considered in teams and as professionals in the wider support system too. What are your patterns of responding to heated situations? What could you do (in the moment and long-term) to press pause to choose a more PACEful way of responding? Could you name it? *"I'm noticing that I'm beginning to feel defensive, can we come back to this later?"*

- Could you ask a safe person to notice and name it?
- Could you set some ground rules in team meetings, where you know things might get tricky?

Those in a position of leadership can consider these supportive steps during protected times of reflection and supervision using the PACE approach to discuss challenges and frustrations, being mindful of shame responses.

Understand the person's story and patterns

As a carer, develop awareness of the person with intellectual disabilities you are supporting and how their history impacts on their current presentation. Increased awareness of a person's experiences, sense of self and patterns of relating, can help increase your empathy and felt sense that *they are a good person and they are doing the best they can* (Hughes *et al*, 2019).

Historically, what have been their experiences of being cared for whilst distressed? How might their early and ongoing attachment experiences and life events shaped their sense of self? What survival strategies have they had to develop to ensure their basic needs are met? How does this all provide context to the person's presentation and interaction when they are distressed or dysregulated? How might you be able to use this understanding of their underlying needs and patterns of coping, to provide a PACEful response and a safe environment to co-regulate?

Two hands of care

As carers, maintain a predictable, available and responsive approach when the person with intellectual disabilities is defensive or unresponsive. Boundaries and limits should always be provided in the context of a safe, connected relationship to communicate accepting and unconditional care (Chapter 8: Two hands of care offers more information around this and the reasons this approach is essential for the person with intellectual disabilities and yourself as a carer).

It can be helpful to develop an agreed 'two hands' support plan with the whole support network that includes specific guidance around:

- Understanding patterns (above) likely to lead to increased dysregulation.
- How to support the person with intellectual disabilities when they show signs of becoming dysregulated.
- When they are dysregulated.
- When they are in crisis.

The two hands of caring approach is also fitting for the staff teams and systems who might be struggling in the face of distress. As a supporter to the team or a member of the system, seek to understand the needs, motives and struggles underlying the team's defensiveness and connect with these needs with a PACEful approach. The aim here is to model regulation and safety in the relationship without judgement to reduce defensiveness and the need for shield of shame responses, modelling the exact balance we hope staff and carers are able to embody themselves. Remember, correction within the caring with two hands approach is likely to be about learning:

- Is it possible to tweak or change something in the team or system to reduce the risk of ruptures and dysregulation?
- Can processes be made clearer?
- Do team meetings need to be facilitated differently to ensure safety to name challenges?
- Do staff from different agencies or disciplines need to consider joint visits?

Repair

The concept of repair will be fitting for carers to consider in their support for the person with an intellectual disability and for staff teams and systems to consider with one another. After difficult experiences, it takes time and effort to rebuild trust and reconnect. When you feel more regulated, put some time aside to consider what happened.

- How has everyone been affected?
- What needs to happen now to fix things?
- How can we repair the relationship?

Consider how things could be different next time or reduce triggers for you and the person you care for to increase chances for success.

Level 4: Empathy and reflection

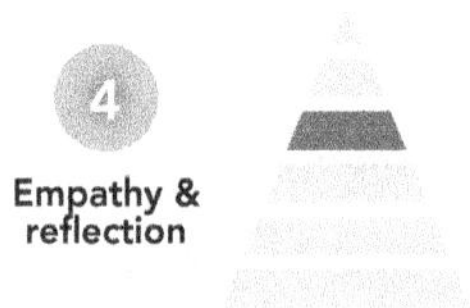

Once someone is starting to feel safe, to trust others, and can accept being comforted by trusted adults, then we notice improvements in their reflective capacity. The ability to reflect and build a deeper, and often more accurate, story of events can enable the development of compassion and understanding initially about oneself, and later for others. It is vital to understand and assess the capacity someone with an intellectual disability has, in order to emphasise with their own experience or with others. Misreading this means that we might mistime support and reduce connection with their experience and any confusion they might be experiencing. Understanding someone's capacity will, in turn, inform our formulation about their interactions with others.

Assessing for signs that a person with an intellectual disability needs support around empathy and reflection

- Noticing that they don't know how to respond to questions like "How are you feeling? or "I wonder why that happened?" – no clear sense of their internal world.
- Their reactions can seem out of step, or not easily matched, with the situation; you might notice over or underreaction.
- Struggling to make sense of their experiences, feelings or physiological needs, and expecting others to both anticipate and be able to meet their needs.
- Struggling to take turns or wait.

- Having no, or very limited insight into another person's experience; underdeveloped theory of mind.
- Shame (such as withdrawal, blaming others, minimising, shutdown and dissociation) – see Chapter 9: Shame and shielding from shame).

Supportive steps to developing empathy and reflection

In drawing on DDP as the core framework and holding an attitude of PACE in mind, the ability for someone to develop empathy for themselves rests on first experiencing empathy for their experience. Over time, this experience of being better understood builds into a version of emotional literacy. Babies first learn about their world through the eyes and reactions of those around them. Using this same method of support, DDP interventions enable a carer to help a traumatised person to better understand their own internal physiological reactions, tied to their affective experiences. By first naming, then not shaming or showing disgust, but offering help and co-regulation around any disquiet the individual is more likely to remain calm. This calm state and just the right support, can help a traumatised person start to understand and empathise with their own experience. This empathy for themselves over time enables reflection about their own experiences and responses. Having an ally reduces the risks of shame and enables more reflective thinking.

Supporting empathy for the self

In creating clarity for their experience, the adults around the person with an intellectual disability will enable them to feel less muddled, but also enable some reflection on these experiences. This pattern of making sense of, and holding, an empathetic view for someone else's experience will need to be repeated many times to help an individual internalise the experience of empathy, and to consolidate their understanding of their own experience.

These interactions with some people with an intellectual disability might be less about words and much more focused on gentleness of gaze, tone of voice, and repeatedly following safe predictable routines, for example, around personal care. The repetition of routine and safety of response can in themselves be orienting, and enable the person receiving such care to better understand their reactions, their responses and why they might be scared.

We first need to support a trauma experienced person to make sense of, or have compassion for, their own experience before expecting they can develop empathy for another. For this reason, it is helpful to avoid moving too quickly to asking someone with an intellectual disability to consider other people's perspectives (e.g. avoid focusing or turning to questions like "How would you feel if....?"). Within a trusting relationship a carer can teach the child or adult about their reactions; what that face change means or what a certain tone of voice means. Over time, a carer can help decipher the world around the person who previously might have felt confused by their own and others' reactions.

It will, at all times, be useful to consider whether the use of Social Stories might assist with these PACE-based conversations.

Assessing for signs of lower empathy and reflection

Immediate caregivers

- Blaming the child or adult with an intellectual disability.
- Showing signs of blocked care.
- Relying on pathways or contracts/agreements rather than talking about connection or coregulation.
- Adults around the person with an intellectual disability are sounding and looking busier but not spending a lot of time in lower-key activities.

Support networks

- Wanting to protect the immediate caregivers, including ending placements.
- Using a critical voice towards the immediate caregivers.
- Focusing on systems and pathways – discussing objectives, service level agreements contracts etc.

The wider system

- Focusing on systems and pathways – discussing objectives, service level agreements contracts etc.
- Service re-organisation or re-structure to improve service delivery.

Supervision to assist reflection

DDP-practice would recommend access to supervision and consultation to help develop an understanding of the experiences of the staff team or parents, and the person with an intellectual disability. By first making sense of the experience of the adults in the network around the focused individual, we can ensure that their experience can be fully explored. If we move too quickly to solutions and strategies, we not only miss the chance to bring support and coherence to the experience of the carers, but we likely miss an opportunity to better understand and reflect on the experience of the individual at the heart of the discussion/concern. Often, when services move to action and strategy, this can move us away from connection and reflection.

Level 5: Resilience and resources

Previously held core beliefs of being bad and unlovable, are now challenged within safe, trusting relationships. The experience of being treated with love and care, being respected and valued will be more powerful than reassuring words. Over time, one's sense of self changes with increasing self-esteem and resilience to better manage future challenges.

Assessing for signs that a person with an intellectual disability needs support with developing their resilience and resources

- Depending on others for comfort and emotional regulation.
- Reluctance to start or finish activities.
- Expressing doubts about being able to do something.
- Handing over things to another person rather than giving it a go.
- Chameleon-like changes – depending on who is in the room/who is the latest best friend as a way of fitting in or being like someone else because they don't have a clear sense of themselves and their worth.

Supportive steps to develop resilience and resources

Clarifying the challenges

To develop resilience, we need to be clear about the challenges someone experiences first. In assessing the needs and experiences we will develop a much more relevant and attuned plan, based on a clearer formulation. Within an empathetic and respectful relationship, drawing on a PACE-based attitude, and the approaches within DDP, it is feasible to track what is currently hard or confusing. In naming and clarifying the challenges together, and when working in partnership, the person with an intellectual disability can be offered co-regulation at times of challenge. Often, a carer or parent will need to be aware of the level of challenge that the person with intellectual disability can cope with and make this very achievable. It can be helpful to consider someone's learning style, whether this is kinaesthetic, visual or verbal. Using a position of curiosity and maybe needing to 'talk for' or 'talk about' the challenge can also be vital when identifying pressures. A curious stance and talking for the person with them can help explore and clarify the challenges for carers and the person with an intellectual disability.

Increasing engagement and success

We can increase engagement and improve self-esteem using approaches such as backward chaining. This technique is commonly considered in supporting someone with an intellectual disability as it allows an individual to start with and learn the final steps in a routine to help them experience immediate success and build self-confidence. In understanding how to both scaffold or structure an activity so that it is more achievable we increase self-efficacy. Also, talking about the experiences, challenges and skills needed, an individual can feel they have an ally in a new endeavour, and this is also reinforced during the process. Again, a lot of repetition is needed to consolidate a skill or to develop a sense of confidence; often, the concern about 'failing' is hard to erode, and the individual will need acceptance and empathy for beliefs about not being good enough. These ideas are relevant in helping someone to recognise their affective experience and how to cope with their feelings and how to rely on others for support. Sometimes, a carer or parent won't time their support or guidance just right which can trigger a rupture to the trust in the relationship. When relational ruptures occur, it is so helpful to offer repair to re-connect and rebuild trust. In focusing on the priorities for the person with an intellectual disability, we increase the likelihood of engagement, and by building in fun or connection, we can increase regulation during a challenge.

Being responsive to needs changing

It is also useful to remember that being able to use the support on a higher level in the Pyramid of Need does not mean the earlier issues of support are resolved. Trauma recovery can be a very active process and it's about being attuned and responsive to the presenting needs at the time.

It can be a helpful part of an assessment process to consider what needs will be triggered by an individual's current demands, environment, the people present or other stressors (such as upcoming reviews, contact with birth families or others moving on from the placement).

Assessing for signs of depleted resilience and resourcefulness

Immediate caregivers

- Feeling they have run out of ideas and have already tried everything.
- Talking about 'nothing works'.
- Increased sense of responsibility and worry that they alone are responsible for resolving things.
- Deterioration in mood: signs of depression, anxiety, difficulty sleeping, weight loss etc.
- Reduction in self-care.

Support networks

- Reducing access to services by narrowing the range or number of people they can support or include within a service.
- Recommending that the person with an intellectual disability would be better suited to another environment/support setting.

The wider system

- Rigidity of focus that often leads to a lack of flexibility or refusal to incorporate new research or evidence into guidelines.

In better understanding the experiences of those offering immediate care, or in more peripheral systems, we can again use a DDP approach to offer co-regulation and support during these more overwhelming experiences. DDP- practice enables a more empathetic and reflective stance, which will enable those in the system to not just feel more regulated, but which, in turn, will facilitate higher order processing. When we draw on the skills in the 'upstairs' brain systems, we can draw on the skills across the whole cortex. In enabling people in the systems to share, listen and collaborate with their partners/colleagues or friends they will feel less isolated. From this perspective, people are better placed to be able to develop creative approaches to dilemmas or challenges. When broader systems stop feeling resilient, there might be huge political changes such as those that in the past have led to more institutional care, or those that trigger a change of government.

Level 6: Explore trauma and mourn losses

6

Explore trauma, mourn losses

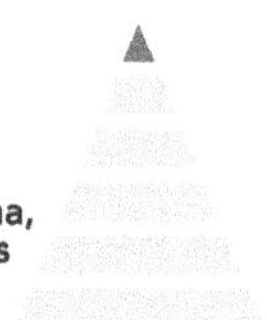

All preceding levels of need as described in the Pyramid model will likely be met, in the main, and in the moment, for someone to be ready to make sense of their traumatic experiences. By making sense of the trauma, the earlier layers of need will, in turn, each be strengthened. As people can make sense of their experiences, integrate their current experiences with the past, they are more likely to have a stronger and more coherent sense of themselves and are less likely to need to draw on self-protective strategies. It is important to assess when is the right time to move into processing trauma as it can be complicated at best, and re-traumatising at worst, to explore events and memories when earlier needs have not been met.

Assessing for signs that an individual needs support around processing trauma and loss

- Repeated mention of memories or flashbacks.
- Questions about why certain events happened to them in particular.
- Lots of fact-finding questions such as who, what, why and when.
- Reliving events as if they are happening today, but tolerating co-regulation and support to make sense of their reactions.
- Struggling with key anniversaries.
- Identifying feelings of sadness or panic and being open to and listening to others about triggers or underlying pressures that lead to these feelings.

Supportive steps to help explore trauma and mourn loss

For those with a trauma or complex relational history, it can be helpful to continue to employ a DDP-focused approach, such as including key attachment figures in therapeutic work. The move at this point can include more traditional therapeutic approaches to help someone process the trauma memories and experiences of loss. This might include Eye Movement Desensitisation-Reprocessing (EMDR) or trauma-focused Cognitive Behavioural Therapy (CBT). These interventions will be delivered PACEfully with all DDP principles helpful to supporting the individual in this work. DDP is an approach that blends well with other interventions, bringing a relational and attachment-focused dimension to the work. Both these approaches have been adapted for use with less profound intellectual disabilities: see Kroese *et al* (2016) work around trauma-focused CBT and Schipper-Eindhoven *et al's* (2024) recent review of the use and adaptations needed for EMDR with people with an intellectual disability.

Assessing for signs in the network for the need to process trauma or loss

Immediate caregivers

- Repeated mention of memories or flashbacks.
- Reliving events as if they are happening today.
- Struggling with key anniversaries.
- Identifying feelings of sadness or panic.
- Having limited time and energy to be able to focus on the person with an intellectual disability.

Support networks

- Disengagement from, or rejection to, working with the immediate caregivers or person with an intellectual disability.

Wider systems

- Avoidance of the issue.

When the immediate and wider networks supporting individuals with intellectual disabilities experience trauma or loss, they too require care and support to effectively provide the care needed. If caregivers or systems around vulnerable individuals become overwhelmed and enter a survival state, they may struggle to recognise their own challenges. In such cases, safeguarding processes may need to be initiated if trauma and loss render families or systems unable to provide good enough care.

Ideally, this safeguarding process would allow key attachment figures, services, or agencies within the wider care system to reflect on their need for support and work toward regaining their capacity for providing safety, relationships and co-regulation.

For those experiencing vicarious or secondary trauma related to relational trauma, it is crucial to:

- Make sense of their experience.
- Seek additional practical help when necessary (such as respite).
- Address any blocks in care caused by the emotional impact of caring for or living alongside someone with a trauma history.

A reflective and accepting system, guided by the principles of DDP, can acknowledge the impact of trauma and loss, increasing the likelihood of recognising the impact of trauma, enabling it to identify and address its own support needs.

- Within families, this may involve arranging additional respite care to support caregivers.
- In schools, it could mean reorganising learning support time.
- In residential or staff settings, increased supervision or working in pairs may provide the necessary support.

By recognising and addressing these needs, the system can better equip itself to care for both the person with an intellectual disability and those supporting them.

Conclusion

In conclusion, addressing the complex needs of individuals with intellectual disabilities, in a DDP framework, is facilitated by Kim Golding's Pyramid of Need, as it allows a structured approach to thinking about a person's current needs and how to enable progress. This model summarises what type of care is needed to increase feeling safe, help develop trusted relationships and offer nurturing co-regulation. Meeting these needs in turn enables the development of empathy and reflection, resilience and resources and, finally, means that the exploration of mourning associated with trauma can start.

Each person's needs depend on a variety of factors and variables. In each area or description of need, we have tried to outline approaches or considerations to bear in mind for someone with an intellectual disability and their caregivers, and the wider system. When caregivers face their own traumas or losses, or feelings of shame or lack of safety, they may struggle to implement the suggestions here and can experience blocks in care, which can compromise their ability to provide effective support. Each network around the traumatised individual will have a direct bearing on the support available to the traumatised individual. The Pyramid of Need can provide a helpful framework to pitch our intervention at the right level, according to need, and signpost us to corresponding DDP-informed intervention to ensure that both individuals with intellectual disability and their caregivers are equipped to navigate challenges and make meaningful relational developments.

Chapter 12: Dyadic Developmental Psychotherapy

Summary

- Dyadic Developmental Psychotherapy (DDP) is the approach that was developed by Dan Hughes to support and deepen connection between parents and their children, where those children have experienced attachment trauma. This therapeutic approach has been adapted for use with birth children, and for use with children alone, or for just parent (or carer) focused work. The purpose of DDP is to build and support connection and so the approaches used are not formulaic but drawn on in response to the presenting needs and challenges.
- We have provided a brief outline of the process that is often followed when offering therapy; the preparation needed and when to make the work dyadic (between the vulnerable person and their attachment figure) and when we just offer DDP-informed parenting support (DDP-parenting).
- Our experience is that we can support people with an intellectual disability with this model; and found it to be an effective way to strengthen the relationships of children or adults with an intellectual disability with their key attachment figures. We share some of the adaptations we have found useful in this work.
- This outline does not and cannot replicate the skills that are learned in the initial training and then developed during the practicum. We would recommend that this approach is only offered by those who have undertaken the first part of training AND actively accessing DDP supervision.

Introduction

This chapter might be of interest to qualified DDP practitioners who feel less familiar with offering support to people with an intellectual disability, or those familiar with supporting people with an intellectual disability and newer to DDP. For those working in services for people with an intellectual disability, the general ideas around therapy adaptations might feel familiar. It is not the intention, in this chapter, to teach or provide a complete overview of approaches that will already be familiar to those working in intellectual disability services. Where additional information is needed for those less familiar with these approaches, we hope to provide some insight in this chapter and also encourage liaison with colleagues in intellectual disability services and with those who know the person well.

People with an intellectual disability are clearly not a homogenous group: there is as much diversity within a group of people with an intellectual disability as there is in any other group. The core principles within DDP do, however, make it an entirely appropriate model for supporting people with an intellectual disability. At the heart of DDP is the intention to build a better understanding between people and by making sense of their experience we can support healing from trauma. The adaptations needed to use DDP to support people with an intellectual disability often sound small or 'doable' and there isn't a prescribed way of offering DDP when working with someone with an intellectual disability; as ever, it's a process of connection.

In this chapter we draw on our experience of working with children and adults with an intellectual disability. Where there are specific considerations for adults these have been drawn out.

This chapter outlines how an assessment for dyadic therapy might begin and be undertaken, and who might be involved and what the process might entail. It moves on to think about the role of parents and carers and how they can be enabled to better understand their connections and relational patterns with the person they are caring for. Finally, an overview of the areas and adaptations for dyadic therapy with people with intellectual disabilities are given.

Reminder of the core approaches in DDP

Figure 12.1 Capturing the approaches available within DDP-based work

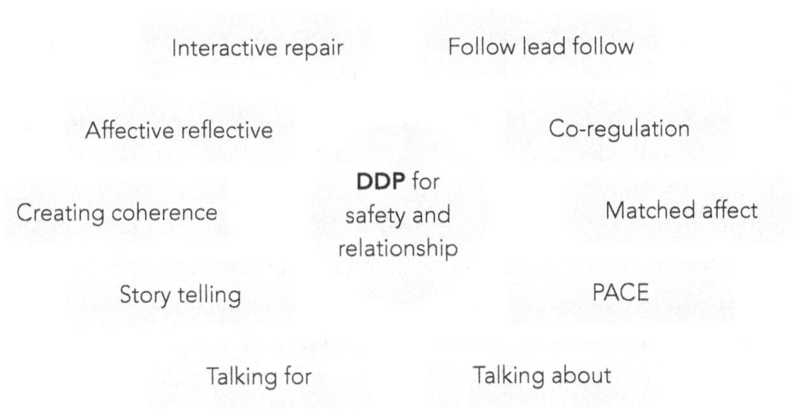

Is it the right time for Dyadic Developmental Psychotherapy?

A trauma-informed assessment will help identify the presence of early trauma, following which, consideration can be given to determine if it might be appropriate to offer DDP through family focused therapeutic work or maybe focus on DDP-informed parenting (DDP-parenting) or prioritise helping the network (DDP-practice), or maybe a combination of these. Too often, these decisions will likely depend on the resourcing available in a service, but for the purposes of this chapter we will consider what the process might look like for therapeutic work. DDP is founded on attachment theory and the theory of intersubjective connection. Both of these theories help outline how safety is created for newborns and how relationships are central in all aspects of a child's development. DDP was developed as a way of creating safety and building connections for children who struggled to trust, because they experienced early gaps in care, adverse childhood experiences, or had parents who were unable to meet their needs. This therapy enables attachment figures around either a child or adult, to better understand the patterns within their relationship, to make sense of any mistrust and to discover the best ways for the person with an intellectual disability to experience co-regulation. In building a strong connection that attunes to the developmental needs of the person in front of them, parents or carers can start to help make sense for, and with, the vulnerable person of their current and past experiences. This process of co-regulation and co-creation of meaning rebuilds trust and enhances safety, and helps individuals to make sense of past traumas while helping them revise their view of themselves. In facilitating safety and in improving connection and regulation we can support reflection, learning and problem solving.

Assessment

Consent around assessments

It will be important to consider whether those you are offering an assessment to are in agreement with the idea of you learning about their past, talking with key people in their lives and that your focus is relational. The explanation about this assessment approach needs to be shared carefully, so that all can fully consent to the idea of better understanding what works, and what hinders, their relationships. This model is very different to many people's previous experience of an assessment, therapy or support, as rather than considering ways to manage or change behaviour, or developing skills for independence, the focus will be on relationships instead. The assessment process relies on a PACE based attitude and requires flexibility as each relationship is unique. The assessment process is about the relationship between people and so the relational trauma is expressed in slightly different ways in each relationship.

The process of assessing capacity to make decisions about accessing an assessment or therapy relies, in part, on access to the right information, and it can take time to make a decision. It is feasible that any child or adult may decline a relational-focused assessment or dyadic therapeutic meetings.

Assessment process

Attachment and relational assessments can be structured in a variety of ways. Ideally, the following three perspectives will provide a clearer sense of the relational dynamics and to help detect the impact of past trauma on current relationships:

Caregivers only/background information

There are advantages to having some time during the assessment process to meet with the key adults around a person with intellectual disability, as this can provide a deeper insight into the relational pressures within the system/family/service. Having this meeting away from the referred person also ensures that you reduce the risk of relational rupture that can be caused by sharing their concerns directly in front of each other.

Caregiver and person with intellectual disability together

It is helpful to organise some time with the referred person and their key family members or closest members of staff. This time enables observation of the current relational dynamics and tensions.

Person with intellectual disability only

It would also be valuable to have time with the person with an intellectual disability to understand their interests and worries and to also clarify their wishes regarding accessing any future therapy. As above, this individual meeting enables them to talk more freely, if needed, about the people who are providing their care.

When offering a relational focused assessment, we are both wanting to observe the existing patterns that emerge without our intervention, but to also note the advantages in drawing on all the key aspects of DDP (shown in Figure 12.1) to inform and enrich our understanding of the presenting patterns. We start with an attitude or approach that is PACEful (Playful, Accepting, Curious and Empathetic). Assessments make some people anxious and so holding a more playful or lighter approach is likely to help others to relax. In offering curiosity, acceptance and empathy, we are more likely to build an accurate picture of their shared experience. We might be able to better identify and build coherence about the systems that work and don't work within relationships, when we talk for, or talk about, their relationship and worries in the moments they feel stuck. In building a coherent story about what interrupts their connection, or in truly accepting and being curious about what they might find upsetting, we can co-create an accurate formulation.

Meeting with the key carers: background information

Prior to meeting for a relational assessment, or observations of the interactions between the dyad, it can be helpful to first talk with the current (and even previous) attachment figures. This meeting enables us to set up the rest of the assessment in the most helpful way.

Carer concerns

It can be helpful to hear from the parents/carers about any current difficulties and successes within their relationship. These conversations do not happen in front of the person with an intellectual disability, to allow carers to talk freely, a space for carers to describe their worries and fears, to talk about the difficult things that are occurring and to describe how hard they might be finding things. In offering this time we can ensure that we do not add to relationship tensions or risk triggering shame for the person with an intellectual disability.

Therapy practicalities

We can also use this time to consider some practical and organisational issues such as, in an ideal world, when is the better time of day to offer meetings, what is the general flow of the week and is there a day to avoid, because it clashes with work, a favourite day at school, or is only used for shopping trips etc. It is important to respect that a change of routine can be particularly challenging for people with an intellectual disability. We can also learn if there are certain activities and interests that the carers already know are needed for regulation. Typically, this includes learning their special interests, and how a 'best day' might be created. This also includes discovering favourite things such as drinks and snacks, and maybe the fiddle toys or sensory resources, such as a big bean bag or rug to hide under during meetings. All of this knowledge will help you to engage someone in therapy by offering soothing, regulating or interesting activities and in being aware of their possible interests.

We can also consider adaptations around known sensory processing difficulties such as lighting, or sensitivities to certain sounds. It can help to know in advance if someone is likely to need to move a lot during their meeting with you. When you have choices about where to meet, this information will help to select the best environment and when there are no alternatives, you will be able to factor in the variables that might be influencing your assessment.

It is also helpful to learn about someone's attentional focus, as setting up a meeting for two hrs of direct talking could be highly aversive and reduce the likelihood of ever meeting again! On a practical note, it is also important to learn, if it's not already been shared, whether any communication tools or aids are needed, and to make sure you are familiar with each person's system.

Case vignette: Mairwen

In setting up my meeting for Mairwen, I learned from her carers Dee and Saeran, that Mairwen found it hard to cope with significant auditory distraction. We spent some time sitting in the two rooms we could use, in order to plan which would provide a better setting for any meetings. When we sat in silence together for a few moments, we noticed that one room had a clock with a quiet but audible tick on the second hand. Also, this room with the 'noisy' clock was next to a main corridor and the general footfall was, we anticipated, likely to cause distraction with the sounds. We also discussed it might add to the worries Mairwen has of being overheard.

We considered the lighting in the quieter room and Dee and Saeran shared that they were both fairly light sensitive and let me know that the overhead lighting was going to be really distracting and hard work for them. I suggested I borrow some lamps that provided softer lighting for the times when we met together in future.

I learned that the range of snacks and drinks that Mairwen liked were considerable but they could change on the day and so Dee and Saeran suggested they gather together the right things in readiness for a meeting.

I also learned that Mairwen's temperature control was not well developed and she might become very cold when thinking about important but difficult or sad things. I offered to have a hot water bottle filled and a soft snuggly blanket ready for any such moments.

Case vignette: Ben

Ben is a child who, prior to our meeting, had fortunately had a helpful Sensory Attachment Intervention assessment which highlighted his marked challenges in some of his sensory processing systems: he has significant vestibular and proprioception (balance and body orientation) needs and these systems struggle more when he is feeling dysregulated and hyperaroused. What his family and school have noticed is that he benefits from having deep muscle pressure to help him feel orientated or grounded. When Ben doesn't have access to this type of support he is more likely to kick out, or grab at or throw things with his hands, as this helps him to better organise and know where his limbs are in the moment. Ben also struggles to sit still and sit upright and often will flop out on a sofa and lie out on the floor.

His parents agreed that I would ask Ben to help me to move the furniture around in the room before we sat down – the reason for this is to provide some deep proprioceptive input that will assist with general regulation. I also suggested we could include a yoga ball as he likes it when his parents roll this up his body to help him feel regulated. We ensured that there was enough space for Ben to move and lie out somewhere, and his parents agreed to bring in his swivel cushion. They bought some Theraputty and selected which soft, silent, fidget toys we should have available in the room.

Building a trauma-nurture timeline

As part of the assessment process, it will be helpful to have access to key reports and previous assessments that provide an overview of current needs, strengths and challenges that the person with an intellectual disability experiences. From the outset, it can be valuable to track interruptions that might have occurred in their sensory or emotional development and identify whether there are indications of relational trauma (covered in Chapter 4: Intersubjective connection, Chapter 5: Attachment theory and Chapter 6: Neuroscience). An attachment-focused perspective will enable consideration of the support available during pivotal moments such as key life events. Understanding early histories, including in utero experiences, can be particularly informative when populating a trauma-nurture timeline. This timeline helps us consider interruptions to developing systems and also helps us better learn about their experience of safety.

As part of this timeline, it can be useful to understand a family's reaction to having a child with an intellectual disability, learning about the age at which a child was diagnosed, whether the family had experience in supporting someone with an intellectual disability, and considering the impact of separations during any medical procedures. It can be helpful to know whether respite was available and if so, whether the family were able to access this and how often. How did their child respond to time away from them? This perspective can enrich our assessment and broaden a formulation that enables us to better understand their experience – positive and negative – of being cared for from the outset. This timeline is not developed to be shared, but to contribute to a formulation and, in therapy, could assist with building coherence for the story of a person's experience.

Questionnaires and screening tools

We have created a list, likely not exhaustive, of some of the available tools that we have noted that help us to understand the sensory and emotional needs of the individual being referred (see Appendix 7). In addition, each service will need to consider what measures they have available to capture the wellbeing of the parents and carers involved. These tools can be used to help deepen our understanding both about the individuals involved and also the relational patterns.

To create a clear formulation or sense of coherence about possible relational trauma, we would encourage use of tools or direct observations that:

1. Focus on the experience and perspective of the carers
2. Hold a focus on the experience of the child or adult
3. Capture the patterns existing within the dyad of the carer and person with intellectual disability

Dyadic assessment

Practical factors

It can make a difference to someone's engagement to share information in an accessible format that provides pictures or a video of yourself, the rooms you will use or what the building looks like. Some people have a fear or worry about specific rooms (often the toilet) and so knowing more about all areas can help reduce anxiety. From the outset, it is important to provide a clear structure and clarify why you are meeting altogether. Sometimes, you might even need to structure things so that you help them work out where they might sit, or how they can move about in order to feel more relaxed. Making things explicit and creating clear boundaries can help manage anxiety around the meeting.

Attuned communication

As with all work with someone with a cognitive impairment, the language used throughout needs to tune into and be accessible to all in the room. However, it is important that simplified language does not lead to a simplification of the nuance or the range of affective or relational complexities experienced by someone with an intellectual disability. As is common with other therapeutic approaches, it is likely that the use of metaphor may be confusing or distracting.

Usually, it is helpful to avoid questions that rely on a well-developed theory of mind, such as asking someone to consider how they would respond to a friend who disclosed similar, upsetting childhood experiences, or "How would you feel if someone spoke to you like that?", or even "What did your parents think of that?" At the start of a meeting, it can be more beneficial to ask questions that only require a "yes" or "no" type response, to reduce the cognitive demand needed when reflecting or in the process of word finding. Sometimes it can help to collaborate and draw on paper to support or illustrate elements of conversations, as it allows simplification, clarity and can help slow the pace of conversation. We would encourage you to take your time and ensure that full use is made of communication boards, photos or video clips to help someone know who you are talking about or to ensure you are learning about the important people or places in their lives. Finding ways to learn about or even engage in someone's interests can be a helpful part of the assessment process. A DDP based approach enables us to follow another's interests, accept and explore their experience, as well as offering support in order to bring coherence or the story together about what you have learned. It will be helpful to check that you are using the right words or making sense to the other person. In these exploratory conversations, you might explore what happens if you describe something for someone (talking for) and then ask if your idea or words sound right: *"I have made a guess about this, sometimes my guesses will be wrong, and sometimes they might be right – how is this guess?"* We notice that even during the assessment process, when we are identifying pressures or worries, we are starting to build a relationship and connection. The pace or rate of the overall conversation will also need to be attuned to all in the room, as it might be that the person with an intellectual disability needs more time to process or consider things than others might assume.

Example: An introductory meeting with a family

Therapist: Hi Kenyl. It's great to meet you. Hi Angus and Alex, it's good to see you again. Follow me into this room and sit where you like on the sofa.

Angus and Alex: Hi Nic. We are pleased to be here.

Therapist: I've brought in a drink and some biscuits, Kenyl – this is what your Dads said you might like today.

Therapist: *Using a lot of non-verbal communication (leaning forward and with a warm smile on my face) I will take time to talk to Kenyl and his parents.* It's great to meet you, Kenyl. I wonder though, do you know why we are meeting today? *Leave time for Kenyl to answer.*

Therapist: *After a pause when Angus and Alex are looking at Kenyl expectantly, I will likely start talking.* Your parents might have said before, but I can say again. We are meeting so that I can learn more about your family *(gesturing to all of them).* I want to learn what you like doing, and what doesn't work well in your family. Does this sound ok?

Kenyl: *Shrugs.*

Therapist: Hey Alex and Angus, I guess this might feel like a lot. Maybe if you and I talk a bit, Kenyl, we can see if this plan feels ok?

Alex: That's ok with us. We have explained why we are meeting today already but go ahead.

Therapist: Oh, that's helpful and maybe a reminder will also help us a bit here. Kenyl might be feeling quiet right now because there is a lot to notice. Kenyl might need to be taking in the sights and sounds of the room – checking where the windows are, where the doors lead, noticing the colours in the room and also what the sofa feels like *(point as you talk)*. These things are important. Have I got that right Kenyl – you are having a look around the room right now? My questions maybe need to slow down?

Kenyl: *Smiles at this last comment.*

Therapist: Kenyl, sometimes I might talk too fast or for too long *(using gestures to mimic this)*. I will try to get this right for all of you. Will you and your parents let me know if I do that?

Kenyl: *Nods a lot.*

Therapist: How will you let me know – shall we come up with a face or a hand signal?

Kenyl and the Therapist explore silly faces they might make for a while! Ok, this is the face we will use. Great.

If you've done some room noticing, shall I talk a bit more? Kenyl, we are meeting so that I can get to know you. I want to learn about your lives together. What you like and what you don't like. Is that ok?

If you've done some room noticing, shall I talk a bit more? Kenyl, we are meeting so that I can get to know you. I want to learn about your lives together. What you like and what you don't like. Is that ok?

Kenyl: Yes.

The assessment will help us to clarify whether there is any likelihood of interrupted care or early trauma experiences, and consider whether these are impacting on current, everyday life and relationships. We can draw on the Pyramid of Need assessment matrix (see Chapter 11) to help us identify the current needs for the person with an intellectual disability, their carers and wider support network. In learning about the impact of trauma and status of current relationships, we can better understand whether carers are experiencing blocked care, or whether a broader system of support is needed. The assessment process will also ideally deepen everyone's understanding of the person with an intellectual disability's sensory and emotional development. Often, we find that the process of a relational assessment and creating a trauma-informed formulation can improve understanding and can alter attitudes and expectations. When an assessment is founded in an attitude of PACE, we can offer a non-judgemental and considered view of the experiences and pressures, for both the carers, and the person with an intellectual disability. A relational assessment can offer an alternative narrative for people with an intellectual disability, as they stop being the referred or 'problem' person and so are not so tied to a process that can be potentially shaming or where they collect more labels or judgements. Instead, offering a relational perspective changes (and reduces) the focus from an individual towards the system.

Feedback after the assessment

In our experience, it has been important to share a summary of the information learnt during the assessment, particularly for young people and adults. This is often completed by creating a report with images and pictures that summarise the issues that are difficult, and the areas that are going well. Some people prefer a verbal description or will need it modelled out, or recorded in a way the person can listen to again. Identifying the correct medium to use will be a part of the assessment process.

When describing the relational aspect to the work, our experience is that many adults with an intellectual disability have been a little confused, but relieved to learn that they haven't done something wrong. There is an important ethical decision to be made when planning for the future for those who struggle with taking turns, impulse control or who find future planning hard; knowing how much to share and when, will likely be informed by those that know the person with an intellectual disability the best, and by your own assessment.

The assessment will indicate whether the traditional therapy model would be introduced, or if DDP-parenting alone might be more suitable. Again, consent for either approach is essential.

Therapy

The traditional DDP therapy process

If, following a relational and trauma-informed assessment, it was identified that family focused DDP is appropriate, the first step is then to set up a meeting for parents/carers. These parent or carer meetings are needed before moving to dyadic meetings, which would include the child or adult with an intellectual disability. Thereafter, parenting meetings continue to be included alongside the dyadic family focused meetings with the aim of supporting parents or carers to move away from traditional parenting approaches into more therapeutic parenting support. The extent and duration of parenting- or carer-focused meetings is adapted to suit the needs of those joining the meetings. We would recommend that DDP is only provided by those who have at least completed Level 1 training and are also accessing DDP supervision (see Training and Supervision section for details).

Therapeutic parenting/caring and readiness for dyadic therapy

Before any dyadic work can commence with a person with an intellectual disability, it is vital to offer support and time for their key attachment figures so that they are regulated and feel fully oriented to this way of reflecting and talking together. From the outset, the focus is on ensuring they feel safe, and able to be open about their experiences with the therapists. Many carers might, at first, feel confused with the model, possibly expecting a list of strategies or approaches to try at home. Often, time is needed to explore this therapeutic model to ensure it continues to feel relevant for all. We are also aware that the carers' experience, and ways of supporting the person with an intellectual disability, might not have been trauma-informed. Hughes (2011) acknowledges three key assumptions in the DDP model: that parents are good people; they are aiming to offer their best care; and they have a genuine desire to love their children. Our experiences in child and adult services for people with intellectual disabilities echo these assumptions and whilst carers may be offering approaches which do not align with DDP, but they are motivated to provide good and protective care to the person with an intellectual disability.

For many people, a part of the focus during these meetings will be to help make sense of the trauma that the person with an intellectual disability has experienced and consider, together, how this impacts on their current presentation. There is a psycho-educational aspect to this discussion, depending on how aware carers might be about trauma in general. Aspects of these discussions might include information about the neuroscientific models, or theories about the development of attachment security or intersubjective connection.

Alongside information sharing and checking, it is also important to clarify how living with someone with complex needs is impacting on the parents' and carers' health and well-being. Often, this type of care has a significant impact on the time and energy carers have available for their hobbies, or to just spend time together; many parents we meet rarely sit down together and often note that the DDP-parenting meetings are the first time in the week when they've had an uninterrupted conversation.

Regardless of other's opinions, there can for many key attachment figures, be moments of self-doubt, self-criticism or even resentment triggered in caring for someone with complex needs. In building a clearer picture of each carer's attachment history, or their expectations of family life or work in a care setting, we can better understand their own internal working model (see Chapter 4: Intersubjective connections) and beliefs about themselves and how they perceive or value their role. We can learn how far away their original hopes and dreams are from their current lived experience. Gaining a deeper understanding of the parent or carer's perspective helps us attune to their needs and builds trust and connection, but can also enable them to reflect with you around the impact of various pressures on their relationship with the person with an intellectual disability.

When we make time to understand the emotional impact of the care they are offering we can learn how family life (or working alongside people with relational trauma) is different to what they originally imagined, based on their previous experience of parenting of siblings/caring for others. They might reflect how different their lives are compared with their friends, or the issues in this residential setting differ from the previous one. Such a discussion can enable consideration about the isolation that intellectual disability can or has brought to their lives, and how they might be feeling about the care they are offering. It is also important, within DDP, to explore carers' own attachment histories and, in particular, to learn about their previous experiences of being cared for, whether they have previously been in a caring role and whether they had prior knowledge of supporting people with an intellectual disability. Each person's attachment history or parented experience will shape and inform their approach to caring for someone else. This will also inform their perceptions and self-judgement about how 'well' they perceive they are doing as a carer, and how they cope and understand during any moments when they might worry they are not doing such a great job. When we offer true acceptance for any biases, concerns or worries, we can offer more meaningful support. This deeper and co-created understanding of their perspective equips us to help people reflect on how their own attachment patterns interact with the person they care for.

To consider

Below are some questions about parent/carer's attachment histories, inspired by Seigel and Hartzell (2014). Building an attachment history might include learning about the following:

- Who was in your family when you were growing up and what was it like?
- How did you get along with your parents when you were little – were you closer to one person when you were small and do you know why that was?
- Were you ill as a young baby or later on? How was that dealt with or talked about much later on?
- Who did you go to for comfort and care when you were hurt or upset?
- Who would you celebrate with and what did that look like?
- Were you ever threatened and did you ever experience life-threatening or changing experiences?
- How were you told off or how did you learn you'd done something wrong?
- Were you ever separated from your parents?
- Was there anyone else around who you would turn to for support/care?
- What was your experience, when you were growing up, of spending time with people with an intellectual disability? Did that change at all before you had your own family?

Sometimes, extended families are ill-equipped to help parents care for the child or adult in the family with an intellectual disability. Sometimes, it can be grandparents, aunts or cousins who are judgemental/critical about the care provided. Other times, these people can be cheerleaders and offer invaluable care and respite. In therapeutic work we need to understand the current context and the history of those providing direct care. Sometimes, the support that is available comes with tension and complexity, such as offering a perspective that isn't so trauma or developmentally attuned. These tensions are helpful to understand, as this is the context in which parents or carers operate, and changing parenting patterns can trigger considerable anxiety or hostility across these important extended networks.

When we offer our focus to caregivers, we endeavour to fully accept their experience of caring, the highs and lows. In joining those conversations, in wanting to learn more and explore their experience and pressures, we might need to hold in mind their experience for them; to talk for, build the story and build coherence around their highs and lows. We need to offer true acceptance of their experience which might include naming the complex or ugly feelings that can be triggered by feeling responsible for another. In establishing a safe and empathetic therapeutic relationship we can allow these feelings to be identified. The relief in this process can be significant, especially when we can make sense of their experience or reaction. In building coherence for, and about, their experience, we can address any feelings of shame that might have arisen. These enquiring steps would be considered in DDP meetings for all carer-focused time, but it is important to also address their unique experience of caring for someone with a significant cognitive impairment where changing and learning might be slower. Carers might doubt whether they are having sufficient impact and worry for the future. When supporting parents with a PACE-based attitude, in helping them out when they are stuck for words, we can help them to explore their worries, to consider and reflect on the impact of their experiences, to describe how complex their lives are and to share their worries about the future for them and the child or adult they care for. A DDP approach offers coherence for their experience and builds the story together about their lives and current concerns or celebrations. When working within a DDP model, the aim is not just for them to experience support around their situation, but also to experience what might happen to their reflective capacity when they are in a connected, attuned relationship. They will have an embodied experience of the model, which will inform their understanding of what their child or adult with an intellectual disability will experience within dyadic meetings; they will also have a model upon which to draw for their own interactions at home.

When working with someone with an intellectual disability it can be very complicated to state opinions or share feelings that we are guessing we 'shouldn't' be experiencing. Caregiving does bring joy, and for many there is a high degree of pleasure, which must be celebrated. However, this doesn't negate the need to be able to share an honest range of reactions arising from this care. In the wider community, parents, foster carers, or staff teams may be told they are 'angels' or 'saints', which is intended to be supportive praise, but it is potentially silencing. How can a parent or member of staff turn around in response to that and share a tough day?

Many caregivers also work in circumstances where there can be long waits for services, or they have access to services or systems that are fundamentally stretched and might not provide the planned backup. Society can also be distancing, and many parents and carers who care for people with high levels of complex disability can experience discrimination and prejudice. In the next chapters, we further explore the risk of hate crime towards people with an intellectual disability and the associated worries and risks for their carers. At times, parents and carers can worry that they are asking for too much and try to work harder to fill gaps in the systems around them. At other times, the need to navigate the complex care systems and bureaucracies can deplete energy, and disrupt the parent or carer's ability to feel regulated (Challenging Behaviour Foundation, 2021). Sometimes, we need to explore the types of barriers that might be interrupting their ability to hold a more relational focus.

In slowing or pausing, our focus is drawn away from finding solutions and we create space to understand the pressures carers are facing. By exploring the scripts or judgements they hold about how they 'should' be supporting someone with an intellectual disability, we begin to understand their experiences and concerns more fully. This process allows us to connect with them more deeply, and to accurately co-create the story of their reactions, worries and successes. In naming affective reactions, that can at times lead to shame, we can support their understanding and empathy for their own experience which can lead to more helpful reflection. Capturing such worries and considering any shame experienced is so very helpful, as these are wearing emotions but will also interrupt the connection and relationship with their loved one. Sometimes these self-doubts or breaks in connection are profound and indicate blocked care. When we can make sense of relational blocks, or even of relational trauma, we help the carers to reflect on their reactions and start to better understand how trauma is impacting all their lives. Having a therapist help identify and make sense of these patterns can be incredibly helpful, as it normalises the experience but also gives hope for the route towards a different and improved connection.

Once parents or carers have a clearer understanding of the relational patterns they bring, develop coherence about the dynamics with the person they care for, and are able to be regulated enough, they can start dyadic work. In preparing them for their role in dyadic meetings, we need to prepare them that these meetings will, initially, focus on the perspective of the person with an intellectual disability. The carer's role, at first, will be to support the person with an intellectual disability, whilst the therapist leads an exploration around the themes and issues that the person with an intellectual disability shares.

Becoming a therapeutic parent or therapeutic carer takes time; the traditional approaches no longer apply! In order to support this more therapeutic approach at home, regular parenting/carer meetings will be scheduled, either prior to or in between meetings with the person with an intellectual disability. However, if new patterns or reactions arise or if there are changes in blocked care, additional parenting or care-focused meetings would be reintroduced as needed.

Dyadic therapy meetings

This next section specifically describes how a therapist would position themselves and adhere to DDP approaches within the dyadic therapeutic meetings with the person with an intellectual disability and their parent/carer. Typically, DDP is organised so that the child/adult with an intellectual disability and the key carers will be in the room together. Ideally these meetings need to be regular such as weekly and likely longer term. Making sense of relational trauma and establishing trust is a long-term process. The focus, at the outset, is on the experience of the person with an intellectual disability.

Some people will opt for this model, but not yet be ready for their parents or carers to join them. Where this is their preference, the therapy focus remains relational and the option to include others in the meetings can continue to be explored. When someone declines to access or join therapy meetings themselves, it can be important to direct support to DDP-parenting or DDP-practice.

Taking a lead

Traditionally in DDP, the therapist follows the issues and patterns that emerge during the early conversations between the dyad and therapist. This is the start of the follow-lead-follow approach in DDP. However, someone with an intellectual disability might need help with starting conversations, and it would be realistic to sometimes turn to the parent or carer and see if there are any particular things they might want to share. However, the emerging themes might be more important to the parent/carers than to the child or adult present. It is important to be sensitive to the overwhelming challenge that comes with talking about things on demand, or because it's therapy time right now. The therapist provides the support needed to help them engage with a topic that is relevant to them.

Many people with an intellectual disability work incredibly hard to navigate the social world around them. In general, they will be in the company of people who are more cognitively able, and might have learned, over time, to fit in or become compliant with the demands around them. Whilst this compliance might enable you to cover a list of topics, they might not necessarily be the issues that the person you are working with would like to consider, or they might be wanting to talk about these issues, but not yet. Attuning to, and working at, the individual's pace is important to maintain trust, but also to facilitate reflection and processing around important issues. A curious stance of checking in will be helpful and might be as simple as: "Is it ok to talk about XX?" or "Is this the thing we need to talk about first? Should it be something different?"

Case vignette: Aisling

Aisling (in her 20s) is joined in a therapy meeting with Nic, by Orla and Oisin who are two keyworkers from her supported tenancy home.

Aisling is playing with the pens and is drawing on some paper. She is not really making eye contact with anyone. The therapist has been talking about how wrapped up they all are in warm jumpers and bright colours which usually engages Aisling, but today Aisling is very quiet.

Orla: Hey Aisling, I think it's time to put the pens down and talk to Nic now.

Oisin: I think that's a good plan, it might be hard but we've got some important things to think about.

Therapist: I notice, Orla and Oisin, that getting going feels quite important for you both today. Ok, let me just do some checking if that's ok? *Moving nearer to Aisling,* So the pens are good? I see the marks they make on paper – you've nearly got a line down for all the pens. *After a while Aisling starts to line the pens up.* All lined up – does that feel or look right? *Aisling nods. She then starts taking things out of her pockets and wants to tell me where they came from.*

Oisin: Aisling, I think we need to talk about you hurting the cat this morning. I know this is hard but Nic will help us.

Therapist: Ah Oisin, I see the pressure for you and I understand that this conversation is really important. Just for now, is it ok if we slow things down a little? What you are describing sounds so important and I don't want to lose that but I might need to get to know how things are more slowly. Is that ok with you both? Hey Aisling, Oisin has some important questions but right now, you are thinking about other things. Is that right?

Aisling: Makes eye contact.

Therapist: These things you've brought with you. They are really great. Can you show me your favourite? *Aisling picks out a fridge magnet her aunt sent her. We then discuss the magnet for a while.* Talking about this magnet is nice, isn't it? *Aisling nods.* Is it better than talking about hard things like the cat? *Aisling nods a bit more.* Ah I see. Would you rather think about the things in your pockets right now or talk about the cat. *Aisling shrugs.* Are you worried you are in trouble?

Aisling: No. I love the cat.

Therapist: Is it hard to know what happened this morning?

Aisling: Yes. I love the cat.

Therapist: So talking about pens or magnets – that is easier?

Aisling: Yes.

Therapist: Is that it? Talking about the cat is too hard?

Aisling: Yes. I don't know how to say what happened. I know about the magnets and pens.

Therapist: Oh, so you don't know where to start, what to say or how to make sense of this morning. I see. Maybe that's a big worry for you? That sounds so hard. You know Orla and Oisin aren't cross but you don't know what to say to them. Shall we work it out together?

Aisling: Yes, that would help.

Indirect communication

You will likely notice how challenging it is for some people with an intellectual disability to continue to focus on a topic once you have started to explore a theme. It is helpful to clarify if this is because it is a sensitive topic, or whether they are just struggling to sustain their attention, or concentrate on one thing, for so long. Making this inquiry helps us to better understand the potential relational pressures (such as how long should a parent/carer try to hold a conversation for) but doesn't make assumptions about why it might be challenging. When we consider ways in which we will be offering co-regulation and connection for an experience, we need to adjust this support, and also the length of our conversation in line with the presenting emotional and developmental needs of the person at the time. When we don't allow time for processing, we can overwhelm the other person. Similarly, when the topic is emotive, we may end up outside of someone's window of tolerance (see Chapter 6: Neuroscience), moving toward dysregulation. Allowing for changes in processing and self-regulation is also important, particularly for those who might struggle to make sense of their affective or interoceptive (bodily) changes themselves. It is important to track all non-verbal communication: to notice changes in attention, the level of engagement, the number or rate at which someone is talking, as well as changes in skin tone or even their skin temperature. These signs provide so much vital information to help inform whether to continue exploring a feeling, a memory or theme, and when it might be time to slow down and move to a topic that is easier to talk about, before leading them back to the main theme again.

The prosody and tone of voice and the types of words we use can also adjust in tune with someone's emotional or developmental presentation in the moment. It can be surprising to observe how much change can occur, in the terms they use and the number of words they might say, but also the type of comfort or help they might need in co-regulation when experiencing distress or upset. In fully accepting or being curious about another person's needs, we are more likely to adjust our lightness of tone, and be able to capture and tell the story of the experience in the most meaningful manner.

Case vignette: Jacob

Jacob has joined a meeting with his foster carers, Jan and Emilia. Jacob tends to agree with and present as very accepting or compliant with the suggestions made. Jacob rarely says no or offers an opinion, but does experience rage and upsets. Jan and Emilia are keen to help Jacob feel more confident to disagree if he wants to and to express an opinion, and are aware that the combination of Jacob's early trauma and intellectual disability likely makes it hard for him to feel confidence in expressing himself.

Therapist: Jacob, when you said you like those crisps I gave you just now, was that right?

Jacob: Yes.

Jan: Oh, I am so surprised by that, Jacob. At home you have the other ones. Have I got that right?

Jacob: YESSS.

Therapist: Oh, so at home when there is a choice it is different. Maybe, here, you are trying to be good? Maybe worrying about keeping me happy? Or maybe you are worried I'll be cross if you don't like my crisps? Can I check: You want it to be ok and calm? *Jacob looks up.* That's a worry. Are you thinking, "I must act happy and ok?" Is it like that? *Jacob nods shyly.* Shall we explain this to Jan and Emilia? Do you want to say or shall I? *Jacob points to the Therapist.* "Jan and Emilia, I don't always know how to say no or no thank you. I worry about those words. So I say yes to keep everyone happy". Have I got that right Jacob?

Jacob: YESSS.

Therapist: What a big pressure. It's hard work keeping everyone else happy. It's helpful for us to understand just how hard it is to say what you like. You worry lots. This is really hard. *Jacob starts to fiddle with a cushion and appears distracted.*

Therapist: Today I think I've also learned that there are two 'yes's – they are different and important. There is the big loud, "I really like this!" YESSSS and the other quieter Yes. Is that right?

Jacob: *Shrugs.*

Therapist: It might be too hard for you to know this right now so I'd like to follow this with Jan and Emilia. And you too maybe? We are going to notice if YESSS means "You are right, Nic" or "I really like this" and if that's different to other 'yes's.

Therapist: There might be one great way to test this idea out! We could set up a huge crisp taste test – find out which ones are a YESSS and which are just ok or more like a Yes. Would you be interested in something like that?

Jacob: YESSS! *and claps his hands together.*

When building coherence about an experience, or drawing together the story around an event, we need to go slowly. There are so many potential challenges around processing information, for misunderstandings, or missing meanings, that we need to be sensitive to the effort involved. It is also important that lighter moments, where we authentically connect and share in joyful or silly moments, are in tune with the moment and not just used for distraction when things become hard or awkward.

Developmental, emotional and chronological age

Trauma experiences, including loving but mis-attuned relationships, can interrupt sensory, emotional and cognitive development (see Chapter 6: Neuroscience). Therefore, the support and conversational pattern at any particular time in DDP will adjust and respond to the presenting need, in that particular moment. Considering the past, thinking about trauma memories and considering certain emotions, is often challenging and might lead to dysregulation, at which point we might notice, and find, that younger focused care is needed. When we attune to the experiences of those in the room, we might offer care and co-regulation that is helpful, but not aligned with an individual's chronological age. It is important to keep monitoring and considering this with all those in the meeting, to ensure the support feels attuned to the presenting needs.

To consider

For one person I worked with, at times when she started to become dysregulated I would offer her a cream that she liked as it smelt of roses. Over time we increased this care, with her permission, to also offer her a hand rub as a way of regulating through safe touch, offering care and co-regulation. I also provided her with a weighted cushion to hold or sit on her lap, and in doing so, she often reported how this helped her feel ok again.

With another person I developed a way of providing a deeply regulating sofa cuddle – where they would be squeezed from sides by a member of staff and myself in order to provide her with felt connection and regulation. We included some other activities associated with sensory regulation, such as blowing feathers away from us or towards each other. In general, this led to a bit of fun and a degree of chaos, but also facilitated intersubjective connection and sensory regulation through blowing. All three of us were in our 30s and we noted together that this type of support was just right for all of us in this situation, but might not suit other 30-year-olds. The person with an intellectual disability also noted how important it was to be able to laugh, how it helped her relax and trust everyone in the room.

Reflecting on feelings and memories

Many people with an intellectual disability struggle with both their autobiographical and episodic memory, which can hinder recall about general life events and specific details about places and timings of events in their lives. Working with an awareness that times, dates, and sequences of events often jumble around, is an important part of the support we might offer to someone with an intellectual disability. Events that occurred in the past can be experienced as recent and vice versa, not just due to the impact of trauma but linked with fundamental cognitive restrictions. In these situations, it can be helpful for the parents/carers or therapists to offer to know the details, in order to help structure conversations about the past, leaving the person with an intellectual disability freer to explore and reflect on their affective reactions to these incidents. Sometimes an affective-reflective conversation develops over a few meetings, requiring the therapist to really keep track of important themes as they re-emerge.

Case vignette: Miles

Miles has a moderate intellectual disability and had masked his difficulties so well that no professionals had guessed just how hard Miles was finding it to live independently. Miles attends therapy meetings with Rose, a long-standing member of staff who is happy to work therapeutically.

Miles and Nic have created a photo book – which includes photos of members of his family and places he had lived. Over a few months they had created an outline of Mile's life – not all the details, but they have been able to build an overarching story about Miles being abused by family members for many years and how his parents were dependent on various substances and encouraged him to drink. He had learned not to trust adults or ask for help.

Miles: *Opened the page to a picture of his flat before coming to live in a supported tenancy.* This was hard.

Therapist: Your flat. Yes, this was hard. You want to think about this for a bit today?

Miles: Yes, it was tidy but hard.

Therapist: You worked so hard to keep it clean. Every day you would clean it with bleach. You worried about people calling round, judging you. They also made it feel unsafe and maybe dirty.

Miles: I worried my aunt would turn up and scare me again. She did that all the time.

Therapist: Your aunt was so scary for you as a child. She died when you were 10 but she was one of the people that scared you. She hurt you so much. Other people also hurt you in that flat, didn't they. It was like your aunt all over again.

Miles: I saw her in the street today.

Therapist: Oh Miles – how horrible. You saw someone like your aunt in the street today. Were you scared all over again? *(Note:not correcting that his aunt is dead and so he cannot have seen her.)*

Miles: Yes, I stopped. My legs stopped.

Therapist: You were having that scared feeling. It was like she was there and you weren't feeling safe. You froze to the spot because you were scared. Was that the same as when the people hurt you – you froze?

Miles: Yes, I didn't talk to her today or in the flat.

Therapist: Can I check this? When you saw someone reminding you of your aunt, you froze. When your aunt hurt you, you froze? And when the people in your flat hurt you, you froze. You couldn't talk and you couldn't move. Have I got this right? *Miles nods*. This is such a horrible big memory about being hurt and feeling so stuck. What is it like to talk about this today with me and with Rose?

Miles: Ok. It's good that Rose knows. She might have been cross.

Rose: I think that helps me understand what happened now. You talked about going to the supermarket to get some cider and we've not talked about that for a while now. I wasn't sure why you needed the cider. This makes sense. AND, this sounds so frightening, Miles. Thank you for letting me know about this and your memories. I really want to work on helping you to feel safe today.

Miles: Thank you.

Rose: You also worried I would be cross. That was probably a big extra worry. I see that now. I am so sorry for missing that. You saw my worried face and thought it was an angry face. Ah, I make that face sometimes. I need to work on my worried face or maybe just let you know a bit sooner. I don't always get that right.

Miles: *Smiles and visibly relaxes.*

Here and now

When working with someone with an intellectual disability we might need to scaffold or help hold an outline of someone's past for and with them, or we might become aware that they prefer or are only able to focus on current experiences. When we offer and co-create coherence with someone, hold their story, help them to reflect on their feelings, we need to work within their attentional range. When people with an intellectual disability feel muddled by lots of words, or in having to hold an abstract idea, like the past, in mind, it can become too complicated. Instead, it can be more helpful to focus on current relational tensions. We can still offer someone support to reflect on affective experiences, to put it into a context of experiences, but the depth of reflection on the past may need to be reduced.

Safety planning

Within all therapy work, there is a need to be clear about safeguarding processes. This is equally important to hold in mind when working with people with an intellectual disability within a DDP framework. The boundaries around disclosures are the same as for all therapy work: if someone is at risk of being hurt, or has previously been hurt, the right agencies need to be informed. Within a relationship-focused model we can move beyond creating a plan that summarises strategies, or practical steps carers or team might take in response to behaviour that is of concern. Golding (2008) again, has led the way in adapting a safety plan that can be used as a therapeutic tool. It was designed to be written for and with children, where the child or young person is included as a central part of the process of outlining what they need and how others can assist when things are escalating. This has been adapted and developed further by Jones (2021) into a pictorial version suitable for children and adults with an intellectual disability, or for those who prefer visual information (and is available in the Appendix 14). Our experience is that people with an intellectual disability have greatly valued being able to use such a form to co-construct and review the support that does and doesn't work for them, adding an additional way for them to feel safe. It is essential that this form is a reminder of helpful steps rather than a contract; centrally, it supports a more relational approach. Within the safety plan there are actions and considerations for the person with an intellectual disability, and for their carers. Contracts or agreements about 'behaving' or not acting in specific ways are often unrealistic for those that are yet to develop emotional regulation. Once someone has become dysregulated, also referred to as 'flipping their lid' (see Chapter 6: Neuroscience) they will no longer be able to draw on their higher order cognitive processes in their prefrontal cortex that manage impulse control, reasoning or problem-solving.

This safety plan can be reviewed and adapted as often as needed, and it would be useful to be clear when it will be reviewed, and at what point it no longer accurately describes the support or actions needed. Safety plans need to be developed with people when they are regulated and able to reason things through together. This collaborative process can increase the connection and sense of safety within a dyad, or across a team, for those living in residential or supported living homes.

Conclusion

DDP places the safety and connection established in relationships as a fundamental therapeutic step to facilitate change, and for this reason, the focus is on enhancing and deepening the relationship between the person with an intellectual disability and their carers. The therapist also needs to connect, be authentic and engage in reciprocal relationships with all those involved in parenting and dyadic meetings; the use of self in being open to intersubjective connection is vital. In offering and supporting more open and engaged relationships, DDP deepens our understanding and attunement to individual needs. The bespoke and attuned nature of this model make it highly suitable and relevant for people with an intellectual disability and their caregivers.

If, from the outset at the assessment phase, we consider and remain open to the possibility of relational trauma we will create more accurate assessments and generic formulations that more fully encapsulate the sensory, emotional, cognitive and relational needs of the person with an intellectual disability, and their carers too. Such assessments can offer clarity about someone's developmental needs in the moment, and how different factors might trigger fluctuations in skills and abilities. We can better understand how feeling safe impacts on their ability to regulate, to reason ideas through or reflect on the past. DDP's focus on the subtleties of communication including our prosody and rate of speech, the need to move in different ways provides vital information about what is meant rather than what might be said.

The support offered to parents and carers helps us better understand the barriers that might have existed or that are ongoing; the barriers that block deeper connection and erode energy and sometimes compassion. We need to prepare carers for their role in therapy meetings, but also, they deserve our support and consideration for all the hours of care they are offering in between therapy meetings. We need to learn about the impact of trauma on their lives to better understand their current and future support needs. Building these stories, creating coherence, can bring a different perspective about their situation, their relationship and their hopes for the future. When we make better sense of their dynamics through distinct time for parents and in our dyadic conversations this improves safety for all. The development of deeper understanding and improved safety in turn allows reflection on affective and trauma experiences; past and present.

The therapist is active in offering co-regulation, learning what each part the dyadic needs for regulation, and will draw on an attitude of PACE to be curious about people's memories or dreams, to accept each person's perspective as it is and will offer genuine empathy for their experience. In being heard, and enabling the dyad to hear or learn about each other, we help carers to be more regulated, to attune their responses and, as a result, to be better placed to offer co-regulation within the dyad. Supporting relational safety and strengthening relationships at home facilitates exploration of difficult moments within their relationships, of their environment and maybe addresses future worries. It is not a sequential process: relationships, especially for those with insecure attachment patterns need nurture and will benefit from ongoing support. This is the strength of offering dyadic meetings as people with an intellectual disability and their carers will be better placed, in the future, to repair ruptures, deepen connection after dysregulation or face future difficulties, during their explorations in therapy.

Chapter 13: Dyadic Developmental Practice in ID Systems: To provide trauma-informed care

Summary

- Having an intellectual disability can make people more vulnerable to experiencing developmental trauma and attachment difficulties.
- Dyadic Developmental Practice (DDP-practice) offers a model and approach for all those working with and in the services connected to someone with an intellectual disability.
- DDP-practice can ensure trauma-informed intellectual disability service provision across health, social care and education to help the person at the centre develop relational security through consistent, connection-based care.

Introduction

Thus far in the book we have discussed how having an intellectual disability can make people more vulnerable to experiencing relational trauma and attachment difficulties. Dyadic Developmental Psychotherapy (DDP) focuses on relational connection to enable 'recovery' from trauma; the emphasis of the systems nature of this work makes it a valuable model to draw on when offering care for those with an intellectual disability. DDP as a model, has developed beyond psychotherapy in a therapy room to also include assistance in parenting and practice for parents, carers and the wider support network within health, social care and education (Golding, 2020); people who have experienced profound challenges with connection, including developmental trauma, need carers who can offer that connection.

DDP-practice interventions need to be systemic and multi-level to tailor support to all those in the support network. This way of working with the system is also an inherent part of intellectual disability practice. In this chapter, we explore ideas around how the DDP model can be most successfully implemented for people with intellectual disability through interactions with their families, carers, and supporters and when it is embedded throughout the wider system which is supporting the person with an intellectual disability and their immediate carers. There is also a growing recognition and interest in trauma-informed care (TIC), and how this can be offered to people with intellectual disabilities, with a focus upon the practicalities of what TIC and relationally-based care looks like for people with intellectual disabilities (see National Senate Guideline 2023; McNally *et al*, 2022). Trauma-informed care is multi-nuanced, and this chapter will explore how DDP-practice across the system can help to add depth and practical ideas to our provision of connection across the layers of care and within the complex systems children and adults with intellectual disabilities often exist within. This chapter explores what DDP-practice and TIC looks like on a micro and macro system levels, exploring different elements of these approaches..

Working within the system

The aim of DDP-practice is to extend the key elements from the therapy room to the day-to-day task of parenting the child or caring/supporting the adult, and also to support the networks around those parenting or caring for the person directly. Essentially, it is about ensuring that the people across the system are aware of DDP, of the fundamentals of attachment theory, intersubjective connection, the importance of safety within relationships, and tailoring support to meet the presenting needs. It also emphasises and offers a framework for those who are undertaking this complex work to in turn receive support. When offered across a broader network, it is referred to as DDP-practice, which emphasises the teams around the dyad and the systems around those teams (see Figure 13.1).

Figure 13.1 DDP-practice in a system supporting people with an intellectual disability (based upon DDP Network, 2013; Golding, 2023)

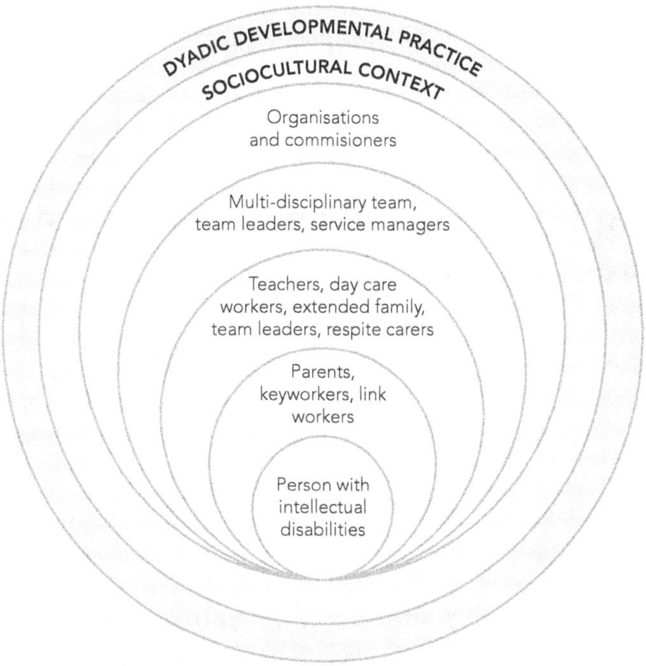

People with intellectual disabilities often find themselves within complex systems: there will be direct carers, such as parents or paid support workers; alongside this there can be respite carers, teachers, day care workers or supported work placements, all with regular contact with the person. More widely, then there are often multi-disciplinary teams which can consist of nurses, psychiatrists, occupational therapists, speech and language therapists, physiotherapists, and psychologists (not an exhaustive list). People in all of these roles can benefit from an understanding of how to take a DDP-informed approach. In engaging the broader system, the aim is to introduce a lasting cultural change. This echoes the broader ideas of a trauma-informed care, needing to have all members of the system, from direct carers, professionals, and managers, able to recognise and respond to trauma, as highlighted in Goad's Hierarchy of Safety (Goad, 2020). Ensuring affective-reflective support and intersubjective connection as well as prioritising and attending to relationships as a way of improving and strengthening safety will be the foundation of DDP-practice and trauma-informed care for systems. Behavioural correction and boundaries will be vital, but relational safety needs to lead before there is a focus on correcting behaviours. Systems that hold a DDP perspective will be oriented towards emotional regulation, connection, and making sense of distress at all levels, in contrast to other intervention models where the focus is more likely to be around 'behaviour', incidents, and management.

> *"While it is a truism that the only person anyone has the power to really change is themselves and (yet)… systemic approaches show us that we are also all part of an interconnected web."*
>
> Jones & Haydon-Laurelut (2019, p.1)

Embedding DDP in the wider support system – working from the outside in

> *"a good functioning team, underpinned by a consistent philosophy of care, is well supported and taken care of so that attention can focus on the care and support that the children [and adults] need".*
>
> Grant *et al* (2024, p.151)

It is imperative that the whole system is engaged in DDP-approaches, as this allows trauma-informed care guidance to be operationalised throughout the complex systems people with intellectual disabilities find themselves in. DDP-practice is highly effective in fostering stronger dyadic relationships surrounding the child or adult with intellectual disabilities. It also ensures that the caregivers providing this support are guided and supported through the same attuned, DDP-informed approach, creating a consistent and cohesive framework of care. Focused on being with rather than doing to (Grant *et al*, 2024). In child work, where children are living at home, this would often look like engaging the family within the DDP informed parenting, whether this is or is not possible there is still a need to engage the wider system. For example, school staff, direct payment workers, overnight breaks providers and social workers (and their managers). In work with adults with intellectual disabilities, or where children with intellectual disabilities are not living in a family home, this can be replicated to some extent by engaging the carers, but we also need to engage those who oversee the system and care within the DDP model – the managers, organisational leadership team, commissioners, and multi-disciplinary team (MDT), as outlined in Figure 13.2.

Figure 13.2 Embedding DDP in the wider support system

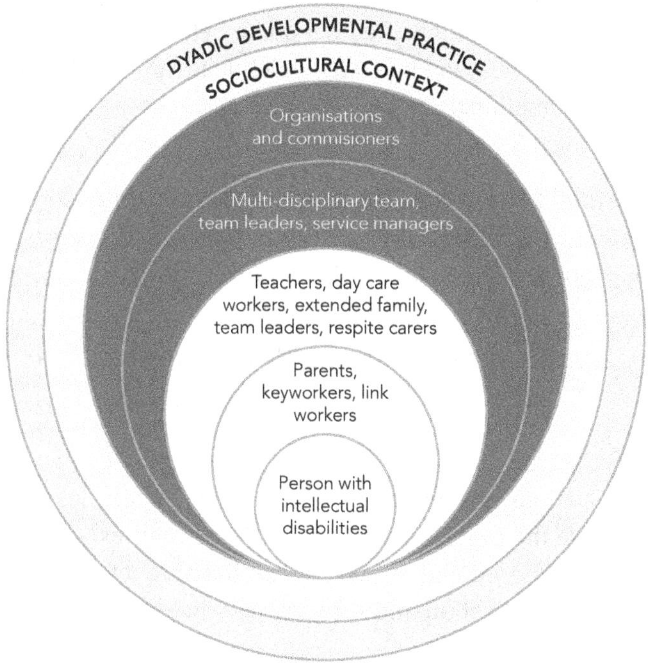

The 'name it to tame it' approach can also support transparency within the system. Its relational and storytelling approach allows processes and emotions to be named, incorporating an affective/ reflective stance. In turn, this promotes greater transparency, self/team-reflection, and awareness of feelings within the wider system, strengthening connection and collaboration. When modelled in MDT meetings, team discussions, or organisational settings, it creates space for the storytelling framework to evolve. This ensures that relational thinking remains central to responses and decision-making. (More on 'name it to tame it' later.)

There is a need for those commissioning, and those overseeing and leading services to understand the broader principles of DDP-practice. This will enable them to not just understand the model but work within it and to act in ways which embody intersubjective, PACE-ful ways and the importance of a relational focus and safety for the care team. There needs to be a skill in identifying the interactions which might be indicative of blocked care and skilful, connected ways of negotiating these, which are non-judgemental and non-blaming for carers and for the person with intellectual disabilities. DDP explicitly talks about embedding safe, positive and genuine relationships with staff. The ways of regulating the system help with this – if carers feel safe in the relationships around them (the wider team and MDT) this will help them be available for connection to the person with intellectual disabilities. In line with trauma-informed care work, this needs to be reflected throughout the systems, with the recording and reporting systems, rostering, key working, and supervision all echoing the attachment/intersubjective bases of DDP. Although we also need to be mindful as embodied the quote below, that we are not over-emphasising relationship building in a way which inadvertently leads to pressure or as if they have done something wrong:

> *"...when we place too much explicit emphasis on relationship building, we risk being yet another service that makes them feel like they're being blamed, like we're trying to correct something rather than just actually hearing them, validating them and being there alongside them."*
>
> Griffiths *et al* (2023, p.43)

We need to avoid relationships being the focus in a way which leads to this feeling like carers/parents are the problems; but rather allows their experiences and emotions to be acknowledged and respected, emphasising relationship building and co-regulation alongside validation and support, in which people feel accepted and not pressured to change.

It is important that in a trauma-informed, systems approach to DDP-practice, organisations are thinking about this for policy, training, supervision, workforce and leadership (e.g. McNally *et al*, 2022; Jackson & Walters, 2015). That these wider elements embody the key principles of DDP and that it is recognised by the wider organisation that these elements, when implemented relationally, are important in the provision of trauma-informed care as well as to the DDP approach. To support this, we should consider training at all levels of the system (see Chapter 16). This approach ensures that the relational aspects of care are prioritised, experienced, and embedded in practice. It also helps maintain a healthy balance of boundaries while addressing challenges such as blocked care. There is a template provided in this text as Appendix 12, which outline how areas of safety, relational support and practical elements can be balanced. This is particularly important within the context of the two hands of care model (see Chapter 8) – the system needs to hold both the compassion, warmth, and connection of the one hand, alongside the structure, boundaries and corrections of the second hand. In orienting the wider network with the principles of DDP, there is a trickle-down ripple that will enable the staff teams to feel safe. In helping staff teams feel safe and allows them to do the same for the people they are providing support for – relationships and boundaries, held together.

Treisman talks about this in her treasury of trauma-informed care, and the importance of thinking about individual and organisational values (see Treisman, 2022). The services being able to clearly state their values is important, and has been shown to alter practice (Whitby, 2020). These practice values need to be about alliance and not compliance to fit with DDP values (Casswell *et al*, 2014). An additional element in both Treisman's work on trauma-informed organisations and shared with DDP is that this is not about teaching approaches, having statements, or learning about attachment but about embodying this way of working as part of interactions that provide trauma-informed care.

In the framework for implementing trauma-informed care (TIC) for people with intellectual disabilities (McNally *et al*, 2022), there is a list of elements which need to be present across the system for this to work well, including supervision, reflective practice and training. It also acknowledges (as does the taking timeframe, Jackson & Waters, 2015) the necessity for this to occur across the layers of the system, including within policy, recruitment, training, and team meetings. The central approach of DDP can offer a route to the operational delivery described in the above TIC outlines.

There are many layers of complexity, of engaging the full system, starting with the tendency that for someone who has experienced developmental trauma, there will most probably be a strong desire not to engage in relationships, as explored in Chapter 10: Blocked care. This can happen when the person does not believe that they can be safe in relationships and/or that it would be unsafe to trust the adults offering care. The added difficulty is that the person may already be in a chaotic lifestyle or have very few connections. For individuals with intellectual disabilities, their reliance on long-term support required across multiple domains can further complicate their situation. While they depend on relationships to receive this support, they may also experience a desire to disengage from these relationships, creating a tension between their need for assistance and their wish to withdraw. With that in mind, one of the first useful things that can happen is to ensure that the person is in a safe place, where there is reliable and attuned support available to them – and then to try and help this support to be DDP-informed.

Embedding DDP with the teams around the person

Figure 13.3 Embedding DDP with caregivers around the person

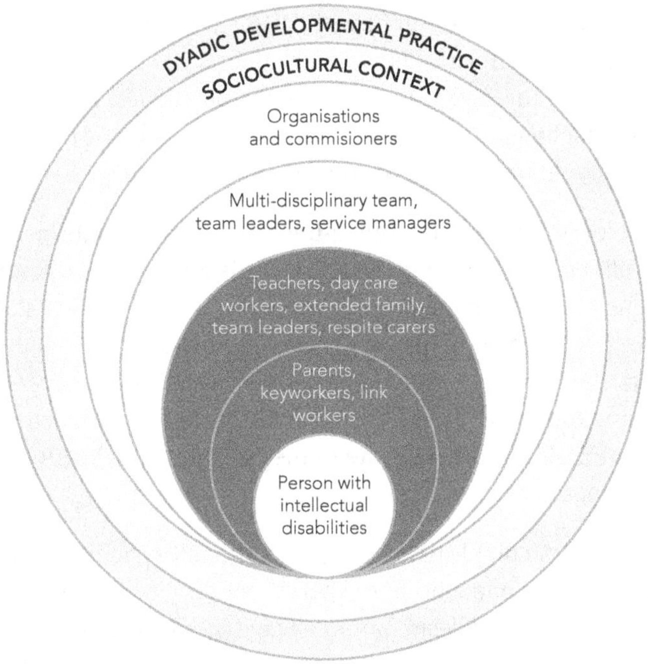

TIC guidance holds centrally the premise that reflective space, debriefing, team meetings and supervision are available for direct care staff working in trauma-informed services (McNally *et al*, 2023). We would suggest that DDP provides the 'how to' ways for this to be provided thoughtfully and relationally.

In addition, Dan Hughes describes three assumptions to hold in mind when working with parents:

1. That they are good people.
2. That they are doing the best they can.
3. That they have a desire to care for/love their child.

This teaching has been extended to leaders within residential (child) services, that all adults in the team are good people, with a genuine desire to do the best they are able to, and that they care (can even come to love) the people that are working with (Grant *et al*, 2024). When Alexis Quinn (e.g. Quinn, 2021; Quinn *et al*, 2023) talks about the terrible abusive experiences of restriction she experienced in a variety of care settings, she also acknowledges that she met very few staff who wished to do her harm, just lots of people who did not know how to connect to and support her or how to help her feel safe.

Grant *et al* (2024) add a fourth assumption to this model – that all parents/carers need support, and some need more support than others. So, for people with intellectual disabilities, with the added layer of cognitive impairment, it seems understandable that their carers and parents will need extra support.

Below are some practical, proactive ways of providing DDP-informed approaches that can be used with a team. There is no strict order to these, although an order has been attempted in this list; it should be acknowledged that very often we would jump ahead a few items and then go back to other areas. This is probably not an exhaustive list and some of these approaches are explored in detail elsewhere in the book, and merely mentioned here to keep them on the radar when practising in this way, within the wider system.

Embedding this practice takes time; improved connections are not achieved in a one-off meeting or a week of contact. Essentially, one of the key messages to take from this is that DDP-practice in the system takes a long time. It therefore also needs to be offered in a timely fashion, not because it will immediately solve the difficulties, but because without a responsive approach, there is a risk of further rupturing attachment relationships.

Establishing a culture of care within the team

Whether the team is composed of parents, educational staff, social workers, or paid carers supporting adults in supported living services, alongside community team professionals, creating a culture of care is essential for implementing DDP approaches effectively. This requires all individuals within the system to prioritise *connection before correction*, fostering an intersubjective, curious, and mind-minded relationship between professionals, those providing DDP knowledge or consultation, and those directly and frequently working with the individual with intellectual disabilities. This is therefore about the culture of care for the staff team – that the reflection is not focused just on the individual person with an intellectual disability but also on the issues arising for the staff team in offering this complex and important support.

It is also crucial to acknowledge existing power imbalances within the system and use this approach to name and contain these. Additionally, opportunities should be created to explore and integrate the emotional experiences of both the person with intellectual disabilities who's being supported and those providing the support. Combining these affective experiences with reflective elements enables real-time co-regulation, helping to embed and sustain other areas of DDP-practice.

The following practical ideas about implementing this culture of care, are aimed at allowing these elements to be delivered and highlighting the DDP emphasis within them.

Training in DDP

Knight and Gurney-Smith (2016) outline several ways in which they introduced a DDP model to the children's residential services they were working in, stating that 'understanding and education are seen as being key to using dyadic developmental practice effectively in residential settings'. In this work, they deliver both DDP and mindfulness training; later results indicate that the DDP learning was the most significant in altering culture of care. It is important that this training notices and understands the needs of people with intellectual disability, and therefore allows consideration of the social, emotional, relational and cognitive skills of the person. In Chapter 16 we further explore how this training could look for people.

Core staff teams

Shackleton's (2016) work on core staff teams talks about 6 or 7 people being within this; to allow attuned care, all these people will probably need to be involved in offering some level of intersubjective relationship, to have some training, understanding and chance to reflect on their work and their implementation of DDP approaches. There is a need perhaps for some key people to lead the way and to be the identified attachment figure, e.g. 2 or 3 key staff. There is also a need to provide support and build the team's capacity to work in this way, especially in paid care settings where the person(s) implementing DDP may not be consistently present. Ensuring the availability of a core staff team is understandably a complex and challenging commitment; and we may be asking them to work very differently than in other roles or circumstances (including reflecting on their own relationship/ attachment experiences, engaging intersubjectively etc). There are risks that staff will change jobs, become ill, or need time off work; the core team helps with these areas (Jones, 2021). DDP-informed reflection and supervision will be essential for core staff teams, to reflect on caring glimmers and challenges. Glimmers are the positive sensory or emotional cues that evoke feelings of safety and connection, in contrast to triggers. In the trauma-informed care context 'glimmers' are used to describe moments that promote well-being and resilience, such as cosy socks, a fluffy or weighted blanket or a sip of your favourite warm drink (see chapter 15).

It is possible some paid carers will not want/be able to engage in the DDP process and so this will need to be discussed with the person with intellectual disability, the care provision managers, and the care team themselves to identify the most suitable, willing and emotionally available individuals.

Regular individual supervision and team meetings

As well as multi-agency meetings and parent consultation, these are informed by the DDP principles of connection, intersubjectivity and reflection on affective experiences. These might be in addition to, or in replacement of, other supervision/ team meetings which may focus upon operational elements. These need to allow the core ethos of support to be modelled, and for this to reflect the PACE approach. There is also an acknowledgement of the need for regular multi-agency meetings and parent consultations. This means team members need to have access to supervision from those skilled in and familiar with a DDP model.

Case workshops/network training and reflection spaces

Rooted in systemic practice, which emphasises connection and curiosity, the Network Training or Case Workshop model is a valuable approach for DDP-informed intellectual disability services (see Jenkins & Parry, 2009; Harding & Hill, 2019). Case workshops focus on bringing together the whole network around a person, using this time to explore multi-perspectives and agree priorities for input and ensuring safety. This can also allow attachment-based information and history to be discussed, shared and connected to by care staff, in relation to the person's current presentation. It ensures that traditionally associated concepts related to intellectual disabilities (for example, choice, capable environments, autism or impulsivity) are understood within the context of early and ongoing relational experiences. Caswell *et al* (2014), discussing children's residential services, reported that DDP-informed services have far more successful placements when there are regular networks consultations in place; this is linked throughout the TIC literature which names the importance of reflection space for carers to think about and discuss how it feels supporting someone and working with them.

Working together agreement

We have learnt that there are emotional and practical complexities when working together as a system around people with intellectual disabilities, with confusion in roles, people feeling blamed, ignored or unsure who to turn to. In response, a working together agreement is developed as a system during an initial network meeting where parents and professionals from all agencies working to support children and families, and adults and staff teams, ensure there is a clear understanding of what each person's role is and who can be approached for what (parenting queries, transport, communication needs, sensory needs, behaviours that challenge, housing, respite). This also includes an agreement of day-to-day communication/handover of what information and an agreement about frequency of multi-agency meetings.

Work alongside us – collaboration not consultation

Agencies we have worked with, such as schools and overnight breaks services, have let us know that they find it more helpful for services to join them and work alongside them for stretches of time, as opposed to spurts of modelling after a training session and purely checking for verbal and practical competence through positive monitoring. Developing a working understanding of the demands and environmental context within which staff are working and genuine relationships with each other throughout the network, is likely to lead to more successful collaborative trusting relationships and embedding of best practice.

Regulate and relate to enable reasoning

All interventions need to be based on Golding's Pyramid of Need (2019) and the 4Rs: regulate, relate, reason and repair. This is based on the neurobiological underpinning of what can be completed at different stages of distress. For example, when areas of learning and skills development are identified as helpful in supporting individuals to have a sense of self and be in relationships that are fulfilling, that support needs to be offered on the foundations of:

1. an environment that is stimulating and safe
2. all those in the system (carers, staff and the person with intellectual disabilities) feeling regulated and in their window of tolerance
3. relationship between the carer and person with intellectual disabilities feeling attuned and non-compromised when supporting any learning or skills development.

Figure 13.1 (p.249) provides an overview of how interactions might be in these different phases of regulation.

Name it to tame it

Modelling alternative communication methods to attune to and name internal needs can help build affective connections and allow collaboration in emotional experiences. The concept of 'name it to tame it' (Siegel & Bryson, 2011) suggests that identifying and labelling emotional experiences can re-engage the brain's thinking areas (pre-frontal cortex), helping to regulate and reduce the intensity of these emotions. This, in turn, allows individuals to recognise, and communicate their internal experiences and manage their reactions more effectively.

For people with intellectual disabilities, tools such as core boards, visuals on a wall, talking mats, or choice boards can be used to name emotions or responses. These tools can also visually link emotions to sensory-regulating activities, based on someone's sensory profile/preferences. These sensory regulating activities might include something organising or calming (as opposed to alerting), whole-body squeezes, time on a swing or trampoline, or deep pressure via a weighted blanket, shoulder compression, gym ball squash; all offered to support or develop sensory regulation and enhance emotional regulation.

Naming big emotions as they start to take hold of us, so we can manage them more effectively.

Naming emotions and adopting a curious stance toward emotional experiences can also play a vital role in the rupture and repair cycle. This is particularly helpful when (not if) disagreements or conflicts arise within staff teams or wider systems. A PACE (playfulness, acceptance, curiosity, empathy) based approach can enable reflection on the emotions being experienced within a care team (see example below). By doing so, it aims to re-engage the thinking brain, encouraging thoughtful responses rather than reactive behaviours, while fostering understanding and connection in challenging situations.

We can use the DDP concept of affective/reflective dialogue as a way to name it to tame it; and reframe it. The affective/reflective dialogue brings a storytelling quality to interactions, characterised by curiosity and a willingness to explore events. This approach conveys the overarching message, *"You are understandable, and I am trying to understand you".* Developing skills in naming difficulties and fostering affective/reflective dialogue can be supported through training, reflective sessions, or real-time guidance with staff and carers.

It is equally valuable to extend this practice into the wider system, particularly within staff teams, by incorporating storytelling and affective/reflective dialogue into '*name it to tame it*' for staff support and reflective sessions. When this approach is modelled in staff supervision and support settings, it provides time and space for the storytelling framework to evolve. It also demonstrates how affective/reflective conversations can unfold naturally, supporting staff in adopting and applying this approach in their own interactions.

Examples of using name it to tame it/affective reflective dialogue within a staff team meeting

"It must have been hard when James threw the dinner you had made and said it was disgusting; I wonder if it made you feel like you were really rubbish at your job, or if it made you feel cross or sad with him..."

"I wonder how it is that you've just spent the first part of this meeting talking about the importance of cleaning and the recycling and now I want to talk to your relationship with James – it feels tricky to think that these things are all important and all need very different skills and time...what do you guys think?"

"When James can't speak with his Mum and then won't get out of bed to do things with you, what do you think that might be like for him....how can we talk to him about that in an accepting and curious way do you think?"

Caring with two hands

In Chapter 8, we explored the cycle of caring in the moment. This approach can have a significant impact on a system level as well. In her work on therapeutic parenting, Kim Golding (2015) talks about the importance of mentalisation – to be mind-minded. This involves being able to connect with the person with an intellectual disability by aiming to make sense of their internal experiences. Holding a space for connecting with underlying experiences and emotions, increases the capacity for regulation. The aim is to focus away from traditional discipline approaches which focus on contingencies and social learning theory and, instead move towards connection before correction, with the focus on curious exploration. This approach still allows for structure, supervision, and consequences, but in the context of connection and co-regulation which builds trust and increases the sense of connection.

The 'parenting in the moment' cycle offers a valuable framework for DDP-focused supervision, fostering reflection on team dynamics and broader systems. It models acceptance of disagreements and differing opinions, emphasising repair and resolution within the system which is key in residential care settings (Casswell *et al*, 2014).

As well as recognising care providers' anxieties or feelings of inadequacy, often tied to shame (Casswell, 2014). The 'parenting in the moment' approach encourages caregivers to first regulate their own emotional responses (e.g. irritation, anger) before addressing the individual's needs. This allows for offering regulation, curiosity, connection, and meaning-making before responding to behaviours and facilitating repair (Golding, 2015). When focusing on the individual's relationships, staff can better understand the impact of past issues and patterns, both for the person with intellectual disabilities and for themselves (Golding, 2015). When supporting those directly caring for a person with an intellectual disability who has experienced relational trauma, it is important to consider the individual's attachment style and how they have historically responded to care. This includes understanding their patterns of aggression when care is offered, the potential influence of their trauma history, and whether there is a recurring pattern of splits within teams or services supporting them.

Examples of parenting/caring in the moment cycle for a staff team

The caring in the moment cycle can be used with a carer or care team to explore their interactions with a person with intellectual disabilities; to step-by step, explore the impact of a certain event or interaction on them and consider their reactions to a situation. In a team meeting people are discussing the difficulties they often having helping Depesh to shower; often, Depesh wants to stay in his pyjamas all day, have food on him and isn't bothered by his matted hair. The carers want to promote choice, but they also want him to be ok to go out and do fun things. People have different views on what to do.

As a facilitator we might:

1. Pause and regulate

Notice that everyone is trying their best for Depesh, aiming for him to have a full life with dignity and opportunity. However, there's a risk of becoming overly restrictive in their aims to achieve this.

Reflection to share with the team

"When you tell me about 'x' happening, I notice my reaction is one of irritation, frustration, or feeling overwhelmed. I wonder if offering you some time to discuss what feelings come up for you might be helpful? To have a think about this first seems really important, and difficult. Let's think about what has been brought up for you before we explore it further."

2. Engage with PACE

Playfulness: *"Gosh, if we're not careful, we might stop Depesh from doing anything until he's scrubbed clean and dressed in a tuxedo!"*

Acceptance: *"I can see that everyone really wants him to have dignity when he goes out. It's such a tricky situation, isn't it?"*

Curiosity: *"I wonder what it feels like as carers if Depesh doesn't have a shower. In some places, that might be seen as the bare minimum for care. I wonder does this make you feel like you aren't doing a good job of caring for him...or maybe makes you feel a bit hopeless as other plans for the day cannot go ahead? For Depesh, though, it's such a hard thing to achieve. Do you think this might be linked to his family environment, where perhaps there wasn't an expectation to wash? Could that be relevant now?"*

Empathy: *"I wonder if you worry that people might think you're not very good at your job if Depesh hasn't showered by lunchtime—or even later?"*

3. Decide on follow-up

"I know there are different ideas about how to help Depesh, but we need to be careful not to make it harder for him to engage in the things he loves. I wonder if increasing visual structure for Depesh might help? What are your thoughts?"

"Have we also been able to explore this with Depesh,what he doesn't like about showering or what makes it tricky for him?"

4. Repair

There might need to be some repair conversations within the team – there might have been ruptures where some people feel that others haven't worked as hard, or been as thoughtful. This can be talked about and explored.

"I know how hard you're all working as a team, and we've talked so much about ways to keep Depesh safe. Now there's a new challenge, and it will take time to understand and resolve. But we've managed some really tricky times together before, and I believe we'll manage this one too."

Ways to support teams to reflect on and draw on DDP approaches

PACE with systems

Within the DDP literature, the PACE approach (playfulness, acceptance, curiosity, and empathy) provides a framework for fostering meaningful connections and building rapport with care networks. This approach emphasises creating an atmosphere of safety and trust, enabling caregivers and support systems to feel more secure and confident in their responses to the behaviours exhibited by the person they are caring for. By focusing on these principles, networks are better prepared to develop a more receptive, collaborative, and attuned environment. This allows for a deeper understanding of the individual's needs; a more curious and compassionate exploration of their behaviours; and a shared focus on empathy and acceptance, which can allow emotional alignment in the team. It is challenging to offer PACE when the people you care for might have high intensity, complex presentations and/or might have developed coping skills and survival strategies that can be difficult to support on a day-to-day basis (once again, remember structure and predictability are essential). It is the carers who spend most of their time with the person with intellectual disabilities, so truly connecting with their experiences, concerns, emotions, and ideas, is central to effective change

PACE allows:

1. An understanding of the system and the way each person within it relates to themselves and one another. This allows intervention to be tailored in a way that works for the system (goodness of fit)
2. Parents and networks to be open and engaged, as opposed to closed and defensive to communicating and new ways of doing, thinking, and relating
3. Identification of personal and organisational barriers that would need to be considered as part of a formulation and intervention plan to improving capable environments and quality of life
4. Progress to be more likely when the relationship feels safe enough to withstand and repair inevitable ruptures whilst the system navigates change. A relationship(s) founded on a connection that supports mutual constructive thinking and openness.

Such an approach needs to be embedded across the system (as in Figure 13.1), with all levels attempting to understand and be curious. If empathy can genuinely be shown for and experienced by the person with intellectual disability and their key carers, it will enable connection, and emotions can be expressed and reflected upon. In parallel, if the MDT can provide a curious and interested response to carers this will aid them with recognising their own emotional responses and cascade this to the person with intellectual disabilities. We know that often families' experiences of services are that they are not reflective or curious (and so embodying the DDP approach will need to be thought about widely. Rather than responding to what people might say in team supervision, or responding to the content of the interactions, offer an intersubjective connection and curiosity: *"I wonder how you felt when that happened; I wonder if when the person did X you felt frustrated, like nothing was working, even though you are working so hard?"*

The PACE approach allows a step back from taking a particular position, from an instructional or an explicit problem-solving stance. Instead, PACE communicates connection and welcomes thoughts, feelings, and reflections. This genuine and non-judgemental stance encourages openness, engagement, trust and team/interagency collaboration. More naturally, within a connected approach, PACE paves a way to any new team approaches based on a shared understanding of any unmet needs.

A DDP-informed approach for people with intellectual disabilities and their network using the Four Rs framework

As discussed in Chapter 6: Neuroscience, the Four Rs framework emphasises the importance of first achieving physiological regulation and then building safe relationships; finally, in engaging in cognitive processes like reasoning and problem-solving. Following this sequence ensures that foundational needs are met before progressing to more complex tasks. This is equally true for direct carers, parents and all in the system. At all times we would aim to ensure that approaches that support regulation are in place. When people are calm/engaged enough we would also look to reconnection within the relationship, , and reason occurs only when people's brains are fully engaged, and they are within their window of tolerance.

Figure 13.4 Working with the system using the Four Rs framework (see Appendix 11)

	What is the focus at this level?	Corresponding focus for family and paid carers at this level
Reason (as well as continued Regulate and Relate)	At this point, the person with intellectual disabilities and their support network feel calm and connected – they have capacity to think and work more clearly to enhance happiness and quality of life. Support can focus on individually tailored support, planning, skills development, and better communication. The focus can be on development as well as on connection. Support choice and agency: expressing preferences.	■ Consider formal therapeutic work – for the individual. ■ Enhancing skills, knowledge, and confidence to implement skills sessions with person with intellectual disabilities and to increase skills and confidence in opportunities to maintain an attitude of PACE, name it to tame it and affective-reflective dialogue ■ Supporting sleep intervention ■ Supporting improved community access and peer activities once carers and the person with intellectual disabilities have developed the skills and environmental context to set this up for success ■ Also to complete the proactive work needed to allow structure and thoughtful interventions at other times ■ Attend regular DDP supervision and team meetings, which model connection and in the moment reflection ■ Also, failures to connect to be seen as learning opportunities, and allow thinking about shame across the system as well as being curious about this for the individual ■ Develop formulation-informed support plans and support implementation

<table>
<tr>
<td>Relate

(as well as continued Regulate)</td>
<td>Genuine connection: relationships that bring comfort, shared joy and improving understanding.<ul><li>Connect with the person with an intellectual disability and their support network to develop enjoyable relationships.</li><li>Ensure care that is nurturing, consistent, calm, and predictable.</li><li>Ensure access to opportunities for shared open interactions: that enable candour, delight, and maybe laughter</li></ul></td>
<td><ul><li>Well-being reflection and support: what helps the person to be able to reconnect with reasoning, such as sensory activities and reducing demands.</li><li>Communication with the person in their way, so intensive interaction should be considered for those with less verbal ability and those with cognitive/emotional disconnect.</li><li>Continuing PACE reflective conversations, staying curious to the person's experiences and verbalising this in a gentle way – which is not necessarily looking for agreement (trying to convince) but rather opening the possibility of curiosity and understanding the message of "You are understandable and I want to understand you"</li><li>Embrace attunement-rupture-repair cycle.</li><li>Remember dysregulation--> co-regulation--> future self-regulation.</li><li>Using supervision/team meetings to also explore shame responses, blocked care and blocked trust and enabling them to embrace PACE</li></ul></td>
</tr>
<tr>
<td>Regulate</td>
<td>At this stage, people are overwhelmed, stressed and tired.

Support the person with intellectual disabilities and their support network to regulate their nervous system, to feel less stressed and more engaged. Consider physical and emotional safety, structure, boundaries, visual schedules, and guidance</td>
<td><ul><li>Keep things simple/concise</li><li>Working together agreement, specifically knowing who to go to for what, effective communication to ensure containment and consistency</li><li>Lower expectations</li><li>Explore the foundations for well-being/capable environment assessment to explore areas in need of attention</li><li>Therapeutic support: Modelling PACE when discussing challenges and frustrations (mostly A&E, with gentle P & C) and Two Hands approach, be mindful of shame responses, blocked care and blocked trust</li></ul></td>
</tr>
<tr>
<td>Repair</td>
<td>Where there have been ruptures in the relationships between carers, or between carers and management or the organisation there needs to be thought given to repair</td>
<td><ul><li>Use 'name it to tame it' and affective/reflective dialogue to attempt a storytelling approach to what has occurred</li><li>Emphasise that everyone was trying to get things right, but noticed it went wrong</li><li>Be mindful of possible shame and blocked care reactions and how to recognise and move away from this</li></ul></td>
</tr>
</table>

Remember:

- Ensure a PACE approach runs through every interaction and intervention, being mindful that playfulness and curiosity might be better timed towards the top of the triangle.
- Ensure intervention never compromises relationships, that genuine connection is maintained to support any skills development.
- Ensure skills development draws on the persons preferred activities, environments, and ways of interacting and feel as natural to everyday life as possible.
- Be mindful of the window of tolerance. If anyone in the system shows dysregulation over expected temporary discomfort due to comfort zones being challenged, consider breaking steps down and moving down a 'level.'

Conclusion

People with intellectual disabilities often live within complex systems and may require lifelong care supported by others. There is a growing emphasis on providing trauma-informed care within these services, and DDP offers an approach to ensure that the principles of this are embedded across the system. This requires a whole-system approach, where commissioners and managers uphold the values of safety, connection, and curiosity in their interactions with others, including multidisciplinary professionals, direct carers, teachers, respite providers, and team leaders.

This systemic approach enables these principles to cascade from higher levels of the system to those providing direct care and, ultimately, to the individual with an intellectual disability. Embodying PACEful interactions helps ensure these values are reflected at every level. Additionally, the Two Hands of Care approach can be applied not only to the person with an intellectual disability, but also to support and guide direct carers. In reflecting on their own emotional reactions and how they may feel compelled to respond, there can be an emphasis on connection before correction; altering interactions and increasing connections within the team and with the person they are supporting.

Incorporating reflective and affective dialogue into team supervision and support sessions increases confidence and equips carers to directly implement these approaches with the individual. It also acknowledges and validates the emotional challenges of caregiving, particularly when the individual's relational style, attachment history, or defences against relationships (e.g. blocked trust) make this work difficult.

To ensure these principles are consistently implemented, key steps include establishing core teams, providing regular supervision and team meetings, and using case workshops to connect the individual's history to current practice or areas of difficulty. These steps are reinforced through PACEful conversations, the 'name it to tame it' approach, and the Two Hands approach, which encourage exploration and reflection across the system. Collaborative working and clear agreements can help services feel more cohesive, moving away from blame culture and fostering clarity about roles and responsibilities. DDP-practice can therefore ultimately support better relational outcomes for individuals with intellectual disabilities and the people who care for them.

Chapter 14:

Dyadic Developmental Practice in ID Systems: Maintaining boundaries, safety and managing risks

Summary

- In our experience, there are particular considerations to be mindful of in the application of DDP approaches when working with people with intellectual disabilities and their system, such as independence, restrictive practice, capacity for paid staff to consider.
- We invite you to be mindful of the systemic context outlined in Chapter 13, with this chapter offering further depth and reflection (and difficulties!), including where DDP-practice can support understanding.
- We wish to acknowledge the areas described here, because they are tricky for all involved in supporting people with intellectual disabilities; they are issues that can evoke feelings of shame in the person with intellectual disabilities and those supporting them, including professionals. If not observed or thought about, these areas can lead to blocks in care.
- Lastly, the following system-wide considerations are included in this book, not to provide neat solutions but to keep the discussion about such important issues present which, through the lens of DDP, may move in a direction where people with intellectual disabilities are able to experience more meaningful relationships and therefore fulfilling lives.

Introduction

This chapter explores key service-wide considerations and examines how DDP-practice can offer alternative narratives and approaches to relationships within these areas. It is presented for the reader's consideration, aiming to expand the influence of DDP- informed thinking and approaches at a higher service level. Additionally, it reflects on areas the authors have personally explored and found beneficial, with the goal of sharing these insights and demonstrating the integration of DDP principles within organisational and strategic systemic practice. These are not always able to provide complete or neat solutions, but rather how DDP can help people with intellectual disabilities and those supporting them to experience more meaningful relationships, even within tricky aspect of care provision.

Figure 14.1 Using DDP in within the context of wider sociocultural factors and organisations

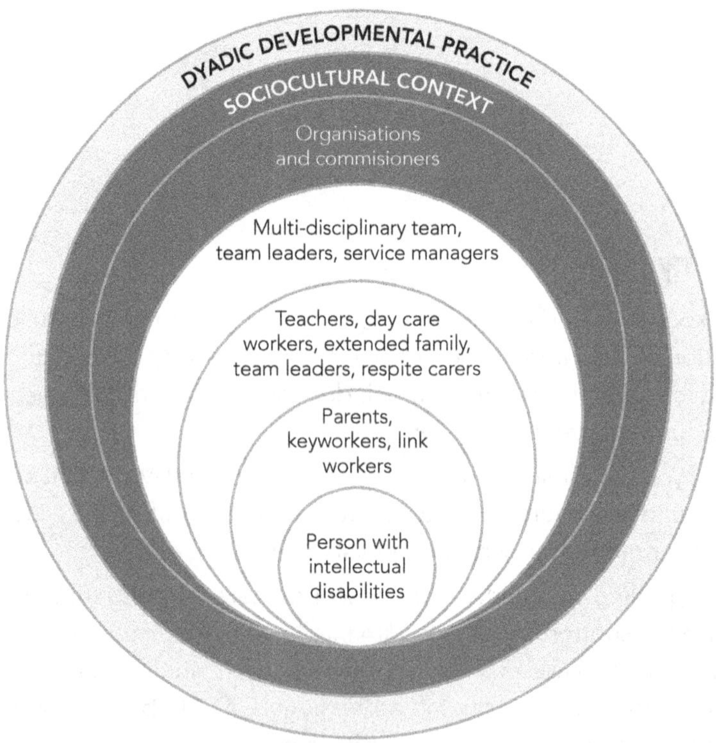

Safety, exploration, and independence

Security and exploration are the inter-related ends of the attachment seesaw. When the child needs comfort and protection, they return to their attachment figure; at other times they can explore and learn about the world. When there has not been the presence of a safe attachment figure or a secure attachment, then there are risks of miscuing in this; that when the person really needs safety, they instead explore or act independently. If someone acts as if they do not need their attachment figure, there is a risk that carers and wider system respond accordingly, perhaps reducing offers of interaction and support respectively. In services this can sometimes occur literally in reducing of funded support hours. Golding (2015) suggests that responding to miscuing is one of the challenges in caring for children with developmental trauma once they are in a safe placement. There is a risk that carers may withdraw when someone expresses they can cope alone, which can reinforce the person's deepest fear—that they are not truly cared for. It also might be that organisations move carers on (or change the care staff) because they organisation misunderstands the need for connection, continuity and predictability. Additionally, the person's lack of trust in relationships may lead them to push others away through their insistence on independence or behaviours that make maintaining connection challenging. In turn, carers might interpret this as a desire for distance and step back, further deepening the person's fear of abandonment (all strategies explored in relation to shame in chapter 9).

In services for people with intellectual disabilities, missed opportunities for connection are perhaps made starker by the rhetoric about independence - that adults with intellectual disabilities need to strive towards independence, and even for those with healthy attachments, we overlook the need to meet their primary safety needs first and for interdependence. Conversely, if someone is being clingy and not soothed easily, the carer can unwittingly reduce experiences that promote autonomy, by staying close and not offering opportunities to experience coping and/or offering co-regulating (or self-soothing). So, we need to be mindful of too many outcomes-focused goals within a service or goals which are actually for others (carers or the wider systems focused on outcomes) not the person with intellectual disabilities.

DDP-informed ways reflecting around this issue

Goals need to be linked with a person's social, emotional, and relational capacity. The goals of relationship-building, co-regulating etc based on the Pyramid of Need are very important.

While a person may have the daily living skills to shop alone, they may lack the emotional or social coping skills to handle unexpected challenges, such as a change in the supermarket layout, being asked a question, or finding their usual item unavailable or packaged differently. In these moments, the presence of a supportive other can provide structure, helping to co-regulate emotions that are being expressed but not yet managed, while also supporting the person in recognising (give voice) to hidden needs. This process fosters interdependence, enabling meaningful problem-solving and progress toward achieving personal goals. This needs to be recognised at an organisational level, and for when there is fluctuation in regulating, reasoning and relating skills to be accepted and adjusted for, so that systems (and carers) can be responsive and cope with changes and temporary adjustments in skills.

Intersubjective care in a subjective care system – boundaries, relationships and capacity

The thoughtfulness about boundaries, structure and connections needs to be present across the entire system - from the carers directly supporting the person with intellectual disabilities to the MDTs, managers, and commissioners involved in their care. The DDP model aims that these boundaries are congruent with connection - again, this requires engagement across the whole system otherwise as funding, placement and systemic pressures risk overtaking individuals with intellectual disabilities attachment needs (Casswell, 2014).

As explored already in Chapter 4, intersubjective connection is not a process whereby the carer evaluates the person with intellectual disabilities, it is rather a comprehensive affective, reflective, and behavioural experience of each other. Within an intersubjective interaction, the carer is influenced by the person they care for and this is acknowledged and celebrated; and in turn the cared for person is influenced by their carer; they are connected. The traditional structure in many care settings can find this level of deep and meaningful connection hard and often worry about boundaries and over-dependence on carers. There can be an expectation that carers are in control; that they set the rules; and the cared for person sticks to them. In DDP- practice, there needs to be a way of enabling staff to connect and care, where the central focus is on developing intersubjective connections, between the person receiving care, their caregivers, and the wider system around the person. For some, this is a huge cultural shift from the dichotomy of independence or dependence to the integration of interdependence. This means that the boundaries and structure provided needs to be intersubjective, and connection based, rather than based on restrictions and control. Through DDP-informed reflection, there can be opportunities to resolve conflict and allow conversations, which help people to identify their different approaches and perspectives and work towards challenging these assumptions, to develop a consistent model.

Grant *et al* (2024) illustrate this as two pillars of residential care – relationship and structure; these are both harder to maintain at times of crisis. They relate to the two hands of parenting/care discussed in the last chapter. Furthermore, when individuals have had significant trauma in their lives, they may not have had regular routines or patterns to their days – this can cause conflict with staff who are trying to implement these (based upon their own models of family routine) and there is a chance of conflict, as these ideas are brought together.

It is also helpful to engage systems, at all levels in thinking, about which behaviours are unacceptable and how the boundaries in relation to these can be held and talked about with the person with intellectual disabilities. Structure and predictability are paramount for all and have been shown to be part of successful DDP (Casswell *et al*, 2014) – daily routines which help all to feel contained, including plans for anniversaries and celebrations – these rituals can allow opportunities for mutual joyful experiences.

There can be a complexity here; DDP emphasises the importance of holding clear boundaries for people in order that they feel safe and contained; and yet, of course adults who have capacity, can make their own decisions, wise or unwise. Fundamental to this is ensuring the person's choices and voice are respected and central, aligning with the core principles of trauma-informed care (TIC).

When people have capacity (always assuming this is the case), it may be helpful to explore *with* them, when they are in their window of tolerance and they are calm and regulated, what they think are suitable boundaries for them (as we might do with an older child/teenager). These boundaries are negotiated when someone is able to be regulated and connected to their upstairs brain (they have their ability to reason); the boundaries may then need to be implemented in a connection-based and non-punitive way for the person, even when they are dysregulated. For this to work, there needs to be a clear plan for when these boundaries will be reviewed, and this needs to be transparently explained and together agree that plans won't be reviewed or changed at times of high distress. Often, regular MDT meetings allow this to be a set time to explore such things. These boundaries can be negotiated with the person with explicit reference to safety and while acknowledging the person's propensity to shame and wish to please the system.

It is helpful to hold in mind, while negotiating boundaries, that we are often trying to support the person with intellectual disabilities to move from a position of environmental safety (where the restrictions within the environment keep them safe) to one of relational safety – where the connection within the relationships helps to keep a person safe.

Restrictive practice and relational safety

Central to providing relationally aware care (Skelly, 2014), and at the foundation of the DDP Pyramid of Need (see Chapter 11) is the idea of safety. Safety encompasses both the reality of being safe and the belief that you are safe; physically, psychologically and in your relationships. Simply stopping the 'bad' things from happening to someone is not enough to repair the damage of them (Hughes, 2017). The times of trauma, although in the past, are joined to the safety of now; '*by the fragmented sense of self with significant challenges to emotional, reflective and relational functioning*' (Hughes, 2017, p.597).

People with an intellectual disability and their support network are at an increased risk of feeling unsafe, which so often is the context within which restrictive practices are most likely to be used. Feeling unsafe, because people with an intellectual disability are more likely to experience unmet needs related to environmental adaptations, sensory, emotional, relational, communication and physiological needs and carers may be more likely to burn out, experience compassion fatigue, vicarious trauma, blocked care and experience/express their own shame responses. Staff can also be motivated to act in this way for fear of criticism for not meeting predetermined goals, actions or targets for the day. These factors all increase the risks of restrictions being put in place for people. People with intellectual disabilities are less able to advocate for themselves, their needs or any unsafe practice.

Restrictive practices are the umbrella term used to describe various types of restraint (see Figure 14.2). They refer to stopping someone from doing something they want to do or forcing someone to do something they don't want to do (RRN, 2023). Restrictive practices often aim to keep people safe, and people's right to life is protected in law by the Human Rights Act (1998). However, we know that restrictive practices are often used disproportionately and even can lead to (re) traumatisation as helplessness and vulnerability surface under power-laden interventions (Quinn & Sheldon, 2025). Additionally, the use of more covertly coercive measures such as psychological restraint and blanket restrictions (generic restrictions applied across a group) can have a damaging cumulative effect (e.g. micro-trauma) and leave people feeling disempowered and objectified (Quinn *et al*, 2023; Quinn, 2025). It is not possible to feel relationally connected and be disempowered. It is important to consider the range of restrictive practices people may be subject to, and the spectrum of lost opportunities in providing timely, bespoke and trauma-informed support. Some examples of restrictive practice are shown in Figure 14.2.

Figure 14.2: Types of restrictive practice *(based upon Restraint reduction network (n.d). Resources: About restraint)*

Type of restrictive practice as outlined by the Restraint Reduction Network	Example of restraint
Cultural restraint	Using cultural norms to restrict, prevent or subdue e.g. stopping a person from stimming, or forcing them to make eye contact.
Psychological restraint is using communication strategies to restrict, prevent or subdue	■ Use of verbal threats e.g. if you do not do X, Y will not happen. ■ Non-verbal threat e.g. turning back on someone, encouraging a person to take medication with 5 or 6 staff standing behind them (communicating a waiting restraint team). ■ Refusing to speak to someone though a shift. ■ Systemic e.g. use of legislation, communication from oppressive building e.g. cannot exit locked doors.
Surveillance is watching people, places and/or property	■ Excessive staffing. ■ CCTV. ■ Observations that invade dignity and privacy, including technological restrictions such as monitoring devices.
Mechanical restraint is the use of equipment to restrict, prevent or subdue	■ Seat belt straps/restraints. ■ Handcuffs. ■ Chairs/beanbags that a person cannot get out of. ■ Bed rails.
Blanket rules is when one rule is applied to a group of people without individual risk assessment	■ Set bed times, meal times. ■ Using diapers unnecessarily (e.g. just in case). ■ Restricted access to items, such as food or activities locking doors, being locked in a room.
Environmental restraint is using the environment to restrict, prevent or subdue	■ Telling someone they must stay in a specific area (e.g. "go to your room".) ■ Locked doors. ■ Windows that do not fully open. ■ Seclusion. ■ Segregation. ■ Parental/staff team withdrawal and confinement.

Physical restraint is using the body to restrict, prevent or subdue	■ Including negligible use of force to brush teeth etc. ■ Clinical holding. ■ Moving someone forcibly from one place to another.
Chemical restraint is using prescribed medication to restrict, prevent or subdue	■ The regular use of antipsychotics and benzodiazepine to sedate. ■ As required (prn) medication – e.g. rapid tranquilisation, or given intra-muscularly.

People's human rights e.g. the right to psychological and physical integrity as well as self-determination are protected by law. Given the evidenced harms of using restraint and our increasing understanding of proactive support, there are extensive drivers to move away from restrictive practice (see RRN, 2023). Restrictive practices should only ever be used as a last resort, proportionate to the risks and occur within a legitimate rights recognising framework. As well as the legal framework, which permits the restrictions (e.g. Mental Health Act or Mental Capacity Act) there also needs to be a justifiable reason to stop the person doing what they are doing – which should clearly be aimed at alleviating harm. The action also needs to be least restrictive and thought needs to be given to how a more supportive and less restrictive intervention can be offered, how care/compassion can be shown, and how restraint can occur of the least amount of time (see Quinn & Sheldon, 2025). We should "*expect people to provide us with agile and timely care… at times when we are distressed… if this does not happen and distress escalates restraint is too frequently relied upon, when providing the right support is what is required*" (Quinn & Sheldon, 2025, p.3).

There is a need to acknowledge that blanket rules are a form of restriction for people with an intellectual disability and that often, psychological restraint inherent in power imbalances e.g. the questions and/or demands placed on people, cause a reduction in a person's ability to be self-determining. Transparency and a willingness to reflect on the subtleties and routine use of restraint within the system is necessary and the Restraint Reduction Network (RRN, 2023) offers advice on this.

In addition, people with intellectual disabilities (adults and children) can be subject to extensive polypharmacy; they may be prescribed a range of medication, primarily concerned with behavioural control and 'neuro-normative' behaviours. In children's services there can be an added layer of power, whereby children are done to ('childism'; Wall, 2019) , which opens the door to restrictive practices, such as gates on bedrooms, movement sensors, harnesses in cars, locked doors in the kitchen, hot water turned off, communication tools in bags, removal of certain things from core boards, so they can't be requested...the list goes on. If adults are deemed to lack capacity, then still careful consideration of best interest is needed. It's an important consideration, in all care systems, but especially in systems that support a potentially vulnerable cohort for the myriad reasons discussed in this book.

The transition from environmental to relational security so often is a tricky one, but in our practice, we have seen this successfully happen for children and adults with an intellectual disability, using the practical steps outline in the previous chapter.

DDP reflections in relation to this issue

DDP-practice can have a role in establishing and naming the needs that underlie behaviours that might be perceived as challenging and may therefore lead to restrictions. Exploring and understanding these underlying and relational needs can be pivotal in changing from reactive to proactive support, thereby eliminating the need for rights restricting measures. Integrated within relational safety is ensuring physical and psychological safety for carers – so they can, in turn, provide this safety for the person with an intellectual disability. DDP-informed reflection helps to better understand and respond to behaviours occurring due to miscuing or efforts to assert extreme independence, offering a framework of PACE and mentalisation across the system.

Following any restrictive practice it will be imperative to consider the 4th R – Repair. We would suggest that repair needs to be offered in a timely way, when both people are regulated. Repair cannot start by engaging with reasoning but needs to absolutely respond to the importance of regulation. Many times the carer wanting to support repair is also the one who also needs to support regulation! It's a fluid process, and carers need to be aware of their own need for regulation and relating. Once the person with an intellectual disability is regulated, it can be helpful to build the story from their perspective about what occurred. This story telling approach draws on PACE-based approaches of deep acceptance for someone else's experience, and curiosity about how it was for them. Being able to make better sense in a co-created way of their reactions, their anger, and their upset with your actions will be important and allow connection and new understanding to emerge. It is likely important to offer empathy rather than a playful or light tone as the latter can be easily misread and increase the risk of inducing shame and further relational disruption. If we slow this process down, re-establish an intersubjective connection then we are more likely to rebuild our relationships and maintain the regulation needed for reasoning, or even considering ways to manage anger differently.

DDP-informed supervision, training and reflection also aims to support carers to develop a better understanding of their own attachment histories and shed light on the blind spots or reasons underlying any less-than-ideal ways of responding to those they are caring for. DDP approaches – by better understanding and meeting individual and relational needs, through a common language and PACE-based approach, two hands of care (and everything discussed in this chapter and the book!), etc – has the potential to play a role in the reduction of restrictive strategies, providing more person-centred care and ensure better planning and training to provide care that prioritises safety through relationships.

Further staffing considerations

Many people with intellectual disabilities live within funded placements with paid staff; this can include residential and supported-living services. These operate under regulatory and commissioning frameworks but here we talk about some of the possible staffing/placement issues that can arise and DDP-informed thoughts on these.

Staff transitions

We acknowledge that staff leave post, and sometimes this happens a lot – it is identified by the British Psychological Society (BPS) as one of the risks of needing lifelong support as many people with intellectual disabilities do (BPS, 2017). In the past, when it was still believed that people with an intellectual disability did not have an emotional world, it would sometimes be commonplace practice for people not to be told about the death of close family relatives, for fear of causing distress (I hope this no longer happens!); now, sometimes, people with intellectual disabilities are not told about the leaving of staff members they are close to. It is as if we think someone will not notice, that a person they were connected with has left and, of course, people always notice. What they may be unable to do, is communicate their level of distress, relief or confusion. Similarly, people might get moved home or foster placement without consent or accessible discussion; these things are, of course, hugely disruptive to attachments and connections.

DDP reflection on this issue

We would urge that there is an individualised (and service-wide) process for how and when people are told about staff leaving post; that this is replicated for people to help them have that feeling of security (it is another example of offering boundaries and predictability). For some key staff, there is an importance in maintaining contact, when either a member of staff or person with intellectual disability leaves a service, so formal care roles ending. This provides a relational thread and overarching connection, in a person's life, someone who is part of and can hold and share the life stories.

Other people with intellectual disabilities who live with the person you are supporting might also leave, for lots of reasons and these peer relationships are important too. Again, this needs to be thought about and planned for and, in both instances, clear messages about why the person has left are necessary. It is highly possible that the person with intellectual disabilities will believe that people leaving is related to them (and their distress) and an alternative message must be clearly communicated; without this (or even with it), there are risks that it reinforces the person's sense of shame and rejection, as well as experiences and, therefore, beliefs that relationships will not last.

When people leave home

There are also times when children, young people and adults move into care as part of a natural transition away from parents or when parents have expressed they can no longer meet their needs at home. At these times it can be a real battle to help the surrounding system agree on the importance of planned, well supported, regular and ongoing contact with parents and other key relationships who were maintained whilst living at home. This transition needs to be considered and allow bespoke transitions which best allow safety and this often includes ongoing contact with key/loved attachment figures. In some services contact breaks, with no contact immediately after transition are still promoted with the view that this will "help the person with intellectual disabilities settle". However, this does not place the safety and regulation of the individual centrally.

DDP-informed reflection on this issue

We would urge that DDP-informed reflection be held around this, perhaps thinking about where an individual might be described or assessed as being on the Pyramid of Need, and how this may be in the new placement/house. What about DDP-informed psychological support before, during and after this transition? How can we use DDP thinking to navigate this transition from being a full-time carer and parent? How can we support the person with intellectual disabilities to manage this transition? To maintain or (re)establish a meaningful relationship and connection through this enormous change and keep contact with individuals whom they wish to maintain these relationships with?

When people are placed far away from their home

It goes without saying that, wherever possible, people should be given the choice and opportunity to live near their families and/or those who love and support them. Unfortunately, in intellectual disability services, people are still often placed in placements (particularly hospital placements) which are many miles from their family, friends and community. The risks of this are discussed in several places and reflected in some of the recent scandals of poor care and abuse in the UK, e.g. Winterbourne and Walton Hall (reflected upon by Oakes, 2012). Of course, this affects connections and the availability of these safe, known and attached people to spend time with the person they care for. Often, there are restrictions of visiting hours and locations, which add to disconnect.

DDP-informed reflection on this issue

As family/relational bonds are important, being in close proximity or accessible by rail/road or transportation connections with those whom they have fulfilling and meaningful connections with. Surely, we all need this more at times of distress, which is just when services might not respond to this. If the system is working in a DDP-informed way, then it is helpful if families are part of training, network consultation/case workshops and reflections. This will ensure that they can be involved in DDP-informed care and contribute to the understanding of the person and their connection needs. We need to think with families who are far away about their feelings of shame, abandonment and powerlessness. This may need to be thought about differently if the family has not been able to provide adequate care for the person with intellectual disabilities, or when there has been abuse, as discussed below.

Respite carers

Linked to societal discourses about independence and family support, parents may experience feelings of shame when they have support from respite carers or educational settings, which can be added to if these adhere to a different model of care from those at home. These feelings might arise, as additional support can sometimes be perceived as judgment, implying that parents are unable to meet their child's needs on their own. Rather than communicating an understanding of the need for a break in caregiving, which is often vital and necessary, it may unintentionally suggest that they are deficient. This can be added to when a child doesn't meet milestones or displays behaviours that challenge societal expectations or norms. There may need to be a shift in expectations from a belief that support is needed because you are failing or not coping, to one of an expectation that you will need and deserve support because you are caring for a child/adult with additional challenges.

As paid staff within intellectual disability services, it is important too to be aware of the narratives that develop when services do not meet the needs of families well enough, resulting in families feeling that they need to fight for services, which comes with the risk of becoming labelled as 'difficult'. All these experiences can be traumatic for families, increasing the risks of them not seeking help and feeling shamed for the help they require for the person with an intellectual disability they support.

DDP-informed reflection on this issue

It is important for professionals and systems to be aware of shame in this context and to name it (to tame it). This can lead to traumas resonating in the system and support the idea that the wider system needs to also be working in a DDP-informed and trauma-informed way – connected with the direct carers and offering them safety and connection before correction and interventions.

Families where abuse has occurred

In adult services there can be times when people choose to have ongoing contact with families and family members who have been abusive to them, and/or failed to protect them from abusive situations; this may occur in children's services as well. Our role, as professionals working within a DDP model, is to help the person to remain regulated and able to bring coherence to and empathy for their feelings before, during and after those visits. We need to ensure that we continue to draw on the elements of connection, curiosity and PACE, in relation to this visit – maintaining connection; helping the person to make sense of any mixed feelings that might arise; and to offer co-regulation as they process the confusion that can occur when spending time with people you love who also cause hurt; whilst also being especially mindful not to evoke shame in the person for their continued need to meet with their family. Where there are ongoing concerns around physical and emotional safety, then of course, discussion with the person and/or safeguarding will need to occur.

Holding the DDP relational perspective to this there is also a need to consider the family's perspective and how we can support them to understand their situation and help them move towards more adequate care. This can be explored through DDP-parenting as well as DDP approaches; this may allow them to develop an understanding of the rupture and make steps towards repair and more co-regulated relationships; of course, ensuring that the person with an intellectual disability is safe while this work is undertaken.

Looking after yourself

As always, it is important that all carers are encouraged to look after themselves, and their own emotional well-being needs. Sometimes, systems are good at this, thinking about staff well-being and ensuring this is prioritised, but too often systems that do not employ a relational-focused model struggle to offer support around well-being. This can include asking people to work long shifts and/or changing shift patterns with little notice, to attend meetings or training that they are not paid to be at, shortening induction processes due to staffing pressures etc. This can be a part of thinking about safety and connection for all in the system. As touched upon, offering this connection to people can lead to feelings of shame arising and struggles with blocked care/trust – and what this says about you as a carer. Some staff will, of course, have their own complex/difficult attachment histories, experiences of abuse or trauma in the past or ongoing. Helping staff to explore their own needs and their own history in thinking about their embodying of the DDP approaches can also help value looking after yourself and connections with wider parts of the system. The essential staff team-meetings and reflection sessions also can include elements of self-care and the importance of a range of elements to this, including looking after one's physical well-being. In the same way we have discussed relationship and structure (boundaries) held in balance for the person with an intellectual disability, it is essential that literature and guidance around this needs to be available, consistent, transparent and fair for all in the system.

Conclusion

This chapter has explored some of the complex service issues that can arise within intellectual disability services and examined how DDP-practice and approaches can contribute to alleviating these challenges by considering a more relational focus. We have considered the importance of issues such as boundaries and capacity, restrictive practices, staff transitions, individuals being placed far from home, respite care, moving out of the family home, and where abuse has occurred within families. Across all these areas, a focus on connection and safety, delivered through the DDP approach, has been highlighted as particularly beneficial. Additionally, the chapter recognises and highlights the importance of parents, carers, and all those within the wider system prioritising their own well-being to provide the most connected and compassionate care possible for individuals with intellectual disabilities.

Chapter 15: Dyadic Developmental Practice in services familiar with Positive Behaviour Support

Summary

- Positive Behaviour Support (PBS) is the dominant model of service provision for people with intellectual disabilities. It was developed to offer a framework to better understand and meet the needs of people with an intellectual disability who might show their dysregulation with responses that can be challenging to those who care for their emotional and physical well-being. PBS intervention aims to support inclusion and equitable participation to quality-of-life enhancing opportunities, environments and relationships.
- Critics reflect that PBS doesn't explicitly consider the neurodevelopmental, emotional, social and relational impact of traumatic experiences on the person with intellectual disabilities and the complexity of relational patterns of interacting with immediate carers and throughout the support network.
- This chapter offers our clinical reflections around how DDP concepts can be considered in a clinical cycle familiar to PBS service provision for people with intellectual disabilities. These reflections are shared in the hope we can bring carers and professionals on a journey with us to, together, move towards an understanding and approach that increases safety for all and supports intersubjective connections.

Introduction

This chapter aims to link the application of DDP concepts and approaches within a PBS framework, as this is widely used within intellectual disability services across the UK. The fit of these two models is not neat, but in an attempt to be practically useful for clinicians, we have tried to outline our thoughts about this. Following a brief description of PBS, we outline the rationale for incorporating DDP principles into PBS. While we do not believe that the PBS framework can significantly contribute to the provision of DDP, we highlight how the behavioural underpinnings of PBS often lack the ability to prioritise safety, connection, co-regulation and intersubjective relationships. In contrast, DDP centralises these elements, making it a crucial model for supporting individuals with intellectual disabilities who express distress or dysregulation through behaviours that challenge and who may pose risks to themselves and/or their caregivers. The question in this chapter is whether they can sit alongside each other.

We then offer a few notes on terminology before delving into how applying a DDP lens to the assessment and formulation processes can deepen our understanding of individuals and inform more relationally attuned PBS plans. The chapter concludes by connecting the Four Rs framework – of Reason, Relate, Regulate and Repair – to trauma-informed care, aligning it with the proactive, secondary, reactive and post-incident stages of a PBS plan. This includes integrating the Pyramid of Need discussed in Chapter 11, demonstrating how these frameworks can enrich our approach to supporting individuals who display behaviour that challenges caregivers and the wider system.

Positive Behaviour Support (PBS)

As clinical leads in services for children and adults with intellectual disabilities, we are aware that a dominant model for supporting people with intellectual disabilities is Positive Behaviour Support (PBS).

PBS was built on the historical context of promoting the rights, inclusion and well-being of people with an intellectual disability. This followed the stigma, discrimination and abuse they experienced, and public enquiries made into the mistreatment and abuse of people with intellectual disabilities in institutional settings. Positive Behaviour Support is a service delivery approach, aiming to offer a system-wide culture of care and person-centred approach to ensuring capable environments that improve quality of life (as opposed to a focus on reducing behaviours that can cause a challenge). PBS can be considered to consist of ten elements (Gore *et al*, 2013) categorised in terms of values, theory and evidence base, and process:

1. Values

The promotion of inclusion, social roles, participation, choice, and equality of opportunity (Gore *et al*, 2013).

2. Theory and evidence base

Evidence-based approaches, such as functional analysis, to support positive changes at multiple levels of a system, based on the premise that behaviours can be understood as responses that meet a need or serve a function (of, for example, connection, communication, sensory regulation or escaping an uncomfortable situation), and quality of life can be enhanced with enriching relationships, environments and skills development

3. Process

A data-driven approach to decision-making at every stage, using assessment to inform multi-component intervention; a PBS plan that describes how a person's quality of life can be improved within a PBS framework of primary (proactive), secondary (active), and reactive strategies.

The PBS model aims to look beyond observable behaviour and better understand and meet a person's unmet needs, through a co-created and implemented plan of support. 'The central independent variable in PBS is systems change' (Carr, 2007, p 4), focusing on principles of environmental adjustments; sensory integration; speech and language support; social support; and skills development.

Why consider DDP concepts in PBS service provision?

PBS has a growing and international body of evidence from systematic and meta-analytic reviews of single-case, small group designs and randomised control trials (RCTs) (as referenced by Gore *et al*, 2013). Policy and professional guidelines have also drawn on PBS as a model of best practice for supporting people who show behaviours that can be experienced as challenging to support (Banks *et al*, 2007; NICE, 2018; CQC, 2018; BILD's Competency Framework, 2015) in residential homes (Grey & McClean, 2007), schools (Goh & Bambara, 2013) and community settings (Durand *et al*, 2012).

However, there are times when the underpinning philosophy does not fully translate into practice (Quinn, 2025). Instances where people are seen as behavioural objects to observe and 'relationships of concern' impact on humanising relationships (Quinn, 2025). National Special Interest Groups for professionals working with people with intellectual disabilities are raising alternative models of service delivery and therapeutic care, including trauma-informed care, systemic approaches, emotion development and DDP. The concept of 'positive social interactions', a foundational aspect of the newly published work promoting Capable Environments (BILD, 2022), does not necessarily equate to mutual, intersubjective relationships. Furthermore, some conversations are turning to the idea of therapeutic love (e.g. Quinn, 2025; Shimmens & Skelly, 2023); where professionals set aside their knowledge in order to offer abundant curiosity and acceptance, manifested through secure attachments and consistent emotional support – similar to DDP.

PBS is making attempts to integrate trauma histories into the understanding of people's presentation (e.g. BILD, 2017). It seems that there are certain assumptions within the behavioural elements of PBS that need to be challenged/reconsidered to more fully understand people's presentations in an emotional and relational way. Explicitly, these are:

Internal states influence responses and behaviour

Firstly, for many years, behavioural work focused only on observable behaviours, reflecting the wider societal assumption that people with intellectual disabilities lacked internal and emotional worlds. There is, of course, an essential need to recognise the emotional experiences of individuals, as internal states significantly influence observable behaviour (Harding, 2025).

Relationships, compassion and empathy must be available at all times to support safety regulation and genuine connection

Behavioural models have mistakenly viewed empathy and compassion as potential reinforcers of undesirable behaviours, sometimes leading to their removal as responses to distress (Sweeney *et al*, 2018). As highlighted in the previous chapter, ensuring a sense of safety is essential and a basic need for all. Safety fosters relationships that eventually enable co-regulation. Relationships must be available proactively and throughout someone's distress; we all rely most on attachment figures during times of distress or dysregulation. Only in connected relationships are people able to be offered abundant curiosity to aid with understanding their distress (Quinn, 2025).

Neurodevelopment, neurobiology, emotions and relationships need to be prioritised

Our understanding of the internal needs/triggers underlying a person's presentation, needs to be intertwined with the impact of neurobiological responses to perceived danger, and the associated experience of fight, flight, freeze and dissociation. It is important to acknowledge the lack of control people have over these responses, as they occur at a biological level; yet we need to adapt our approach or levels of support accordingly. Although the Time Intensity Model (Kaplan & Wheeler, 1983) and accompanying proactive, secondary and reactive strategies are an attempt to acknowledge what support a person might need when they are within, on the edges of and outside of their window of tolerance, this is not always explicitly linked to potential changes in processing and regulatory needs at times of distress. PBS doesn't explicitly consider the neurodevelopmental, emotional, social and relational impact of traumatic experiences on the person with intellectual disabilities.

Figure 15.1 highlights the developmental sequence and therefore how, if we focus purely on behavioural regulation, we are assuming that all the previous levels of development are in place – this may not be true and may not be consistently true. These ideas are explicitly explored later in this chapter.

Figure 15.1: The sequence of the seven pieces of developmental trauma (inspired by Lyons *et al*, 2020)

Carers need guidance and tools to understand and support emotional and relational needs

PBS is a framework which provides person-tailored interventions, and a service delivery approach. It is possible to integrate a range of models within the framework. A central part of this is to help carers and the wider system gain a better understanding of the underlying needs driving distressed behaviours. PBS encourages carers' responses dependent on the person's level of arousal and distress, and this can include how we can continue to offer safety and connection to people at these times. However, PBS does not inherently provide the theoretical guidance or practical tools to build secure attachment relationships or to understand, connect with and support emotional and relational needs. Behavioural support is unlikely to be effective when provided within relationships that are not connected (Sterkenburg *et al*, 2008).

Behaviour can be best understood in the context of a relationship, not just an individual

The final assumption is that traditional approaches often risk attributing behaviour solely to the individual. Notably, PBS seeks to address this issue by promoting capable environments and focusing on systems change (as mentioned above). Some clinicians have also begun to reconceptualise what has traditionally been seen as factors 'reinforcing' behaviours, within the context of relationships, and the impacts of wider societal issues. For example, Hastings *et al* (2013) note an inter-relationship between behaviours that challenge and carers' behaviours, including the importance of understanding the beliefs about and the emotional impact of these behaviours that challenge (both in witnessing the behaviours and the increase in stress caused by them).

In this chapter, we propose enriching the PBS framework by integrating DDP-practice principles throughout the clinical cycle to better reflect upon these relational dynamics. We attempt to offer a way to integrate DDP concepts into the PBS framework, with DDP offering an approach to understanding and supporting these important ideas. Yet, also allowing the PBS framework to be present, which in some organisations is the current service configuration and may fit with constraints and commissioning regulations, supporting both compliance and effective practice.

Proposing a transformation of thinking and practice

As highlighted by Beth Greenhills' powerful and provocative article title 'They have behaviour, we have relationships' (2011), we need to reformulate behavioural approaches in a more emotionally resonant and relational context. It is important to consider the emotional experiences that underlie observable behaviour and actions. In keeping with a dyadic position, the emotional experiences of the person with an intellectual disability *and* their carers. For example, triggers and consequences need to also be understood within patterns of relating and the relationship between the person with an intellectual disability and individuals caring for them in their support network. These patterns might include control, power (powerlessness) and rejection. Separately, triggers and consequences also need to incorporate what we know about neurobiological needs for safety, including the role of co-regulation, the impact of hypervigilance to danger, and the foundational principles of the Four Rs (Bombèr, 2020; Perry, 2006). These elements are essential for trauma-informed PBS practice that fosters trust, and promotes meaningful engagement, particularly for individuals affected by developmental trauma or heightened states of distress.

One of the aims of PBS is the focus on quality of life to help move away from 'measuring the misery' and equating success only to reductions in behaviours; instead, measuring skills and happiness. We propose that quality of relationships needs to be prioritised too (Harding, 2024). Boelé (2017) argues that it is not enough for interventions to attempt to make the individual with intellectual disabilities more 'acceptable' or conform to society (i.e. through increasing independent living skills) or even to simply remove some of the access barriers so that people can participate. Instead, we would argue 'relationships heal relational trauma' (Treisman, 2016) and when working within a PBS framework, this needs to incorporate the areas discussed in this book, for people whose relationships are difficult and/or scary and who show their dysregulation through behaviours that challenge.

Rather than a predominant focus on improving quality of life, happiness or complex behaviour, we propose that services for people with intellectual disabilities consider a paradigm shift: a focus on supporting people with intellectual disabilities, their carers and support network to (re)build a felt sense of emotional and physical safety, trust and unconditional acceptance within relationships. We propose this can be achieved through integrating the knowledge of the intra-related connections between attachment, experiences the brain, behaviour and developmental models throughout our work, to truly accept and care for the underlying relational and emotional needs of the person with intellectual disabilities and their care network; ultimately, responding relationally.

We discuss how DDP can enhance the PBS framework, not because we think that DDP benefits from thinking more about reinforcement or proactive working and capable environments, but because PBS can lack the tools to focus on relationships and connection. We accept that many services have invested heavily in PBS and that this model has become familiar to many, including families, paid carers and commissioners. Familiarity can be useful, but this does not mean we should stop progressing these ideas. In this chapter we urge that our assessment, formulation and intervention (including support plans) become more relationally focused, more invested in connection and include key DDP concepts such as PACE, exploring affective-reflective dialogue, and the Two Hands of care as an approach to (behaviour) support.

Terminology

This chapter deliberately uses terminology which is more closely related to the PBS model, such as 'triggers' and 'long-term maintaining factors'. This is so that those familiar with a PBS model can see how the ideas they are more familiar with can link with the DDP approach.

Dysregulated responses that are also known as behaviours that challenge

Barriers to the development of a secure attachment relationship are likely to adversely impact on the child's sense of a safe haven and secure base. This, combined with the child's disability-related factors, may make it harder for them to engage in relationships that support their ability to explore the world and can interfere with their attempts to be playful, independent and productive. This means children and the adults they grow into, may be more likely to be hypervigilant, show frequent displays of protest, increased levels of distress and dysregulated/distressed behaviours. This can look like being shut down, withdrawn, disconnected, showing self-neglect, showing clingy or demanding patterns of relating or causing injury to themselves, others or their environment. It is starting to be widely recognised that developmental trauma is presenting in children and adults as behaviours that are challenging (in the general population and in individuals with an intellectual disability; see Chapter 9: Shame and shielding from shame;, Kezeler & Stavropoulos, 2012; Harding, 2021).

In most intellectual disability services, such dysregulated responses are referred to as behaviours that challenge. Behaviours that challenge can be understood as behaviour of such an intensity, frequency or duration as to threaten the quality of life and/or physical safety of the individual or others and risk leading to responses that are restrictive, aversive or result in exclusion (Banks *et al*, 2007). Behaviour can be thought of as a response to and communication of an internal need (Emerson & Einfield, 2011). In this chapter, we have referred to behaviours that challenge as an inclusive term. This encompasses behaviours arising from distress or dysregulation, and what services may refer to as challenging behaviours, behaviours of concern, and behaviours that pose challenges to the system. It includes actions that cause distress to the individual and those supporting them, as well as behaviours that place the individual, their carers, or their social inclusion at significant risk.

Reinforcement

Reinforcement, in behavioural terms, refers to the factors that maintain a behaviour, traditionally categorised as tangible, escape, sensory, or social attention based. Unlike traditional reinforcement models, the concept of safety plays a foundational role in determining whether an individual can engage with any sort of correction. In behavioural terms safety can be thought of as reinforcement. DDP clearly states that there is a need for connection before (during and after) correction. It is possible that the positive aspect of safety and connection can in themselves become reinforcers of attachment security and relational development.

It is highly unlikely that any learning from contingencies will occur when someone is dysregulated or dissociated; when they have 'flipped their lid' (Siegel, 2024). A key distinction lies in the role of relational and practical safety as a prerequisite for reinforcement. According to polyvagal theory, if the autonomic nervous system does not perceive safety, the individual cannot fully engage in social interaction, learning, or process reinforcement effectively. Humans, as inherently social and meaning-making beings, find social engagement itself to be a powerful reinforcer, but it must be (in the language of PBS) provided proactively and within an environment that nurtures regulation and relational safety. This can be achieved, in time, through co-regulation, where the caregivers help another achieve a state of calm and safety (see p.304 (intervention planning)). Praise and naturally occurring rewards may have their place, but we have to be mindful of unintended consequences, such as shame or dysregulation, which can lead to relationship rupture. Praise, as a positive reinforcer, can also be problematic. Praise has an evaluative element, which, in Polyvagal terms, can push people into a defensive position and therefore reduce their social engagement and learning. A relational approach minimises attention on external rewards and instead emphasises joy and comfort in relationships; connection which leads to an increase in prosocial behaviours because the person feels of value and interest (Golding, 2025). So, a relational approach does not immediately focus on behaviour, but instead focuses on the relationship, prioritising its endurance and presence even at times of behaviours that challenge.

More recently, in PBS practice, there has been an acknowledgement of the importance of considering longer-term reinforcers or maintaining factors such as how our interactions may shape an individual's experiences of themselves, relationships, trust, and sense of safety (Paterson, 2020; Dunn & Bolton, 2004). Considering the broader influence of longer-term reinforcement can be a helpful part of a trauma/attachment-informed PBS process (e.g. Harding, 2025). Part of this shift allows consideration and curiosity about the unintentionally longer-term impacts on the sense of self of the person with an intellectual disability and the care-giving system around them; as well as these impacts cascading to and from the caring dyad and the wider system.

DDP-informed assessment, formulation, intervention planning and support plans in a PBS framework

The following section explores how DDP-practice can be tied into the clinical cycle of assessment, formulation and intervention, in addition to the ways this is already discussed within this book. To help bring our thinking to life, we introduce the following case vignette to help consider the application of our writing to a person with intellectual disabilities and their support network. Within the PBS framework, assessment, formulation and intervention planning is often considered in context of the time intensity model. This model considers how people may present differently depending on whether they are at baseline, escalation or in crisis; and considers how people may need different types of support, practically and emotionally. This can be related to polyvagal theory and the window of tolerance (see Chapter 6: Neuroscience); it allows people to gauge/formulate how to best support someone depending on their level of regulation.

Case vignette: Jay

Jay is a 13-year-old boy with severe intellectual disabilities. He is reliant on others to prompt for all his personal care and most of his daily living skills. He can communicate with people who understand his idiosyncratic gestures and sounds. He lives at home with his mother and older sibling. Jay spent a lot of time in hospital as a premature baby and throughout his early childhood, due to feeding problems. His mother left a domestically violent relationship when Jay was 4 years old. He has seen many professionals and has always attended special school. He is referred to an NHS community child and adolescent learning disability child service, due to an increase in behaviours that challenge which include biting, scratching and hitting out at his mum and the respite carers who support him in the community. School is also seeing this behaviour. There is a concern around keeping his peers safe. Jay enjoys watching cartoons on TV, people-watching and being in the midst of the excitement. He has an older brother who has recently left home and with whom Jay remains very close.

Assessment

Central to PBS is the assessment of behaviours that challenge to learn when, where and how a person shows these, and what factors might be causing them to be maintained. Traditionally/behaviourally, this involves a functional assessment of antecedents (slow and fast triggers), the behaviour and the maintaining factors (consequences or reinforcers). These assessments lead to developing an understanding of the function of the behaviour (i.e. how it helps the person to cope or meet their needs). The behavioural model would suggest that through changing biological, social and environmental triggers and consequences, behaviours can change. DDP recognises a complex interaction involved in people's behaviours, which considers current and past relationships, interactions, internal working models, survival strategies, feelings of safety, powerlessness and choice, as well as levels of regulation and attachment patterns of the person with intellectual disabilities and those who care for them.

This means that DDP-informed assessment and formulation needs to take account of the seen, and unseen, the verbally expressed and the emotionally felt elements of the interaction between two people, while also acknowledging sensory differences/needs. In fact, it moves the focus away from focusing on the individual's behaviours in isolation and encourages a deeper focus on someone's response to their situation – the dyad of interaction. It aims to establish with the individual and/or their system, the internal triggers alongside the observable ones (Harding, 2021). In this way, we would align with the work of Delahooke (2022) and the developmental iceberg of factors which underlie the seen behaviour. However, in keeping with the dyadic nature of DDP, we have extended this, so that alongside the seen behaviours above the water, we can represent both the person with an intellectual disability and their care givers elements as underlying the seen presentation (see Figure 14.2). These elements interact seen and unseen and are felt for both the person with intellectual disability and their carer(s). They can also interact more broadly throughout the wider team of people who are supporting the person.

Assessments around communication, sensory regulation, physical needs, skills for living, processing and any other additional needs are crucial when developing an understanding of a person's needs. For the purposes of this chapter, we describe how to ensure PBS assessment can be more relational in nature. For example, we include a relational naturalistic observation template (see Appendix 13), which aims to gather information with a relational lens examining safety and attachment-seeking behaviour. While we see the usefulness of traditional monitoring and analysis of behaviours that challenge; it is also essential to acknowledge the underlying, unobservable, and interactional aspects of behaviour, as illustrated by the Dyadic Iceberg model in Figure 15.2 (see template in Appendix 8).

Figure 15.2: Dyadic Iceberg of behaviours that challenge – showing the underlying factors for the person with an intellectual disability and their carer

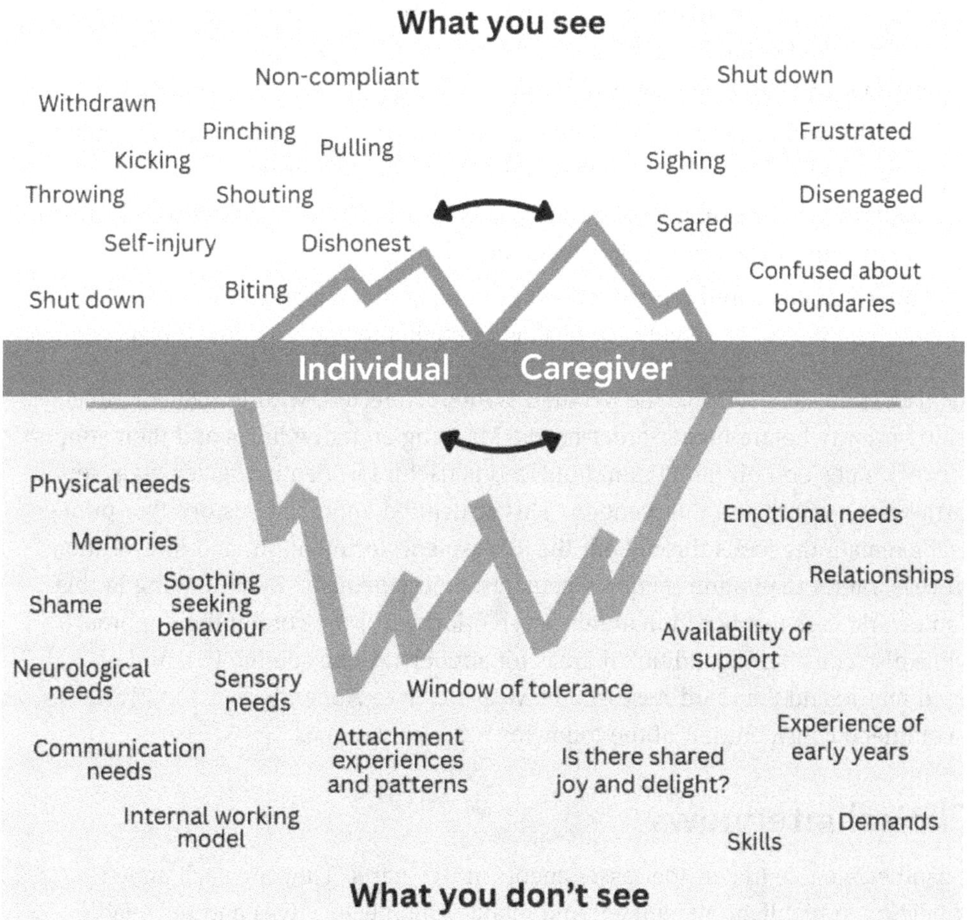

Pyramid of Need

The Pyramid of Need (Golding, 2013), is discussed in detail in chapter 11 and provides a six-level framework that can be used to understand presenting needs and tailor a plan of intervention for the person with intellectual disabilities, their caregivers, the support network and wider system. Therefore, the first stage of an enriched and more attachment-informed assessment would include mapping presentation based on the Pyramid of Need:

1. **Feeling safe:** Developing physical, emotional and sensory safety.
2. **Developing relationships:** Developing trust in availability and responsiveness of relationship.
3. **Comfort and co-regulation:** Using support from trusted adults to begin regulating emotions and behaviours. This aids the co-regulation when experiencing emotions at high or low arousal levels.
4. **Empathy and reflection:** Building reflective capacity and enhancing the ability to process and reflect on experiences and manage behaviour in relation to others.
5. **Resilience and resources:** Previously held core beliefs are revised within trusting relationships, developing self-esteem and identity.
6. **Explore traumas and mourn losses:** Processing past experiences, acknowledging pain, and supporting emotional healing through attuned, trust-based relationships.

As discussed, each stage of the pyramid is interconnected, with foundational needs taking priority before higher-order needs. Mapping an individual's and their support network's position on the Pyramid of Need is useful for identifying key areas for further assessment and intervention. This structured approach ensures that primary needs remain the focus throughout the assessment, formulation, and intervention process, rather than addressing all elements simultaneously. By grounding in this framework, care teams can maintain these priorities at the core of their approach while also considering additional areas for support. Alongside the Pyramid of Need matrix and Standard Assessment Measures (see Appendices 6 and 7), we recommend consideration of the following assessment areas.

Clinical interviews

It can be valuable to consider assessments in two parts. They are each aimed at helping to highlight attachment and relationship perspectives and the dyadic relationship and interaction between the two:

1. **Individual meaning-making:** Person with intellectual disabilities
2. **System meaning-making:** Parents, carers and professional network and the wider context.

As discussed in Chapter 12 Dyadic Developmental Psychotherapy, there is a need to assess people in their dyad as much as possible, so that you are focusing on their relational strengths and challenges.

1. Individual meaning-making: Questions relating to the person with intellectual disabilities

We have built upon suggestions by Fletcher (2016) and the BPS (2017) to develop what we hope is a useful way to explore individual meaning-making. This approach can involve the person themselves as well as others who can contribute insights into these areas.

1. **Early experiences:** What were early relationships and experiences like for the person with intellectual disability (in utero, birth and beyond)? What was the person's temperament like? Were there particular social/cultural elements of the person's upbringing to consider? What was the person's early development like? Were they able to meet key developmental milestones? What were their early relationships like with caregivers, and were there key disruptions in family life when the person was young? How did the family/ the person learn about their disability?
2. **Emotional expression:** How does the person respond to events or activities that might be expected to be highly distressing for them – do they communicate an emotional response or appear outwardly unaffected? Has this always been the pattern? Do they seek comfort and how?
3. **Trust and regulation:** Does the person develop trust in those who support them and respond positively to reassurance in unfamiliar situations?
4. **Interaction and expectation:** How does the individual interact with people around them? What style of interaction do they enjoy? What expectations do they appear to have of those interactions?
5. **Comfort:** How does the person seek support from others during times of distress, anxiety or discomfort? Do individuals around the person recognise these as support-seeking behaviours?
6. **Separation:** What is the person's response to separating from and being reunited with relatives who have had primary caregiving roles? If supported by paid carers, how does the person respond to support staff beginning and ending shifts, taking leave from work or leaving the job?
7. **Attachment preferences:** Does the person show a strong preference for a particular caregiver? Does this cause difficulties or concerns? Has this always been the pattern?

Whenever possible, the person themselves should be consulted and these areas discussed with them directly via genograms, 10 picture method (McKensie, 2023) or Talking Mats™, as appropriate. (Talking Mats™ are a visual communication tool to help individuals express their views, thoughts and preferences using visuals.) Sometimes this information is not available, or the person is only partially able to present their story. The approach of curiosity and connection needs to be genuinely held in a truly DDP-informed way whilst completing this assessment and ensuring the person with an intellectual disability is central to their care and, when this is not possible, their experiences and history is still held centrally to the process and developing understanding. DDP is not a technique, talking about the elements in the PBS framework can make it seem like a series of techniques, but it needs to be held as an overarching approach for individuals, immediate carers, wider networks and consultants – as explored throughout this book. It can be helpful to use video to review some questions to help more closely observe and analyse interaction (Fletcher, 2016).

2. System meaning-making: Questions for the support network

The following questions are combined from those suggested by Fletcher (2016), Skelly's Conditions for Safety (Skelly, 2016) and relational risk questions (Skelly, 2014) and those developed by the authors. It remains important to consider the parental/carer attachment history as well, as outlined in detail in Chapter 12: Dyadic Developmental Psychotherapy.

Parents/carers and siblings

- Conception, pregnancy, birth and early days and years – what was each parent's experience of pregnancy and birth – and what were the experiences of the wider family?
- Parental reactions to their child's diagnosis and resolution of any feeling of loss or grief that they might have experiences. Also, when did they find out/realise about their child's disability? What were the responses? Of them and others?
- Experiences of sibling relationships and impact of disability on such relationships
- Family's culture and religious beliefs concerning disability, parenting and caregiving
- Experiences of early separations, losses or traumas of parents/carers
- Intergenerational attachment experiences of parents/carers
- Parental mental health and emotional distress
- Social support available to parents from their own families/support for carers within their teams
- Parent-child interactions and attunement. What's the last fun thing you did together? When was the last time you had a good time together?

Parents/carers and wider network

- *Relationship expectations:* What has been the experience of getting to know the person? What hopes or expectations did individuals in the support network have around getting to know and work with the person with intellectual disability? What does it feel like to be in a relationship with this person? What does the carer expect will happen in relationships based upon their previous relational experiences, with professionals and personally?
- *Shared joy and delight:* How do individuals in the network feel when they spend time with the person with intellectual disability? When do individuals in the support network feel attuned? When are interactions fun and playful? When the person shows behaviours that are confusing or challenging, does the support network feel able to be curious about the underlying thoughts, feelings and needs? Do people already have ideas about what's going on and what are these ideas – how do they link to historical experiences?
- *Comfort and co-regulation:* How does the person seek support during times of distress, anxiety or discomfort? Do carers recognise these as support seeking behaviours? How does this look and how does this feel for those supporting?
- *Support for the supporters:* How and with whom are the parents/carers/wider support networks needs being noted and checked? Who is containing and offering support to them currently? Are they able to have breaks and is this predictable or ad hoc (or both); how does the carer feel about accessing support?
- *Relationship stress and blocked care:* What internal and external response do individuals in the network notice themselves having to different behaviours of concern (thoughts and emotions)? When supporting the person with intellectual disabilities, when do individuals notice being within/outside their window of tolerance (frustrated/upset/annoyed)? Does the person's behaviour threaten to break or damage relationships? Do individuals in the support network experience feeling hostile, ambivalent, unavailable cut off from the person they are working with? Are there any patterns of rejection or relationship breakdowns? How might this fit with individuals internal working model, shame and rupture and repair experiences?

Environmental/wider contextual meaning-making

- *Resources:* What were familial resources and support like growing up? How does this look now? Are there any financial circumstances to consider?
- *Carer understanding:* What are the gaps in understanding for parents and carers to increase their insight into attachment behaviour and identify helpful ways to respond (possibly using video to review these interactions)?

- *Environmental and social enrichment:* Is the environment enriching, with opportunities to freely access activities, food and relationships to meet basic needs of nurture, comfort, joy, nutrition and stimulation?
- *Safety:* Are all environments the person accesses safe, emotionally and physically? Does everyone in the system feel safe and confident to provide physical, environmental and emotional safety for the person with intellectual disabilities? Do the staff and wider system feel safe themselves? Is the person's day predictable or changeable or even chaotic? What support structures are in place in the attempt to ensure safety/reduce risk of harm? Are there any restrictions in place in an attempt to ensure safety?

(See Appendix 7 for a Summary table of attachment-informed clinical interview considerations.)

Glimmers

In trauma-informed care, 'glimmers' are being introduced as the opposite to triggers. They are small, positive moments or experiences that help to activate a sense of safety and calmness or connection. In services where the focus is often on challenges and difficulties, glimmers offer an opportunity to capture and celebrate the alternative narratives and experiences. While capturing glimmers can sometimes feel like 'catching stars in the dark', or trying to learn a dance without music, they can also provide energy, reduce burnout, and a light a more hopeful path. These glimmers may include positive physical sensations, such as warmth or a cool breeze, a soothing sound, or feelings of connection and safety. Unlike triggers, that activate our nervous system into fight flight or freeze, glimmers help activate the vagal nerve which support return to calm and regulation (Dana & Porges, 2018). We would encourage glimmers to be formally captured as part of the assessment process, for people with intellectual disabilities and their carers.

Formal assessment measures

In addition to the areas of clinical interview above, we have created a list, likely not exhaustive, of some of the available tools that helps towards developing an understanding of relational/attachment patterns of the person with intellectual disability and their caregiver(s), as well as their sensory, emotional and developmental needs. These tools are listed at the end of the book (see Appendix 7). Measurements of attachment have flaws and the pros and cons of this type of measurement is reviewed elsewhere (see Walker *et al*, 2016). We suggest that such measures are considered alongside other assessments completed as standard PBS assessment, such as behavioural monitoring forms, for example.

For Jay we have presented the assessment information in the dyadic iceberg model, for him and his carer/mother. Assessment directly with caregivers and with the person with an intellectual disability use creative communication methods to support their ability to engage. Through this and caregiver discussions and relational observations, we can begin to make tentative guesses about 'what you don't see' and internal working models. These guesses would ideally be done together with the person with intellectual disabilities and their caregivers (see Chapter 12: Dyadic Developmental Psychotherapy), again through creative communication methods, such as Talking Mats™.

The details of this assessment for Jay are beyond the scope of this chapter, however the outcomes are presented as the beginning link of the assessment information into the formulation (see Figure 15.3).

Figure 15.3: Understanding Jay's experiences following assessment of Jay and his carer

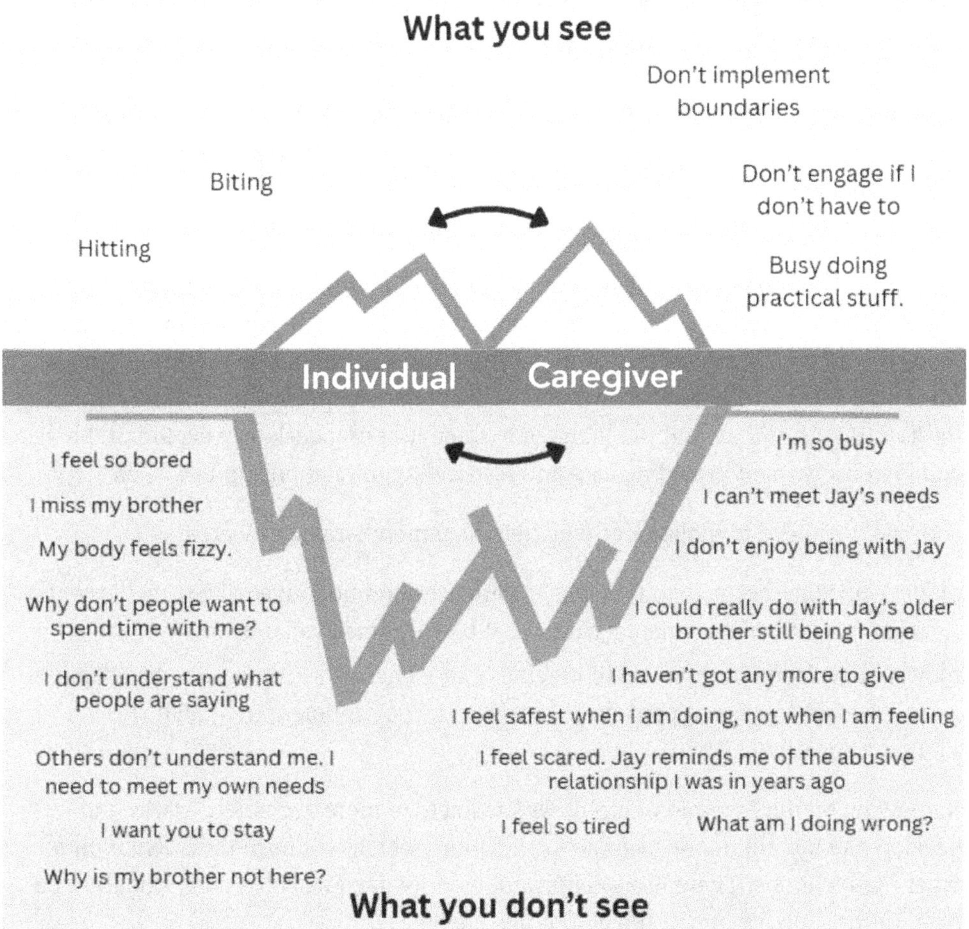

Formulation

Formulation is the way of understanding someone's presentation. Traditionally, PBS might focus on behavioural summary statements to provide a formulation summary of the slow triggers, fast triggers, description of dysregulated behaviour and any observable maintaining functions. Figure 15.4 summarises an alternative attachment and trauma informed version of the PBS behaviour summary statements, which we name a Dyadic Interaction Summary Statement (not a fuller formulation). Demonstrating how a behaviour of concern can be formulated as a reflection of an interaction of individual and carer needs, internal triggers and relational factors, (which also account for longer term maintaining factors). A blank template of this DDP-informed interaction summary statement can be found in Appendix 9.

Of note, the DDP-informed interaction summary statement is an initial summary formulation around specific interactions relating to behaviours of concern, which you are likely to add to and review as you learn more.

Any understanding of behaviour that stems from and/or elicits distress, needs to consider what each person in the dyad brings to patterns of interaction and how this might be understood in the context of early and ongoing experiences and their position on the Pyramid of Need. We propose the use of a comprehensive DDP formulation model that enables behaviour to be understood in the context of individual and system factors and the interaction between them (see Figure 15.5). A template of this formulation model can be found in Appendix 10.

This formulation model can also be applied to staff teams – here you might work with key individual carers to curiously explore the areas of their needs and internal working models from which they operate and provide care. You could also do this in a wider team way, using the ideas for the previous chapters to explore with a staff team using the Two Hands of Care and the 'name it to tame it' ideas; curiously exploring the team and systems ways of providing care and responding to relationship needs, etc.

Formulations need to make clear whether attachment strategies were:

a) developed in response to previous experiences and no longer reflect the current relational and environmental safety that has become available, or
b) were developed in response to previous experiences and continue to be adaptive in response to current perceived threats in the environment or system (British Psychological Society, 2017).

In drawing on the Pyramid of Need, we are likely to more accurately assess and develop a richer and more accurate formulation, which will form the orientation for other interventions. There is a brief formulation for Jay presented alongside the PBS plan information for him at the end of this chapter.

Figure 15.4: Dyadic interaction summary statement

Underlying context (PBS calls this Setting events or Slow triggers)	**When** (PBS calls this Fast Triggers)	**Concern** (PBS calls this Behaviour of Concern)	**Why does it continue?** (PBS calls this Maintaining Consequences)
Stimulation and sensory needs: Preferred activities and foods that offer stimulation and sensory feedback are locked away, as Jay will consume/use these endlessly without the boundaries needed, which Mum struggles to implement (see attachment patterns and shame). **Cognitive and communication needs:** Jay needs extra processing time, struggles to initiate interaction and to understand what others are asking. Mum struggles to communicate in a way Jay understands. **Attachment patterns, burnout, blocked trust and blocked care:** Mum is busy running the household and struggles to be available. Mum is fearful to implement boundaries, as this is often met with responses that are hurtful and reminders of past abusive relationship. Mum struggles to find joy in her relationship with Jay and interactions are mostly practical. Jay struggles to initiate interaction and when Mum does communicate, Jay struggles to understand, trust or feel connected in a relaxed way. These experiences lead to a relational pattern of mis-attunement, confusion and lack of emotional connection. Jay has learnt to meet his own needs and developed strategies accordingly. **Shame:** Mum feels some shame that she is unable to meet Jay's needs and is struggling to implement boundaries. Now toileting is becoming difficult too, she worries that even the most basic of tasks will become difficult. She avoids the shame by asking Jay to do fewer things with her and doesn't uphold boundaries, to reduce interactions that lead to feeling shame.	When the underlying context cues key triggers to challenging interactions: **Under-stimulation and lack of connection:** when Mum is busy and struggles to support Jay's engagement in activities or interactions he enjoys Mum: *"I'm exhausted and scared."* Jay: *"My body feels fizzy. I'm bored. Mum doesn't like me."* **Demands:** When Mum shows tension in her face and prompts Jay to do something he doesn't enjoy, like using the toilet. Jay: *"I can't trust you to know my needs. You don't like me. I don't understand you."*	Jay hitting and biting carer's upper arms *(might be a traditional way of summarising the concern).* **OR** Mum is struggling to understand and therefore attune to Jay's needs. Mum is burnt out with the load of caring responsibilities and is experiencing blocked care. When a demand, such as going to the toilet is placed on Jay and he does not understand this, he becomes dysregulated and seeks a way to regulate himself in the best way he knows how. The consequence is that Jay will hit and bite his Mum's arms.	**It provides interaction, sensory regulation and stimulation:** hitting and biting provides sensory regulation. It also provides stimulation when feeling alone, bored and unregulated without needs proactively being met. **Support is not tailored to regulate and communicate**: Mum struggles to tailor communication according to Jay's window of tolerance. Jay needs extra processing time and adapted communication support, especially when dysregulated. **Escaping something unpleasant**: It could be that biting carers' upper arm stops the demand. Interactions have started to feel unpleasant for Jay and carer – so both are avoiding these, limiting connection. **Longer term** **Internal working model narratives strengthen:** Jay: *"Others are too busy for me, so I need to find my own ways of meeting my needs. People do not enjoy being with me – I am not fun".* Mum: *"I am not able to meet Jay's needs, so he's better off without me trying. I cannot interact with Jay without risking getting hurt. Boundaries and fun interactions all increase this risk."* **Blocks in care increase:** Ongoing experiences of mis-attunement and relationship ruptures increases experiences of blocked trust and blocked care, with a risk of family breakdown

Figure 15.5: A proposed DDP-informed formulation model for dysregulated responses shown by people with an intellectual disability

Pyramid of need position: Feeling safe, developing relationships, comfort and co-regulation, empathy and reflection, resilience and resources, explore trauma and mourn losses

Person with intellectual disability

Attachment pattern

Internal Working Model
I am...
Others are...
The world is...

Physical needs
Emotional needs
Cognitive/processing needs
Communication needs
Relationship needs
Sensory needs
Skills and knowledge

Behaviour/
Response/
Interaction

Parent/siblings/ (professional) carers

Attachment pattern

Internal Working Model
I am...
Others are...
The world is...

Physical needs
Emotional needs
Cognitive/processing needs
Communication needs
Relationship needs
Sensory needs
Skills and knowledge

Early and ongoing context: Strengths and needs relating to wider personal and professional experiences and support, educational experiences, financial security, opportunities for activities, access to environmental stimulation, structure, routine and safety

Intervention planning

DDP is an overarching approach rather than a set of interventions. Intervention planning should prioritise timing and process within each system level, guided by the Pyramid of Need (see Chapter 11) and DDP-Practice for the system (see Chapters 13 and 14). Following the clinical cycle model in this chapter, our assessment and formulation should help deepen our understanding of behaviours that challenge, recognising them as observable outcomes of past and ongoing influences on the individual, their caregivers, the wider environment and the relationship between these. Based on the assessment and formulation, we recommend thought be given to what DDP input is appropriate for the person with an intellectual disability and/or their carers; whether that be DDP-psychotherapy and/or DDP-parenting. It is also important to consider whether DDP-informed supervision or training is needed within the system. By linking this process to the Pyramid of Need, we can identify key areas for intervention and determine what needs to be in place across the environment, system, care teams, caregivers, and the individual to enhance safety, foster connections, and support long-term development. These elements form the foundation of PBS plans. All interventions will need to uphold the key DDP principles, such as PACE, responding to shame-inducing situations, adopting 'name it to tame it', and using a storytelling and curious approach to explore situations with the person with intellectual disabilities and the wider care system. The Two Hands of Care approach and reflection on blocked care and trust are also essential. Therefore, this chapter should not be viewed in isolation, as the PBS-based understanding, and interventions must integrate all the DDP key concepts covered in this book. All DDP elements should be incorporated into a person's PBS plan, and, more importantly, in the approach embodied throughout the system. The intervention section of this chapter specifically focuses on how DDP-practice links with a PBS support plan, as this is often the cornerstone of PBS interventions. Towards the end of this chapter, we provide examples of how these elements are applied, using Jay as a case study.

Support plans

DDP-informed intervention recognises that intersubjective connections, playfulness, acceptance, curiosity, empathy, comfort and development, relies on brain systems to not be compromised or disengaged (see Chapter 6: Neuroscience; Golding & Hughes, 2012; Perry, 2006; Porges, 2022). Accordingly, the 4Rs approach (Perry, 2006; Bombèr, 2020) can provide a tiered framework, supporting regulation first to enhance relationship building, which in turn, sets the system up for success in learning new patterns of relating (social, emotional, occupational and communication skills and environmental management), to experience more meaningful relationships and fulfilling quality of life (see Chapter 6: Neuroscience for further information about the 4Rs approach). A DDP focus within support plans is about both building and being in a relationship with the person - and their caregivers/systems and not focused on the behaviour itself. Figure 14.6 shows how the 4Rs approach maps on to the PBS plan stages of proactive, secondary and reactive support; this needs to sit alongside the wider aims for the person with intellectual disabilities and their support system, based on the Pyramid of Need. Intervention plans should consider how the experiences of need according to the pyramid, alter as a person's levels of regulation fluctuate.

Figure 15.6: The Four Rs framework, linked to the PBS model

Primary preventative →	Secondary preventative →	Reactive strategies →	Post-incident
Regulate Relate Reason	Regulate Relate	Regulate	Regulate Relate Repair

Figure 15.7 below shows how DDP principles might fit within a PBS plan, including the framework of regulating, relating, reasoning and repair which might need varying levels of emphasis depending on window of tolerance and area of priority in the Pyramid of Need. Whilst difficult to separate these entities, as they are so interdependent, this chapter offers a description of key DDP principles to consider within each stage of a PBS plan.

Figure 15.7: DDP-informed PBS plan

Below is a summary of how DDP is integrated in the areas of a PBS plan.

Typical PBS plan sections	Suggested DDP emphasis
Understanding me, my needs, and my behaviour ■ My likes and dislikes ■ Understanding my needs and behaviours	Use DDP-informed assessment tools and formulation to describe a person's needs, including understanding of: ■ Where the person is on the Pyramid of Need (and when this alters how we know) ■ Internal working model ■ Early and ongoing experiences and relationships (and relationship patterns) ■ Upstairs and downstairs brain or window of tolerance ■ Internal emotional triggers (including shame and blocked trust) ■ Ensure emphasis on behaviour reflecting individual and system factors and the interaction between them ■ Reflect strengths and needs of the person and carers/system experiences and support ■ Recognise that behaviours can be a coping strategy and/or a way of regulating and meeting sensory or safety needs

Primary/proactive strategies:	**Regulate, relate and reason**
What you need to do so I feel happy and safe ■ Personal and health needs ■ Structure, routine and boundaries ■ Communication ■ Sensory regulation	*At this stage, the person (and support network) has capacity to learn new skills, to explore, be in relationship and reflect and use all the areas of their upstairs brain. All DDP approaches are potentially useful here.* ■ PACEful stance and interactions, that bring genuine shared joy, comfort and delight ■ Emphasise the importance of curiosity to learn about a person's internal experiences and internal working model to increase system understanding and empathy ■ Consider the impact of any blocked care and blocked trust ■ Think of providing structure and boundaries alongside compassion and connection so that these are established and clear while the person is able to reason (and potentially engage in these).
■ Positive interactions and relationships ■ Meaningful activities ■ Choice ■ Physical environment ■ Transport needs ■ Skills development plan ■ Active support	■ Think of providing structure and boundaries alongside compassion and connection so that these are established and clear while the person is able to reason (and potentially engage in these). ■ Ensure skills development draws on preferred activities, environments, and ways of interacting for the person with intellectual disabilities and encapsulates acceptance and therefore is naturalistic and within everyday life as possible. Ensure skills development intervention never compromises safety in the relationship; genuine connection forms part of any skills development. ■ Working with person's internal working model and experience of shame and helping people with intellectual disabilities to experience emotions and interactions through connection and relational predictability ■ 'Talking for' by gently exploring and naming their feelings for and with them when they might seem uncertain or just don't know. This can help the person to link their feelings and experiences (past and present) ■ Aid the person in staying regulated and within their window of tolerance, considering interventions that maintain a regulated nervous system, including sensory regulating activities (alerting, calming and organising) ■ Activities that allow meaningful connection and choice ■ Interventions that represent Capable Environments, supporting communication, allowing independence, opportunities for choice and a good physical environment etc. Alongside positive and connected relationships ■ Emphasise any clinical intervention from different disciplines, never compromises relationships, that genuine connection forms part of any development

Secondary/active strategies *What you need to do to help when I feel wobbly* ■ Triggers ■ Early warning signs ■ Help me and others feel safe ■ Help me regulate	**Regulate and relate** *At this stage the person (and possibly support system) will be less able to reason and so we need the strategies to focus on regulate and relate.* ■ When detailing triggers, emphasise the emotional and internal elements and the interaction in presentation such as in the dyadic iceberg ■ Two Hands of Care: Hold a safe emotional and physical space for the person. Show genuine connection and curiosity of the emotional needs underlying the visible behaviour ■ Remember: dysregulation requires co-regulation, before expecting future self-regulation. What would help bring the person back into their window of tolerance? ■ Still offer activities that allow meaningful connection ■ Limit choice to ensure achievable level of agency ■ Maintain boundaries to increase feelings of safety ■ Increase predictability and simplify language/use visual supports to support regulation (people will need more visual supports the more distressed they become) ■ If person with an intellectual disability moves out of their window of tolerance whilst learning a new skill, consider breaking steps down to smaller more manageable steps and/or change support as described above to ensure coregulation and increase safety and connectedness
Reactive strategies *Supporting me through crisis* ■ What I might do in crisis ■ Help me regulate ■ Ensure safety	**Regulate** *The priority here is helping the person to feel safe and regulated.* ■ Personalised parenting/caring in the moment cycle ■ Ensure carers and the wider system understands that when the person is out of their window of tolerance, they are unlikely to problem solve and use skills they otherwise might ■ Emphasise the impact of behaviours that challenge on carers internal working model, regulation/window of tolerance, relational connection and levels of confidence ■ Holding a safe emotional and physical space-quiet, personal and accessible space away from expectation with the freedom to move. Emphasis on movement and food, interactions and sensory activities that offer a sense of safety and regulation ■ Ensure safety for all

Post-incident support *What to do after an incident* ■ What I need after an incident ■ Support for parents and staff ■ Paperwork	**Regulate, Relate and Repair** (see secondary/active strategies section) ■ PACE: After an incident, our window of tolerance remains compromised. What can help bring the person back into their upstairs brain? How can you show acceptance for the needs that underlie the behaviours that were tricky to manage? How can carers help the person to experience emotional responses safely? How does this impact on everyone's sense of safety and how can we return to safety quickly? ■ Consider individually-tailored attunement-rupture-repair cycle and ensure connection (before correction once a person feels safe and connected and back at baseline). Do I need to repair the relationship so that the person I care for knows what has happened has not affected our relationship? When the person is back at baseline, do I need to help the person I care for repair a relationship with others and with me? ■ Consider network communication and relationships (see Chapter 13) ■ Reflect: how might the incident impact internal working models and patterns of relating (longer term maintaining factors)? How might this shape understanding and support moving forward?

Finally, there is a version of the 4Rs framework presented for Jay (Figure 15.8). Some areas of the plan will be very familiar to intellectual disability practitioners; however, the shift lies in their role in fostering safety and relationships. There is a strong emphasis on choice and predictability to create a sense of felt safety, supporting the Two Hands approach (connection before correction). Visual supports enhance processing, especially when individuals struggle with reasoning, when their 'upstairs brain' is offline. While the interventions may appear similar, the underlying rationale has subtly shifted. This shift of rationale is important as it is relationally focused and supports regulation and relationships first rather than addressing behaviours on the surface. For this reason, regulation is offered first in the table, before relate, reason and repair. The system's understanding of this will also be important in allowing this shift to a DDP approach.

Figure 15.8: DDP-informed intervention ideas within 4Rs framework

Formulation summary	■ **Relationships:** Carers are busy, fearful and struggling to find joy interacting with Jay ■ **Attachment pattern:** Based on Mum's early experiences of being asked to be independent from a young age, and messages from extended family members, Mum believes Jay shouldn't be so dependent on her. Likewise, Jay has learnt to meet his own needs. There are currently very few joyful interactions, the Mum and carers are apprehensive about being hurt so do not offer interaction for fear of this – only when they need Jay to do something. Jay feels disconnected but then overwhelmed when asked to complete a task ■ **Environment:** Preferred activities and foods that offer stimulation and regulation are locked away. Jay is bored and dysregulated, with a decreased window of tolerance. ■ **Consequences:** Hitting and biting provides connection and sensory regulation, but causes physical and emotional hurt and strengthens internal working model and attachment patterns in an adverse way. ■ **Communication needs:** Jay has developmental needs, including communication, processing and sensory needs ■ **System:** The support network is feeling stuck, but are engaged and keen to help
(Co) Regulate	■ **Explore respite** to give Mum a break from caring role, with a view to review whether this is helpful and exploring additional day to day ways in which Mum might have time for non-caring tasks ■ **DDP-informed carer consultations:** Connect with the Mum's experience of caring and explore any signs of blocked care and own past experiences in relation to this. Similarly, do this with other carers. ■ **Network Training:** Ensure a multi-agency formulation and working together agreement. Discuss (if the system is open and engaged) key principles of creating DDP-informed interactions to all immediate caregivers, including how to implement boundaries using Two Hands Approach ■ **Safe objects, places and sensory regulation:** Support Mum and carers to support an increase in activities, foods and environments that support Jay's regulation and felt safety. Ensure Jay has free access to a space he feels safe and able to regulate in. ■ **Routines and Structure:** Provide predictability and structure for Jay with routines, boundaries and choice, using visual support. ■ **Communication:** Ensure Jay can express needs and wants using objects of reference and visual communication methods ■ **Consistency:** Share a formulation informed support plan, which includes clear proactive (regulate, relate and reason), secondary (regulate and relate) and reactive strategies (regulate). This can be a Two Hands support plan, 4Rs Plan or PBS plan.

Relate	■ **Ongoing connection before correction:** Support Mum and carers to find meaningful activities that bring mutual joy and delight to increase opportunities for genuine connection and alternative experiences that will challenge negative internal working models, shame and blocked care. Make these predictable and freely available (not contingent on behaviour). ■ **Meaningful activity:** Ensure opportunities for community access and peer relationships. ■ **Ongoing network communication and support:** Will maintain collaborative approach and reflection
Reason	■ **DDP-psychotherapy:** Ongoing DDP-parenting support (and consideration of DDP-psychotherapy) to support Mum and carers to explore trauma experiences in caring role and consider ways for meaningful connection. ■ **Skills development:** Consider Jay's developmental needs to seek out meaningful activities, regulation and interaction and support skills development accordingly, such as use of visual communication support to make requests, especially for activities and sensory input. To also consider his emotional and social development and how to build these skills through play activities that encourage this. ■ **Improved access to community and social activities:** Once Mum, carers and Jay have developed the skills and planning to set this up for success and he enough safety in his key caregiving relationships.
Repair	■ **Re-establishing safety (regulate):** How do incidents of behaviours of concern impact on everyone's sense of safety and how can we return to safety quickly? It is helpful for Mum and carers to have spaces where they can talk about the impact on them. ■ **Connect (relate):** After incidents of behaviours of concern, Mum and carers to offer/make available a favoured and sensory regulating activity, to allow opportunities for regulation and potential positive interaction and development of trust. This connection (before, during and after correction) demonstrates a repair whereby Jay understands "You matter, no matter what" and "We are okay". ■ **Only when Jay is feeling safe, regulated and connected:** Check whether it can be helpful for Jay to be supported to repair a relationship with others

Review and evaluation

PBS tends to evaluate intervention effectiveness by reviewing PBS plan implementation, skills progress, quality of life and behaviours that challenge through ongoing intervention, data collection, observation and specific monitoring documentation. In line with neuroscience and the impact of meaningful connections, we propose that attachment-informed assessment measures (See Appendix 7), DDP-parenting sessions, caregiver reflections, DDP-informed supervisions and network meetings can also be used to review relational change. We would encourage evaluation to be sought from the wider support network too, supporting ongoing collaborative and DDP-informed working relationships.

"It's been so useful reflecting at my own pace in a safe environment. I'd gotten too drawn in to the mundane everyday tasks, which are still essential to keep our heads above the water, but my connection with my boy was lost. Pausing on the powerful positive emotion that grew between us through playfulness has helped our relationship thrive. Allowing ourselves the time to support our boy in his home environment with new skills when we were ready, without judgment, allowed us to implement the skill he'd already learnt at school, in the home. The PBS team and their approach creates synergy."

Parent feedback of DDP-informed PBS service provision

"The relationship between staff and the family…this has allowed trust to build up…building up the foundations for support…without this we probably would not have seen the positive progress."

Social worker feedback around DDP-informed PBS service provision

Conclusion

We propose that a shift from traditional behavioural approaches to a more relational framework can be beneficial for those keen to understand and respond to behaviours that challenge, a shift that acknowledges the dyadic nature of behaviours and the role of internal triggers, including neurobiological dysregulation, emotions and relational patterns. Behaviour should be seen as an observable expression of underlying emotional, historical, and environmental influences, rather than an isolated issue within the individual. The PBS framework can accommodate these ideas. By integrating the Pyramid of Need, we can prioritise foundational needs such as safety, co-regulation, and meaningful relationships, ensuring interventions are developmentally appropriate and responsive to both the individual and their support network.

DDP-practice enriches our understanding by acknowledging the relational complexity and intersubjectivity of care systems. It moves beyond merely modifying behaviours to fostering secure attachments and acknowledging how this might maintain patterns of relating in the long-term (longer term maintaining factors). This perspective also challenges outdated assumptions, such as the idea that empathy and compassion reinforce undesirable behaviours, instead recognising these as fundamental to emotional healing and behavioural stability. In this chapter we have also proposed that the 4Rs framework, which aims to offer a model around supporting (dys)regulation can be understood within the PBS framework of primary, secondary, reactive and post-incident support guidance, while emphasising that DDP is not a technique but an approach which needs to be incorporated across a system.

Ultimately, we propose that assessment, formulation, and intervention planning needs to be attuned and responsive to individual needs, system-wide considerations, and a commitment to creating environments that promotes regulation, connection, and well-being. The Positive Behaviour Support (PBS) model, informed by DDP principles, provides a structured yet flexible approach, ensuring that interventions are meaningful, sustainable, and person-centred. By embedding these principles into practice, we can support individuals with intellectual disabilities in achieving greater stability, inclusion, quality of life and quality of relationships whilst also empowering caregivers and teams to respond with understanding, consistency, and compassion. We hope this discussion- based chapter informs the further development of PBS plans to be able to deliver these more relational, attachment and trauma-informed elements.

Chapter 16:
Training and supervision

We would encourage those who are interested in this model to access Dyadic Developmental Psychotherapy (DDP) training with a qualified DDP trainer. The basic training will provide a theoretical foundation and help you learn how to use this model for therapy, parenting support or in everyday practice. The eight days training (split into two distinct courses, called Level 1 and Level 2) is, however, just the start! Those who have attended the training days can describe themselves as *'offering DDP informed approaches'*. If at this point you are interested in offering therapeutic support we would recommend accessing an accredited DDP supervisor.

Those wishing to further develop their skills and become a qualified practitioner can embark on the practicum route. A DDP consultant will assess when you are ready to join the practicum and support you through to the point of qualifying. Once qualified, you can describe yourself as a 'DDP practitioner'.

We cannot overstate the importance of accessing supervision; it will improve your practice and use of this model. We would encourage anyone who is drawing on this model to inform their work to access supervision from an accredited DDP supervisor (either an experienced practitioner or DDP consultant).

DDP training

Level 1 training: introduces the model, overarching theory and includes practice relevant to your workplace.

Level 2 training: builds on Level 1 to deepen understanding and practice.

Available training courses are listed on the DDPI website:
https://ddpnetwork.org/professionals/training/

PACE training

Many recognise how important and significant a PACE-based attitude is in their work and often want to know more. We would recommend accessing a course run by a qualified DDP practitioner:
https://ddpnetwork.org/professionals/training/ddp-pace-training/

Practicum

To become a qualified DDP practitioner you will need to complete the DDP practicum. Prior to starting the practicum, you will need access to an accredited DDP supervisor. For further information about the practicum process, go to:
https://ddpnetwork.org/ddpi/practitioner-certification-ddp/.

Supervision and workshops

The DDP team holds a list of all available accredited supervisors. Please state in your email request that you would like supervision for your work with people with intellectual disability; the team works hard to match the right supervisor with the right supervisee where possible. It is possible to access 1:1 supervision or to join a supervision group.

DDP also runs study days for those interested in meeting with others in their region, or to consider DDP when working with people with specific needs. When DDP is running workshops they will be listed on the main website regarding support for professionals.

Supervision, groups, study days, workshops and future conference can be found on the DDPI website:
https://ddpnetwork.org/professionals/supporting-professionals/

Special interest groups

DDP to support people with intellectual disabilities:
https://ddpnetwork.org/events/categories/special-interest-group/

or contact Nic for further links or information about DDP and intellectual disability focused work:
https://www.drnicjones.co.uk/

Outcome measures and evaluation

We are keen to develop a clearer evidence base in this field specifically around the impact of DDP, DDP-parenting and Dyadic Developmental Practice (DDP-practice) for people with an intellectual disability and their parents and carers. In the Appendix 7, we have listed a range of tools for consideration to review the impact of DDP based interventions; we understand that services will vary in their access to such measures, but we hope this provides a useful starting point.

To access existing research, go to: https://ddpnetwork.org/research/

This webpage, amongst lots of other helpful information, refers to the Measurement in DDP Guidance and recommended measures (Gurney-Smith & Phillips, 2017).

It also refers to the NICE requirements for DDP RCTs, including:

Primary outcome measures may include:

- Attachment.
- Parental sensitivity.
- Placement disruption.
- Educational performance.
- Behavioural problems.

There should be at least a 6-month to 1-year follow-up.

Chapter 17: A final conclusion

We hope this book has been thought-provoking, supportive, and insightful, inspiring you to consider the importance of the clinical application of Dyadic Developmental Psychotherapy in providing relational support for people with intellectual disabilities and their caregivers and supporters.

Through reading this book – alongside any training or supervision you may choose to undertake – we hope that whatever your role in providing support to individuals with intellectual disabilities, you will hold at the heart of your work the importance of connection. It is through attuned, playful, curious, fun and compassionate relationships that individuals with intellectual disabilities who have experienced trauma, attachment difficulties, or mismatches in relational experiences can develop the ability to regulate, relate, and reason. The process of repair plays a crucial role in mediating this process.

While some of these approaches may seem simple, they can be challenging to sustain, especially over long periods, full days, or demanding shifts. We encourage you to adopt a PACE attitude not only in your work but also with yourself – being playful, accepting, curious, and empathetic about your own experiences. Reflecting on what makes this work difficult for you, at times, using some of the approaches we suggest, as a parent or practitioner can help with the connection and empathy to yourself.

People with intellectual disabilities deserve 'good enough care that is reliable, containing, empathetic, and attuned' (Hughes, 2019). Your commitment to fostering these connections is invaluable and we hope this book helps strengthen that commitment and provides practical approaches to support its application in your relationships with people with intellectual disabilities and the teams around them.

Appendices

Appendix 1: Potential complicating factors to attachment security for people with intellectual disabilities

Individual factors

- Premature birth and additional physical needs. alter the time they have with their parents and the availability of soothing touch.
- Altered sensory experiences.
- Communication difficulties.
- Need increased physical proximity to feel safe and secure.
- Smaller social circles and attachment relationships.
- Challenges in experiencing co-regulation.
- Challenges in expressing their needs.
- Less responsive to parents' attachment cues.
- Need longer to process and respond to stimuli.
- Physical disabilities.
- Lifelong support needs.

Parental factors

- Dejection and overcompensating in context of diagnosis.
- Missing delayed or difficult to read attachment cues.
- Smaller social circle and isolation.
- Parental grief and feelings of loss.
- Overwhelm, guilt, frustration, helplessness, shame.
- Experiencing blame.
- Attachment history.
- Relationship to seeking help.
- Cognitive needs.
- Sensory preferences.
- Neurodiversity.
- Economic strain.
- Additional layers of practical care impact on emotional connection and reflection.
- Increased risk of mental health difficulties and marital strain.

System factors

- Potential lack of available and/or quality professional and practical support in the context of needing lifelong support.
- Changeable and professional support network, who lack adequate support and guidance in negotiating relationship boundaries.
- Living amongst discriminatory and stigmatising cultural discourses.
- Social exclusion.
- Placement insecurity and multiple placements.
- More likely to live in low socio-economic households and be exposed to poverty.
- More likely than non-disabled peers to experience violence, abuse and neglect.
- More likely than non-disabled peers to be exposed to a greater number of potential adverse life experiences.
- Ongoing misunderstanding of needs and support offered.

Appendix 2: What might Two Hands of Care look like when supporting someone with an intellectual disability?

Appendix 2: What might Two Hands of Care look like when supporting someone with an intellectual disability?

Hand one

Provides warmth, nurture, connection and is attuned to needs of the person with an intellectual disability, communicating *"you matter, no matter what"*.

- **Be open and engaged**, calm and regulated. Watch, be with, listen, really listen (with intention). Be playful, allowing for light exploration without pressure or expectation.
- **Spend time with and delight** in the person you care for.
- **Attunement and mind-mindedness:** View the person you care for as an individual, with their own thoughts, feelings, needs and motivations. Wonder, be curious and aim to understand and meet both hidden and expressed needs and any shield against shame.
- **Acceptance and empathy:** Show acceptance for the thoughts and feelings underlying their actions (remember, this doesn't mean you accept the behaviour, but you accept the underlying feeling).
- **Coregulate:** Help person you care for to manage emotions and feelings of shame with empathy and acceptance.
- **Intersubjective interaction:** Interaction that maintains the key links between you both as a dyad whether this is around sensory, emotional, social and communication needs.
- **Repair**: Help the person you care for to know and feel they are cared for and liked. Your relationship is stronger than whatever has just happened within it.

Hand two

Provides structure, boundaries, opportunities for learning and making corrections that are carer-led, communicating *unconditional love, with conditions on behaviour* (Golding, 2015).

- **Safety first:** Boundaries for harmful behaviour to maintain a sense of safety.
- **Time in** (as opposed to time out). Stay near the person you care for and ensure they feel safe. Although this will not always be appropriate. It might look like an explicit offer of space and **time** instead for the person to be regulated before considering other correction-based strategies below to ensure correction is not reactive.
- **Set limits and routines:** Consider what structure, routines, boundaries and limits are needed for the person you care for to feel safe and thrive in the context of (dys)regulation and developmental needs.
- **Problem-solve:** Consider what corrections/adjustments you need to make to your own approach, the environment and activities to better meet the needs of the person with intellectual disabilities. Start with addressing and meeting the presenting dysregulation. For example, where a person is struggling to manage an activity, you can offer to assist to maybe just be near them to help them manage their anxiety or sense of feeling overwhelmed.
- **Teach** (not to punish) in a calm, clear and empathic manner.
- **Logical teaching:** Ensure any correction/consequence is logical and linked to fixing/making right/repairing the behaviour, not abstract consequences. For example, where a person is struggling to manage an activity on their own, you will offer to support them and be closer to them in that activity in future.
- **Cause and effect:** Help the person you care for understand cause and effect with "if-then" statements. For example, "if you break the tablet, then it won't be there when you want to watch your programme. That will be so sad you won't be able to watch your programme".
- Provide **guidance** and **suggestions** and opportunities to **practise** new adaptive behaviours.

X Delay conversation about behaviour.

X Avoid leaving the person.

X Delay problem solving.

X Avoid punishments (e.g. withdrawing a planned and much anticipated activity because of distress earlier in the day).

X Avoid relationship-based consequences (withdrawing love, attention, interaction).

X Avoid responding with anger or shame- ensure you have taken a deep breath and any other necessary steps, so you are in your upstairs brain, feeling regulated and calm.

X Avoid giving complex or unrelated consequences (e.g. if you break the tablet then we won't be able to go out later).

X Avoid lecturing or talking at the person you care for.

Questions to consider when exploring connection before correction

Connection

- How can I stay calm in stressful situations?
- How can I calm the nervous system of the person I care for?
- How can I let the person I care for know that I am here and I care – no matter what?

Correction

- Why did the person with intellectual disabilities do this?
- What do I want to teach? A skill? What are my hopes for this person?
- What would the person with intellectual disabilities like to learn?
- What do I need to learn? What are my fears? What do I need to change?
- What would the person with intellectual disabilities like to be different?
- Can we reframe a 'no' into a 'yes', with conditions? What are the reasons for limitations?

Dyadic Developmental Practice and Intellectual Disabilities © Pavilion Publishing and Media, 2025

Appendix 3: Parenting/Caring in the Moment Cycle

1. Notice

What is happening?
Do I need to step in? Do I need to take any immediate steps to ensure everyone is safe? Try not to shout, criticise or lecture. If you do, repair later.

2. Connect with yourself

Calm yourself: Take a breath and check your own response

Am I regulated? Can I stay open and engaged? Am I becoming irritated, angry or defensive? Do I feel useless? Do I need a break? Can I be compassionate to myself?

3. Calm the other person

Are they in upstairs or downstairs brain?

Give a simple acceptance and empathy response – NO curiosity yet! Then consider: Do they need me to help them **regulate** their emotions or senses?

4. Show curiosity

Real interest through tentative exploring

Even if you know they did something 'wrong', stay curious about *their* experience:
"I wonder what was going on when ...?"
"How come...?"
"No wonder you did...if you felt..."

5. Connect

via acceptance, empathy and meaning-making

Explore thoughts, desires, urges and motives underneath the behaviour. How can I help the person I care for to know and feel that I'm trying to get it? This is a deepened acceptance and empathy based on your increased understanding

6. Correct

Respond to the behaviour

Do I need to do anything further based on what I understand now? What should I approach this situation differently next time? Are there skills I can support the person I care for to develop?

7. Relationship repair

Do I need to repair the relationship so that the person I care for knows what has happened has not affected our relationship?

Parenting in the Moment Cycle. Adapted with permission from: Golding, K. S. (2017) *Foundations for Attachment Training Resource*, 'The six-session programme for parents of traumatized children', Jessica Kingsley Publishers, p. 289.

Appendix 4: Reflecting on your experience of shame – a worksheet for parents, carers or professionals

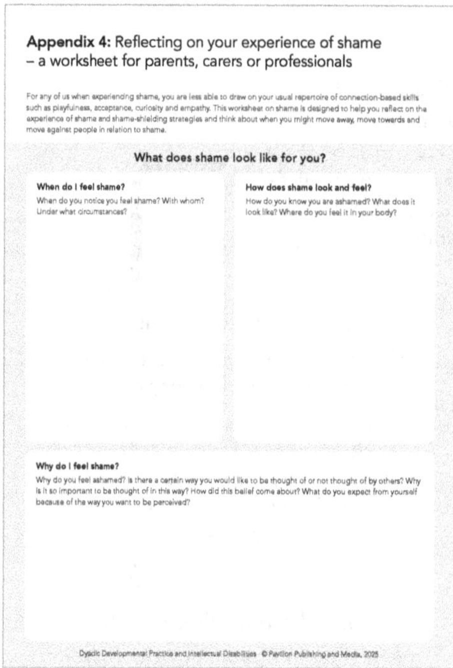

Appendix 4: Reflecting on your experience of shame – a worksheet for parents, carers or professionals

For any of us when experiencing shame, you are less able to draw on your usual repertoire of connection-based skills such as playfulness, acceptance, curiosity and empathy. This worksheet on shame is designed to help you reflect on the experience of shame and shame-shielding strategies and think about when you might move away, move towards and move against people in relation to shame.

What does shame look like for you?

When do I feel shame?
When do you notice you feel shame? With whom? Under what circumstances?

How does shame look and feel?
How do you know you are ashamed? What does it look like? Where do you feel it in your body?

Why do I feel shame?
Why do you feel ashamed? Is there a certain way you would like to be thought of or not thought of by others? Why is it so important to be thought of in this way? How did this belief come about? What do you expect from yourself because of the way you want to be perceived?

Dyadic Developmental Practice and Intellectual Disabilities © Pavilion Publishing and Media, 2025

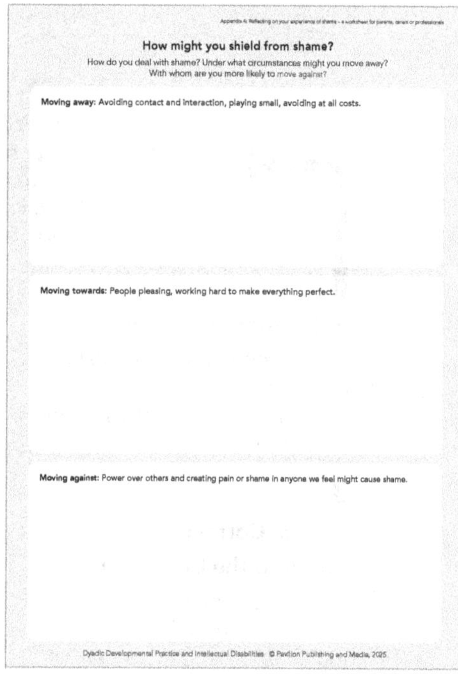

Appendix 4: Reflecting on your experience of shame – a worksheet for parents, carers or professionals

How might you shield from shame?

How do you deal with shame? Under what circumstances might you move away? With whom are you more likely to move against?

Moving away: Avoiding contact and interaction, playing small, avoiding at all costs.

Moving towards: People pleasing, working hard to make everything perfect.

Moving against: Power over others and creating pain or shame in anyone we feel might cause shame.

Dyadic Developmental Practice and Intellectual Disabilities © Pavilion Publishing and Media, 2025

Appendix 5: DDP-informed Support Plan templates

Appendix 5: DDP-informed Support Plan templates

Caring for someone with an intellectual disability using the 4Rs

To help a vulnerable person to learn, think and reflect, we need to intervene in this simple sequence (Beacon House, 2022; Bombèr, 2020; Perry, 2006). This plan is applicable in DDP-practice, system-focused work and when weaving DDP into PBS.

Step 1 **Regulate** The person you care for will struggle to listen, learn or do activities when they are overwhelmed, stressed, or tired. Before trying anything else, regulate nervous systems (flight/ fight/ freeze/ fawn response). **Why do you need to do this first?** Scan QR code	**Safe response:** When things go wrong, take a few deep breaths and swap with someone if possible. Create a consistent and calm safe response (no language, step back, provide a safe space, access to things they find physically regulating). **Get the environment right:** Ensure access a quiet space, enjoyable things, privacy, sensory equipment, low lights/noise **Predictability:** Structure, routine and a reliable calm adult reduces chaos and creates a feeling of safety. Write down (so everyone can follow consistently) existing and new routines and daily structure, especially considering transitions in/out of the house and key activities). No matter what verbal ability, use objects or pictures alongside activities to show what's happening now and next. This will help create emotional safety. Use a communication book (celebrations, challenges, sleep/diet, etc) across different carers and places and talk altogether in person when you can! **Move!** Provide opportunity for *at least* 30 minutes of big movement: swing, walking, pacing in and out of house/rooms, sensory workouts. **Go outside!** Every day, come rain or shine! Fresh air, space, movement, and natural light are all brain and body calmers. If the person you care for does this in a way that doesn't feel safe, talk to someone in your professional team to make a plan. **Sensory needs:** Most of us process sensory input (words, sounds, the way things feel, pictures, light, etc) automatically, but sensory input is often amplified and processed differently when in distress, especially for people with intellectual disabilities and autism. They may need to manually process through climbing, deep pressure, extra movement, pacing, balancing, adjusting the light. What does the person you care for do? Make sure they get opportunities to do these things throughout their day! If they do this in a way that doesn't feel safe, talk to someone in your professional team. **Food and drinks:** Ensure regular drinks (low sugar and drinks with a straw are regulating) and regular snacks and routine mealtimes. **Sleep** (if possible!): Make sure you both have a sleep routine that looks the same every day e.g. warm drink, shower, story, kiss, cuddle and sleep. When waking at night, use sleep associations to restart the sleep cycle. If not asleep in 30 minutes, do something low key together for a while before starting the sleep routine again.

Step 2 **Relate (and repair)** When we are with people we trust, our bodies produce oxytocin, the hormone responsible for calming our nervous system. Increase positive interactions with the person you care for.	**Connect!** Because of their additional needs, you are likely to do lots **for** and **to** the person you care for. Practise being **with** them instead, delight in who they are and what they do; fill their cup to overflowing! Every day, plan 3 minutes, 3 times a day of uninterrupted play/interaction/ intensive interaction led by them. This will help with processing the day, deepen your connection, ensure shared joy and support discovery and learning (for you both!). **Intensive Interaction** Scan QR code **Give choice:** Because of their needs, the person you care for is likely to have much less control and choice than their peers without additional needs. Making choices gives a sense of autonomy and freedom. Give opportunities for choice (between 2 things is best!) of clothes, snacks, drinks and activities **whenever possible**, using objects or pictures if needed. **Play and engage:** Watch, play alongside, be present and available and join their world/way of playing/doing something **Develop trust:** Play ready, steady, go and stop/start games to develop trust, people are fun and to allow others to also take a lead
Step 3 **Reason (and repair)** When we feel calm and connected, you will both be in the right place to learn new skills to live a happier life.	**Repair:** After a difficult experience, it takes time and effort to rebuild and reconnect. What needs to happen now to fix things? How can we help repair the situation? This does not mean being permissive. Instead consider whether it's possible for things to look or be different next time to reduce triggers for you both, increase connection and set you both up for success. **What happened and why**: After a difficult experience, once you are both calm, be curious about the reason(s) behind the behaviour. Where possible, together, consider: What happened (including thoughts and feelings)? How have others been affected? *Why are they doing that? What are they trying to communicate?* Then, learn how to do things differently. **Communication**: Imagine being unable to tell someone what you want/need using language – you will find a way! Help the person you care for to tell you their wants and needs using pictures, photos, objects. Teach pointing, so they can make choices. Show an object/picture alongside each thing you do- shoes for outside, keys for car, bowl for eating, etc. **Waiting:** Consider the use of sand-timers, visual timers or offer something enjoyable to help with waiting.

This plan is applicable in DDP-practice, system-focused work and when weaving DDP into PBS.

[insert child name]'s Therapeutic Support Plan

Understanding me and my needs

What I need from you

Appendix 6: Assessing for signs according to the Pyramid of Need

Appendix 6: Assessing for signs according to the Pyramid of Need

Assessing for signs according to the Pyramid of Need

These 'assessing for signs' tables are designed to support understanding of presenting needs at each level of the Pyramid of Need for the person with an intellectual disability, their caregivers and the wider support system. It is hoped that this understanding can contribute to a wider formulation and tailor intervention using the corresponding suggested steps detailed in Chapter 11 of this book.

The Pyramid of Need consists of six levels, with each level building on the foundations being created by needs being met at the earlier stages for the next. It is not a linear or sequential process as individuals' needs and support varies depending on their environment, what is happening and who is present at the current time. It is also important to note that it is possible to be at different levels at the same time and to move up and down depending on what is happening, who is around, how regulated someone is and what the environment is like at any moment.

Level 1: Feeling safe: Assessing for signs that a person with intellectual disabilities, their carers or support networks are not feeling safe

Person with intellectual disability

☐ Almost constantly distressed or dysregulated.
☐ Finding it difficult to feel safe away from parent(s) or primary attachment figure; struggling to separate from carers.
☐ High levels of fear and anxiety, displayed through anxious (often distracted and fearful of change, new situations or places) or angry behaviours towards self and others.
☐ Often closed off and/or defensive.
☐ In blocked trust of relationships, often taking charge, demanding or conversely falling into submission; isolated, withdrawn and superficial in interactions; seeking out places to hide and lack of eye contact.
☐ Moving quickly; always on the 'go' and chaotic or conversely static and a bit sedentary.
☐ Hungry and never satiated or indifferent to food offered.
☐ Poor temperature control.

Immediate caregivers, teams and support networks

☐ Home/placement at risk or broken down.
☐ Difficult interactions with others in the support system.
☐ Information concealing and/or incoherent with the rest of the system or person with intellectual disabilities.
☐ Often reactive and emotional in responses and emotional in interactions with others in the support network and in meetings; showing signs of hopelessness and negativity.
☐ Saying they do not feel heard and supported.
☐ Feeling unsafe in their care of the person with intellectual disabilities, for example:
  ☐ Struggling to use boundaries, for fear of the reaction of the person with intellectual disabilities.
  ☐ Having to manage high levels of violence and risk with the person with intellectual disabilities.
☐ Struggling to use boundaries, for fear of the reaction of the person with intellectual disabilities.
☐ Having to manage high levels of violence and risk with the person with intellectual disabilities.
☐ Not engaged in discussion, starting to work as individuals as opposed to part of a team.
☐ Socially isolated and unsupported.
☐ Showing signs of blocked care or struggling to be attuned to and engaged with the person with intellectual disabilities, quickly defensive, irritated or hopelessness.

☐ Hypervigilance to signs of anger or rejection.
☐ Finding it hard to be available for, enjoy being with and caring for the person with intellectual disabilities.
☐ Difficulty attuning to and understanding the inner world of the person with intellectual disabilities.
☐ Struggling to provide safety and containment in parenting style, by being too strict or too lenient.

Additional signs that the support network doesn't feel safe

☐ Often unavailable to others in the system and missing correspondence from others.
☐ Showing signs of blocked care or struggling to be attuned to, and engaged with, the person with intellectual disabilities; quickly defensive, irritated or hopelessness.
☐ Not enough capacity in the team, so often seeing unmet needs, feeling responsible to fill gaps in service provision; not taking breaks; working longer hours than contracted or double shifts.
☐ Work environment not meeting needs of the carers or person with intellectual disabilities – lack of office space, training space, meeting space, kitchen, space for breaks.
☐ Jobs not secure; shift patterns given at late notice.
☐ Management struggling to use boundaries, for fear of staff leaving.
☐ No clear risk management and safeguarding processes or training to manage highly risky situations.
☐ No clear understanding of job role.
☐ Too much responsibility in context of resources available, skill and training.
☐ Lack of appropriate supervision structures, reflection or debrief structures, or that these are in place but not attend.

Level 2: Developing relationships: Assessing for signs that a person with intellectual disabilities, their carers or support network need support to develop relationship

Person with intellectual disability

When a person with intellectual disabilities is struggling to develop (trust in) relationships, it might look like they are:

☐ Struggling to manage own emotions; struggling to accept others' efforts of being present or offer comfort during times of dysregulation.
☐ Drawn to inappropriate interactions or social groups.
☐ Struggling to trust the availability of parents/carers, which can result in behaviours that appear to be a communication to want to push away efforts of connection or are testing boundaries.
☐ Struggling to initiate interactions.
☐ Struggling to allow others to be present or join in play or activities the person with intellectual disabilities is engaged in.

Immediate caregivers

☐ When carers are struggling to support the person with intellectual disabilities to develop trust in their relationship, and when carers struggle to relate to the support network around them, it might look like they are:
☐ Struggling to be and make themselves available for interactions.
☐ Struggling to make connections, with responses often being irritable and defensive instead of light and playful.
☐ Struggling to stay calm and open when the person with ID is dysregulated (potentially defensive, shut down, pushing away), and needs them most.
☐ Struggling to understand the needs and communications of the person with ID; struggling to read their cues and make meaning.
☐ Struggling to feel and offer empathy to the person with ID or colleagues and their internal experiences, to acknowledge their struggles; instead, quick to offer solutions, shutting down or minimising expressions of need. For example, *"There's no need to be upset. Come on, let's watch some TV"*.
☐ Relationship with person with ID feeling more functional and practical, whilst struggling to find joy, delight or fun in the interactions together.
☐ Struggling to navigate social interactions and people in their support network (partner, colleagues, professionals).
☐ Feeling unsupported and defensive.
☐ Struggling to manage whilst also struggling to trust or other personal barriers to accessing support from others.

Whole teams and services

Teams and systems struggling to relate to one another might look like:

☐ Services struggling, but practising in isolation as opposed to sharing the load or and working collaboratively.
☐ Lack of genuineness; systems blaming (*"they would never understand"*) and passing responsibilities (*"that's not our remit"*), as opposed to thinking creatively about meeting needs.
☐ Struggling to navigate social interactions.
☐ Defensiveness in interactions, shutting down creativity and flexibility.

Level 3: Comfort and coregulation: Assessing for signs that a person with intellectual disabilities, their carers or support network need support to accept comfort and coregulation

People with an intellectual disability

☐ Person with intellectual disabilities is increasingly regulated and finding moments of joy and some sadness, and are becoming more secure with their main carers, but they still struggle when experiencing strong emotions, with this often leading to them coming out of their window of tolerance, dysregulated or dissociating.

Immediate caregivers

Carers are struggling to provide comfort and co-regulation when the person with intellectual disabilities is experiencing dysregulation and needs them. This might look like:

☐ Withdrawing or shutting down.
☐ Trying to talk the person with intellectual disabilities out of their sadness or anger, distracting them or minimising the emotion (as opposed to showing acceptance and empathy).
☐ Becoming dysregulated themselves and showing, for example, frustration or anger.
☐ An imbalance in the two hands of care: providing discipline or corrections when the person with intellectual disabilities needs connection first, or being too lenient and not upholding limits.
☐ Struggling to repair after there has been a rupture in the way they might usually respond.

Teams and systems

Teams struggling to remain PACEful when the person with intellectual disabilities or others in the support network show distress or dysregulation. This might look like:

☐ Teams or support networks no longer open and engaged with one another.
☐ Splitting and becoming fragmented.
☐ Staff withdrawing and isolating themselves.
☐ Staff or systems being defensive and showing shame responses, minimising, blaming, judging, anger, with-holding information.
☐ An imbalance in the 'two hands of care': providing discipline or corrections when the person with intellectual disabilities needs connection first, or being too lenient and not upholding limits.
☐ Teams struggle to meet one another, name challenges and repair.

Level 4: Empathy and reflection: Assessing for signs that a person with intellectual disabilities, their carers or support network need support around empathy and reflection

Person with an intellectual disability

- ☐ Noticing that they don't know how to respond to questions like "How are you feeling?" or "I wonder why that happened?" No clear sense of their internal world.
- ☐ Their reactions can seem out of step with or not easily matched with the situation; you might notice over or underreaction.
- ☐ Struggling to make sense of their experiences, feelings or physiological needs, and expecting others to both anticipate and be able to meet their needs.
- ☐ Struggling to take turns or wait.
- ☐ Having no, or very limited insight into another person's experience; underdeveloped theory of mind.
- ☐ Shame

Immediate caregivers

- ☐ Blaming the child or adult with an intellectual disability.
- ☐ Showing signs of 'blocked care'.
- ☐ Relying on pathways or contracts/agreements rather than talking about connection or coregulation.
- ☐ Adults around the person with an intellectual disability are sounding and looking busier but not spending a lot of time in lower-key activities.

Support networks

- ☐ Wanting to protect the immediate caregivers; including ending placements.
- ☐ Using a critical voice towards the immediate caregivers.
- ☐ Focusing on systems and pathways; discussing objectives, service level agreements contracts etc.

The wider system

- ☐ Focusing on systems and pathways; discussing objectives, service-level agreements (SLA) contracts etc.
- ☐ Service re-organisation or re-structure in order to improve service delivery.

Level 5: Resilience and resources: Assessing for signs that a person with intellectual disabilities, their carers or support network need support with developing resilience and resources

Person with an intellectual disability

- ☐ Depending on others for comfort and emotional regulation.
- ☐ Reluctance to start or finish activities.
- ☐ Expressing doubts about being able to do something.
- ☐ Handing over things to another person rather than giving it a go.
- ☐ Chameleon-like changes – depending on who is in the room/who is the latest best friend, as a way of fitting in, or being like someone else because they don't have a clear sense of themselves and their worth.

Immediate caregivers

- ☐ Feeling they have run out of ideas and have already tried everything.
- ☐ Talking about "nothing works".
- ☐ Increased sense of responsibility and worry that they alone are responsible for resolving things.
- ☐ Deterioration in mood: signs of depression, anxiety, difficulty sleeping, weight loss etc.
- ☐ Reduction in self-care.

Support networks

- ☐ Reducing access to services by narrowing the range or number of people they can support or include within a service.
- ☐ Recommending that the person with an intellectual disability would be better suited to another environment/support setting.

The wider system

- ☐ Rigidity of focus that often leads to a lack of flexibility or refusal to incorporate new research or evidence into guidelines.

Level 6: Explore trauma and mourn losses: Assessing for signs that a person with intellectual disabilities, their carers or support network need support around processing trauma and loss

Person with an intellectual disability

- ☐ Repeated mention of memories or flashbacks.
- ☐ Questions about why certain events happened to them in particular.
- ☐ Lots of fact-finding questions such as 'who, what, why and when' type questions.
- ☐ Reliving events as if they are happening today, but tolerating co-regulation and support to make sense of their reactions.
- ☐ Struggling with key anniversaries.
- ☐ Identifying feelings of sadness or panic and being open to and listening to others about triggers or underlying pressures that lead to these feelings.

Immediate caregivers

- ☐ Repeated mention of memories or flashbacks.
- ☐ Reliving events as if they are happening today.
- ☐ Struggling with key anniversaries.
- ☐ Identifying feelings of sadness or panic.
- ☐ Having limited time and energy to be able to focus on the person with an intellectual disability.

Support networks

- ☐ Disengagement from, or rejection of, working with the immediate caregivers or person with an intellectual disability.

The wider system

- ☐ Avoidance of the issue.

Appendix 7: Attachment-informed assessment

Appendix 7: Attachment-informed assessment

Attachment-informed assessment measures

Please see a list of assessments which are attachment-informed and can be helpful in assessment of individuals with an intellectual disability and those within their wider system in a DDP informed way. They can also help with tracking progress within DDP and DDP informed practice. This list is not exhaustive and many of these assessment measures required training and supervision. They are listed here rather than repeatedly referenced across chapters.

Sensory

Assessment name	Detail	What does it assess?
Sensory Processing Measure (Parham et al, 2007)	Useful for tracking sensory development. Carer report. All age.	Sensory development.
Sensory Attachment Intervention (SAI) (Bhreathnach, 2013)	Carer report scoring sensory and attachment patterns. All age.	Sensory and attachment patterns.

Assessments suitable for use with children only

Assessment name	Detail	What does it assess?
Assessment Checklist for Children/ Adolescents (ACC or ACA) (Tarren-Sweeney, 1997)	No normative data available for people with an intellectual disability but useful for tracking relational patterns impacted by trauma. Carer report.	Child and Adolescent versions available only.
The Mother's Object Relations Scale- short form (MORS-SF) (Oates & Gervai, 2019)	A 14-item questionnaire that looks at the caregiver's perception of the thoughts, feelings and intentions of their child towards them, based on evidence of this shaping how the caregiver behaves and interacts, with consequences for the development of the child.	Carer perception of child/carer attachment relationship.
Secure Base Have Observation (SBHO) (De Shipper and Schuengel, 2006)	Rating for indications of secure attachment, rating by carers. For use with children and adolescents.	Attachment relationship.
Carer Questionnaire/ Thinking about your Child Questionnaire (TAYC) (Adoption plus, CPLAAC, Golding)	Understanding carer priorities and key concerns about their children. Has been adapted into the TAYC. (Nic is currently talking to researcher about developing a version for children and adults with an intellectual disability).	Carer priorities and concerns.
Part 1 of the Sheffield Learning Disability Outcome Measure (Girgis, 2013)	An 8-item questionnaire which relate to understanding the child's behaviour and looks at the relationship between carer/parent and child, level of confidence and views about the future.	■ Child behaviour. ■ Attachment relationship. ■ Carer confidence and hope.

Assessments suitable for children and adults

Assessment name	Detail	What does it assess?
Scale of Emotional Development Short (SED-S) (Sappok, Zeppertiz & Hudson, 2022)	Carer report on the closeness between carer and cared for person enables developmental areas to be assessed and development milestones to be incorporated into the understanding of behavioural presentation, assessment, and later interventions.	Attachment relationship and emotional development.
Self-report Assessment of Attachment Security (SRAAS) (Smith and McCarthy, 1969)	Self-report exploration of attachment style. Individualistic focus rather than specifically relational. All age.	Attachment relationship.
The Secure Base checklists (University of East Anglia, 2024)	Exploration of the carer and cared for person (children and adults) relationship across a range of elements and areas including, availability, sensitivity, acceptance, co-operation, and family membership.	Attachment relationship.
Foundations for Well-being Assessment (Gwillim et al, 2023 in press)	Based on McGill et al (2020) framework of capable environments which enable the promoting of physical and emotional safety with a relational focus on the context in which behaviour occurs within the following domains.	Pre-requisites for regulation, safety, relationships and learning.
The quality of early relatedness rating scale (*QuERRS-2*: Skelly et al, 2020) and the self-report version of this same scale (SQuERRS; Skelly et al, 2021).	Likert scale which aims to examine the person's early attachment history and their judgements about this (their or their staff's thoughts on this). The authors of the scale recommend that a psychologist or Psychotherapist is part of interpreting the results which can also be used to assess readiness for therapy.	Early attachment history and impact on presentation.
Challenging Behaviour Needs Assessment Scale (Wilcox et al, 2021)	The assessment is based on the Brief Behavioural Assessment Tool (BBAT) (Smith & Nethell, 2014); the Functional Behaviour Needs Assessment Tool (Nethell, 2019); and Reducing Restrictive Practice Toolkit (Edwards, Nethell & Jones, 2021). A needs-based assessment of behaviours that challenge which includes emphasis on needs and preferences, a rating scale of behaviour, triggers and maintaining factors and information round the use of restrictive practice.	Cared for person's needs, preferences behaviours, communication and use of restrictive practice.

Assessments suitable for adults only

Assessment name	Detail	What does it assess?
Adult Attachment Projective Picture System (AAP) (George & West, 2001)	Exploration of an attachment-based narrative through interpretation of various picture stories. For use with adults.	Attachment narrative.
Manchester Attachment Scale - Third Part (MAST) (Penketh et al, 2014)	Rating for indications of secure attachment, rating by carers. For use with adults.	Attachment relationship.
The Frankish Assessment of the Impact of Trauma in Intellectual Disability (FAIT) (Frankish, 2019)	Formal observational assessment of interaction and trauma indicators. Designed to be used with people with Profound and multiple learning disabilities as well as across the range of intellectual disabilities.	■ Attachment Relationship. ■ Trauma.

Observational assessments of relational interactions

Assessment name	Detail	What does it assess?
Marshak Interaction Method (MIM) (Marshak, 1960)	Structured observation-based assessment where a parent/carer – child dyad complete a series of activities to observe and assess the overall quality and nature of relationship. Can be used to inform Theraplay.	■ Observation of attachment relationship.

Attachment-informed clinical interview considerations

This table summarises some of the individual and system meaning making assessment elements which support an attachment-informed formulation in a PBS framework. It will also be important to note individual differences within each relationship.

Individual meaning making	System meaning making
Early experiences and development: in utero, birth and their early years experiences. Socio-cultural elements to be considered? Was/is there stability, predictability, consistency or chaos, changes and confusion? What do we know about the person's neurosequential processing? How does this affect their emotional, social and cognitive needs? Were they able to meet their developmental milestones? Early relationships with caregivers? Disruptions/separations in family life? How did the family/ the person learn about their disability? **Internal working model:** Based on the person's relational experiences, intellectual disability and additional needs what are the person's expectations of themselves, others and the world around them. **Window of tolerance and needs:** How might early and ongoing relationships and experiences affect the person's window of tolerance and neurosequential processing? Does the person feel safe? Within what relationships and contexts, is the person's window of tolerance bigger (needs met) or smaller (needs unmet)? **Triggers (internal and external, Harding, 2020):** How do external events, activities and relationships trigger difficult internal experiences and relate to their internal working model, and associated physiological and emotional response or sensory experience? Including an experience of **toxic shame**? For example, a person with intellectual disability might show a learnt survival strategy in response to their experience of shame (that could be perceived as a behaviour that is challenging). This behaviour, in turn, can trigger a carer's internal working model of not feeling good enough and a subsequent shame response. This can perpetuate an unhelpful pattern but also enact a trauma cycle with the person with intellectual disabilities and throughout the wider support network.	**Relationship expectations:** What has been your experience of getting to know the person? What were your hopes or expectations? What are the strengths? **Emotional availability and regulation:** Can the person with intellectual disabilities come to you for interaction and comfort? Do individuals around the person recognise support seeking behaviours? How does this look and how does this feel for you? When are you attuned? When do you have fun? How do you feel when you spend time with the person with intellectual disabilities? Are interactions joyful? When things are tricky, do you feel curious about underlying thoughts, feelings and needs? Do you notice whether it is hard work or enjoyable being together? **Safety and support:** Does everyone in the system feel able to provide physical and emotional safety for the person with intellectual disabilities? Are there systemic barriers to safety, predictability, consistency and positive/ joyful interactions? How and with whom are the parents/ carers/wider support networks needs being supported? **Window of tolerance, shame and blocked care** What internal and external response do individuals in the network notice themselves having to different behaviours of concern (thoughts and emotions)? How does it feel when the person seeks/accepts comfort (or not!)? When do you notice you stay in your window of tolerance and when do you notice you are not? When do individuals in the network notice they feel frustrated, upset, annoyed? What sense do they make of that in terms of their own IWM, shame rupture and repair experience?

Attachment patterns: What does the person expect from interactions, based on the relational experiences? Words to describe these can be given e.g. caring, nurture, abusive, rejecting, as well as details of experiences which are known. How does this impact their pattern of relating and their emotional presentation? For example, *"When I used to express a need, others responded in a certain way, so in anticipation of my needs perceived like that, I think, feel and act a certain way"*. Does the person seek/accept comfort when in distress? What style of interaction do they enjoy?

Responses/behaviours of concern: How do internal triggers and physical, emotional and relational needs impact on the persons response to cope? How might you expect the person with intellectual disabilities to respond in the context of their previous relational experiences (and IWM)? How does this give context to relationships that are helpful and relationships that are challenging/tricky?

Long-term impacts of patterns of relating and how these exacerbate distress: For example, when I throw things because a demand is placed on me, people run away. In the short term, this behaviour is a successful coping strategy, as the person escaping from the demand, reducing their distress whilst, long-term, carers might avoid placing demands, increase shame-related beliefs, such as "people do not like being with me" (Dunn & Bolton, 2004) and increase blocked connections.

Agency: What are the person's strengths, skills? What would they say would improve their quality of life and relationships?

Environment: What role do environmental factors play in relationships, reactions and responses? What are the strengths? Are there restrictions? Are preferred activities and interactions freely available and accessible? Is everyone's day predictable? Are there financial or cultural circumstances to consider?

Support: What support, formal and informal, is available to the carer and the system? Is there a way to have breaks from caring? Is there practical or predictably support as well as ad hoc support? How does the carer feel about asking or accessing this?

Appendix 8: Dyadic iceberg of behaviours that challenge

While we see the usefulness of traditional monitoring and analysis of behaviours that challenge; it is also essential to acknowledge the underlying, unobservable, and interactional aspects of behaviour, as illustrated by the Dyadic Iceberg model.

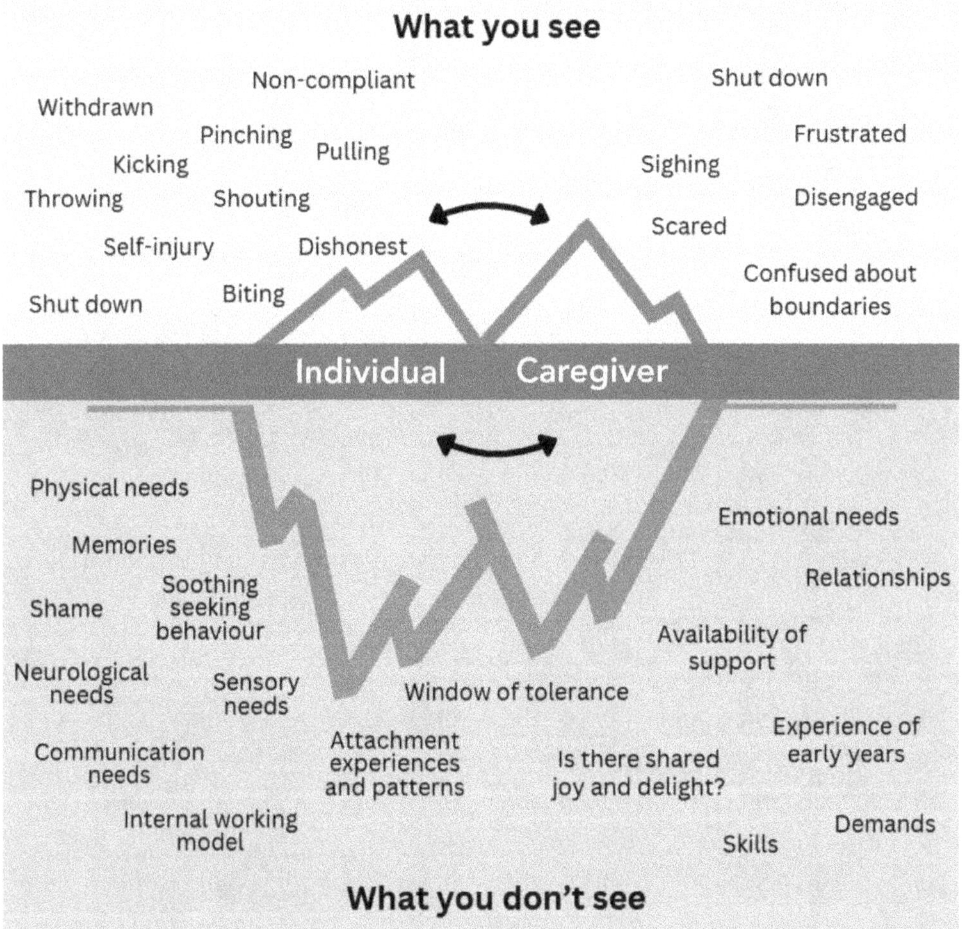

Appendix 9: Dyadic interaction summary statement

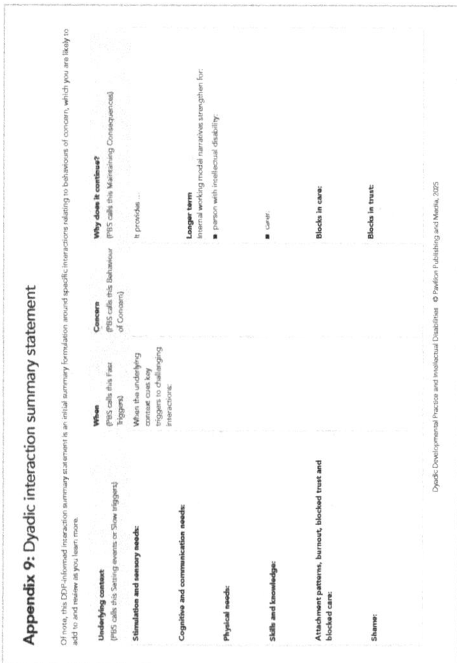

Appendix 9: Dyadic interaction summary statement

Of note, this DDP-informed interaction summary statement is an initial summary formulation around specific interactions relating to behaviours of concern, which you are likely to add to and review as you learn more.

Underlying context (PBS calls this Setting events or Slow triggers)	**When** (PBS calls this Fast Triggers)	**Concern** (PBS calls this Behaviour of Concern)	**Why does it continue?** (PBS calls this Maintaining Consequences)
Stimulation and sensory needs:	When the underlying context cues key triggers to challenging interactions:		It provides …
Cognitive and communication needs:			**Longer term** Internal working model narratives strengthen for: ■ person with intellectual disability:
Physical needs:			
Skills and knowledge:			■ carer:
Attachment patterns, burnout, blocked trust and blocked care:			**Blocks in care:**
Shame:			**Blocks in trust:**

Dyadic Developmental Practice and Intellectual Disabilities © Pavilion Publishing and Media, 2025

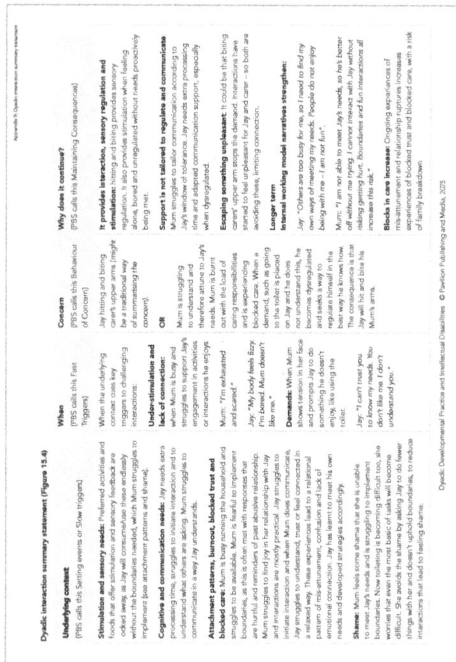

Appendix 9: Dyadic interaction summary statement

Dyadic interaction summary statement (Figure 15.4)

Underlying context (PBS calls this Setting events or Slow triggers)	**When** (PBS calls this Fast Triggers)	**Concern** (PBS calls this Behaviour of Concern)	**Why does it continue?** (PBS calls this Maintaining Consequences)
Stimulation and sensory needs: Preferred activities and foods that offer stimulation and sensory feedback are ocked away, as Jay will consume/use these endlessly without the boundaries needed, which Mum struggles to implement (see attachment patterns and shame). **Cognitive and communication needs:** Jay needs extra processing time, struggles to initiate interaction and to understand what others are asking. Mum struggles to communicate in a way Jay understands. **Attachment patterns, burnout, blocked trust and blocked care:** Mum is busy running the household and struggles to be available. Mum is fearful to implement boundaries, as this is often met with responses that are hurtful and reminders of past abusive relationship. Mum struggles to find joy in her relationship with Jay and interactions are mostly practical. Jay struggles to initiate interaction and when Mum does communicate, Jay struggles to understand, trust or feel connected in a relaxed way. These experiences lead to a relational pattern of mis-attunement, confusion and lack of emotional connection. Jay has learnt to meet his own needs and developed strategies accordingly. **Shame:** Mum feels some shame that she is unable to meet Jay's needs and is struggling to implement boundaries. Now toileting is becoming difficult too, she worries that even the most basic of tasks will become difficult. She avoids the shame by asking Jay to do fewer things with her and doesn't uphold boundaries, to reduce interactions that lead to feeling shame.	When the underlying context cues key triggers to challenging interactions: **Under-stimulation and lack of connection:** when Mum is busy and struggles to support Jay's engagement in activities or interactions he enjoys Mum: *"I'm exhausted and scared."* *Jay: "My body feels fizzy. I'm bored. Mum doesn't like me."* **Demands:** When Mum shows tension in her face and prompts Jay to do something he doesn't enjoy, like using the toilet. *Jay: "I can't trust you to know my needs. You don't like me. I don't understand you."*	Jay hitting and biting carer's upper arms *(might be a traditional way of summarising the concern).* **OR** Mum is struggling to understand and therefore attune to Jay's needs. Mum is burnt out with the load of caring responsibilities and is experiencing blocked care. When a demand, such as going to the toilet is placed on Jay and he does not understand this, he becomes dysregulated and seeks a way to regulate himself in the best way he knows how. The consequence is that Jay will hit and bite his Mum's arms.	**It provides interaction, sensory regulation and stimulation:** hitting and biting provides sensory regulation. It also provides stimulation when feeling alone, bored and unregulated without needs proactively being met. **Support is not tailored to regulate and communicate**. Mum struggles to tailor communication according to Jay's window of tolerance. Jay needs extra processing time and adapted communication support, especially when dysregulated. **Escaping something unpleasant**: It could be that biting carers' upper arm stops the demand. Interactions have started to feel unpleasant for Jay and carer – so both are avoiding these, limiting connection. **Longer term** **Internal working model narratives strengthen:** Jay: *"Others are too busy for me, so I need to find my own ways of meeting my needs. People do not enjoy being with me – I am not fun"*. Mum: *"I am not able to meet Jay's needs, so he's better off without me trying. I cannot interact with Jay without risking getting hurt. Boundaries and fun interactions all increase this risk."* **Blocks in care increase:** Ongoing experiances of mis-attunement and relationship ruptures increases experiences of blocked trust and blocked care, with a risk of family breakdown

Dyadic Developmental Practice and Intellectual Disabilities © Pavilion Publishing and Media, 2025

Appendix 10: DDP-informed formulation template

Any understanding of behaviour that stems from and/or elicits distress, needs to consider what each person in the dyad brings to patterns of interaction and how this might be understood in the context of early and ongoing experiences and their position on the Pyramid of Need. We propose the use of a comprehensive DDP-informed formulation model that enables behaviour to be understood in the context of individual and system factors and the interaction between them.

Pyramid of need position: Feeling safe, developing relationships, comfort and co-regulation, empathy and reflection, resilience and resources, explore trauma and mourn losses

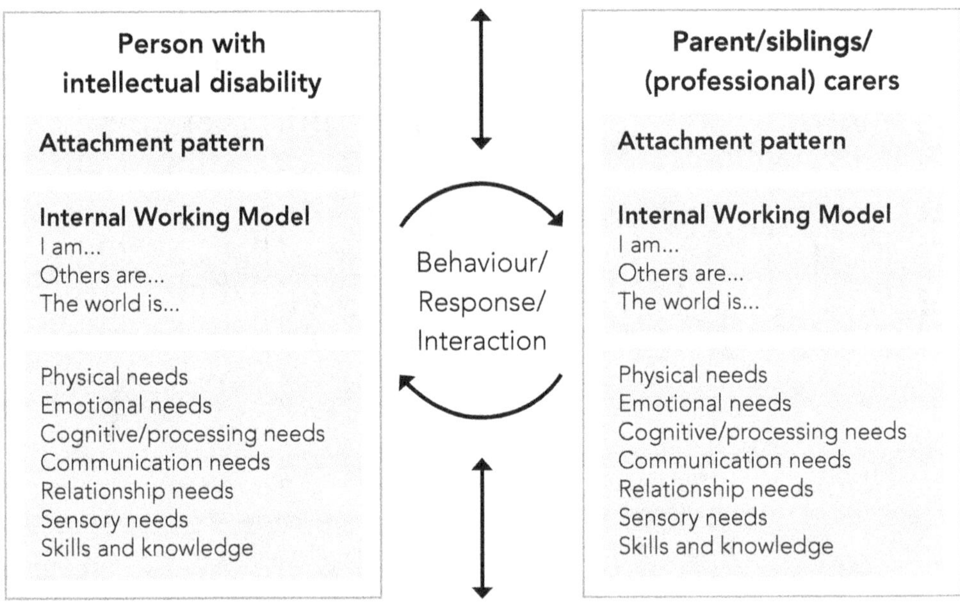

Early and ongoing context: Strengths and needs relating to wider personal and professional experiences and support, educational experiences, financial security, opportunities for activities, access to environmental stimulation, structure, routine and safety

Appendix 11: Working with the system using the four Rs framework

Appendix 11: Working with the system using the four Rs framework

	What is the focus at this level?	Corresponding focus for family and paid carers at this level
Reason (as well as continued regulate and relate)	At this point, the person with intellectual disabilities and their support network feel calm and connected – they have capacity to think and work more clearly to enhance happiness and quality of life. Support can focus on individually tailored support, planning, skills development, and better communication. The focus can be on development as well as on connection. Support choice and agency: expressing preferences.	■ Consider formal therapeutic work – for the individual. ■ Enhancing skills, knowledge, and confidence to implement skills sessions with person with intellectual disabilities and to increase skills and confidence in opportunities to maintain an attitude of PACE, 'name it to tame it' and affective-reflective dialogue. ■ Supporting sleep intervention. ■ Supporting improved community access and peer activities once carers and the person with intellectual disabilities have developed the skills and environmental context to set this up for success. ■ To complete the proactive work needed to allow structure and thoughtful interventions at other times. ■ Attend regular DDP supervision and team meetings, which model connection and in the moment reflection. ■ Failures to connect to be seen as learning opportunities, and allow thinking about shame across the system as well as being curious about this for the individual. ■ Develop formulation-informed support plans and support implementation.
Relate (as well as continued regulate)	Genuine connection: relationships that bring comfort, shared joy and improving understanding. ■ Connect with the person with an intellectual disability and their support network to develop enjoyable relationships. ■ Ensure care that is nurturing, consistent, calm, and predictable. ■ Ensure access to opportunities for shared open interactions that enable candour, delight, and maybe laughter	■ Well-being reflection and support: what helps the person to be able to reconnect with reasoning, such as sensory activities and reducing demands. ■ Communication with the person in their way, so intensive interaction should be considered for those with less verbal ability and those with cognitive/emotional disconnect. ■ Continuing PACE reflective conversations, staying curious to the person's experiences and verbalising this in a gentle way – which is not necessarily looking for agreement (trying to convince) but rather opening the possibility of curiosity and understanding the message of "you are understandable, and I want to understand you". ■ Embrace attunement-rupture-repair cycle. ■ Remember dysregulation--> co-regulation--> future self-regulation. ■ Using supervision/team meetings to also explore shame responses, blocked care and blocked trust and enabling them to embrace PACE.

Appendix 11: Working with the system using the four Rs framework

Regulate	At this stage, people are overwhelmed, stressed and tired. Support the person with intellectual disabilities and their support network to regulate their nervous system, to feel less stressed and more engaged. Consider physical and emotional safety, structure, boundaries, visual schedules, and guidance.	■ Keep things simple, concise. ■ Working together agreement, specifically knowing who to go to for what, effective communication to ensure containment and consistency. ■ Lower expectations. ■ Explore the Foundations for Well-being/Capable Environment Assessment to explore areas in need of attention. ■ Therapeutic support: Modelling PACE when discussing challenges and frustrations (mostly Acceptance &Empathy, with gentle Playfulness & Curiosity) and Two Hands Approach, be mindful of Shame responses, blocked care and blocked trust.
Repair	Where there have been ruptures in the relationships between carers, with carers and management or the organisation there needs to be thought given to repair.	■ Use 'name it to tame it' and affective/reflective dialogue to attempt a storytelling approach to what has occurred. ■ Although some formal learning may be needed to emphasise that all were trying their best and aims of what they were hoping to achieve. ■ Be mindful of possible shame and blocked care reactions and how to recognise and move away from this.

Appendix 12: Relational Management Supervision Template

Appendix 12: Relational Management Supervision Template

Relational Management Supervision
Recording Template

Name of Supervisee:

Name of Supervisor:

Date:

Agenda

Actions from previous meeting

Emotional well-being

This is not intended to come across as a judgemental space. Rather a check-in to gauge whether the system is in a good enough place for staff to feel safe and emotionally well. We can hold your sense of well-being in mind throughout the discussion and focus on re-establishing safety and well-being, or maintaining well-being, depending on how things are feeling.

☺ Feeling happy in job and can hold empathy understanding and compassion — Feeling sad, annoyed, stressed and/or anxious ☹

1 2 3 4 5 6 7 8 9 10

Appendix 12: Relational Management Supervision Template

Sense of safety

Work environment
- Is the environment comfortable and meeting your needs to do undertake your role?

Capacity
- Number of families on caseload?
- While at times challenging, is there generally enough capacity in the team to carry out the key tasks?

Risk management
- Are risk management processes clear?
- Risk assessment up to date?
- Feeling physically safe in challenging situations?
- Buddy system in place?

Job role
- Annual leave/sickness/TOIL

Record keeping
- Is it clear?
- Do you have adequate time?
- Do you need support?

Job role
- Is the role clear?
- Have there been any changes?

Relationships and dynamics
- Does the team feel supportive?
- Are there aspects of relationships that need some support?
- What are relationships like with our partner agencies?

Emotional load
- What emotional impact does the role have day to day? Is there time and space for reflection on more emotionally challenging aspects of the job?

Appendix 12: Relational Management Supervision Template

Professional development
- What achievements can we celebrate since last supervision?
- Anything, in particular, you've learnt?
- What challenges have you faced since last supervision?
- How have you managed these?
- What challenges that remain?
- Would it be helpful to discuss?
- Any training/general opportunities to take up?
- Skills and training needs (inc. mandatory training)
- Professional Development Plan date and action update

Appendix 12: Relational Management Supervision Template

Outcomes/Actions

Next Meeting:

Signed Supervisor:

Signed Supervisee:

Appendix 13: Attachment-informed Naturalistic Observation Record

Appendix 13: Attachment-informed Naturalistic Observation Record

Naturalistic Observation Record for (initials):

Completed by:

Date:	**Day:**	**Observation time:**
General location:		**Exact location(s) in which observing:** 1 2 3

The environment at time of observation:
(please indicate the corresponding location number behind every ticked box)

☐ Very quiet	☐ Very Cold	☐ Deserted	☐ Very relaxed	☐ Very friendly
☐ Quiet	☐ Cold	☐ Almost deserted	☐ Quite relaxed	☐ Quite friendly
☐ Somewhat noisy	☐ Comfortable	☐ Some people about	☐ A little tense	☐ Indifferent
☐ Noisy	☐ Hot	☐ Somewhat crowded	☐ Quite tense	☐ Quite hostile
☐ Very noisy	☐ Very hot	☐ Very crowded	☐ Very tense	☐ Very hostile

Describe other environmental factors observed

Look:	Smell:
Listen:	Touch:

Other people in the same location (number people, initials and factors of importance as required):

Physical health presentation

Emotional presentation

☐ Calm	☐ Disinterested	☐ Tense	☐ Quiet
☐ Excited	☐ Happy	☐ Withdrawn	☐ Tearful
☐ Agitated	☐ Anxious	☐ Angry	☐ Sad

Communication (Requesting)

1. **What communication system does the person you are observing already have in place? Please note how this looked in naturally occurring activities and routines. Can the person you are observing use more than one method of getting needs met?**

   What types of things is the person you are observing requesting? How are they requesting (different forms of communication for different requests)?

   Frequency of requests during observation (tally):

   Percentage of independent requests v prompted requests during observation:

2. **Can the person you are observing say "no" in a functional way?**

   Frequency of requests during observation (tally):

   Percentage of independent requests v prompted requests during observation:

3. **Can the person you are observing request attention/interaction from others in a functional way and what did this look like?**

   Frequency of requests during observation (tally):

   Percentage of how many independent requests v prompted requests during observation:

Communication (Receptive understanding)

1. **Can the person you are observing follow simple one step health and safety instructions in context? Can the person you are observing follow two step instructions? Does the person you are observing need visual cues to follow an instruction?**

   Types of instruction followed independently:

   Types of instructions followed with prompts:

Relationships

1. **Thinking about attuned interactions and seeking comfort and support, how does the person you are observing express a want/need?**
2. **Does the person you are observing approach adults for social interaction, comfort, delight? How is this expression received and responded to** (consider concepts of taking charge where necessary, following a need, acceptance, curiosity, playfulness, empathy, availability)?
3. **Will the person you are observing engage in joint play with an adult?**
4. **Does the person you are observing approach peers for social interaction? Will the person you are observing engage in joint play with a peer?**
5. **Does the person you are observing engage in play alongside peers? How long is this sustained?**
6. **What types of interactions does the person you are observing appear to enjoy/not enjoy?**

Appendix 14: An example of a Relational Safety Plan

This plan is a variation on the safety plan originally outlined by Kim Golding (2008), adapted in turn from Spragus (1997), *Clinical management of suicidal behaviour in children and adolescents*, Sage Publishing.

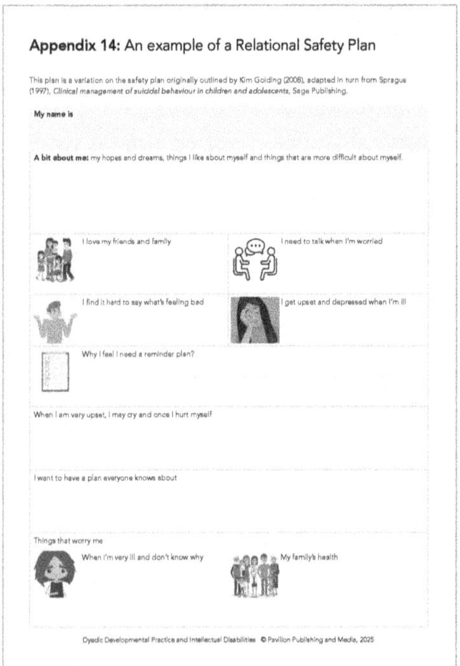

Appendix 14: An example of a Relational Safety Plan

This plan is a variation on the safety plan originally outlined by Kim Golding (2008), adapted in turn from Spragus (1997), *Clinical management of suicidal behaviour in children and adolescents*, Sage Publishing.

My name is

A bit about me: my hopes and dreams, things I like about myself and things that are more difficult about myself.

I love my friends and family

I need to talk when I'm worried

I find it hard to say what's feeling bad

I get upset and depressed when I'm ill

Why I feel I need a reminder plan?

When I am very upset, I may cry and once I hurt myself

I want to have a plan everyone knows about

Things that worry me

When I'm very ill and don't know why

My family's health

Dyadic Developmental Practice and Intellectual Disabilities © Pavilion Publishing and Media, 2025

Appendix 14: An example of a Relational Safety Plan

Signs that I am worried in my body

Crying

Headache

Sweating

Feel sad/depressed

Blame myself for stuff

Call myself bad names

What helps?

Talking

Check my health with GP

Chocolate

How can others help me?

Get out of the house – visit a friend

Watch TV with me

Listen to music and dance with me

See if someone will go for a walk

Cook a meal

Go to the group

Dyadic Developmental Practice and Intellectual Disabilities © Pavilion Publishing and Media, 2025

References

Adoptionplus, CPLAAC, Golding https://ddpnetwork.org/resources/library/authors/adoptionplus/

Ainsworth, M. D. S. & Bell, S. M. (1970). Attachment, exploration, and separation: illustrated by the behavior of one-year-olds in a strange situation. *Child Development*, 41, 49–67.

Alexander, S. L., Frederico, M., Long, M. & Vincendese, D. (2024). Attachment security in children with disability or developmental delay: systematic review of quality and interventions. https://doi.org/10.1080/19411243.2023.2177237

Ali, A., Hassiotis, A., Strydom, A., & King, M. (2012). Self-stigma in people with intellectual disabilities and courtesy stigma in family carers: A systematic review. *Research in Developmental Disabilities, 33*(6), 2122–2140. https://doi.org/10.1016/j.ridd.2012.06.013

Andrai, E., Duhamel, J., Zalla, T., Herbrecht, E., Lebauyer, M. & Sirgiu, A. (2010). 'Promoting social behavior with oxytocin in high autism spectrum disorders.' Proceedings of the National Academy of Sciences. Published online before print February 16, 2010, doi: 10.1073/pnas. 0910249107 PNAS February, 16, 2010.

Astor, K., Lindskog, M., Forssmann, L., Kenward, B., Fransson, M., Skalkidou, A., Tharner, A., Cassé. J. & Gredebäck, G. (2020). Social and emotional contexts predict the development of gaze following in early infancy. *Royal Society Open Science*, Sept 7(9), 201178.

Atkinson, L., Chisholm, V. C., Scott, B., Goldberg, S., Vaughn, B. E. & Blackwell, J. (1999). Maternal sensitivity, child functional level, and attachment in Down syndrome. *Monographs of the Society for Research in Child Development*, 64(3), 45–66.

Balbernie, R. (2001). Circuits and circumstances: the neurobiological consequences of early relationship experiences and how they shape later behaviour. *Journal of Child Psychotherapy*, 27 (3), 237–255.

Banks, R., Bush, A., Baker, P., Bradshaw, J., Carpenter, P., Deb, S., Joyce, T., Mansell, J. & Xenitidis, K. (2007). *Challenging Behaviour: A unified approach.* London: Royal College of Psychiatrists, British Psychological Society & Royal College of Speech and Language Therapists.

Barnett, D., Clements, M., Kaplan-Estrin, M. & Fialka, J. (2003). Building new dreams: supporting parents' adaptation to their child with special neEds *Infants and Young Children*, 16(3), 184–200. https://doi.org/10.1097/00001163-200307000-00006

Baylin J. (2024). 'From Us vs Them to WE: Overcoming the Neurobiology of "The Other" and Implications for DDP'. DDPI Worldwide Conference 2024.

Beacon House, 2022, https://youtu.be/0ehq5-P5OSs.

Beadle-Brown, J., Richardson, L., Guest, C., Malovic, A., Bradshaw, J. & Himmerich, J. (2014). *Living in Fear: Better Outcomes for People with Learning Disabilities and Autism.* Main research report. Canterbury: Tizard Centre, University of Kent.

Behrman, R. E. & Butler, A. S. (Eds) (2007). Institute of Medicine (US) *Committee on Understanding Premature Birth and Assuring Healthy Outcomes*, Washington (DC): National Academies Press (US).

Bhreathnach, E. (2009). 'Innovative Body Based Interventions with Traumatised Children', conference paper. Trauma, Sensory Processing & Attachment: Sensory-Attachment Intervention, Family Futures Conference, London.

Bhreathnach, E. (2013). 'Sensory Attachment Intervention: Sensory Processing Trauma and Attachment.' SAI Level One Professionals Course.

BILD (2022). British Institute of Learning Disabilities. Capable environments. BILD. Retrieved February 2, 2025, from https://www.bild.org.uk/resource/capable-environments/

Boelé, A. (2017). In search of community: lessons from idealized independence for adults with disabilities. *Harvard Educational Review*, 87(3), 380–403.

Bombèr, L. M. (2020) *Know Me To Teach Me: Differentiated Discipline for those recovering from Adverse Childhood Experiences.* Worth Publishing.

Booth, P. B. & Jernberg, A. M. (2010). *Theraplay: Helping parents and children build better relationships through attachment-based play.* (3rd Edition). Wiley and Sons.

Bowlby, J. (1969). *Attachment and Loss.* Volume 1 Attachment. Hogarth Press.

British Psychological Society (2017). *Incorporating Attachment Theory into Practice: Clinical practice guidance for clinical psychologists working with people who have learning disabilities.* British Psychological Society.

British Institute of Learning Disabilities (BILD) (2017). *Positive Behavioural Support: A competence framework.* BILD. https://www.bild.org.uk/resource/positive-behavioural-support-competence-framework/

British Psychological Society (2004). *Challenging Behaviours: Psychological interventions for severely challenging behaviours shown by people with learning disabilities.* Clinical Practice Guidelines. Leicester: BPS.

Brown, B. (2007). *I thought it was just me (but it isn't): Making the journey from "What will people think?" to "I am enough".* Gotham Books.

Brown, B. (2012). *Daring Greatly: How the Courage to Be Vulnerable Transforms the Way we Live, Love, Parent and Lead.* Avery.

Care Quality Commission (2018). *Positive behaviour support for people with behaviours that challenge: Brief guide.* CQC. 20180705_900824_briefguide-positive_behaviour_support_for_people_with_behaviours_that_challenge_v4.pdf

Carpendale, J. I. M. & Lewis, C. (2004). Constructing an understanding of mind: the development of children's social understanding within social interaction. *Behavioral and Brain Sciences*, 27, 79–151. doi: 10.1017/s0140525x04000032

Carr, E. G. (2007). The expanding vision of positive behavior support: research perspectives on happiness, helpfulness, hopefulness. *Journal of Positive Behavior Interventions*, 9, 3–14.

Casswell, G., Golding, K. S, Grant, E., Hudson, J. & Tower, P. (2014). Dyadic Developmental Practice (DDP): a framework for therapeutic intervention and parenting. *British Psychological Society*, 2, 19–27.

Challenging Behaviour Foundation (2021). *Broken: The psychological, emotional, and mental health needs of children and young people with learning disabilities and their families – Final report (Strand 1).* https://www.challengingbehaviour.org.uk/wp-content/uploads/2021/03/brokencbffinalreportstrand1jan21.pdf

Chaudhary, N., Salali, G. D. & Swanepoel, A. (2024). Sensitive responsiveness and multiple caregiving networks among Mbendjele BaYaka hunter-gatherers: potential implications for psychological development and well-being. *Developmental Psychology*, 60(3), 422–440.

Cozolino, L. (2006). *The Neuroscience of Human Relationships: Attachment and the developing social brain.* W. W. Norton & Co.

Davis, K., & Gavidia-Payne, S. (2009). The impact of child, family, and professional support characteristics on the quality of life in families of young children with disabilities. Journal of Intellectual & Developmental Disability, 34(2), 153–162. https://doi.org/10.1080/13668250902874608

Dana, D. (2018). *The Polyvagal Theory in Therapy: Engaging the rhythm of regulation.* Norton.

De Shipper, J. C. & Schuengel, C. (2006) Secure Base Safe Haven Observation list for child attachment behaviour. Unpublished work, VU University, Amsterdam. Cited in Fletcher, H. K., Flood, A. and Hare, D. J. (2016). *Attachment in Intellectual and Developmental Disability: A clinician's guide to practice and research.* Wiley.

Delahooke, M. (2022). *Brain-Body Parenting: How to stop managing behavior and start raising joyful, resilient kids.* First edition. Harper Wave.

Derbyshire, L. (2013fc) A mug or a teacup? In Curran T and Runswick-Cole, K (eds) (2013, fc) Disabled Children's Childhood studies: Critical Approaches in a Global context, London Sage.

Ditchman, N., Werner, S., Kosyluk, K., Jones, N., Elg, B. & Corrigan, P. W. (2013). Stigma and intellectual disability: potential application of mental illness research. *Rehabil Psychol.*, 58(2), 206–216. doi: 10.1037/a0032466.

Down Syndrome International. (2024). *Assume That I Can* – World Down Syndrome Day 2024. Retrieved from https://ds-int.org/assume-that-i-can/

Bernard-Bonnin, A. (2004). Maternal depression and child development. *Paediatrics & Child Health*, 9(8), 575–583.

Dunn, B. & Bolton, W. (2004). The impact of borderline personality traits on challenging behaviour: implications for learning disabilities services. *British Journal of Forensic Practice*, 6(4), 3–9.

Durand, M., Heineman, M., Clarke, S., Wang, M. & Rinaldi, M. (2012). Positive family intervention for severe and challenging behaviour – a multisite randomised control trial. *Journal of Positive Behavioural Support Interventions*, 15(3), 133–143.

Emerson, E., Vick, B., Rechel, B., Munoz-Baell, I., Sørensen, J. & Färm, I. (2015). 'Health Inequalities and people with Disabilities in Europe. Disadvantage. vulnerability and health inequalities: A task group supporting the Marmot region review of social determinants of health and the health divide in the EURO region'. DOI:10.13140/RG.2.1.4521.3606 Accessed 5th January 2025.

Emerson, E. & Einfeld, S. L. (2011). *Challenging Behaviour* (Third edition). Cambridge University Press.

Ewards, R., Nethell, G. & Jones, J. (2020). Reducing Restrictive Practice Toolkit – unpublished.

Fletcher, H. (2016). 'Attachment relationships between parents and their children: The impact of 'The Loss of the Healthy Child'.' In H. Fletcher, A. Flood and D. Hare (Eds) (2016). *Attachment in Intellectual and Developmental Disability: A clinician's guide to practice and research (pp. 33-58).* Wiley.

Fletcher, H. K. & Gallichan, D. J. (2016). An overview of attachment theory: Bowlby and beyond. In H. K. Fletcher, A. Flood and D. J. Hare (Eds), *Attachment in Intellectual and Developmental Disability: A clinician's guide to practice and research* (pp 8–32). Wiley-Blackwell.

Frankish, P. (2019). *Frankish Assessment of the Impact of Trauma in Intellectual Disability (FAIT)*. Pavilion Publishing.

Furnivall, J. & Grant, E. (2014). *Trauma-Sensitive Practice with Children in Care.* Insights.

George, C. & West, M. (2001). The development and preliminary validation of a new measure of adult attachment: the Adult Attachment Projective. *Attachment & Human Development*, 3(1), 30–61.

Giltaij, H. P., Sterkenburg, P. S. & Schuengel, C. (2015) Psychiatric diagnostic screening of social maladaptive behaviour in children with mild intellectual disability: differentiating disordered attachment and pervasive developmental disorder behaviour. *Journal of Intellectual Disability Research*, 59, 138–149.

Girgis, E. (2013). Sheffield Learning Disabilities Outcome Measure (SLDOM). Sheffield Children's NHS Foundation Trust & CORC. Available from: https://www.corc.uk.net/outcome-experience-measures/sheffield-learning-disabilities-outcome-measure-sldom/

Glenn, F. E. (2007). *Growing Together, or Drifting Apart? Children with disabilities and their parents' relationship.* One Plus One.

Goad, E. (2020). Trauma informed care in a service context. In N. Beail, P. Frankish and A. Skelly (Eds), *Trauma and Intellectual Disability: Acknowledgment, identification and intervention.* Pavilion Publishing.

Goh, A. E. & Bambara, L. M. (2013). Individualized positive behaviour support in school settings: a meta-analysis, *Remedial & Special Education*, 33(5), 271–286.

Golding, K. S. (2008). *Nurturing Attachments. Supporting Children Who Are Fostered or Adopted.* London: London: Jessica Kingsley Publishers.

Golding, K. S. (2013). Nurturing attachments training resource. Running parenting groups for adoptive parents and foster or kinship carers. London: Jessica Kingsley Publishers.

Golding, K. S. (2015). Connection Before Correction: Supporting Parents to Meet the Challenges of Parenting Children who have been Traumatised within their Early Parenting Environments. *Children Australia*, 40(2), 1-8.

Golding, K. S. (2017). Foundations for Attachment Training Resource: The Six-Session Programme for Parents of Traumatized Children. London: Jessica Kingsley Publishers.

Golding, K. S. (2019). https://ddpnetwork.org/backend/wp-content/uploads/2019/04/Pyramid-with-DDP-assessment-matrix581.pdf

Golding, K. S. (2020). Understanding and helping children who have experienced maltreatment. *Paediatrics and Child Health*, 30(11), 371–377.

Golding, K. S. (2023) Living with a constant feeling of dread. Dyadic Developmental practice (DDP) with families who foster or adopt children with developmental trauma experience. *The Child and Family Clinical Psychology Review*, 1(8), 63–69.

Golding, K. 2025, personal communication

Golding, K. S. & Hughes, D. A. (2012). *Creating Loving Attachments: Parenting with PACE to Nurture Confidence and Security in the Troubled Child.* Jessica Kingsley Publishers.

Gore, N. J., McGill, P., Toogood, S., Allen, D., Carl Hughes, J., Baker, P., Hastings, R. P., Noone, S. J. & Denne, L. D. (2013). Definition and scope for positive behavioural support. *International Journal of Positive Behavioural Support*, 3(2), 14–23.

Gouin, J-P., Carter, C., Pournajafi-Narzarloo, H., Glaser, R., Malarkey, W., Loving, T., Stowell,

J. & Kiecolt-Glasser, J. (2010). Marital behavior, oxytocin, vasopressin, and wound

healing. *Psychoneroendocrinology*, 35(7), 1082–1090.

Grant, E., Thompson, G. & Golding, K. (2024). *Working with Relational Trauma in Children's Residential Care: A guide to using Dyadic Developmental Practice*. Jessica Kingsley Publishers.

Green, J. & Goldwyn, R. (2000). Annotation: Attachment disorganisation and psychopathology: New findings in attachment research and their potential implications for developmental psychopathology in childhood. *Journal of Child Psychology and Psychiatry*, 41(6), 831–846. https://doi.org/10.1111/1469-7610.00671

Greenhill, B. (2011). They have behaviour, we have relationships? *Reformulation,* Winter, 37, 10–15.

Grey, I. & Mcclean, B. (2007). Service user outcomes of staff training in positive behaviour support using person-focused training: a control group study. *Journal of Applied Research in Intellectual Disabilities*, 20, 6–15.

Griffiths, J., Harrhy, E. & Wilcox, M. (2023). Beyond words: A reflection from health professionals around the meaning of 'hear me, don't blame me' in relation to meeting the needs of young people with learning disabilities and autism spectrum conditions. *Child and Family Clinical Psychology Review*, 8, 41–45.

Gwillim., L., Griffiths, J. & Wilcox. M. (2023). 'Foundations for Well-being'. Unpublished.

Hamadi, L. & Fletcher, H. K. (2021). Are people with an intellectual disability at increased risk of attachment difficulties? A critical review. *Developmental Disabilities Research*, 25(1). https://doi.org/10.1177/sagepub.com

Hamadi, L. & Fletcher, H. K. (2021). Are people with an intellectual disability at increased risk of attachment difficulties? A critical review. *Developmental Disabilities Research, 25*(1). https://doi.org/10.1177/sagepub.com

Harding, 2025 reference to be con

Harding, C. 2025. Relational safety in every interaction: Practical approaches to trauma-informed care with support teams. In Gallichan, D., Fletcher, H., Crabtree, J. & Theodore, K. *Working with Support Teams around People with Intellectual Disabilities: Collaborative approaches to psychological interventions.* Pavillion Publishing.

Harding, C. (2024).' Attachment and Trauma-Informed PBS Plans'. Faculty Conference, London, 14 May 2024.

Harding, C. (2020). Providing emotionally aware care in the positive behavioural support framework. In N. Beile, P. Frankish and A. Skelly (Eds) *Trauma and Intellectual Disability: Acknowledgment, identification and intervention.* Pavilion Publishing.

Hartling, L. M., Rosen, W., Walker, M. & Jordan, J. V. (2000). *Shame and Humiliation: From Isolation to Relational Transformation.* Work in Progress, No. 88. Wellesley, MA: Stone Center Working Paper Series. Accessed 9th December 2024 from: https://www.humiliationstudies.org/documents/hartling/HartlingShameHumiliation.pdf

Hastings, R. P. (2002). Parental stress and behavior problems of children with developmental disability. *Journal of Intellectual & Developmental Disability*, 27(3), 149–160. https://doi.org/10.1080/1366825021000008657

Hastings, R. P., Allen, D., Baker, P., Gore, N., Hughes, J. C., McGill, P., Noone, S. & Toogood, S. (2004). Stress in parents of children with an intellectual disability. *Current Opinion in Psychiatry*, 17(5), 349–352. https://doi.org/10.1097/00001504-200409000-00007

Health and Social Care Committee. (2016). *Written evidence submitted to the Health Committee inquiry into suicide prevention* [Report]. UK Parliament. https://committees.parliament.uk/writtenevidence/74082/pdf/

Herman, J. L. (1992). *Trauma and Recovery: The aftermath of violence—from domestic abuse to political terror.* Basic Books.

Hill, C. & Harding, C. (2019). Working systemically with multidisciplinary teams. In V. Jones & M. Haydon-Laurelut (Eds), *Working With People With Learning Disabilities: Systemic approaches.* Bloomsbury.

Horner-Johnson, W. & Drum, E. C. (2006). Prevalence of maltreatment of people with intellectual disabilities: a review of recently published research, *Mental Retardation and Developmental Disabilities. Research Reviews*, 12, 57–69. http://dx.doi.org/10.1002/mrdd.20097

Hughes, D. A. (2009). *Attachment-Focused Parenting: Effective strategies to care for children.* W. W. Norton.

Hughes, D. A. (2011) Attachment - Focused Family Therapy Workbook. New York, NY, Norton.

Hughes, D. A. (2017). Dyadic Developmental Psychotherapy (DDP): An Attachment-focused Family Treatment for Developmental Trauma. *Australian and New Zealand Journal of Family Therapy,* 38, 595–605.

Hughes, D. A. & Baylin, J. (2012). *Brain Based Parenting: The neuroscience of caregiving.* New York: Norton.

Hughes, D. A. & Golding, K. S. (2024). *Healing Relational Trauma Workbook: Dyadic developmental psychotherapy in practice.* Norton Professional Books.

Hughes, D.A., Golding, K. S. & Hudson, J. (2019). *Healing Relational Trauma With Attachment-focused Interventions: Dyadic developmental psychotherapy with children and families.* New York: W. W. Norton & Company.

Human Rights Act 1998, c. 42. (1998). London: The Stationery Office. Retrieved from https://www.legislation.gov.uk/ukpga/1998/42/contents/enacted

Jackson, A. L. & Walters, S. E. (2015). *Taking Time Framework: A trauma-informed framework for supporting people with intellectual disability.* Melbourne, Australia: Berry Street.

Jacobs, E. & Nader-Grosbois, N. (2020). Affective and cognitive theory of mind in children with intellectual disabilities: how to train them to foster social adjustment and emotion regulation? *Journal of Education and Training Studies,* 8 (4), 80–97.

doi:10.11114/jets.v8i4.4757 URL: https://doi.org/10.11114/jets.v8i4.4757

Jansen-van-Vuuren, J. & Aldersley, H. M. (2020). Stigma, Acceptance and Belonging for People with IDD Across Cultures. *Current Developmental Disorder Reports,* 7 (3), 163-172.

Jenkins, R. & Parry, R. (2006) Working with the support network: applying systemic practice in learning disabilities services. *British Journal of Learning Disabilities,* 34(2), 77–81.

Jones, N. (2021) Adapting Dyadic Developmental psychotherapy (DDP to support adults with an intellectual disability who experience complex developmental trauma. In N. Beile, P. Frankish and A. Skelly (Eds) *Trauma and Intellectual Disability: Acknowledgment, identification and intervention.* Pavilion Publishing.

Jones, V. & Haydon-Laurelut, M. (Eds)(2019) *Working With People With Learning Disabilities: Systemic approaches.* London: Bloomsbury.

Joseph Rowntree Foundation (1998). *Paying to Care: The costs of childhood disability.* York: JRF Publications.

Kaplan, H. S. & Wheeler, E. G. (1983). The assaultive psychiatric patient: prevention and treatment. *The Journal of Clinical Psychiatry,* 44(5), 26–31.

Keller, H. (2022). *The Myth of Attachment Theory: A critical understanding for multicultural societies.* Routledge.

Kessler, R. C., McLaughlin, K. A., Green, J. G., Gruber, M. J., Sampson, N. A., Zaslavsky, A. M., Aguilar-Gaxiola, S., Alhamzawi, A. O., Alonso, J., Angermeyer, M., Benjet, C., Bromet, E., Chatterji, S., de Girolamo, G., Demyttenaere, K., Fayyad, J., Florescu, S., Gal, G., Gureje, O. & Williams, D. R. (2010). Childhood adversities and adult psychopathology in the WHO world mental health surveys. *The British Journal of Psychiatry,* 197(5), 378–385.

Kezelman, C., & Stavropoulos, P. (2012). *Practice Guidelines fFor Treatment Of of Complex Trauma And and Trauma-Informed Care And and Service Delivery.* Blue Knot Foundation. Retrieved from https://blueknot.org.au/resources/blue-knot-publications/guidelines/

Kildahl, A. N., Helverschou, S. B., Bakken, T. L. & Oddli, H. W. (2020). "If we do not look for it, we do not see it": Clinicians' experiences and understanding of identifying post-traumatic stress disorder in adults with autism and intellectual disability. *Journal of Applied Research in Intellectual Disabilities, 33*(3), 552–562. https://doi.org/10.1111/jar.12734

King, R. 2005. CAT, the therapeutic relationship and working with people with learning disability. *Reformulation.* Spring p.10-14.

Knight, D. & Gurney-Smith, B. (2016, October). *Navigating a way for DDP in residential care.* Presented at The Power of DDP – International DDP Conference, Glasgow, Scotland.

Kroese, B, S., Willott, S., Taylor, F., Smith, S., Graham, R., Rutter, T., Stott, A. & Willner, P. (2016). Trauma-focussed cognitive-behaviour therapy for people with mild intellectual disabilities: outcomes of a pilot study. *Advances in Mental Health and Intellectual Disabilities,* 10(5), 299–310.

Larkin, H., Felitti, V. J. & Anda, R. F. (2014) Social work and adverse childhood experiences research: implications for practice and health policy. *Social Work in Public Health,* 29(1), 1–16.

Lanarkshire EVA services: Trauma and the Brain (https://www.youtube.com/watch?v=4-tcKYx24aA. 8th August 2024.

Larson, F., Alim, N. & Tsakanikos, E. (2011). Attachment style and mental health in adults with intellectual disability: self-reports and reports by carers. *Advances in Mental Health and Intellectual Disabilities*, 5(1), 15–23. https://doi.org/10.5042/amhid.2011.0100

Lloyd, S. (2016). *Improving Sensory Processing in Traumatized Children: Practical ideas to help your child's movement, coordination and body awareness.* Jessica Kingsley Press.

Lyons, S., Whyte, K., Stephens, R. & Townsend, H. (2020) Developmental Trauma: Close up. Beacon House Therapeutic Services and & Trauma Team. https://beaconhouse.org.uk/resources/

Madigan, S. Fearon, R. M. P., Van Ijzendoorn, M. H., Duschinsky, R., Scheungel, C., Bakersman-Kranenburg, M. J., Ly, A., Cooke, J. E., Deneault, A-A., Oosterman, M., Verhage, M. I., (2023). The first 20,000 strange situation procedures: A meta-analytic review. *Psychological Bulletin*, 149 (1-2), 99-132 https://doi.org/10.1037/bul0000388

Main, M. & Solomon, J. (1986). Discovery of a new, insecure-disorganized/disoriented attachment pattern. In M. Yogman and T. B. Brazelton (Eds), *Affective Development in Infancy*, pp 95–124. Norwood, NJ: Ablex

Marsha, K. M. (1960). A method for evaluating child-parent interactions under controlled conditions. *The Journal of Genetic Psychology*, 97, 3–22.

Maslow, A. (1954). *Maslow's Hierarchy of Needs.*

Available at: https://www.google.com/search?q = maslow + hierarchy + of + needs&client = firefox-b-d&source = lnms&tbm = isch&sa = X&ved = 2ahUKEwixltWqh67nAhXEQEEAHXZdDJMQ_AUoAXoECA4QAw&biw = 1366&bih = 654#imgrc = fwO_G_1bKLAU8M:

McGill, P., Bradshaw, J., Smyth, G., Hurman, M. & Roy, A. (2020). Capable environments. *Tizard Learning Disability Review*, 25(3), 109–116.

McKensie, C. (2023). 'Quality Matters, Says Who? An exploration of the lived experience of autistic people with a focus on what in their life is good, what contributes to this and whether this differs from regulating standards.' IPBS conference, 2023.

McNally, P. (2022). A framework for the implementation of trauma-informed care in residential and supported living services for adults with learning disabilities. *Trauma-Informed Care* (ulster.ac.uk). https://www.ulster.ac.uk/__data/assets/pdf_file/0004/1446412/A-framework-for-the-implementation-of-Trauma-Informed-Care-in-residential-and-supported-living-services-for-adults-with-a-learning-disability.pdf Accessed August 1, 2024.

Michael, T., Kinsella, M. T. & Monk, C. (2009). Impact of maternal stress, depression and anxiety on fetal neurobehavioral development. *Clinical Obstetrics and Gynecology*, 52(3), 425–440.

Mongan, D., Shannon, C., Hanna, D., Boyd, A., Mulholland, C., (2017) The association between specifc types of childhood adversity and attenuated psychotic symptoms in a community sample. Early Intervention in Psychiatry, 13:2, 281-289.

National Institute for Health and Care Excellence, (2018). *Learning Disabilities and Behaviour that Challenges: Service design and delivery* (NICE Guideline NG93). NICE. https://www.nice.org.uk/guidance/ng93

National Learning Disability Professional Senate CLDT Guidance. (2023). Delivering effective specialist community learning disabilities health team support (September). [https://bild.org.uk] Accessed September 5, 2024.

Nethel, G. (2019). 'Functional Behaviour Needs Assessment Tool.' unpublished

Nind, M. & Hewett, D. (1994). *Access to Communication: Developing the basics of communication with people with severe learning difficulties through intensive interaction.* London: David Fulton.

Nirje, B. (1969). The normalization principle and its human management implications. In R. Kugel and W. Wolfensberger (Eds) *Changing Patterns in Residential Services for the Mentally Retarded*, pp 179–195. Washington, DC: Government Printing Office

Oakes, P. (2012). Crash: What went wrong at Winterbourne View? *Journal of Intellectual Disabilities*, 16(3), 10–17.

Oates, J. & Gervai, J. (2019). Mothers' perceptions of their infants. *Journal of Prenatal and Perinatal Psychology and Health*, 33, 282–300.

Parham, L. D., Ecker, C., Miller Kuhaneck, H., Henry, D. A. & Glennon, T. J. (2007). *Sensory Processing Measure.* Pearson.

Pattison, B. (2016). 'Attachment Trauma and PBS'. BILD Training Day. Birmingham. May 2016.

Payne Bryson, T. & Siegel, D. (2012). *The Whole-Brain Child: 12 revolutionary strategies to nurture your child's developing mind, survive everyday parenting struggles, and help your family thrive.* Random House.

Pelchat, D., Levert, M. J. & Bourgeois-Guérin, V. (2009). How do mothers and fathers who have a child with a disability describe their adaptation/transformation process? *Journal of Child Health Care, 13*(3), 239–259. https://doi.org/10.1177/1367493509336684

Penketh, V., Hare, D. J., Flood, A. & Walker, S. (2014) Attachment in Adults with intellectual disabilities: preliminary investigation of the psychometric properties of the Manchester Attachment Scale – Third Party Observational Measure. *Journal of Applied Research in Intellectual Disabilities*, 27(5), 458–470.

Perrot, A. & Horn, R. (2023). Preserving women's reproductive autonomy while promoting the rights of people with disabilities? The case of Heidi Crowter and Maire Lea-Wilson in the light of NIPT debates in England, France and Germany. *Journal of Medical Ethics*, 49(7), 471–473.

Perry, B. D. (2006). Applying principles of neurodevelopment to clinical work with maltreated and traumatized children: the neurosequential model of therapeutics. In N. B. Webb (Ed) *Working With Traumatized Youth in Child Welfare*, pp27–52. The Guilford Press.

Phillips, A. (1988). *Winnicott*. Fontana Press.

Porges, S. W. (1995). Orienting in a defensive world: mammalian modifications of our evolutionary heritage. a polyvagal theory. *Psychophysiology*, 32(4), 301–18.

https://doi.org/10.1111/j.1469-8986.1995.tb01213.x

Porges, S. W. (2011). *The Polyvagal Theory: Neurophysiological Foundations of Emotions, Attachment, Communication and Self-Regulation*. W.W. Norton & Company.

Porges, S. W. (2022). Polyvagal theory: a science of safety. *Frontiers in integrative neuroscience*, 10(16), 871227. doi: 10.3389/fnint.2022.871227

Powell, B., Cooper, G., Hoffman, K. & Marvin, B. (2014). *The Circle of Security Intervention: Enhancing Attachment in Early Parent-Child Relationships*. Guilford Press.

Quinn, A. (2021). *UNbroken – Learning to live beyond diagnosis*. Welbeck Publishing.

Quinn, A. & Sheldon, J. (2025). *Restraint and Human Rights*. Available at: Restriantreductionnetwork.org

Quinn, A. (2025). Relationships of concern: the perils of the progress paradox in positive behaviour support. *BILD, International Journal of Positive Behavioural Support*, 15, 1, pp.35-44.

Quinn, A., Wood, A., Lodge, K. & Hollins, S. (2023). Listening to the experts: person-centred approaches to supporting autistic people and people with an intellectual disability in the mental health system. *BJPsych Advances*, 29(5), 308–317. doi:10.1192/bja.2023.31

Restraint Reduction Network. (2023). *Six Core Strategies and Human Rights*. Retrieved from https://restraintreductionnetwork.org/wp-content/uploads/2023/09/Six-Core-Strategies-and- Human-Rights.pdf. Accessed 24th January 2025.

Ross, H. E. & Young, L. (2008). Oxytocin and the neural mechanisms regulating social cognitive and affiliative behavior. *Frontiers in Neuroendocrinology*, 4, 534–547.

Rothschild, B. (2018). *The Body Remembers, Volume 2 Revolutionising Trauma Treatment*. W. W. Norton.

Rubeis, G. & Steger F. (2019). A burden from birth? Non-invasive prenatal testing and the stigmatization of people with disabilities. *Bioethics*, 33(1), 91–97. doi: 10.1111/bioe.12518.

Sappok, T., Zepperitz, S. & Hudson, M. (2022). *Meeting Emotional Needs in Intellectual Disability: The developmental approach*. Hogrefe.

Schipper-Eindhoven, S. M., de Knegt, N. C., Mevissen, L., van Loon, J., de Vries, R., Zhuniq, M. & Bekker, M. H. J. (2024). EMDR treatment for people with intellectual disabilities: a systematic review about difficulties and adaptations. *Frontiers in Psychiatry*, 14, 11–14. doi: 10.3389/fpsyt.2023.1328310

Schuengel, C. & Janssen, C. (2006). People with mental retardation and psychopathology: stress, affect regulation, and attachment. *International Review of Research in Mental Retardation*, 32, 229–260.

https://doi.org/10.1016/S0074-7750(06)32008-7

Scior, K. & Werner, S. (2016). *Intellectual Disability and Stigma*. Palgrave Macmillan.

Séassau, A., Munos, P., Gire, C., Tosello, B. & Carchon, I. (2023). Neonatal care unit interventions on preterm development. *Children* (Basel). 2023 Jun 2; 10(6), 999.

Shackleton, A. (2016). Have a Heart: Helping services to provide emotionally aware care. In H. Fletcher, A. Flood and D. J. Hare (Eds), *Attachment and Intellectual and Developmental Disability: A clinician's guide to practice and research*. Wiley.

Shevlin, M., McAnee, G., Bentall, R. P. & Murphy, J. (2015). Specificity of association between adversities and the occurrence and cooccurrence paranoia and hallucinations: evaluating the stability of childhood risk in an adult environment. *Psychosis*, 7(3), 206–216.

Shemmings, D. (2024, September 30). *'The need to revisit how we think about attachment.'* [Webinar]. Traumatic Stress Wales.

Shimmens, C. & Skelly, L. (2023). *Love, Attachment and Intellectual Disability: Meeting emotional needs and developmental trauma*. Pavilion Publishing.

Shore, A. N. (2000). Attachment and the regulation of the right brain. *Attachment and Human Development*, 2(1), 23-47.

Siegel, D. (2020). *The Developing Mind (3rd Ed). How relationships and the brain interact to shape who we are.* Routledge.

Siegel, D. (2024). Daniel Siegel Hand Model. Flipping your lid: https://www.youtube.com/watch?v=qFTljLo1bK8 (accessed 22nd October 2024).

Siegel, D. & Hartzell, M. (2005). *Parenting From the Inside Out: How a deeper self-understanding can help you raise children*. Scribe.

Silver, S. M. (1986). An Inpatient Program for Post-Traumatic Stress Disorder: Context as treatment. In C. R. Figley (Ed.), *Trauma and Its Wake, Volume II: Post-Traumatic Stress Disorder: Theory, Research and Treatment*. New York: Brunner/Mazel.

Sinason, V. (2021). The History of Disability is a History of Trauma. In N. Beail, P. Frankish and A. Skelly (Eds), *Trauma and Intellectual Disability: Acknowledgement, identification, and intervention.* Pavilion Publishing.

Singer, G. H. S. (2006) Meta-analysis of comparative studies of depression in mothers of children with and without developmental disabilities. *American Journal on Mental Retardation* 111, 155–169.

Skelly, A. (2014). 'Attachment, Trauma and Relationships.' One-day training, May 2014. BILD.

Skelly, A. (2016). Maintaining the Bond: Working with people who are described as challenging using a framework based upon attachment. In H. K. Fletcher, A. Flood and D. J. Hare (Eds) *Attachment and Intellectual and Developmental Disability*, pp 104–129. Wiley.

Skelly, A. (2021). Self-Rated Quality of Interpersonal Relatedness Scale (SQUEERS). In N. Beail, P. Frankish and A. Skelly (Eds), *Trauma and Intellectual Disability: Acknowledgment, identification, and intervention*, pp 80–81. Pavilion Publishing.

Skelly, A., Usher, R. & Windebank, P. (2020). *Quality of Early Relationships Rating Scale (Version 2)*. Cumbria, Northumbria, Tyne and Wear NHS Foundation Trust.

Sloper, T. & Beresford, B. (2006). Families with disabled children: Social and economic needs are high but remain largely unmet. *British Medical Journal*, 333(7575), 928–929. https://doi.org/10.1136/bmj.39017.633310.BE

Smith, P. & McCarthy, G. (1996) The development to a semi-structured interview to investigate the attachment related experiences of adults with learning disabilities. *British Journal of Learning Disabilities*, 24, 54–160.

Smith, M. & Nethell, G. (2014) The Brief Behavioural Assessment Tool – preliminary findings on reliability and validity. *International Journal of Positive Behavioural Support*, 4(2), 32–40.

Sobsey, D. (1993). Sexual abuse of individuals with intellectual disability. In A. Craft (Ed.), *Practice Issues in Sexuality and Learning Disabilities* (1st ed., pp. 137-150). Routledge.

Sobsey, D. & Doe, T. (1991). Patterns of sexual abuse and assault. *Sexuality and Disability*, 9(3), 243–259. https://doi.org/10.1007/BF01102395

Spencer, N., Devereux, E., Wallace, A., Sundrum, R., Shenay, M., Bacchus, C. & Logan, S. (2005) Disabling conditions and registration for child abuse and neglect: a population-based study. *Paediatrics*, 116(3), 609–614.

Spring, C. (2015). 'Dealing with distress: Working with self-harm and suicide.' Positive Outcomes for Dissociative Survivors, training day.

Sterkenburg, P. S., Janssen, C. G. C. & Schuengel, C. (2008). The effect of an attachment-based behaviour therapy for children with visual and severe intellectual disabilities. *Journal of Applied Research in Intellectual Disabilities*, 21(2), 126–135.

Substance Abuse and Mental Health Service Administration (SAMHSA) (2014) *Concept of Trauma and Guidance for a Trauma Informed Approach*, SAMHSA Trauma and Justice Strategic Initiative July 2014. U.S. Department of Health and Human Services, Office of Policy, Planning and Innovation.

Sullivan, P. M. & Knutson, J. F. (2000) Maltreatment and disabilities: a population-based epidemiological study. *Child abuse and neglect*, 24(10), 1257–1273.

Swain, J., Lorberbaum, J.P., Kose, S. & Strathearn, L. (2007) Brain basis of early neuroimaging studies. *Journal of Child Psychology and Psychiatry*, 48, 262–287. https://doi.org/10.1111/j.1469-7610.2007.01731.x

Sweeney, A., Filson, B., Kennedy, A., Collinsion, L. & Gillard, S. (2018). A paradigm shift: relationships in trauma-informed mental health services. *British Journal of Psychiatric Advances*, 24(5), 319–333. doi: 10.1192/bja.2018.29.

Tarren-Sweeney, M. (2007). The assessment checklist for children – ACC: a behavioral rating scale for children in foster, kinship and residential care. *Children and Youth Services Review*, 29(5), 672–691.

Thompson, B. L., Levitt, P. & Stanwood, G. D. (2009). Prenatal exposure to drugs: effects on brain development and implications for policy and education. *National Review of Neuroscience*, 2009 Apr; 10(4), 303–312.

Tomsa, R., Gutu, S., Cojocaru, D., Gutiérrez-Bermejo, B., Flores, N. & Jenaro, C. (2021). Prevalence of sexual abuse in adults with intellectual disability: Systematic review and meta-analysis. *International Journal of Environmental Research and Public Health*, 18(4), 1980. https://doi.org/10.3390/ijerph18041980

Treisman, K. (2021). A treasure box for creating trauma-informed organizations: A ready-to-use resource for trauma, adversity, and culturally informed, infused, and responsive systems (Therapeutic Treasures Collection). An ebook, available at [PDF] A Therapeutic Treasure Box for Working with Children and Adolescents with Developmental Trauma by Karen Treisman | 9781785922633, 9781784505530

Treisman, K. (2016). *Working with Relational and Developmental Trauma in Children and Adolescents.* Routledge.

Trevarthen, C. (2012). Embodied human intersubjectivity: imaginative agency, to share meaning. *J. Cogn. Semiot*, IV, 6–56.

Trevarthen, C. (1979). Communication and Cooperation in Early Infancy: A description of primary intersubjectivity. In M. Bullowa (Ed), *Before Speech: The beginning of human communication*, pp 321–347. Cambridge: Cambridge University Press.

Trevarthen, C. & Aiken, K. (1991). Infant intersubjectivity: research, theory, and clinical applications. *Journal of Child Psychology and Psychiatry*, 20042(1), 3–48.

Tronick, E. (2007) *The Neurobehavioral and Social-Emotional Development of Facts and Children.* New York: Norton.

Tronick, E., Als, H., Adamson, L., Wise, S. & Brazelton, T. B. (1978). The infant's response to entrapment between contradictory messages in face-to-face interaction. *Journal of the American Academy of Child Psychiatry*, 17(1), 1–13. https://doi.org/10.1016/S0002-7138(09)62273-1

UK Government (n.d.) *Learning Disabilities: Applying All Our Health.* Available at: https://www.gov.uk/government/publications/learning-disability-applying-all-our-health/learning-disabilities-applying-all-our-health (Accessed: 11th February 2025).

Van Ijzendoorn, M. H. & Kroonenberg, P. M. (1988). Cross-cultural patterns of attachment: a meta-analysis of the strange situation. *Child Development*, 59, 147–156.

Wall, J. (2019). From childhood studies to childism: reconstructing the scholarly and social imaginations. *Children's Geographies*, 17(5), 563–576.

WECIL (Supported Independent Living)(n.d.). 'The importance of authentic representation of disability in the media.' Retrieved September 22nd, 2024, from https://wecil.org.uk/the-importance-of-authentic-representation-of-disability-in-the-media/

Wellman, H. M., Cross, D. & Watson, J., (2001). Meta-analysis of theory-of-mind development: the truth about false belief. *Child Development*, 72, 655–684. doi: 10.1111/1467-8624.00304

Westoby, P. (2024, October 9). 'The dark, desire, and community development'. [Conference presentation]. Community Psychology Festival, Newport, UK.

Whitby, P. (2020). *Good Care Leadership: A leadership development course for frontline health and care staff.* Pavilion Publishing.

Wigham & Emerson, (2015). Trauma and Life Events in Adults with Intellectual Disability. *Current developmental disorders reports.*

Wigham, S., Hatton, C. & Taylor, J. L. (2011). The effects of traumatizing life events on people with intellectual disabilities: a systematic review. *Journal of Mental Health Research in Intellectual Disabilities*, 4(1), 19–39. doi.org/10.1080/19315864.2010

Wilcox, M., Davies, K. & Williams, C. (2021). 'Challenging Behaviour Needs Assessment Scale.' Unpublished.

Wilczek, R. Please stop people going through what I went through – and am still going through. In N. Beile, P. Frankish and A. Skelly (Eds) *Trauma and Intellectual Disability: Acknowledgment, identification and intervention*. Pavilion Publishing.

Winnicott, D. W. (1964/1991) The Child, The Family, and The Outside World. First published in 1964 by Pelican books and recently published in 1991 by Penguin books.

Wiseman, P. & Watson, N. (2022). "Because I've got a learning disability, they don't take me seriously:" Violence, wellbeing, and devaluing people with learning disabilities. *Journal of interpersonal violence*, 37, 13–14. doi: 10.1177/0886260521990828

Wolfensberger, W. (1983). Social role valorization: a proposed new term for the principle of normalization. *Mental Retardation*, 21(6), 234–239.

Index